P9-AQT-419

917.
441
STE
2006

A COMPLETE GUIDE

8TH EDITION

# The Berkshire Book

Lauren R. Stevens

FINKELSTEIN
MEMORIAL LIBRARY
SPRING VALLEY, N.Y.

The Countryman Press
Woodstock, Vermont

3 2191 00782 8204

We welcome your comments and suggestions. Please contact Great Destinations Guide Editor, The Countryman Press, P.O. Box 748, Woodstock, VT 05091, or e-mail countrymanpress@wwnorton.com.

Copyright © 1986, 1991, 1994, 1997, 1999, 2000, 2003 by Berkshire House Publishers
Copyright © 2006 by Lauren R. Stevens

All rights reserved. No part of this book may be reproduced in any form, or by any electronic or mechanical means, including information storage and retrieval systems, without permission in writing from the publisher, except by a reviewer, who may quote brief passages.

Library of Congress data has been applied for.
ISBN-13: 978-1-58157-033-5
ISBN-10: 1-58157-033-3

Maps by Ron Toelke Associates and Mapping Specialists Ltd., © The Countryman Press
Book design by Bodenweber Design
Text composition by Melinda Belter
Interior photographs as credited
Cover photograph by of the Norman Rockwell Museum grounds © Jeff Greenberg/Alamy

Published by The Countryman Press, P.O. Box 748, Woodstock, VT 05091

Distributed by W. W. Norton & Company, Inc., 500 Fifth Avenue, New York, NY 10110

Printed in the United States of America

10 9 8 7 6 5 4 3 2 1

## Great Destinations travel guidebook series

Recommended by *National Geographic Traveler* and *Travel + Leisure* magazines.

[A] crisp and critical approach, for travelers who want to live like locals.
— *USA Today*

**Great Destinations™** guidebooks are known for their comprehensive, critical coverage of regions of extraordinary cultural interest and natural beauty. The authors in this series are professional travel writers who have lived for many years in the regions they describe. Each title in this series is continuously updated with each printing to insure accurate and timely information. All the books contain more than one hundred photographs and maps.

**Current titles available:**

The Adirondack Book

The Berkshire Book

Big Sur, Monterey Bay & Gold Coast Wine Country

The Charleston, Savannah & Coastal Islands Book

The Chesapeake Bay Book

The Coast of Maine Book

The Finger Lakes Book

The Hamptons Book

The Hudson Valley Book

The Nantucket Book

The Napa & Sonoma Book

Palm Beach, Miami & The Florida Keys

Playa del Carmen, Tulúm & the Riviera Maya: Great Destinations Mexico

The Santa Fe & Taos Book

The Sarasota, Sanibel Island & Naples Book

The Seattle & Vancouver Book: Includes the Olympic Peninsula, Victoria & More

The Shenandoah Valley Book

The Texas Hill Country Book

Touring East Coast Wine Country

If you are traveling to, moving to, residing in, or just interested in any (or all!) of these enchanting regions, a Great Destinations guidebook is a superior companion. Honest and painstakingly critical, full of information only a local can provide, Great Destinations guidebooks give you all the practical knowledge you need to enjoy the best of each region.

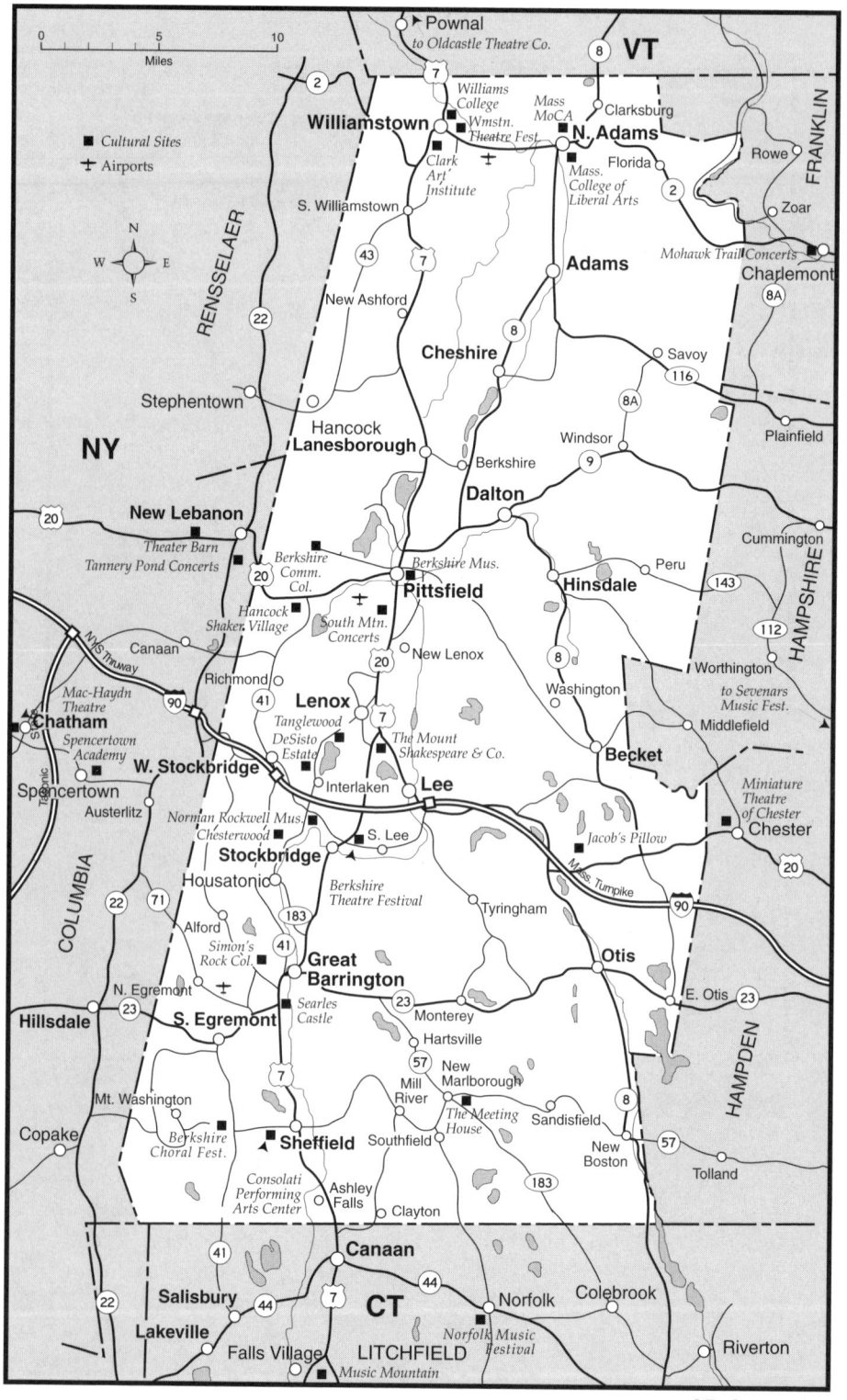


© The Countryman Press

# Contents

Map: Berkshire County 6

Acknowledgments 9

The Way This Book Works 10

**1**
History
*From the Glaciers to the Present*
12

**2**
Transportation
*Getting Here, Getting Around*
24

**3**
Lodging
*The Keys to Your Room*
40

**4**
Dining
*Pleasing the Palate*
80

**5**
Arts & Pleasures
*What to See, What to Do*
130

**6**
Body & Spirit
*Spas & the Spiritual Life*
188

**7**
Outdoor Recreation
*For the Fun of It*
195

**8**
Shopping
*Fancy Goods*
238

**9**
Information
*Practical Matters*
266

**10**
If Time Is Short
286

Index 290
Lodging Index 307
Restaurant Index 309
Maps
Berkshire County 6
Berkshire Towns 11
Berkshire Access Maps 27
Berkhire Town Maps
Great Barrington 34
Stockbridge 35
Lenox 36
Pittsfield 37
Williamstown 38
North Adams 39

## Acknowledgments

The eighth edition of *The Berkshire Book*, like the seventh, has been perpetrated upon an unsuspecting public by a dubious cast of characters who have in common that they live, work, or play in Berkshire County. Jean Jacques Rousseau provided invaluable information on the changing South Berkshire scene. Judith Monachina took many of the photographs. Joyce Monachina wrote chapter 6, "*Body & Spirit*." Carol Bosco Baumann wrote chapter 8, *Shopping*, and investigated the galleries in chapter 5. Seth Rogovoy wrote the "Nightlife" section of "*Arts & Pleasures*." Thanks to them all for their wealth of knowledge and professionalism. Philip Rich edited the whole in his usual thorough and informative way.

*The Berkshire Book* is more of an ensemble production than the work of any individuals. Fortunately this group worked well together. Any errors, however, should be attributed to the author. Readers could help by forwarding comments to:
The Countryman Press
PO Box 748
Woodstock, VT 05091

— LRS

# The Way This Book Works

## Organization

Entries are located by subject in the appropriate chapters. Among the chapters, arrangements vary to suit the needs of subject matter. Most material is arranged in three geographical groupings, with South County offerings first, followed by those in Central County, and finally North County. A few nearby listings that are located Outside the County are given, as well.

Within these geographic groupings, listings are arranged alphabetically—first by town or topic, and then by establishments' names. Some entries, such as those in *Shopping*, are arranged by type; hence all the crafts shops appear together. Each chapter has its own introduction, and the specific arrangement of that chapter is spelled out there.

Factual information was researched at the latest possible time before publication, but be advised that chefs and innkeepers come and go, hours change, shops appear and disappear. When in doubt, phone ahead.

Specific information (such as address and location, telephone number, hours of business, and a summary of special features or restrictions) is presented in a block above each entry or otherwise shown, usually within parentheses, adjacent to descriptions of various entries throughout the book.

## Prices

With few exceptions, specific prices are not given. Because pricing is constantly changing, generally we have noted price ranges.

Lodging prices are on a per-room rate, double occupancy, in the high season (summer, fall foliage, and ski months). Low-season rates are likely to be 20–40 percent less. We urge you always to phone ahead for updated prices and other information and for reservations.

Restaurant prices indicate the cost of an individual's meal, which includes appetizer, entrée, and dessert but does not include cocktails, wine, tax, or tip. Restaurants with a prix fixe menu are noted accordingly.

## Price Codes

| | *Lodging* | *Dining* |
|---|---|---|
| Inexpensive | Up to $100 | Up to $15 |
| Moderate | $100 to $150 | $15 to $30 |
| Expensive | $150 to $200 | $30 to $50 |
| Very Expensive | Over $200 | $50 or more |

**Credit Cards are abbreviated as follows:**

| | |
|---|---|
| AE — American Express | DC — Diner's Club |
| CB — Carte Blanche | MC — Master Card |
| D — Discover Card | V — Visa |

## Area Code

There is one telephone area code for all of Berkshire County: **413.**

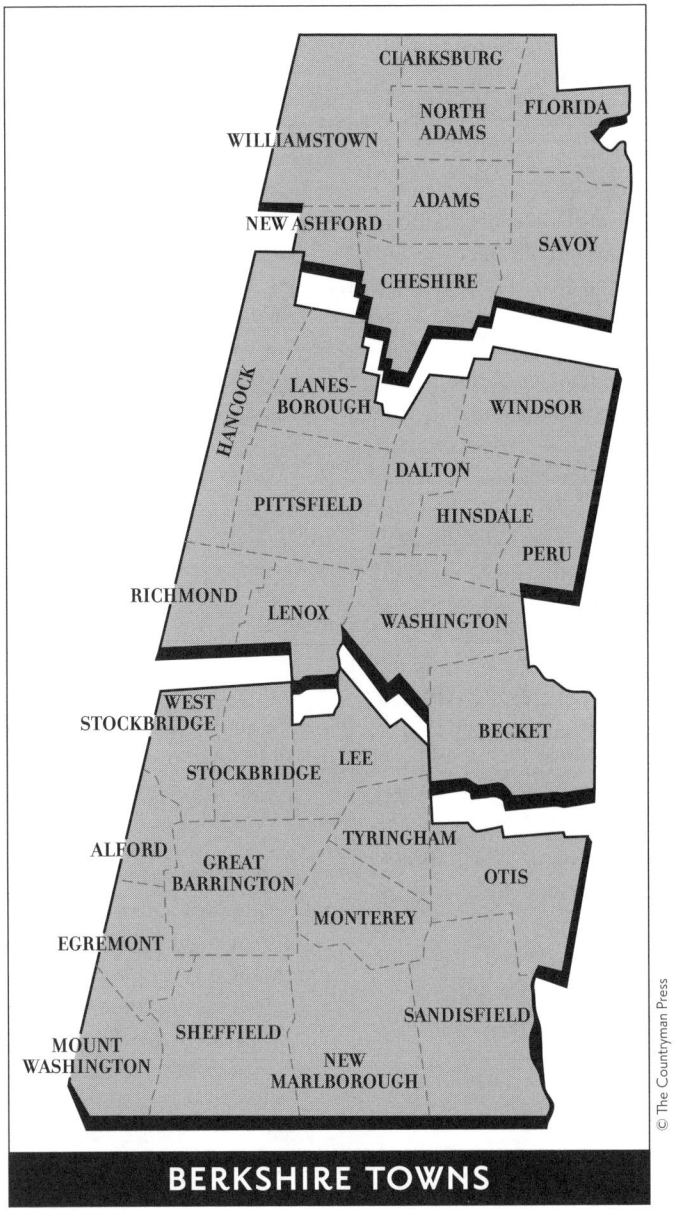


BERKSHIRE TOWNS

## Information Booths

Volunteers in several Berkshire towns staff tourist information booths in the summer and early fall. Often information is available at the site even when volunteers aren't. Year-round tourist information can be obtained from the **Berkshire Visitors Bureau** (800-237-5747; www.berkshires.org; 3 Hoosac St., Adams, MA 01220). The bureau is open Mon.–Fri., 8:30–4:30.

For a more detailed list of information sources, see "Tourist Information" at the end of chapter 9, "Information."

# 1

# History

## *From the Glaciers to the Present*

**To hardworking** Berkshire settlers, much of what we prize today as beauty was at the least unproductive and at the most an absolute impediment to making a living. Jeremiah Wilbur who, at age 14 in 1767, began farming on the sides of Mount Greylock, could not have had a lot of time to admire the view. This prodigious worker built a carting road over the notch between Ragged Mountain and Greylock into Adams, built a road to near the summit of Greylock that was the forerunner of today's Notch Road, cleared enough land to grow and cut 100 tons of hay in a year, tapped enough maples to produce 1,800 pounds of sugar in a year, protected his herd of free-roaming cattle from wolves, maintained the best sheep herd in the county, built a cider mill, a gristmill, and a sawmill on Notch Brook, increased his holdings to 1,600 acres—and died in 1813 a very tired but relatively wealthy man. It may have been the promise of waterpower that lured this early farmer out of the valley and onto the wildest land around, but that same water was a constant threat to his road, the wildlife threatened to destroy his livelihood, and the steep terrain was hard to negotiate and tougher to plow.

We're fortunate to know a bit about this "active and industrious man" who lived in a remote part of what was still nearly frontier. In 1800 the president of Yale College, Timothy Dwight, toured the area, publishing *Travels in New England and New York* in 1822. At the time, people traveled to settle, trade furs, convert Indians, survey boundaries, or fight a war. The concept of taking a recreational spin through remote and unsettled places was unheard of. Dwight may, in fact, have been America's first native tourist. Our good fortune is that he was an intelligent, observant, literate man.

**Berkshire, the Berkshires, the Berkshire Hills**

Even residents are confused about the name of this place. The original Berkshire is in England, south of Oxford. There it's pronounced BARK-SHUR. *Shire* refers to an Anglo-Saxon administrative district.

Strictly speaking "Berkshire Hills" is the handle for south-county hills and plateau, including the adjacent Taconics in New York State and northwestern Connecticut. As time wears on, however, the term seems to be generalizing to all the high ground in and around the county.

Residents may refer to the area politically as "Berkshire County," poetically as "Berkshire" and, in relation to tourism, as "the Berkshires." This book is similarly inconsistent.

*Benedict Pond, Beartown State Forest* Lauren R. Stevens

When Dwight rode his horse into Williamstown in October, he looked up the president of Williams College, Ebenezer Fitch (a fellow Yalie who had written about Wilbur's remarkable sheep), suggesting a trip up Greylock. Fitch led him to Wilbur's home, partway up the mountain. Wilbur not only allowed the men to cross his land, he also "willingly accompanied" them up the road he had built to carry salt to his cattle. "We alighted from our horses within 20 feet of the summit, and found our path better than a great part of the town and country roads throughout the hill country of New England," Dwight wrote. The summit of Mount Greylock was tree covered as, of course, no one had yet built the tower that now graces it. So, to get the view, the two college presidents and the farmer each picked out a wind-battered fir tree and shinnied up.

"The view was immense and of amazing grandeur," Dwight wrote. "You will easily suppose that we felt total superiority to all the humble beings who were creeping on the footstool beneath us. The village of Williamstown shrunk to the size of a farm; and its houses, church, and colleges appeared like the habitation of martins and wrens."

Dwight recognized the Adirondacks "west of Lake Champlain," the Green Mountains, Mount Monadnock, Mount Tom, and the Catskills. He discovered the joy of the third dimension that we, who so easily drive over hills or fly above them, take for granted. For Dwight's generation and those to follow, Mount Greylock was spectacular, as most people did not visit higher peaks—just as Bash Bish Falls, at the southwest corner of Berkshire, inspired more awe when few had been to Niagara.

Forty-four years later, when writer-naturalist Henry David Thoreau climbed past the old Wilbur homestead, Mount Greylock was still wild country, still an adventure. He exchanged a few pleasantries about reaching the summit that night with Smith Wilbur, Jeremiah's grandson. Thoreau used the trip to overcome his grief over his brother's death, his disappointment at being turned down in matrimony by a cousin, his guilt for having accidentally burned 300 acres of woodlands in Concord, and to answer his need to find his own transcendent vision. All of these things, he implies, he accomplished on his walk up Greylock, awaking the next morning to a Technicolor sunrise above the clouds. The trip was his preparation for Walden, pond and book, the next year.

(Thoreau must have read Dwight, for he makes the same mistake of identifying Williamstown and its colleges from the summit. Can't be done: Mount Prospect is in the way. Thoreau admitted, in his account of the trip in *A Week on the Concord and Merrimack Rivers*, that he had only a very quick view out before the sun set.)

While Wilbur may deliberately have chosen his site for the grand view, what Dwight began (and 19th-century writers and painters continued) was to instruct hardworking, practical farmers and shopkeepers in appreciation of the landscape. For a farmer occupied with the daily grind of growing food for his family, someone had to say (as Thoreau did more than once): Slow down, enjoy, observe the values nature maintains without any human labor.

Thus the Hudson River school of painters created large, inspiring landscapes and toured them through the towns and cities. "Look what we have here!" they exclaimed to folk who had seen little beyond the back forty. Furthermore, these artists turned around the religious view of the landscape. When the Puritans arrived, they saw the woods as dark, evil, and aligned with the devil. When Thoreau described his July sunrise on Mount Greylock or Thomas Cole painted the sun breaking through the clouds, they depicted trees, fields, and falling water as infused with heaven. Thoreau solved his own problems on Greylock, but he also taught his readers to appreciate the marvels of this godly place.

Building on this tradition, the arts in Berkshire excel and expand, still teaching residents and visitors to appreciate our surroundings.

## NATURAL HISTORY

*Tell me your landscape and I will tell you who you are.*
—ORTEGA Y GASSET

Artists taught us to appreciate this gentled landscape. Erosion turned jagged peaks to rolling hills in much the same way that culture has smoothed the rough edges of its people—whom Edith Wharton once called her "granite outcroppings."

Six hundred million years ago, however, the region lay flatter, covered by a shallow sea. Lapping waves built up beaches that turned to sandstone, which in turn metamorphosed into quartzite—the erosion-resistant backbone of many of the county's ridges. Shelled marine animals built coral reefs, which calcified into limestone. Deposits of this alkaline agent, which are still mined on the side of Mount Greylock today, buffer the area against the worst ravages of acid precipitation. Some of the limestone recrystallized into marble, snowy chunks of which grace hiking trails and can be inspected at Natural Bridge in North Adams. Muddy, offshore sediments settled to form shales and then schists, crystalline rocks that fracture cleanly. The bands of granite that run through the southern part of the county antedate the sedimentary rock.

Then, at a speed of an inch a year over 150 million years, the landmasses that would one day be North America, Africa, and Europe moved toward each other, closing the proto-

Atlantic Ocean. Several arcs of offshore volcanic islands were shoved onto the continent by a series of slow but cataclysmic collisions known as the Taconic orogeny (*orogeny* means "mountain building"). The entire continental shelf was squeezed into a series of folds, the monumental forerunners of the Appalachian Mountains. Then, slowly, the continents began to pull apart, as they are still doing.

Even as the mountains were rising to Himalayan heights, the process of erosion began. Rain fell, forming streams that raged through a landscape unrooted by vegetation. Over the eons water and wind tamed the rugged land forms, preparing them for the plants that would further soften them.

Less than 2 million years ago the first in a succession of four ice sheets ground down in response to a cooling climate. These mile-high glaciers deposited debris, gravel, and rocks around the relative nubbins of mountains that remained. Glacial lakes covered Great Barrington, Tyringham, and the valley from Williamstown to Adams, forming gravel beaches on their shorelines. But the glaciers only iced the Berkshire cake; the great work of diminution had begun—and continues—through erosion. Two great landslides on Mount Greylock in the summer of 1990 were simply more dramatic instances. The Hoosic, Housatonic, and Westfield river valleys existed before the glaciers and remained largely the same, although glacial debris forced the Farmington River to swing north to meet the Connecticut.

As the climate warmed, as recently as 11,000 years ago, the vegetation returned and further tempered the climate. From the boggy marshland an evergreen forest moved north, lingering now only on the tops of the highest ridges. In its place, the broad-leaved deciduous forest moved in, characterized by oak and its associated species in South County, and, sugar maple in the north.

As the glaciers withdrew, animals returned—and perhaps a few of the earliest North American human inhabitants, whose Asian ancestors had boated the Pacific or walked across the Bering land bridge, were in Berkshire to bid farewell to the ice. The first Americans here were initially foragers, but after developing tools, they crafted weapons and became hunters. In South Egremont recently the remains of a 12,000-year-old mastodon were found; around it, arrowheads of the same age.

Seen from above, Berkshire County presents its ridges as north-to-south-running folds: the Taconics along the New York boundary, the Green Mountains protruding south from Vermont, the Hoosacs filling the northeast quadrant, and the Southern Berkshire Plateau filling the southeast quadrant. Tributaries of the two main Berkshire rivers, the Housatonic and the Hoosic, nearly meet at Brodie Mountain, flowing in opposite directions to form the extended north–south valley that U.S. Route 7 now follows. The Greylock massif stands as a peninsula to the Taconics, as indeed it was when glacial Lake Bascom filled the Hoosac Valley to the 1,300-foot elevation. Greylock rises 3,491 feet, the highest point in southern New England, visible from most of the county. Mount Everett is the 2,264-foot sentinel of South County. It is possible to see the one from the other.

The rocky steepness of the county does not lend itself to leisurely flowing water and big lakes. With the exception of the southern reach of the Housatonic, which meanders through Sheffield, Berkshire rivers rush to their destinations. We owe the lakes we have now, excepting Stockbridge Bowl, to 19th-century industrialists who either dammed small ponds to make them larger—as with Otis, Pontoosuc, and Onota—or created reservoirs out of rivers—as with Cheshire Reservoir. They wanted a supply of water upstream they could let out in low-water times to turn the mill wheels.

This geology follows Lauren R. Stevens's *Hikes and Walks in the Berkshire Hills,* for which Williams College geologist Paul Karabinos consulted. The pamphlet *A Canoe Guide to the Housatonic* comments on the local ecology. Berkshire Sanctuaries Director René Laubach, in his *Guide to Natural Places in the Berkshire Hills,* invokes the flora, fauna, geology, and ecology. The Berkshire Museum, the county's center for natural-history study, displays Bartlett Hendrick's wall-sized raised relief topographic map of the county. For field trips, try any of the "Outdoor Sites" (see chapter 7, "Recreation").

The two branches of the Housatonic River rise in the Greylock range and in Washington, the northernmost part of the Southern Berkshire Plateau. They meet in Pittsfield and flow south to enter Long Island Sound at Stratford, Connecticut. The Hoosic River, flowing northward from Cheshire Reservoir (aka Hoosac Lake) through Adams, joins with its north branch in North Adams and passes through Williamstown and a corner of Vermont on its way to the Hudson River, above Albany. The Westfield forms in the Hoosac Plateau, joining the Connecticut River in Westfield, while the Farmington forms in the Southern Berkshire Plateau, mostly in Otis Reservoir—the largest recreational body of fresh water in the commonwealth.

Although settlement and deforestation of the county once drove off the larger animals, today they are returning. One hundred years ago the county was 75 percent cleared; now, as the farms grow in, it is 75 percent wooded, providing habitat for the prolific deer, the occasional moose, black bear, red and gray fox, coyote, bobcat, beaver, and mink. Tales of eastern cougar sightings are making the rounds again; the last cougar in these parts was thought to have been shot in Vermont 100 years ago. Berkshire hosts rare salamanders that thrive only in these wetlands because of the area's high lime content. Wild turkey flap about in the woods, while in 1999 a bald eagle was born in Sandisfield. Great blue heron, with wings 6 feet across, scurry along the streams; ruffed grouse and quail explode out of the woods.

Although formal gardens at historic homes are beautiful, so are the ephemeral spring flowers at Bartholomew's Cobble and the delicate boreal blooms on Greylock. In our post-glacial melt, accelerated by global warming, a tamed Berkshire is green and welcoming.

## Social History

*History is to the community what memory is to the individual.*
—Shaker saying

As recent archeological digs in south country have confirmed, American Indians settled and farmed in the area before the time of Europeans. The words *Housatonic* and *Hoosic* have a similar linguistic root, which may have meant "beyond place," beyond the Hudson. In prehistory, the Mahican Indians entered the area from the Hudson Valley by way of the Green River, a tributary of the Housatonic, and the Hoosic River to hunt and farm. They fished shad, herring, and salmon in the springtime. They built weirs to trap fish in the Housatonic's tributaries and also fished with hand nets from dugout canoes on the river. They gathered mussels from the rocky river bottoms and smoke-cured them, together with

*A farmhouse and split-rail fence still grace the Tyringham Valley.* Judith Monachina

their surplus fish, for winter storage. They hunted duck and goose, and they maintained gardens in the river's floodplain, which were fertilized annually by the spring flood.

After the Dutch established a fur-trading outpost at Fort Orange (now Albany, New York) in 1624, the Mahicans and the neighboring Mohawk went to war over who would be gatekeepers to the valuable fur trade. By 1628 the Mahican, had been driven to the east of the Hudson, some settling in Berkshire.

In 1676 the first European of record set foot in Berkshire, when Major John Talcott overtook a raiding band of about 150 Indians "neare unto Ousatunick" (Great Barrington). It was the last significant battle of King Philip's War, Major Talcott preserving both colonial security and his unbeaten battle record. Smallpox brought by the Europeans dramatically reduced Mahican ranks by the late 17th century.

As the numbers of Indians shrank, a few Dutch settlers infiltrated from the Hudson Valley to what is now the town of Mount Washington. Dutch town names, such as Van Deusenville (in Great Barrington), still exist in South County, together with traces of Dutch architecture in the stepped gable ends of old buildings.

In 1724 a small band of Mahicans led by Chiefs Konkapot and Umpachenee sold their lands along the Housatonic River, including what is now Sheffield, Great Barrington, Egremont, Mount Washington, Alford, and parts of Lee, Stockbridge, and West Stockbridge. The price: "£460, 3 bbls. of cider, and 30 qts. of rum." While the first land buyers were speculators from the Massachusetts Bay Colony, the first settlers tended to come from Connecticut because it was easier to move from south to north along the river valleys than from east to west over the mountains.

English settlers moved to the Sheffield grant, building the earliest homesteads at some distance from the Housatonic, on the second river terrace. This allowed the fertile floodplain to be used for agriculture and kept the settlers away from the malarial lowlands or floods. In the mid-1730s, the Reverend John Sergeant came from Yale College to proselytize and educate the hundreds of Mahicans who lived around *W-nahk-ta-kook* (Great Meadow), later called Indian Town and then Stockbridge. He learned their language and won their respect.

In 1744 Berkshire was opened to cross-country travel for the first time, when the "Great Road" was laid out between Boston and Albany, crossing the county at Great Barrington. John Sergeant died in 1749. The Reverend Jonathan Edwards came to Stockbridge two years later. His zeal had offended parishioners at his previous pulpit in Northampton, and Edwards had been dismissed. Exiled, in effect, to Stockbridge, his relation to the Indians did not compare to Sargeant's. One of America's earliest philosophers of religion, Edwards published *Freedom of the Will* in 1754, Berkshire's first book. With his fiery preaching style, Edwards stirred up the Great Awakening, a religious revival that swept New England.

When the 1759 British victory over the French at Quebec marked the conclusion of the French and Indian War, western Massachusetts was no longer as vulnerable to invading Indian attack and was considered safer for settlement. On July 1, 1761, the royal governor, Sir Francis Bernard, created the county by striking off a section from the already-existing Hampshire County. He declared this one "Berkshire," after his home county in England. Although the line between New England and New York wasn't settled until the 1790s, Berkshire boundaries correspond remarkably to the mountain ridges.

In early 1773 a group of townspeople and lawyers met in the Sheffield study of Colonel John Ashley. There, in one of the earliest public assertions of American freedom, they drafted the Sheffield Declaration, stating to Great Britain and all the world that "Mankind in a State of Nature are equal, free and independent of each other. . . ." In the following year, ferment in the county against the British intensified. In July a county convention met under the chairmanship of Colonel Ashley. From this meeting, the Stockbridge Non-Intercourse Articles of 1774 were drafted, complaining that "whereas the Parliament of Great Britain have of late undertaken to give and grant away our money without our knowledge or consent, . . . we will not import, purchase, or consume" any British goods. British oppression mounted. On August 16 some 1,500 people of Berkshire staged a peaceful sit-down strike around the Great Barrington Courthouse, preventing the Royal judges from meeting. It was the first open resistance to British rule in America.

And in April 1775 a regiment of Berkshire Minutemen under Colonel John Paterson of Lenox started out for Cambridge to aid in the Revolutionary effort. That May former Sheffield and Connecticut resident Ethan Allen led his Green Mountain Boys, with 57 Berkshire men, in a successful surprise attack on Fort Ticonderoga on Lake Champlain. That winter (1776), General Henry Knox, Continental troops, and over 100 oxen, dragged captured Ticonderoga cannon through Berkshire on the way to General George Washington in Cambridge. Aided by this additional weaponry, Washington was able to drive the British from Boston.

In a kind of Revolutionary hangover, Daniel Shays led a revolt of western Massachusetts veterans disappointed in their lot. In 1786 they closed courthouses and released debtors from jail. Mum Bet, Colonel Ashley's slave freed by Theodore Sedgwick and then employed at the Sedgwicks', hid the family silver during the fighting. An attempt to take the Springfield arsenal the following January failed. Most of the "regulators" were killed or captured.

With peace and growing prosperity, the 1790s saw the beginnings of a number of county institutions. The Shakers established colonies in Hancock and Tyringham. Marble quarrying started in West Stockbridge. Williams College's faltering beginnings in 1793 eventually led to its position as one of the finest liberal arts colleges in the United States.

The American Indian community in Berkshire had collapsed socially and economically. As Konkapot's tribe dwindled to fewer than 400 members—including stray Indians from other tribes and rechristened "Stockbridge Indians"—in 1771, at age 94, he stepped down as chief. Beginning in 1784 the Stockbridge were forced into westward migration, leaving only their Housatonic legends—and a Bible—behind them. Their descendants returned to the Mission House for the Bible in 1984.

The farmers of Cheshire pooled the entire town's milk production for a day in 1801 to produce the Great Cheshire Cheese, a 1,235-pound, barrel-shaped cheddar that was hauled by oxen to Albany and then by boat to Washington for presentation to President Jefferson.

Elkanah Watson introduced Spanish Merino sheep—and incidentally the agricultural fair—into Berkshire in 1807, tethering two of the animals on the Pittsfield common. Their wool, spun into fine worsted yarn and woven into Berkshire broadcloth in the county's state-of-the-art mills, was fashioned into President Madison's inauguration suit in 1809. Shortly thereafter, the first stage route in the county was established, running from Greenfield to North Adams, Williamstown, and Albany.

The mill on the farm became the mill in town. Plants of a new sort sprouted by the sides of Berkshire's rivers. Industry took a firm hold in Berkshire when Zetas Crane began paper production in Dalton and David Estes opened the first textile mill in North Adams.

Writers and painters arrived soon after. William Cullen Bryant spent a year at Williams College and then practiced law in Great Barrington. As he attempted to divine the art of

*The paper industry has thrived in the Housatonic Valley, including Lee.* Judith Monachina

**Hawthorne and Thoreau**

Nathaniel Hawthorne was one of 19th-century Berkshire's greatest admirers. During his year-and-a-half residency in the "Red Cottage" at Tanglewood, overlooking Stockbridge Bowl, he kept a journal, recording the fullness of his affection for the landscape.

OCTOBER 16, 1850

A MORNING MIST FILLING UP THE WHOLE LENGTH AND BREADTH OF THE VALLEY, BETWIXT HERE AND MONUMENT MOUNTAIN; THE SUMMIT OF THE MOUNTAIN EMERGING. THE MIST REACHES TO PERHAPS A HUNDRED YARDS OF OUR HOUSE, SO DENSE AS TO CONCEAL EVERYTHING, EXCEPT THAT, NEAR ITS HITHER BOUNDARY, A FEW RUDDY OR YELLOW TREE-TOPS EMERGE, GLORIFIED BY THE EARLY SUNSHINE; AS IS LIKEWISE THE WHOLE MIST CLOUD.

H. D. Thoreau shared Hawthorne's reverence for these hills, saying of Williams College's position at the foot of Greylock—or anyone's willingness to learn from nature:

IT WOULD BE NO SMALL ADVANTAGE IF EVERY COLLEGE WERE THUS LOCATED AT THE BASE OF A MOUNTAIN, AS GOOD AT LEAST AS ONE WELL-ENDOWED PROFESSORSHIP. . . . SOME WILL REMEMBER, NO DOUBT, NOT ONLY THAT THEY WENT TO COLLEGE, BUT THAT THEY WENT TO THE MOUNTAIN.

poetry while earning his living as a lawyer, his new Stockbridge friend Catherine Sedgwick published her first novel, *A New England Tale* (1820), to critical acclaim. Hudson River artist Thomas Cole painted Mount Greylock over Pontoosuc Lake, while other artists depicted the lower Housatonic and Bash Bish Falls. Alexis de Tocqueville visited the Sedgwicks by stagecoach in Stockbridge in 1831. Not long after, trains huffed into the hills, one of them bringing Henry Wadsworth Longfellow to honeymoon in Pittsfield. Dr. Oliver Wendell Holmes, the "autocrat of the breakfast table," built a home on ancestral lands at Canoe Meadows to spend his summers in Berkshire. Nathaniel Hawthorne moved from Salem to Lenox and took up residence at a property he called Tanglewood. Then in 1850 Herman Melville bought Arrowhead Farm in Pittsfield. David Dudley Field introduced Melville to Hawthorne on the occasion of a climb up Monument Mountain; the two great writers' imaginations were entwined thereafter.

In 1851 construction began on the Hoosac Tunnel between the Berkshire towns of Florida and North Adams, a project that was to take 195 lives. The 4.75-mile tunnel, longest in America and the one in which nitroglycerin was used for the first time, was completed in 1875.

Before those explosions were silenced, shells were fired in hate in the Civil War. Five days after the Confederate forces opened fire on Fort Sumter, Berkshire militiamen were on their way south to defend the indivisibility of the Republic. These first county recruits stayed 3 months and saw little action; other Berkshire regiments took their place, fighting through 1865 as far south as the state of Florida.

In 1866, after two unsuccessful attempts, Cyrus Field of Stockbridge and his engineers laid a cable across the Atlantic, connecting America with Europe. A year later in America's leading paper town, Lee, paper fabrication from wood pulp rather than rags was demonstrated for the first time in the United States.

Industry was now booming in Berkshire, with textile and paper plants lining the rivers. Fueled by the county's abundant forests, iron smelters, railroads and other heavy industries

*The gardens at the Mount* Judith Monachina

cut deep into the Berkshire woodland. It was not long before nearly 75 percent of the county's timber was gone, and the hills were nearly bald. In 1879 Crane & Co. of Dalton obtained an exclusive contract with the federal government involving a lot of money: to produce American currency.

In 1886 William Stanley installed the world's first commercial electric system, lighting 25 shops along Main Street, Great Barrington. The General Electric Company visited Stanley in his Pittsfield workshop and, soon after, moved nearby. Five years later an electric trolley system was introduced in Pittsfield, running from Park Square to Pontoosuc Lake. Soon this quiet, reliable transport would connect most of the county—and the county with the region.

The decade of the 1880s ushered in Berkshire's Gilded Age, during which millionaires came to the hills to play and build their dream "cottages." Mrs. Mary Searles had just completed her $2.5 million castle in Great Barrington; Anson Phelps Stokes had spent nearly as much in completing the largest home in America just then, his 100-room Shadowbrook in Stockbridge. A mile away, the 33-room Italianate palazzo called Wheatleigh was being finished, a gift of H. H. Cook to his daughter on the occasion of her marriage to "Count" Carlos de Heredia. The 90-plus-room Elm Court was nearby, too, in Lenox, built by rug magnate W. D. Sloane; and across town, Giraud Foster had erected his multimillion-dollar likeness of Le Petit Trianon in France at his estate, Bellefontaine. Also in Stockbridge was Naumkeag, Ambassador Choate's homey mansion, along with sculptor Daniel Chester French's splendid Chesterwood. Soon, in Lenox, Robert Paterson built Blantyre, and novelist Edith Wharton oversaw the design of the Mount. In all, some 75 extraordinary mansions graced the Berkshire landscape. European and urban tastes had arrived in the hills.

Yet William C. Whitney, secretary of the navy under President Grover Cleveland, acquired more land than all of these. In 1896 Whitney established an 11,000-acre game preserve in the Berkshire town of Washington, stocking it with buffalo, moose, Virginia deer, and elk. The estate later became October Mountain State Forest, a giant reserve in the center of the county. Two years later North Adams industrialists donated 400 acres at the summit of Mount Greylock to the commonwealth, creating the first state reservation.

In North Adams a "normal school," or teachers' college, was established in 1894. Over the following century it evolved into the Massachusetts College of Liberal Arts.

President James Garfield was assassinated on his way to his 25th Williams College reunion, so his vice president, Chester A. Arthur, took over. Both men had taught in the same one-room schoolhouse in nearby Pownal, Vermont, in the 1850s. In the fall of 1902, President Teddy Roosevelt visited Berkshire, sustaining minor injury after his coach overturned near the Pittsfield Country Club. That next summer, both ex-President Grover Cleveland and humorist Mark Twain summered in Tyringham. Eight years later, on July 4, 1911, as Pittsfield observed its gala 150th anniversary, President Taft spoke before a crowd of 50,000 at the railroad station. And later that same year, Edith Wharton's novella *Ethan Frome* was published, a critical and popular success that derived many of its dramatic and scenic details from life in the Berkshires.

Twentieth-century Berkshire was marked with events principally in industry and the arts. Since 1903 General Electric has played a significant role in the county's industry. In 1914 GE established a high-voltage laboratory in Pittsfield, and 7 years later the lab made electrical history by producing a million-volt flash of artificial lightning. While GE developed a large transformer business and produced naval armaments, Sprague Electric met the country's enormous need for capacitors during World War II and expanded to fill former mills in North Adams. Both manufacturers declined significantly in the second half of the century, although Commonwealth Sprague and GE Plastics remain.

*Public fountain by Daniel Chester French, in the town park, Lee* Judith Monachina

In the arts, the Stockbridge Playhouse (now the Berkshire Theatre Festival) opened in 1928 with Eva LeGallienne in *Cradle Song*. Ted Shawn established his School of Dance at Jacob's Pillow in Becket in 1933. The 1930s heard the first Berkshire Symphony Festival concerts, a prelude to Tanglewood.

Downhill skiing debuted in Berkshire in 1933, as Bousquet opened runs in Pittsfield and arranged for "ski trains" from New York. After the Civilian Conservation Corps carved the Thunderbolt Trail on Greylock in the

1930s, it was the scene of eastern championships before and after World War II. Soon half a dozen mountains in the county were crisscrossed by trails.

The 1950s saw the arrival of artist Norman Rockwell in Stockbridge and the creation of the Sterling and Francine Clark Art Institute in Williamstown, a collection and facility of international import. The Williamstown Theatre Festival began performances, enlivening all of Berkshire with star-studded drama. In the 1960s two more colleges joined Williams and MCLA: Berkshire Community College in Pittsfield, the first in a series of state junior colleges, and Simon's Rock Early College in Great Barrington, a progressive school that is now part of Bard College. Speaking of bards, Arlo Guthrie, scion of a folk legend and a former student at Stockbridge School, wrote a song about littering, the draft, and a community of friends in Stockbridge, "Alice's Restaurant."

The last Shaker sisters left their village in Hancock in 1960. A group of visionary citizens led by Amy Bess Miller managed to purchase their property and turn it into a living museum, today one of the county's premier attractions. And the great estates, too, have been recycled since the mid-20th century, opening Berkshire's fiefdoms to the public. In addition to uncounted B&Bs and restaurants, the arts lead in the adaptive reuse of former manors. The Mount, now owned by Edith Wharton Restorations, Inc., is open to tours in-season, sponsoring lectures and other events. Shakespeare & Co. struts the stage at Springlawn. In the Glendale section of Stockbridge, the gracious Linwood estate was transformed into the new home of the Norman Rockwell Museum. Looking back toward Tanglewood from this splendid site, the visitor gets a fresh view of unspoiled 19th-century Berkshire. In the early 1990s, Tanglewood expanded at another former estate, as well, creating a $10 million arched concert hall, where 1,200 music lovers enjoy both acoustic intimacy and fidelity.

The Massachusetts Museum of Contemporary Art—MASS MoCA—in North Adams, resides not in an old estate but an old mill complex. It opened in the summer of 1999 to large crowds and international press coverage. Critics, even those who have reservations about individual works of art, cheer the space created and the imaginative performances of film, theater, dance, and music presented.

Berkshire citizens discuss the changes in their county: condos, shopping malls, bypasses, even traffic signals. The Wal-Marting of Berkshire has begun, first in North Adams and then in Pittsfield. Some say the big-box stores create jobs and bring low prices; others point out that the Berkshire Mall drained life from downtown Pittsfield, just as Prime Outlets appears to have pulled business from the Lenox shops. Once again the Berkshire barrier has been broken—this time by the nitroglycerin of mass marketing.

Environmental issues are being addressed head on. A variety of ecologically aware groups continue to oversee efforts to clean up Berkshire's principal river, the Housatonic. And the Hoosic River appears to be on its way to be cleansed of PCBs for good. The Berkshire Natural Resources Council and other environmental protection groups guard and preserve the splendor of the landscape. With the gradual shrinking of industry here and tourism among the most stable of Berkshire businesses, protecting the rolling hills makes economic and aesthetic sense. Once the hills were decimated, shaved bald by paper and lumber mills and charcoal manufacturers. Now the hills are once more alive, fully forested and soothing to the eye.

# 2

# Transportation

## *Getting Here, Getting Around*

**Although bus lines** bring some visitors to and from Berkshire County and the "B Bus" (Berkshire Regional Transit Authority) carries some through the county, most people rely on automobiles. Travel was more colorful if less comfortable in the past.

First we walked or rode horseback on county roads that were choked with dust, buried in snow, or clogged with bottomless mud, depending on the season. Then the Hudson and the Connecticut rivers carried passengers toward Berkshire aboard sailing ships, and by 1825 steamboats began regular service. Both Albany and Hartford were connected to New York City by steamboat runs, the upper Connecticut and the Hudson rivers being outfitted with an elaborate system of locks to bypass the rapids.

With the harnessing of steam for riverboat power, it wasn't long before the iron horse galloped into the Berkshire Hills. The Housatonic Railroad brought visitors from New York City and Connecticut. Two lines competed to the west: the Albany–West Stockbridge Line and the Hudson and Berkshire Line. From Boston, construction of the Western Railway up from Springfield was reportedly "delayed by competition between Stockbridge and Pittsfield for fixing of the route through their town. After surveys, Pittsfield won." During the summers of 1840–41, laborers, mostly Irish, dug deep cuts in the hills and built many bridges. When the lines were completed, Berkshire was 9 hours by train from Boston and about 3 hours from Albany. Many who had come to work on the railroads never took the train back.

Sons of these rail workers may have labored on a remarkable system of track and overhead electric wires running from Williamstown south through North Adams and Adams, through Pittsfield, Lenox, Lee, Great Barrington, and Sheffield. Quiet and reliable, this Berkshire Street Railway grew so popular that opulent parlor cars were constructed and put into service, running till 1932. When automobiles and buses were refined, the possibilities for public transport changed; paved roads were improved, and unpaved ones were surfaced. Passenger rail and street railroad service to and within the Berkshires withered.

### Present Possibilities

The roads to Berkshire are smooth and scenic, so an automobile, if available, is useful to explore the back roads and byways. Buses run regularly from New York City, Hartford, Boston, and Albany. Those in a hurry to get to these hills can fly in but, alas, only by private or charter plane to Great Barrington, Pittsfield, or North Adams. Closest commercial air

*A small park near the Intermodal Center in Pittsfield* Judith Monachina

service is to Bradley International, north of Hartford and the Albany International Airport; from there, car rentals or limousine and bus service are available. The future of Amtrak's once-a-day service to Pittsfield is questionable. For convenience, a host of details about Berkshire transportation follows—none of it as up-to-date as a telephone call, however.

## Getting to These Hills

### By Car

**From Manhattan:** Take the Major Deegan Expressway or the Henry Hudson Parkway to the Saw Mill River Parkway, and then proceed north on one of the most beautiful roadways in the world, the Taconic State Parkway. For southern Berkshire, exit the Taconic at "Hillsdale, Claverack, Route 23," and follow Route 23 east, toward Hillsdale and on to Great Barrington. For Stockbridge, Lee, and Lenox, proceed up Route 7. For Pittsfield and northern Berkshire, exit the Taconic at Route 295 and head east to Route 22, following Route 22 north to Route 20 for Pittsfield or to Route 43 through Hancock to Williamstown and North Adams.

**From New Jersey, Pennsylvania, and south:** Take the New York Thruway to I-84 east; at the Taconic Parkway exit, turn north, following "From Manhattan" instructions. If local color is high on your list, or you'd rather ramble than scurry northward, Route 22 north is a good choice, and you can pick it up as far south as Armonk or Bedford in Westchester County, New York. Route 22 is a road still proud of its diners: Of particular note is the Red Rooster in Pawling, just north of I-684's end. Farther upstate on Route 22, turn right at

Hillsdale on Route 23 east toward Great Barrington, on Route 20 to Pittsfield, or on Route 43 to Williamstown.

**From Connecticut and/or the New York Metro area:** Route 7 north was an early stagecoach thoroughfare to Berkshire, and you join the same trail at Danbury, via I-684 and I-84. Driving up Route 7, you'll wend your way along the beautiful Housatonic River, north through New Milford, Kent, and Canaan and into Massachusetts through Ashley Falls (an especially good ride for picnics and antiques). To arrive in southeastern Berkshire, Route 8 is a quick and scenic drive as it follows the Farmington River north.

**From Boston and east:** The scenic Massachusetts Turnpike (MassPike, I-90) is the quickest, easiest route west to south Berkshire and Pittsfield, and from Boston there's no better bet. West of the Connecticut River, you can get off the turnpike at Exit 3, and take Route 202 south to Route 20 west, and pick up Route 23 west at Woronoco for the best route to Otis Ridge, Butternut Basin, and Catamount ski areas. Most people stay on the turnpike right into the Berkshires, exiting either at Lee or West Stockbridge.

A less rapid but more colorful route westward from Boston is Route 20, which cuts across southern Massachusetts, connecting with Lee. If you're coming west to the Berkshires from more northern latitudes, Route 9 from Northampton is a splendid drive, a high road, with long lovely vistas and few towns. Still farther to the north, eastern entry to Berkshire County can be gained by driving the most scenic of them all, the Mohawk Trail, originally an Indian byway. Also known as Route 2, this is the most direct way to North Adams, Williamstown, and north Berkshire ski areas. Warning: some people do not take kindly to the twists, turns, and dropoffs of the trail as it crosses Florida Mountain.

**From Hartford:** The quickest route is I-91 north to the Massachusetts Turnpike west. Then proceed as in directions for Massachusetts Turnpike travel from Boston. A slower but more pleasant drive is Route 44 west, up through Avon, Norfolk, and Canaan, where you take Route 8 or Route 7 north into Berkshire County.

**From Montreal or Albany:** Leaving Canada, take I-87 (known as "the Northway") south to Albany, and exit at Route 7 to Route 2 toward Williamstown, to Route 20 to Pittsfield, or continue on I-87 south to I-90 east, connecting then to the Massachusetts Turnpike, which is the continuation of I-90 east. Exit at either Canaan, New York, or Lee.

## By Bus

**From Manhattan** (3.5 hours): **Bonanza** (800-556-3815) serves the Berkshires out of New York City's **Port Authority Bus Terminal** (212-564-8484) at 40th Street between 8th and 9th avenues. Tickets may be purchased at the **Greyhound** ticket windows (212-971-6363), near 8th Avenue. Several buses a day. Boarding is down the escalators at the center of the terminal, and then to the right, usually at Gate 13. Berkshire locales marked with an asterisk are Flag Stops, where you must wave to the bus driver in order to be picked up.

### Berkshire Phone Numbers for New York Buses

**Canaan, CT:** Brooks Pharmacy, Main St., 888-751-8800

**Gt. Barrington:** Bill's Pharmacy, 362 Main St., 413-528-1590

**Hillsdale, NY:** *Junction Rtes. 22 & 23, 800-556-3815

## BERKSHIRE ACCESS

Using Tanglewood (on the Stockbridge–Lenox line) as the Berkshire reference point, the following cities are this close.

| City | Time | Miles |
|---|---|---|
| Albany | 1 hr | 50 |
| Boston | 2.5 hrs | 135 |
| Bridgeport | 2 hrs | 110 |
| Danbury | 1.75 hrs | 85 |
| Hartford | 1.5 hrs | 70 |
| Montreal | 5 hrs | 275 |
| New Haven | 2.5 hrs | 115 |
| New York City | 3 hrs | 150 |
| Philadelphia | 5 hrs | 230 |
| Providence | 2.5 hrs | 125 |
| Springfield | 0.75 hr | 35 |
| Washington, DC | 7 hrs | 350 |
| Waterbury | 1.5 hrs | 75 |
| Worcester | 1.75 hrs | 90 |

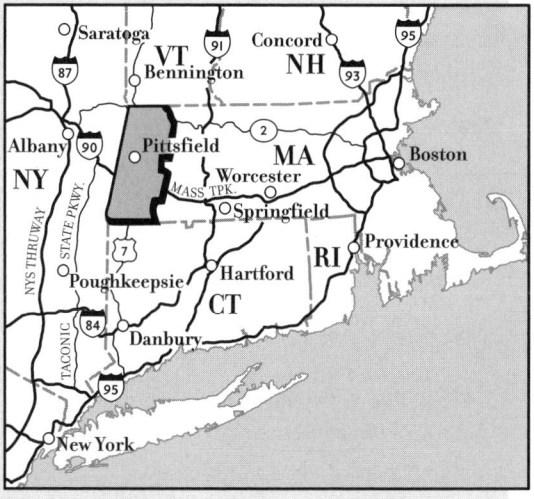


© The Countryman Press

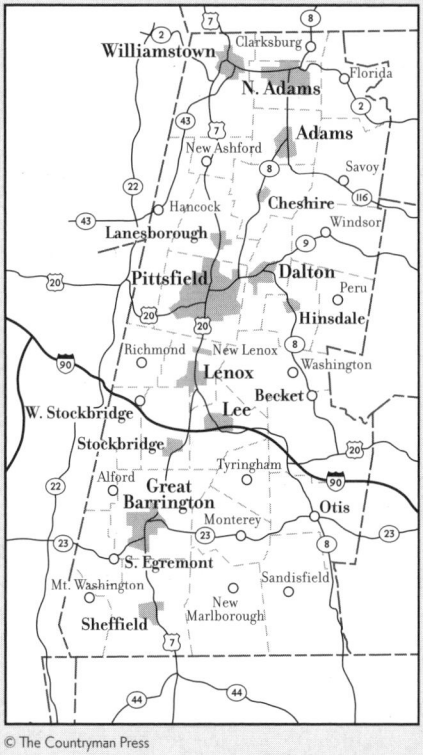


© The Countryman Press

Berkshire County is 56 miles in length from Sheffield to Williamstown, and, depending on the season and the weather, it normally takes 1.5 hours to drive along Route 7. Because of the mountain ranges that also run north to south, east-west travel across the county remains more difficult. All of the county's east-west routes (2 in the north, 9 midcounty, and 23 in the south) are tricky drives in freezing or snowy weather. Back roads in particular vary tremendously in condition and type, ranging from smooth macadam to rough dirt. On these back roads especially, drivers should keep an eye out for bicyclists, horseback riders, hikers, joggers, in-line skaters—and deer, bear, moose, and bobcat.

**Lee:** McClelland Drugs, 43 Main St., 413-243-0135

**Lenox:** Lenox News & Variety, 39 Housatonic St., 413-637-2815

**New Ashford:** *Entrance to Snowy Owl Development, Rte. 7, 800-556-3815

**Pittsfield:** Intermodal Center, Columbus Ave., 413-442-4451

**Sheffield:** *Bank of Boston, Rte. 7, 800-556-3815

**Stockbridge:** Chamber of Commerce Booth, Main St., 413-298-3344

**Williamstown:** The Williams Inn, Main St., 413-458-2665

**From Boston** (3.5 hours): **Peter Pan/Trailways** runs daily to Pittsfield and Lee–Lenox out of the **Trailways Terminal** at South Station. Change to **Bonanza** in Springfield for North Adams–Williamstown. Contact 800-343-9999 or www.peterpanbus.com for prices and schedules.

Pittsfield's Intermodal Center brings local and long-distance buses together with Amtrak on Columbus Avenue between North and Center streets.

#### Berkshire Phone Numbers for Boston Buses

**Lee:** McClelland Drugs, 43 Main St., 413-243-0135

**Lenox:** Lenox News & Variety, 39 Housatonic St., 413-637-2815

**Pittsfield:** Bus Terminal, 57 S. Church St., 413-442-4451

**Williamstown:** The Williams Inn, 1090 Main St., 413-458-9371

**From Hartford** (1.75 hours): The **Greyhound Line** (800-231-2222) runs two buses to Pittsfield daily, with a transfer at Springfield, from the **Greyhound Terminal** at 1 Union Place (in the train station), Hartford.

**From Montreal** (6 hours): **Greyhound** runs south to the Albany **Greyhound Terminal.** Connect to Pittsfield as noted below.

**From Albany** (1 hour): **Bonanza** runs two buses daily from Albany to Pittsfield. **Greyhound** runs one bus daily.

## By Train

**From Manhattan:** Commuters ride at a fraction of the regular rate if they take **Metro North** (800-METRO-INFO) out of Grand Central Station and get off at Wassaic, New York (on Route 22 near Sharon, Connecticut). A bus connects to South County on **summer weekends. Amtrak** (800-USA-RAIL, 413-872-7245) can also help you get to the Berkshires. Their Turboliner from Pennsylvania Station runs frequently and smoothly along the Hudson River, a splendid ride. For southern Berkshire, stay aboard till Hudson, a river town recently restored; for northern Berkshire, stay on to Rensselaer. For travel connections from Wassaic, Hudson, or Rensselaer to the Berkshires, see "By Taxi or Limousine."

**From Boston: Amtrak** *may* continue to run a single train daily through the Berkshires, starting from Boston's South Station, although the run is threatened. The station in

Pittsfield is part of the Intermodal Center, on Columbus Avenue between North and Center streets. The round-trip ticket prices vary, depending on time of travel and seat availability. Private compartments are available. Note: Because this train is "borrowing" tracks from ConRail, freight trains take priority, resulting in delays.

**From Montreal: Amtrak** runs one train daily from Montreal through Albany. There is no same-day train connection from this run to the Berkshires; see "By Limousine or Taxi"; or see "By Bus."

**From Albany: Amtrak** may continue a single Pittsfield-bound (to the Intermodal Center; see "From Boston") train daily from the Albany/Rensselaer station on East Street (2 miles from downtown Albany).

## By Plane

If you own a small airplane or decide to charter one, you can fly directly to the Berkshires, landing at Great Barrington, Pittsfield, or North Adams airports.

**From New York City:** Feeling rich, traveling high with some friends, or riding on the corporate account? There are several charter air companies in the metropolitan New York area that will fly you from La Guardia, JFK, or other New York metropolitan airports near to any of the Berkshire airports. Charters currently flying these routes include

**American Air Charter:** 800-645-9572

**Chester Air:** Chester, CT; 800-752-6371

**First Flight:** Horseheads, NY; 800-221-1802

**And from Westchester County:**

**Panorama:** White Plains Airport, 914-328-9800

**Richmor Aviation:** 800-331-6101, 518-828-9461

**From Boston:** Numerous charter flight companies fly from Beantown to Berkshire.

**From Hartford:** Bradley International Airport in Hartford handles numerous domestic and international airlines, so you can fly to Bradley from nearly anywhere. From there, charter air service to the Berkshires is available through any of the companies from Boston or through the Berkshire County companies listed below.

**From Albany:** Albany is terminus for a substantial volume of domestic jet traffic and, being under an hour from the Berkshires by car, is the closest you can get to these hills by big plane. Charter connector flights are available from Albany to the Berkshires, based at Albany International Airport or through the Berkshire County companies listed below.

**In Berkshire County:** Three aviation companies in Berkshire County operate air taxi service to just about any other northeastern airport:

**Berkshire Aviation:** Great Barrington Airport, 413-528-1010, 413-528-1061

**Esposito Flying Service:** Harriman & West Airport, North Adams, 413-663-3330

**Lyon Aviation:** Pittsfield Airport, 413-443-6700

### By Limousine or Taxi

If you're with a group or want to pamper yourself, a limousine direct to Berkshire is the smoothest approach. Many limousine services will whisk you away from urban gridlock to the spaciousness of this hill country.

**From New York City and its airports:**
**Carey:** 212-935-9700
**Kabot:** 718-545-2400

**From Boston and Logan International Airport:**
Numerous services are available.

**From Hartford and Bradley International Airport:**
**Carey Chauffeured Service:** 860-666-9051, 800-RELIMOS
**Avalon Transportation:** 800-395-LIMO

**From Albany, Albany International Airport, and Rensselaer:**
See "By Taxi or Limousine" below.

**From Hudson, NY, and its Amtrak Station:**
**Star City Taxi:** 518-828-3355

## GETTING AROUND THE BERKSHIRES

Route 7 is Berkshire County's main roadway, connecting cities and towns from south to north. Driving in winter, you'll certainly need snow tires. In summer the cruising is easy, but on certain weekends during Tanglewood and fall foliage seasons, temporary traffic delays in popular villages are likely. Whenever possible, park and walk. Friendly but firm traffic police will suggest outlying parking areas. And motorists beware: State law requires a full stop for pedestrians in crosswalks.

**Note:** Individual town maps of Great Barrington, Stockbridge, Lenox, Pittsfield, North Adams, and Williamstown can be found on pages 34–39.

### By Bus

Berkshire County is no longer served by the electrified Berkshire Street Railway, but the **"B,"** a public bus system, has in some ways filled the gap. The buses run from early morning to early evening. Information can be obtained from the **Berkshire Regional Transit Authority** (413-499-2782; from Massachusetts phones, 800-292-2782). Fares vary by distance. If you're visiting without a car, the B will provide plenty of access to other communities, but Sunday service is not available.The Intermodal Center in Pittsfield brings local and long-distance buses together with Amtrak on Columbus Avenue between North and Center streets.

### By Rented Car

Car rental agencies abound in Berkshire. Most will not deliver cars—you must first go to their place of business to do the paperwork. Berkshire car rentals are available through the following agencies:

NORTH ADAMS
**Berkshire Rent-A-Car:** 413-664-1000
**Enterprise:** 413-664-7120

PITTSFIELD
**Affordable:** 413-445-5795

**Berkshire Rent-A-Car:** 413-447-8117

**National:** 413-442-4200

**Pete's Leasing:** 413-445-5795; 800-651-7383, 800-499-8117

## By Taxi or Limousine

Numerous taxi and limo companies serve Berkshire County. The following is a listing by town, with notations indicating if they have only taxis (T), only limos (L), or both (B).

DALTON
**Jenkins Livery:** 413-684-1893 (T)

GREAT BARRINGTON
**AA Transport Car Services:** 413-528-6778 (B)
**Taxi Company:** 413-528-0911, 413-528-0567 (T)

LEE
**Abbott's Limousine & Livery:** 413-243-1645 (L)
**Park Taxi:** 413-243-0020 (T)

LENOX
**Alston's Livery & Limo:** 800-286-3674 (L)

**Berkshire Taxi:** 413-637-1737 (T)

**Tobi's Limousine Service:** 413-637-1224 (L)

NORTH ADAMS
**American Cab Co.:** 413-662-2000 (T)

**Berkshire Livery Service:** 413-662-2609 (L)

**Norm's Limousine Service:** 413-663-8300 (L)

**Transport the People:** 413-664-3200 (B)

PITTSFIELD
**Airport Limousine Service:** 413-443-7111 (L)

**Arrow Taxi:** 413-499-8604 (B)

**Berkshire Limousine:** 413-499-3232, 800-543-6776 (L)

**Classic Coach Limo:** 413-448-2258 (L)

**Rainbow Taxi:** 413-499-4300 (T)

## By Bicycle

Bicycling in the Berkshires gives an exciting intimacy with the rolling landscape. Depending on your willingness to bundle up, biking from town to town is possible nearly year-round. Bike rental prices vary widely. Bikes for rent or purchase are available through

ADAMS
**Berkshire Outfitters:** 413-743-5900

GREAT BARRINGTON
**Berkshire Bike & Blade:** 413-528-5555

LENOX
**Arcadian Shop:** 413-637-3010

**Mean Wheels:** 413-637-0644

NORTH ADAMS
**Sports Corner:** 413-664-8654

PITTSFIELD
**Mike's Bike Shop:** 413-443-1166

**Ordinary Cycles:** 413-442-7225

**Plaine's Bike & Ski Center:** 413-499-0294

WILLIAMSTOWN
**The Mountain Goat:** 413-458-8445

**The Spoke:** 413-458-3456

## On Foot

For those with the time, we've got the trail. The **Appalachian Trail** enters southern Berkshire in the town of Mount Washington and runs over hill and dale, past Great Barrington, through Monterey, down into Tyringham Valley, then up near the town of Washington, through Dalton and Cheshire, over Mount Greylock, and into Vermont. See "Walking, Hiking, Camping, X-C Skiing" in chapter 7, "Outdoor Recreation."

Most Berkshire towns have a system of local trails, and many comunities are small enough for walking exploration. Four in particular are well suited to visiting without a vehicle: Lee, Lenox, Stockbridge, and Williamstown. All are lovely villages, with good accommodations, fine dining, interesting shopping, and first-rate cultural attractions within easy walking distance.

# NEIGHBORS ALL AROUND

Just as the name "Berkshire" has spread to adjacent areas, the county and its people frequently have close ties with neighboring communities, counties, and states. Travelers will want to connect with the neighbors, too, for Berkshire is surrounded by areas of extensive natural beauty. Certain nearby towns are loaded with good restaurants, old inns, and cultural attractions.

### To the South

The Litchfield Hills of northwest Connecticut are gentler than the Berkshire Hills but still make for good hiking. There is lovely architecture in this area, with many stately homes in Salisbury, Lakeville, Sharon, Litchfield, and Norfolk. And there are music festivals, as well, such as the ones at Norfolk and at Music Mountain in Falls Village. See "Music" in chapter 5, "Arts & Pleasures."

### To the East

Halfway over the Berkshire highlands between the Housatonic River Valley and the Connecticut River lies the jagged eastern county border, shared with Franklin County up north and Hamden and Hampshire counties. Besides this eastern area's natural splendor, an attractive array of cultural possibilities is located here. The "Five College Area" of Amherst, South Hadley, and Northampton (a cultural mecca all by itself) offers all the aesthetic and academic action anyone could want with the presence of Amherst, Hampshire, Mt. Holyoke, and Smith colleges, and the University of Massachusetts.

### To the North

The Green Mountains of Vermont offer great skiing, hiking, and camping. The town of Bennington makes an interesting stopover, with its museum (featuring Grandma Moses paintings), an arts center, and poet Robert Frost's grave behind the historic Old Bennington Church. A new Frost museum has opened on Historic Route 7-A north of town. There is also the extraordinary Bennington Pottery, where a visitor can both buy and dine on handsome stoneware. Route 7 up here continues to architecturally stunning Manchester: well worth the time, even dawdling along Historic Route 7A.

### To the West

The farms and small towns of Columbia County, in New York State, hold treasures for antiques and "untiques" hunters. Berkshire is not far from the Hudson Valley, an area rich with history and vineyards worth visiting. And then there's Albany, which offers big-city cultural entertainment such as the touring New York Metropolitan Opera, performing at the capital city's structurally unique theater, the Egg. A bit farther north is Saratoga with its spas, its springs, its own summer arts festival (Saratoga Performing Arts Center, known as SPAC), and its elegant and justly famous racecourse.

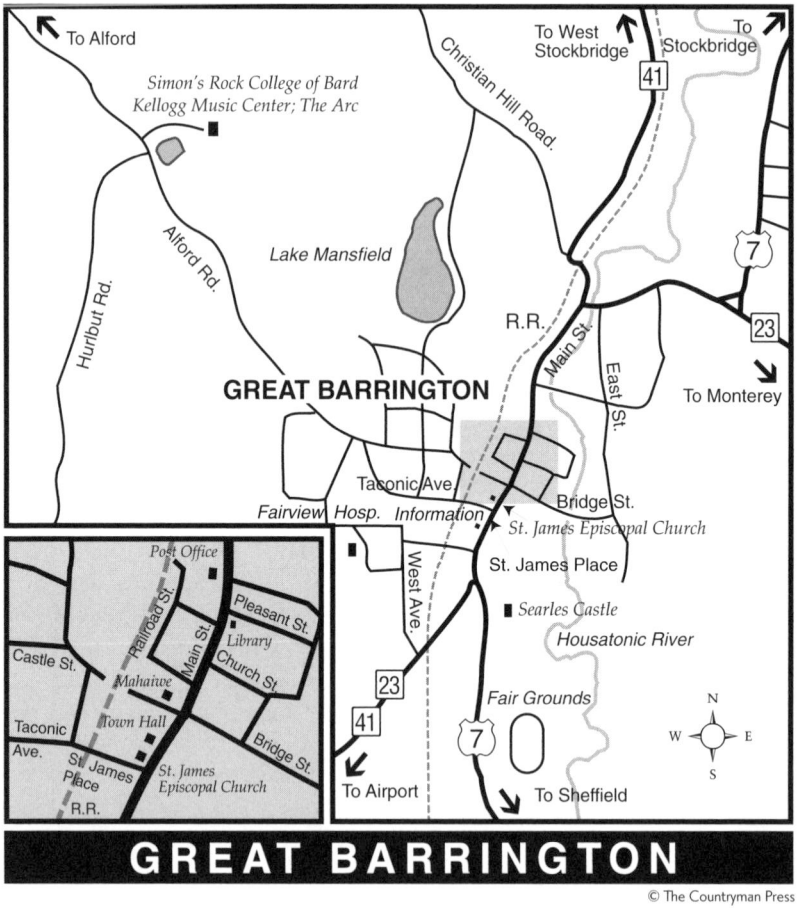


GREAT BARRINGTON

© The Countryman Press

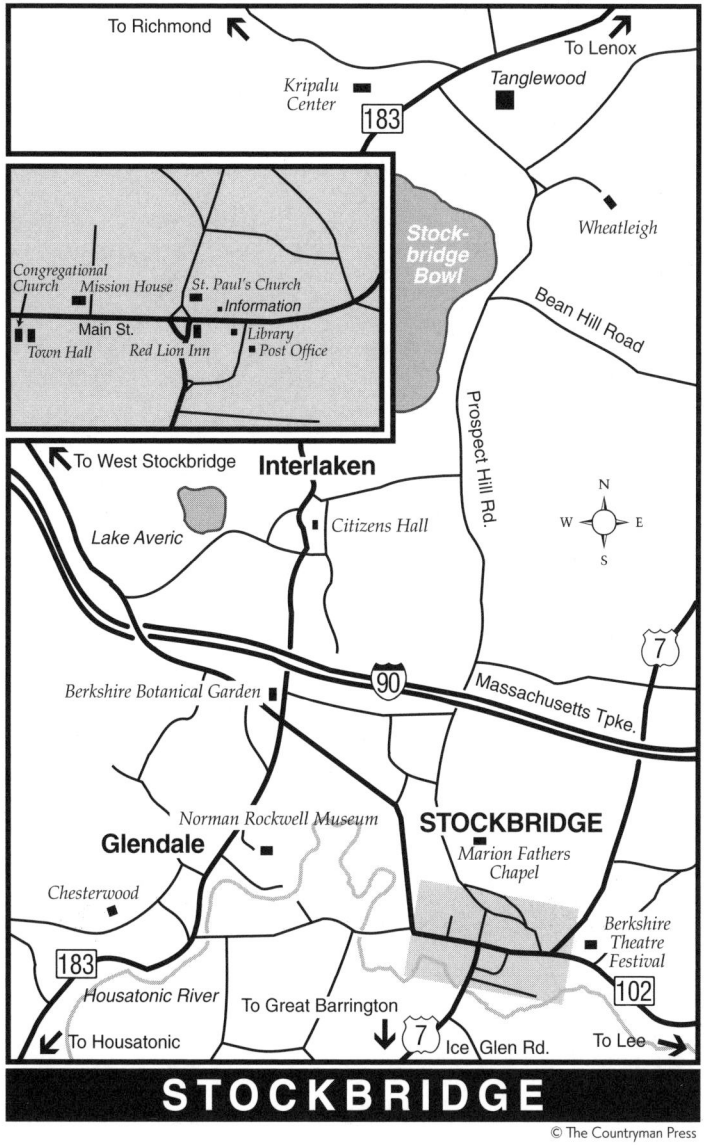


© The Countryman Press

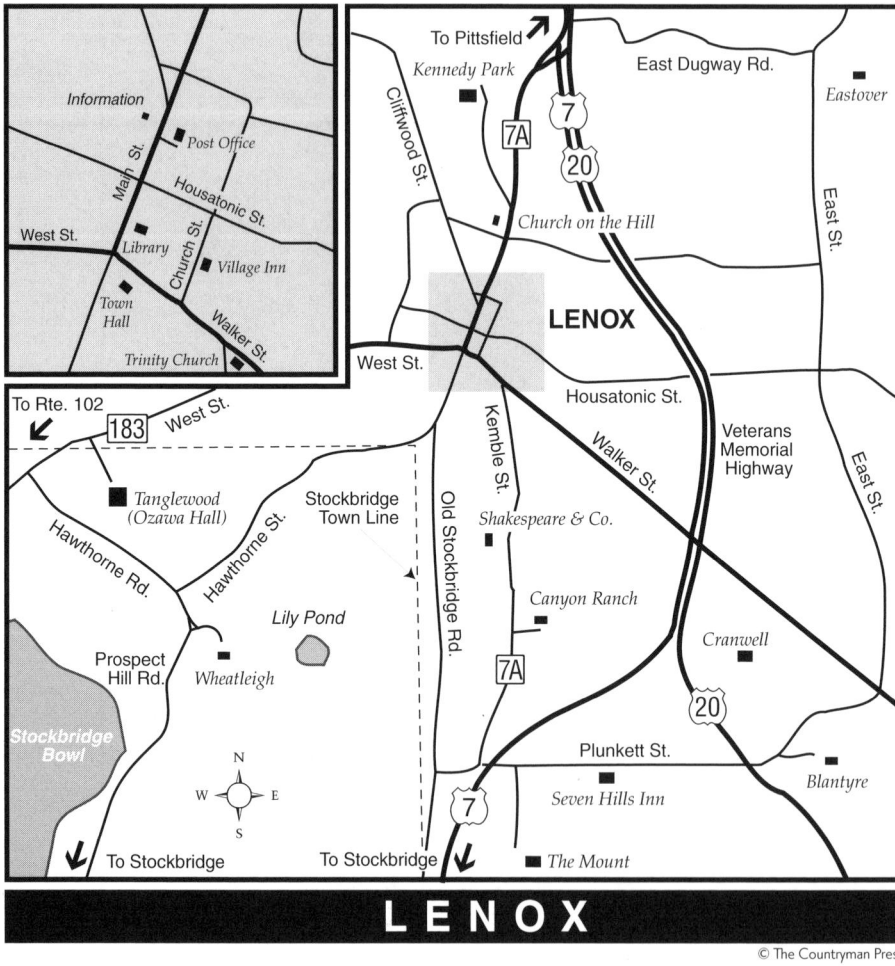


LENOX

© The Countryman Press

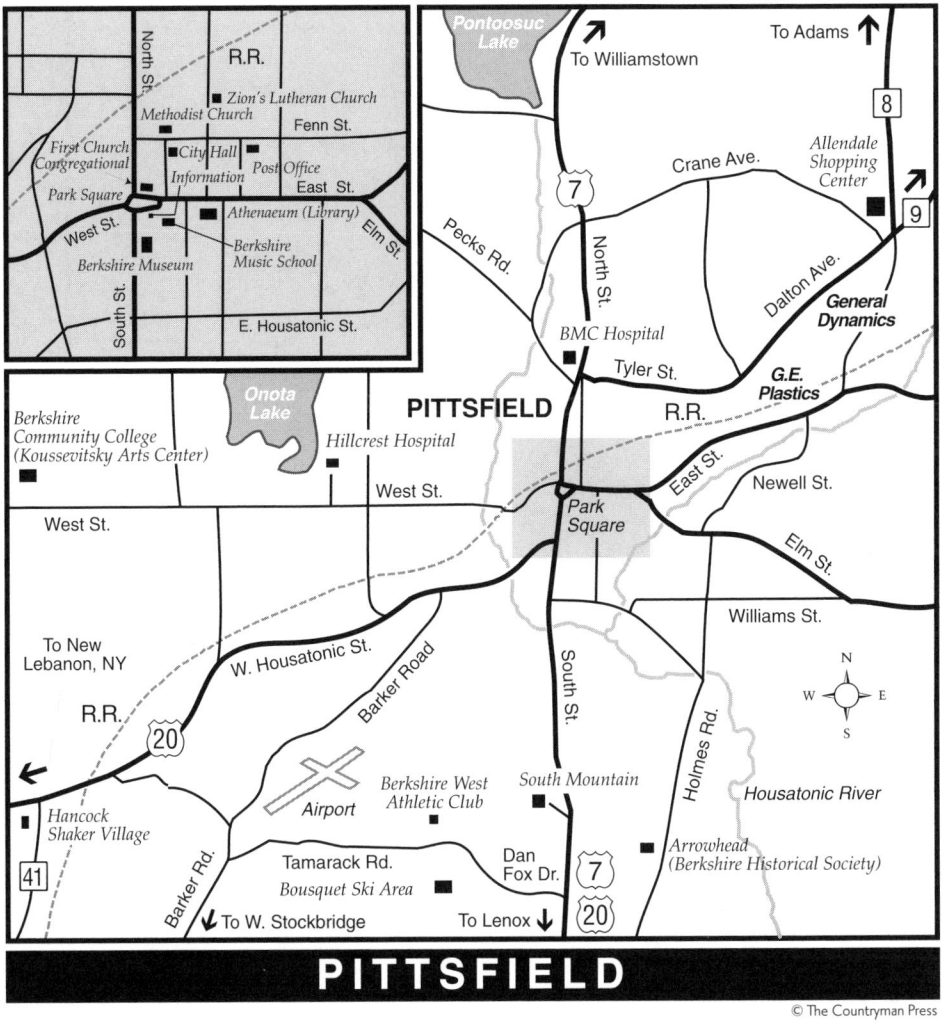


© The Countryman Press

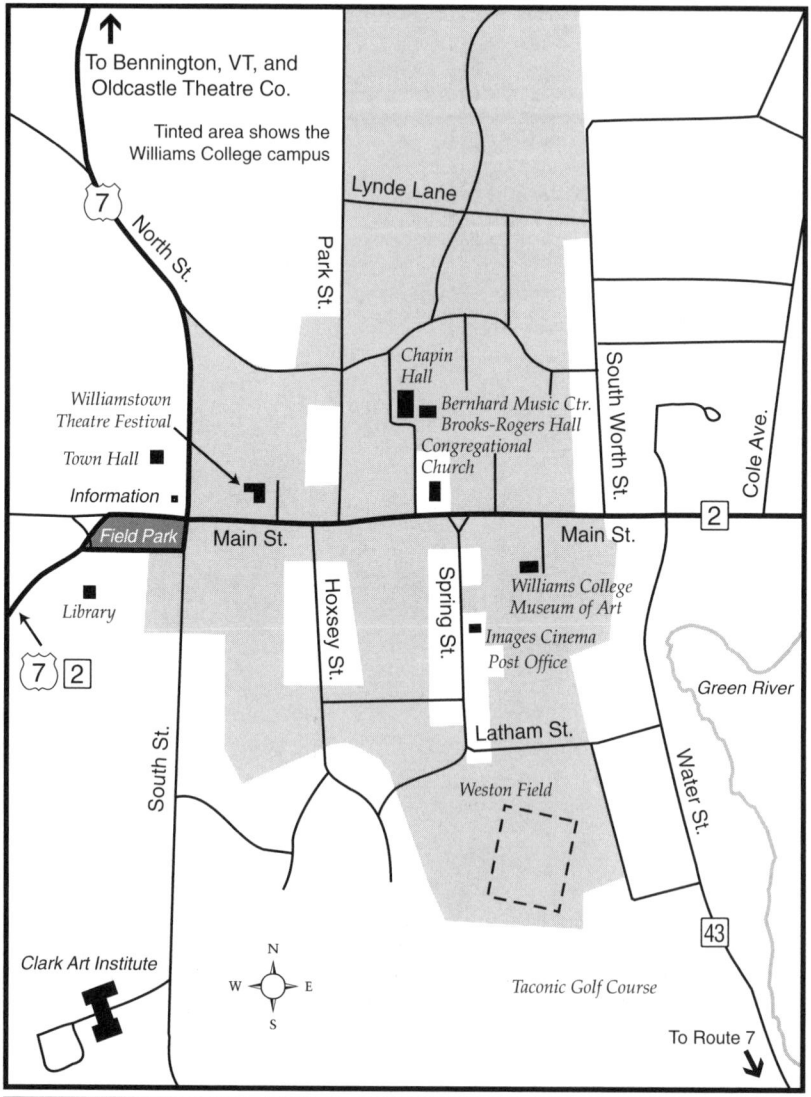


WILLIAMSTOWN

© The Countryman Press

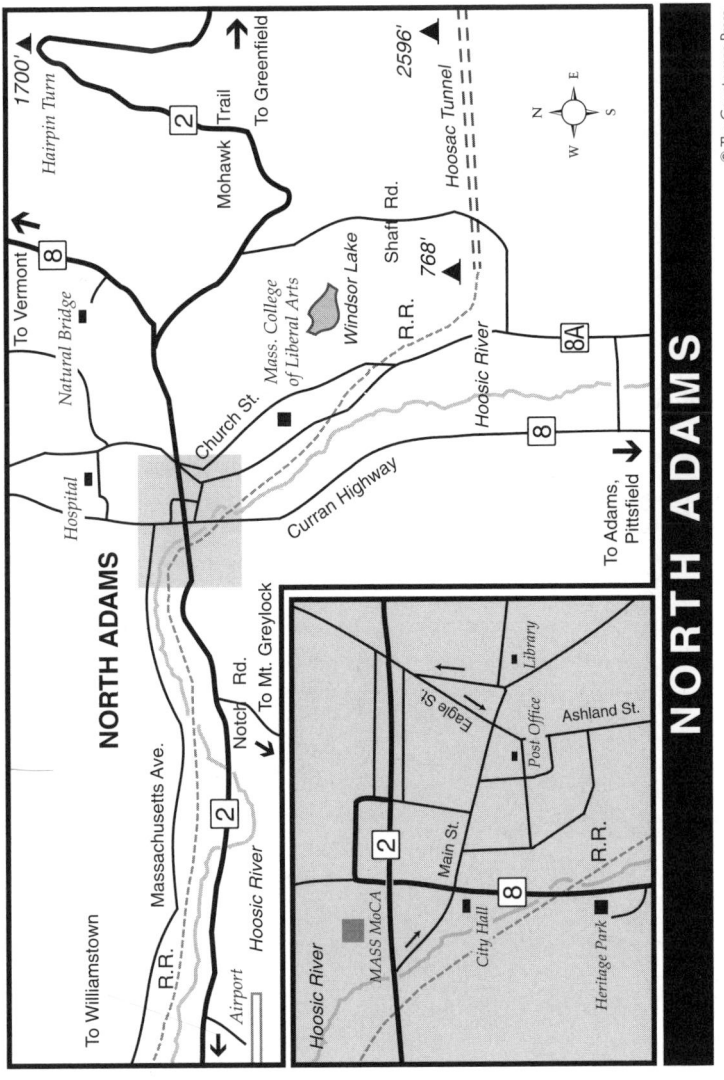


© The Countryman Press

# 3

# Lodging

## *The Keys to Your Room*

**As stagecoach travel** through Berkshire developed in the 18th century, the need for roadside lodgings grew. The **New Boston Inn** in Sandisfield, still welcoming travelers, was likely the first extant one. Built in 1737, this restored inn is about as authentic an Early American lodging experience as can be found in New England. Close in age and attention to period detail is the **Old Inn on the Green** (1760), in New Marlborough. This inn served as a tavern, a store, and later as a post office. Today it comforts travelers with a small number of authentically colonial rooms and a superlative restaurant. In 1770 Colonel Benjamin Simonds established **Riverbend Farm** in Williamstown, now a B&B meticulously restored by David and Judy Loomis. Next came the **Red Lion Inn** (1773) in Stockbridge, which provided not only housing for sojourners but also a meeting place for pre-Revolutionary political activists eager to communicate their grievances to Britain. More than 225 years later, distinguished guests still communicate from the Red Lion . . . around the world.

Many other 18th-century Berkshire inns continue to offer warmth, hospitality, and a good night's sleep, often in a four-poster bed—among them, the **Village Inn** in Lenox, built as a farmhouse in 1771; the **Egremont Inn** (1780) and the **Weathervane Inn** (1785) in South Egremont; the **Elm Court Inn** (1790) in North Egremont; and the **Williamsville Inn** in West Stockbridge, originally a farmhouse dating from 1797.

Or if the 19th century's sumptuous Gilded Age stirs our stirrup cup, Berkshire offers, among other possibilities, an Italian palazzo called **Wheatleigh** and a Tudor castle called **Blantyre,** both in Lenox. Strikingly different in style, these palatial estates-turned-hotels share the ability to satisfy even the most refined of tastes and to do so with panache.

About 300 Berkshire lodgings exist today, some shorter perhaps on romance but more reasonably priced than others. Berkshire Visitors Bureau executive director William R. Wilson Jr. estimates 4,000 "heads in beds" capacity for the county. There are an ever-growing number of guesthouses, both in town and out, many offering bed and breakfast ("B&B"); there are simple inns where precious quiet is an everyday experience; and there are modern hotels and all grades of motels.

We present a representative sampling, in terms of price, geography, and architecture. To include lodgings, we place a high value on hospitality, the personal attention and sincere care that can turn a visit into an unforgettable sojourn. We also assign value and significance to the architectural qualities of a property, to its history and traditions and care

*Tea time at Crabtree Cottage, in Lee. Many small inns and B&Bs have tea time or offer early-evening snacks or place chocolates on guests' beds.* Judith Monachina

in furnishing and use of antiques or other art, and to the views and the natural beauty right at its doorstep. As always, we would appreciate hearing about disappointments—or pleasant surprises.

## Berkshire Lodging Notes

**Rates:** Rate cards are generally printed in the spring and will change slightly from year to year. Reminder: Price codes are based on a per-room rate, double occupancy, during weekends in the high seasons (summer, fall foliage, skiing). Off-season rates are usually lower. Many establishments adjust for midweek, as well.

| | | | |
|---|---|---|---|
| Inexpensive | Up to $100 | Expensive | $150 to $200 |
| Moderate | $100 to $150 | Very Expensive | Over $200 |

These rates exclude required room taxes or service charges, which may be added to your bill. Suites tend to distort the scale.

**Minimum Stay:** Many lodgings require a minimum stay of 2, 3, or even 4 nights in summer and autumn. For a single night's stay in Berkshire at such times, motels are the best bet. During the off-season, minimum-stay requirements relax.

**Deposit/Cancellation:** Deposits are usually required for a confirmed reservation. Policies regarding deposits, cancellations, and refunds vary. It is always wise to inquire about these in advance. In the high season, including college graduation weekends in late May and early June, lodging demand exceeds supply, so reservations for the more popular places need to be made months or even years ahead.

**Special Features:** Wherever pertinent, we mention special features of lodgings, along with any caveats. Few establishments allow smoking indoors. Many limit pets or ages of children. This information is intended as a general guide only, and it is always best to call and inquire as policies may be flexible.

**Other Options:** We include Web sites. We do not list e-mail addresses as these are usually available on Web sites. Visitors may also want to browse general lodging or community sites, such as **www.berkshirelodging.com**, **leelodging.org**, **berkshireweb.com**, or **greatbarrington.org**.

For last-minute or emergency lodging arrangements in Berkshire, here are some numbers to phone:

**Berkshire Bed and Breakfast Reservation Service:** 413-731-8785

**Berkshire Lodgings Association:** 413-298-4760, 800-298-4760

**Berkshire Visitors Bureau:** 800-237-5747

For single-night stays in the high season or spur-of-the-moment arrangements at other times, visit any of the **tourist information booths** listed in the introduction.

## INNS AND B&BS SOUTH COUNTY

### EGREMONT

#### BALDWIN HILL FARM B&B

Owners: Richard and Priscilla Burdsall.
413-528-4092, 888-528-4092; fax 413-528-6365.
www.baldwinhillfarm.com.
121 Baldwin Hill Rd. N-S, Gt. Barrington, MA 01230.
N. on Baldwin Hill Rd. (off Rte. 23 & 41) to S. Egremont, 1.5 mi. to inn on left.
Price: Moderate.
Credit Cards: AE, D, MC, V.
Special Features: View; heated pool; no smoking; no pets; children over 10 welcome.

Baldwin Hill provides a 360-degree view of its magnificent surroundings. The establishment, a dairy farm, includes an 1820s farmhouse-turned-B&B and barns galore. It provides an opportunity for guests to stay at what they think farms were like. Peace, quiet, and tranquility abound on 300 acres perfect for hiking, cross-country skiing, or simply observing the wildlife. Guests enjoy reading by the fieldstone fireplace in winter or on the screened porch in summer. Four rooms, two with private baths, have views across fields to the mountains beyond. Full country breakfast, from a menu with numerous choices, is served by friendly innkeepers. They take pride in this farm that has been in Richard's family since 1910.

#### THE EGREMONT INN

Owners: Steven and Karen Waller.
413-528-2111, 800-859-1780; fax 413-528-3284.
www.egremontinn.com.
10 Old Sheffield Rd., P.O. Box 418, S. Egremont, MA 01258.
Side street off Rte. 23 in village center.
Price: Moderate.

Credit Cards: AE, D, MC, V.
Special Features: Pool, 2 tennis courts.

Coziness, low ceilings, five—count 'em, five—fireplaces downstairs, broad porches, 20 delightful rooms furnished with antiques: These set the tone for this historic 1780 stagecoach inn nestled on a quiet side street in the heart of a classic village. All rooms have private baths and central air-conditioning. Both two-room suites have fold-out sofas. Scenery ranges from lovely to gorgeous. Tavern and fine restaurant located on main floor. Live music 2 nights a week.

### THE WEATHERVANE INN

Owners: Maxine and Jeffrey Lome.
413-528-9580, 800-528-9580; fax 413-528-1713.
www.weathervaneinn.com.
Box 388, S. Egremont, MA 01258.
Rte. 23 just E. of the village.
Price: Expensive to Very Expensive.
Credit Cards: AE, MC, V.
Handicap Access: Limited.
Special Features: Pool; no pets; children welcome.

This is a comfortable, clean, and well-run operation set within a 1785 farmhouse. The 10 rooms and two suites all have private baths and air-conditioning. The hosts are skilled at their trade and provide their version of colonial lodging and catered fine dining for groups of 10 or more. The Weathervane's location is convenient to some of the best antiques shopping in the Berkshires, including one shop just behind the inn. Weekends in July and August have a 3-night minimum stay.

## GREAT BARRINGTON

### SEEKONK PINES INN B&B

Owners/Innkeepers: Lefkowitz Family.
413-528-4192, 800-292-4192.
www.seekonkpines.com.
142 Seekonk Crossroad, Gt. Barrington, MA 01230.
Rte. 23 between S. Egremont and Gt. Barrington.
Price: Moderate to Expensive.
Credit Cards: MC, V.
Special Features: Pool; bicycles; no smoking; no pets.

Originally the main house for a large estate, this 170-year-old house surrounded by meadows and well-groomed acreage keeps getting better and better. It must be the legacy of the wild goose for which the place was named. Furnished in country antiques and collectibles, the six guest rooms, all with private baths, are filled with personal touches. A guest pantry has a refrigerator, hot-water dispenser, and sink, with complimentary beverages available. Guests can dip in the swimming pool on hot summer days and walk or read in the formal gardens. A hearty breakfast is served.

### THORNEWOOD INN

Owners/Innkeepers: Terry and David Thorne.
413-528-3828, 800-854-1008; fax 413-528-3307.
www.thornewood.com.
453 Stockbridge Rd., Gt. Barrington, MA 01230.
Rte. 7 just N. of Gt. Barrington.
Price: Expensive to Very Expensive.
Credit Cards: AE, MC, V.
Special Features: Pool; no smoking; no pets; children over 11; packages include dinner.

Creativity and imagination are evident throughout this inn. Having purchased an old run-down but handsome Dutch colonial, the Thornes restored and expanded it to create 15 guest rooms, all with private baths, and four public rooms—picturesque right down to the uneven floors. The antiques used throughout include canopy beds, pier mirrors, and original sinks, yet the rooms have wireless cable access. The three-room carriage house, refurbished in

1992, is convenient for families. The full breakfast might include strawberry-stuffed french toast or apple pancakes. The inn enjoys hosting banquets and weddings.

### TURNING POINT INN

Owners: Dennis, Rachel, and Tava O'Rourke.
413-528-4777.
www.turningpointinn.com.
3 Lake Buel Rd., Gt. Barrington, MA 01230.
Jct. of Lake Buel Rd. and Rte. 23 E. of Gt. Barrington.
Price: Inexpensive to Moderate.
Credit Cards: None.
Special Features: Children welcome.

Turning Point is a well-regarded lodging in a handsome brick-and-clapboard former stagecoach inn that's 200 years old. An informal atmosphere prevails. Full breakfast served; Saturday-evening dinner can be arranged (Rachel is a chef and Tava a pastry chef who also cater). Stay in one of six inn rooms (four with private baths); a separate two-bedroom cottage is perfect for families. The popular Butternut Basin ski area is a third of a mile down the road.

### WAINWRIGHT INN

Innkeeper: Marja Tepper Grader.
413-528-2062; fax 413-644-6410.
www.wainwrightinn.com.
518 S. Main St., Gt. Barrington, MA 01230.
Rte. 7, 1 block S. of jct. with Rte. 23.
Price: Expensive to Very Expensive.
Credit Cards: MC, V.
Handicap Access: Yes.
Special Features: No smoking; dining room reserved for guests; no pets; inquire about children.

This beautiful gabled house built by Peter Ingersoll in 1766 was the Tory Tavern and Inn until David Wainwright purchased it in 1790, and then it passed down through his descendants as a family home. The present owners purchased it in 2000, keeping it open year-round with nine guest rooms/suites with private baths, some with fireplaces. One guest room has been renovated to be entirely wheelchair accessible. The carriage house is now available, either as a suite or two rooms with common area. Full breakfast served.

### WINDFLOWER INN

Owners: Liebert and Ryan Families.
413-528-2720, 800-992-1993.
www.windflowerinn.com.
684 S. Egremont Rd., Gt. Barrington, MA 01230.
Rte. 23 just E. of S. Egremont.
Price: Expensive.
Credit Card: AE.
Handicap Access: Limited.
Special Features: Pool; no pets; children welcome.

One of the prettiest settings in South Berkshire complements the soothing, comfortable interior of this gracious and respected inn. Antiques furnish the common rooms as well as the bedrooms. All 13 rooms have private baths, and six have fireplaces. Full breakfast and afternoon tea and cookies served. The inn and its restaurant are available for special catered occasions. The inn is across from the country club, which is open to the public.

## HOUSATONIC

### CHRISTINE'S B&B

Innkeepers: Steve and Christine Kelsey.
413-274-6149, 800-536-1186; fax 413-274-6296.
www.christinesinn.com.
325 N. Plain Rd., Housatonic, MA 01236.
Rte. 41, 4 mi. N. of Gt. Barrington.
Price: Expensive.
Credit Cards: MC, V.
Special Features: No smoking; children over 11; business-traveler discount.

A little jewel (four rooms, all with private baths) off the beaten path between Great

Barrington and West Stockbridge. The rooms and the innkeepers are delightful. Two rooms have queen canopy beds, and the third has a high-poster. All are filled with antiques and are air-conditioned. Table-served breakfast. Afternoon tea; tearoom open to the public except in the summer.

LEE
(See also *South Lee*)

### APPLEGATE INN

Owners: Len and Gloria Friedman.
413-243-4451, 800-691-9012.
www.applegateinn.com.
279 W. Park St., Lee, MA 01238.
Off Rte. 7, between Stockbridge and Lenox.
Price: Expensive to Very Expensive.
Credit Cards: MC, V.
Special Features: Heated pool; no pets; children over 12.

This magnificent white-pillared colonial is special in every way, and a stay at Applegate will be cherished. Public rooms are large, with fireplaces and bay windows. The puppets that appear to be part of the décor are also for playing. Guests are greeted in their room with fresh flowers, a crystal decanter of brandy, and Godiva chocolates. The main house has six large guest rooms with private baths and fireplaces. Two suites in the main house and two suites in the carriage house with private patios, whirlpool tubs, and wet bars. The house has central air-conditioning. From the screened-in porch filled with wicker furniture, a tranquil view across the pool reveals 6 landscaped acres. If anyone wishes to go farther afield, the Friedmans have four bicycles to loan.

### AUNTI M'S BED & BREAKFAST

Owners: Michelle and Phil Celentano.
413-243-3201.
www.auntimsbnb.com.
60 Laurel St., Lee, MA 01238.
On Rte 20.
Price: Inexpensive to Expensive.
Credit Cards: None.
Special Features: No smoking; no pets; children over 15.

Aunti M's is a restored Victorian within walking distance of a historic downtown. All five comfortable rooms—named for nieces and nephews of the owners—have period furnishings, floral wallpapers and borders, and oak floors. One has a private bath, and the others share two baths. The rooms are air-conditioned. The homey feeling is exemplified as Michelle Celentano says of her guests, "Whatever is ours is theirs." An elegant full breakfast is served; the piano in the foyer is the focal point for after-breakfast camaraderie.

### BEST WESTERN BLACK SWAN INN

Owner: Shatish Desai.
413-243-2700, 800-876-SWAN (7926).
435 Laurel St., Lee, MA 01238.
Rte. 20 on Laurel Lake N. of town.
Price: Very Expensive.
Credit Cards: AE, D, DC, MC, V.
Handicap Access: Yes.
Special Features: Pool; exercise room and sauna; no pets.

From the outside, this 52-room inn looks decidedly like a motel, but its location on placid Laurel Lake, its private balconies, Colonial décor, and hospitality provide an innlike atmosphere. Lovely restaurant, swimming pool, and exercise room with sauna. There are boat rentals for boating on the lake. Close to Tanglewood, hiking trails, countless other Berkshire amenities. Conference facilities are available. In the summer, meals are not included; in winter a continental breakfast is served.

### CHAMBÉRY INN

Owners: Joe and Lynn Toole.
413-243-2221, 800-537-4321.
www.chamberyinn.com.
199 Main St., Lee, MA 01238.

On Rte. 20.
Price: Moderate to Very Expensive.
Credit Cards: AE, D, MC, V.
Handicap Access: Yes.
Special Features: No smoking; no pets; children over 15.

The Chambéry Inn began life as a schoolhouse in 1885, when five nuns arrived from France to teach the youngsters of St. Mary's Parish in Lee. Joe Toole's grandfather was in the first class. Concerned that it was scheduled for the wrecker's ball and enchanted by its history, Joe moved the schoolhouse to its present location. He left the proportions of the rooms as they were, which is *big*, with 13-foot ceilings and massive windows. There are nine rooms, including three schoolhouse suites and three deluxe suites; all king or queen beds and large private baths with whirlpools. The furniture, including canopy beds, is Amish handcrafted cherry. A charming feature of the suites is the original blackboards. All the rooms have central air-conditioning, telephones, and cable TV (including HBO). Breakfast is delivered to the room.

### CRABTREE COTTAGE

Owner: Janis Monachina.
413-243-1780.
www.crabtreecottage.com.
65 Franklin St., Lee, MA 01238.
Off Main St.
Price: Moderate.
Credit Cards: AE, MC, V.
Special Features: Pool; children over 12.

This lovely Greek Revival home on a quiet residential street is handsomely garbed in Victorian furnishings. The single room, one-room suite, and efficiency suite all have private baths, air-conditioning, and television with VCR. The option of a kitchen goes with the suite. Guests have access to a common room, deck, and swimming pool. Janis's husband, contractor Jeffrey Keenan, who grew up in the home, has done much of the extensive refurbishing. Cordials and treats in the afternoon; full candlelit breakfast.

### DEVONFIELD B&B

Owners/Managers: Jim and Pam Loring.
413-243-3298, 800-664-0880; fax 413-243-1360.
www.devonfield.com.
85 Stockbridge Rd., Lee, MA 01238.
Off Rte. 20 just outside village.
Price: Very Expensive.
Credit Cards: AE, D, MC, V.
Special Features: Heated pool; tennis; bicycles; Jacuzzis and fireplaces.

No expense was spared in renovating this 1800s house, built by a Revolutionary War soldier and initially restored by George Westinghouse in the early 1900s. The small estate became the 1942 summer sanctuary for Queen Wilhelmina of the Netherlands, her daughter Princess Juliana, and granddaughters Beatrix and Irene. The house is secluded, with 10 air-conditioned rooms, all with private baths. Full breakfast.

### INN ON LAUREL LAKE

Innkeeper: Thomas Fusco.
413-243-1436, 413-243-9749; fax 413-243-2936.
www.laurellakeinn.com.
615 Laurel St., Lee, MA 01238.
Rte. 20, 2 mi. N. of MassPike Exit 2.
Price: Expensive to Very Expensive.
Credit Cards: AE, D, MC, V.
Handicap Access: Limited.
Special Features: Private beach with canoes, paddleboats; tennis; no smoking.

On the shore of Laurel Lake, this 120-year-old country property has attracted a loyal following with its 19 comfortable bedrooms (17 with private baths) and 2 sitting rooms filled with an impressive collection of record albums, books, and games. The tennis court and private beach add to guests' playtime possibilities. Full breakfast buffet served.

### JONATHAN FOOTE 1778 HOUSE

Owner: JoAnn Zarnoch.
413-243-4545.
www.1778house.com.
1 East St., Lee, MA 01238.
Cor. East and Maple sts.
Price: Expensive to Very Expensive.
Credit Cards: MC, V.
Special Features: No children under 12; no pets; no smoking.

Although near town, the Jonathan Foote 1778 House is in a distinctly rural setting, located on the road to October Mountain State Forest. Its lovely grounds are host to large honey locust trees, part of the view from a comfortable front porch. Inside are five spacious guest rooms, two with fireplaces, and two suites. All have their own bathrooms and air-conditioning. The house retains distinctive features from its early construction, and much of the furniture is also antique. A great room downstairs has a large fireplace and two seating areas. Full breakfast served in the dining room or on the porch.

### THE MORGAN HOUSE INN

Owners: Sean and Emlyn Diggein.
413-243-3661; fax 413-243-3103.
www.morganhouseinn.com.
33 Main St., Lee, MA 01238.
On Rte. 20, 0.8 mi. N. of MassPike Exit 2.
Price: Expensive.
Credit Cards: AE, MC, V.
Special Features: No pets; children welcome.

The Morgan House, built in 1817 and a stagecoach stop beginning in 1853, has a bustling and convenient in-town location. This full-service inn, totally refurbished in 1999 and now under new owners, offers 12 comfortable rooms in a variety of shapes and sizes, 7 with private baths. The dining room has also been spruced up; light fare is available in the tavern. The spirit of former guests remains to provide a patina for a modern inn. Lunch and dinner served 7 days a week in summer, 6 otherwise.

### PARSONAGE ON THE GREEN

Innkeepers: Barbara and Don Mahony.
413-243-4364.
www.bbhost.com/parsonageonthegreen.
20 Park Pl., Lee, MA 01238.
On the green, adjacent to church.
Price: Expensive.
Credit Cards: None; checks accepted.
Special Features: Access to Laurel Lake beach; no smoking; no pets; children over 12.

This 1851 Colonial, originally the parsonage for the church next door, was entirely refurbished by the present owners, who have run it since 1997. Three sunny rooms upstairs, each with private bath, have comfortable four-poster beds, family memorabilia, and other nice touches. Also downstairs are a parlor and a library (with games and TV), both filled with pictures of the Mahony family and early occupants of the house. Although the inn sits in the middle of Lee, it is on the opposite side of the green from the main drag, so visitors enjoy quiet as much as easy access to the town. Coffee and tea available upstairs after 7:00 in the morning; continental breakfast served in the dining room downstairs.

## SOUTH LEE

### THE FEDERAL HOUSE

Owners: Jim Finnerty & Carole Merko.
413-243-1824, 800-243-1824; fax 413-243-1828.
www.federalhouseinn.com.
1560 Pleasant St., P.O. Box 248, S. Lee, MA 01260.
On Rte. 102 just E. of Stockbridge.
Price: Expensive.
Credit Cards: MC, V.
Special Features: No smoking; no pets; children.

Thomas Hurlbut built this house in 1824, when he came to South Lee to operate the paper mill on the Housatonic River. In this historic property, which has been beautifully restored, the 10 graceful and charming guest rooms feature antique furnishings. Some rooms have fireplaces; all have private baths and air-conditioning. Full breakfast included.

### HISTORIC MERRELL INN

Innkeepers: George and Joanne Crockett.
413-243-1794, 800-243-1794; fax 413-243-2669.
www.merrell-inn.com.
1565 Pleasant St., S. Lee, MA 01260.
On Rte. 102 just E. of Stockbridge.
Closed: Christmas and week preceding.
Price: Moderate to Expensive.
Credit Cards: AE, MC, V.
Special Features: No smoking; no pets.

Those who walk through the massive door of this striking 1794 brick inn will find themselves transported back in time. For years it served as a stagecoach stop on the busy Boston–Albany Pike. It lay idle and boarded up for over 100 years until late 1980. Now lovingly and carefully restored, the inn is listed on the National Register of Historic Places. Of the nine bedrooms and one suite, some are furnished with four-poster and canopy beds, and all have private baths, air-conditioning, and telephones; four have fireplaces. Wireless Internet service available. The Old Tavern Room features the original circular colonial bar. A groomed lawn in back leads through old foundations to a screened gazebo on the banks of the Housatonic River. A full breakfast is served from a menu.

NEW MARLBOROUGH

### GEDNEY FARM AND MAPLE MANOR & SPA

Innkeepers: Bradford Wagstaff and Leslie Miller.

*The rustic ambiance at Gedney Farm in New Marlborough belies the elegance one finds inside.* Judith Monachina

413-229-3131, 800-286-3139; fax 413-229-8236.
www.gedneyfarm.com.
34 Hartsville–New Marlborough Rd., New Marlborough, MA 01230.
On Rte. 57, center of village.
Price: Expensive to Very Expensive.
Credit Cards: AE, MC, V.
Special Features: Spa.

A beautiful village rich in unaffected nostalgia is the setting for Gedney Farm, with 16 guest rooms including four suites, carved out of a Normandy-style barn, which was built around 1900 as a showplace for Percheron stallions and Jersey cattle. All suites feature fireplaces in the living rooms, large bedrooms, and whirlpool tubs in the master baths. Maple Manor, 12 rooms all with private baths, is 0.5 mile down the road and the most deluxe. The restored second horse barn serves as space for weddings, parties, meetings, and concerts. The restaurant in the nearby inn is one of the finest in the Berkshires.

### THE RED BIRD INN

Managers: Barbara and Doug Newman.
413-229-2349; fax 413-229-2433.
16 Adsit Crosby Rd., New Marlborough; mail: Rte. 57, Gt. Barrington, MA 01230.
From Gt. Barrington, Rte. 23 E. to Rte. 57.
Price: Expensive.
Credit Cards: MC, V.
Handicap Access: Limited.
Special Features: No smoking; no pets.

A former stagecoach stop, the 1791 Red Bird Inn is a classic New England Colonial with Greek Revival trim. The inn, located on 10 acres on a quiet country road, has six rooms, all with private baths. The rooms are furnished with antiques and retain their original wide-plank floors, fireplaces, and old ironwork. Luxurious linens and bathrobes are laid out. A newly renovated, separate cottage suite has one huge room with a queen-sized bed, two twins, a sitting area, and private bath. The large screened porch is a popular feature with warm-weather guests. Doug, a chef, prepares a full country breakfast.

## SANDISFIELD

### NEW BOSTON INN

Innkeeper: Susan and Conrad Ringeisen.
413-258-4477, 888-774-7666; fax 413-258-4234.
www.newbostoninn.com.
P.O. Box 601, Sandisfield, MA 01255.
Jct. Rtes. 8 and 57 in village of New Boston.
Price: Moderate–Expensive.
Credit Cards: AE, MC, V.
Special Features: 1737 pub and full-service restaurant.

The owners of this remarkable old stagecoach inn, built in 1737 and listed on the National Register of Historic Places, continue to make improvements. The seven guest rooms are—true to the period—snug. Low ceilings, wide-board floors, and multipaned windows hark back to the 18th century and, in most cases, are original. All rooms feature private baths and are decorated with early pine furniture and stenciling. All closets are cedar lined. After wandering through the cozy bedrooms on the second floor, we enter the spacious ballroom—now called the Gathering Room—complete with an antique billiards table and a barrel-vaulted ceiling. The matching fireplaces at either end accent the sense of openness and grace. Another historic delight is the taproom, now open as a pub, which adjoins the low-ceilinged dining room. The 22-inch-wide pine boards on the wall are called "king's wood." The trees were cut by the colonists in spite of being reserved for masts for the Royal Navy. In this room as throughout the inn, the wooden moldings, plaster walls, slanted floors, venerable windows and doorways (there is hardly a right angle in the place) provide a powerful charm and sense of history. What's more, the New Boston Inn has resident ghosts, know as the friendly spirits. One is real enough to have been reported in *Yankee* magazine: an Irish maiden, dressed in bridal black, who was shot by a scorned suitor in an upstairs room. Breakfast is included.

SHEFFIELD

### BIRCH HILL BED & BREAKFAST

Owners: Michael and Wendy Advocate.
413-229-2143, 800-359-3969; fax 413-229-3405.
www.birchhillbb.com.
254 S. Undermountain Rd., Sheffield, MA 01257.
On Rte. 41, 4 mi. S. of Rte. 23.
Price: Expensive to Very Expensive.
Credit Cards: None.
Special Features: Pool; dogs welcome; children over 9.

Set along one of the most scenic roads of South Berkshire, Birch Hill (formerly Ivanhoe Country House) provides seven comfortable rooms, all with private baths and refrigerators, some with fireplaces. Guests may take a dip in the pool before dinner, play the piano, enjoy the fire in the chestnut-paneled room, and select from the many fine area restaurants for an evening meal. At the base of Race Mountain, traversed by the Appalachian Trail, 20 wooded acres hug this 1780-vintage country house. "Mouthwatering" breakfast served.

### BROKEN HILL MANOR

Owners: Michael Farmer and Gaetan Lachance.
413-528-6159, 877-535-6159; fax 413-644-8872.
www.brokenhillmanor.com.
771 West Rd., Sheffield, MA 01257.
From Rte. 7, W. on Lime Kiln Rd. to N. on West Rd.
Price: Expensive.
Credit Cards: All major.
Special Features: No smoking; no pets; children over 14.

A long drive leads to the top of the world: Broken Hill Manor rests with its 12 acres atop a hill, totally surrounded by woods—a fine place to view the stars. And perhaps hear them, in the quiet. Stars there are: Each of the eight rooms is named for an opera heroine, from Aida to Violetta. The rooms are air-conditioned and contain CD players, with an ample supply of disks. The 100-year-old rambling house, wood and peanut-brittle stone, was inhabited by two playwrights until 1997. Renovated since then, it offers seclusion, comfortable beds, and a full cooked breakfast, served either inside or on the terrace.

### ORCHARD SHADE

Owners: Debbie and Henry Thornton.
413-229-8463, 877-672-4233; fax 413-229-2711.
www.orchardshade.com.
999 Hewins St., Sheffield, MA 01257.
E. side of the Housatonic, between County Rd. and Rte. 7.
Price: Inexpensive to Moderate.
Credit Cards: MC, V.
Special Features: No smoking; no pets; children welcome.

The Thorntons' small B&B, built in 1850, is truly set in the trees—and located a bit farther from Route 7 than expected. They furnished their three bedrooms with antiques. One room has a private bath. The fireplace in the common room wards off the chill on cooler evenings. The large porch is perfect for relaxing after a busy day of Sheffield antiquing, as are the 2 acres and gardens.

### RACE BROOK LODGE

Innkeeper: Allegra Graham.
413-229-2916, 888-725-6343.
www.rblodge.com.

864 S. Undermountain Rd., Sheffield, MA 01257.
On Rte. 41, 2 miles S. of Berkshire School.
Price: Moderate to Expensive.
Credit Cards: MC, V.
Handicap Access: Limited to ground-level entry to many rooms.
Special Features: No smoking; well-behaved dogs accepted; children welcome.

This rustic lodge beside Race Brook has its own trail leading to a state forest with waterfall, ravine, and the Appalachian Trail. A large rambling barn, dating from the 1790s, embraces rooms and suites in what were once haylofts, with exposed original beams, stenciling, nooks and alcoves, and windows and stairs in unexpected places. The variety of bedroom, bathroom, and entrance arrangements can work for couples, family groups, or friends traveling together. Having converted a garage into the Meeting House and built a new post-and-beam barn, the lodge owners emphasize team-building retreats and other group meetings.

The interiors have been specifically designated a "chintz-free zone" to maximize informality. The rooms are also smoke free, phone free, and TV free. More rooms and suites, 32 in all, are in nearby cottages. In the lofty common rooms at the heart of the barn is the well-stocked, always-open Horseshoe Wine Bar—run on the honor system—along with tables and a TV corner, and a horseshoe bar. The lodge will produce lunch, suppers, and catering for groups on request. A hearty breakfast buffet is served. The adjacent Stagecoach Tavern serves dinner Thursday, Friday, and Saturday.

### RAMBLEWOOD INN

Owners: Cliff and Nadine Hawver.
413-229-3363, 800-854-1862; fax 413-229-5942.
www.ramblewood-inn.com.
400 S. Undermountain Rd., Box 729, Sheffield, MA 01257.
On Rte. 41.
Price: Expensive.
Credit Cards: MC, V.

Up a short hill off scenic Route 41, this alpine structure at the edge of the woods has an attractive rustic look, with all the comforts of home, including central air-conditioning. The Hawvers offer six guest rooms (four with private baths), including a ground-floor suite with full kitchen, bedroom, living room, and bath. The inn owns pond-front property across the road, where guests may swim, canoe, and fish.

A full gourmet breakfast is served. The Berkshire School, site of the Berkshire Choral Institute (see the "Music" section in chapter 5, "Arts & Pleasures"), is a mile down the road.

### SHEFFIELD INN

Owners: Florence Liberman and Gail Ullman.
413-229-9992.
www.sheffieldinn.com.
84 Maple Ave.
Price: Moderate to Expensive.
Credit cards: All major.
Special features: Pet room; heated pool.

This rambling house with a nicely set pool and a front porch made for rocking has been an inn or guesthouse in continuous use since 1848. The six rooms all have private baths and air-conditioning. Along with breakfast, the innkeepers serve wine and cheese in the afternoon.

### STAVELEIGH HOUSE B&B

Innkeeper: Ali A. Winston.
413-229-2129.
www.staveleigh.com.
59 Main St., Sheffield, MA 01257.
On Rte. 7 just S. of village center.
Price: Moderate.
Credit Cards: All major.

Handicap Access: Limited.
Special Features: No smoking; inquire about pets or children.

The Reverend Bradford, minister of the oldest church in Berkshire, built his lovely house in 1817 in the heart of Sheffield. The Staveleigh family acquired the property at the turn of the 20th century. *House & Garden* magazine has documented Ali's old-fashioned welcome: "The hospitality at Staveleigh House is deeper and more thoughtful than any you will find elsewhere." All seven guest rooms are air-conditioned. Five have private bathrooms; terry-cloth robes are provided. The grounds feature perennial beds, an herb garden, and a place to sit under the trees. Ali serves an elegant breakfast and afternoon tea.

STOCKBRIDGE

### ARBOR ROSE BED & BREAKFAST

Owner: Christina Alsop.
413-298-4744, 877-298-4744.
www.arborrose.com.
8 Yale Hill Rd., Box 114, Stockbridge, MA 01262.
Off E. Main St. (Rte. 102).
Price: Moderate to Expensive.
Credit Cards: MC, V.
Special Features: No smoking; children welcome.

The first thing one hears on entering the driveway to Arbor Rose is the soothing sound of rushing water. The large white house sits on a hill overlooking an early 1800s sawmill and millpond. The house has three guest rooms, all with private baths and air-conditioning. The mill contains a three-room apartment that sleeps six. The décor is highlighted by colorful paintings by the owner's mother, Suzette Alsop, a noted local artist. Full breakfast includes magnificent muffins (continental breakfast midweek).

### BLUE WILLOW

Owners: Lila and Joseph Ruggio.
413-298-3018; fax 413-298-0009.
www.bluewillowbb.com.
2 Lincoln Lane, P.O. Box 843, Stockbridge, MA 01262.
Off Rte. 102, 0.5 mi. E. of Red Lion Inn.
Price: Expensive.
Credit Cards: None.
Special Features: Secluded road; on Housatonic River across from Laura's Tower.

The Ruggios purchased an abandoned house more than 20 years ago, gutted it, redid it, added to it, and opened it seasonally for guests. Then they began hosting visitors year-round in their tidy B&B. The theme: a collection of Blue Willow china they began many years ago and have been adding to that depicts the daughter falling in love with the gardener, which angers the father, who kills them both; but they fly off as birds. The three rooms (one with deck, one in the carriage barn) have television, air-conditioning, and private baths. They are furnished with antiques, including brass beds. Full breakfast.

### CONROY'S B&B

Owners: James and Joanne Conroy.
413-298-4990; fax 413-298-4990.
www.conroysinn.com.
11 East St., Box 191, Stockbridge, MA 01262.
On Rte. 7 about 1.5 mi. N. of village.
Price: Expensive to Very Expensive.
Credit Cards: MC, V.
Special Features: No smoking; no pets; families welcome; special-events catering.

Located just north of Stockbridge in a handsome 1830s Federal-style house, Conroy's B&B is well situated for cultural attractions. The Conroys offer five double rooms year-round in various configurations, some with private baths, some shared, all air-conditioned. Two rooms

*The gracious front porch of the Red Lion Inn.* Judith Monachina

have working fireplaces. Four seasonal rooms and an apartment/suite are located in an air-conditioned detached barn. In busy summer and fall months, dining is extended from tables in the great room in the front house into a wonderfully renovated, equally old attached barn section in its rear. Period charm is not compromised. Full breakfast is included. Families with well-behaved children are welcome.

### THE INN AT STOCKBRIDGE

Innkeepers: Alice and Len Schiller.
413-298-3337, 888-466-7865; fax 413-298-3406.
www.stockbridgeinn.com.
Box 618, Stockbridge, MA 01262.
On Rte. 7 about 1 mi. N. of village.
Price: Expensive to Very Expensive.
Credit Cards: AE, D, MC, V.
Handicap Access: Limited.
Special Features: Heated pool; no smoking; no pets; children over 12.

A marvelous, secluded inn run by friendly, professional people. The large, white-columned, 1906 house features priceless antiques and many thoughtful touches. All seven rooms in the main house have private baths and are air-conditioned. Barn and cottage contain eight suites with fireplaces; six have whirlpool baths. Exercise and fitness equipment is available as is a massage room. Wine and cheese are served in the living room—warmed by a fire in chilly weather—and breakfast in the formal dining room includes homemade pastries, with croissants, french toast, and cinnamon buns possible offerings. Special private dinners can be arranged on request.

### THE RED LION INN

General Manager: Bruce Finn.
413-298-5545; fax 413-298-5130.
www.redlioninn.com.
30 Main St., P.O. Box 954, Stockbridge, MA 01262.
Village center, jct. Rtes. 7 and 102.
Price: Expensive to Very Expensive (some shared baths less expensive).
Credit Cards: AE, D, DC, MC, V.
Handicap Access: Yes.
Special Features: Outdoor pool; fitness room; massage therapist.

In 1773 (or so) the Red Lion Inn first opened its doors to travelers on the stagecoach route linking Albany, Hartford, and Boston. Two hundred thirty-five years later, the Red Lion still welcomes visitors and locals with consummate colonial charm. The present inn, rebuilt in 1897 after a fire, is an icon of the Berkshires, representing graceful country lodging at its best.

Antique furniture and a fine collection of china teapots adorn the lobby. Each of the 108 private rooms (including 25 suites) is decorated with unique period appointments, carefully coordinated by the inn's owners, the Fitzpatrick family, who also own Country Curtains. Recent improvements have concentrated on refurbishing the rooms. Wireless Internet service is available. Throughout the inn, the loving attention to detail is evident in every aspect of its operation. It's easy to feel at home here because all of the inn's top-quality services are offered by a vibrant, eager-to-please staff. In summer, one's porch or courtyard company may be an actor or actress of note who spends evenings nearby on the boards of the Berkshire Theatre Festival.

The atmosphere is faithful to the rhythms of a simpler, slower time while providing all contemporary comforts. Sipping a cool drink on a hot summer's day on the Red Lion's famous porch or meeting a companion in front of the cheery fireplace in the lobby in winter is to beat to the heart of the Berkshires. The Red Lion Inn is not, however, a particularly tranquil place. The main building is full of activity and people, and the streets outside are sometimes noisy with traffic. There's a conviviality and gaiety about the lobby that some folks love. Others might prefer the cottages that form a complex around the inn: Stafford House, O'Brien House, Meadowlark (at Chesterwood), Yellow Cottage, Stevens House, Fire House, McGregor House, and Two Maple Street.

Reservations should be made in advance, especially in the summer. The rooms are complemented by an excellent formal dining room; casual or informal dining in the Widow Bingham Tavern; nightly entertainment in the Lion's Den, a pub; a courtyard for summer meals under the trees, surrounded by bushels of impatiens; the Red Lion Inn Gift Shop; and a Country Curtains retail store.

### SEASONS ON MAIN B&B

Innkeepers: Pat and Greg O'Neill.
413-298-5419, 888-955-4747.
www.seasonsonmain.com
47 Main St., Box 634, Stockbridge, MA 01262.
On Rte. 7, E. end of town center.
Price: Expensive to Very Expensive.
Credit Cards: AE, MC, V.
Special Features: No smoking; no pets or children; 3-night minimum during Tanglewood season.

This gracious house is within an easy walk of Stockbridge shops, restaurants, and the Berkshire Theatre Festival. Downstairs, the inn offers three sitting rooms with Victorian-inspired furnishings and wallpaper, and a dining room with a Duncan Phyfe–style dining table and Larkin sideboards. Upstairs, the four air-conditioned guest rooms follow a seasonal motif; one has a king-sized sleigh bed, fireplace, TV, and large bath. Guests have the use of a comfortable, west-facing porch that affords a view of Main Street and handsome gardens.

### TAGGART HOUSE B&B

Owners: August and Sandra Murko.
413-298-4303.
www.taggarthouse.com.
18 Main St., Stockbridge, MA 01262.
Price: Very Expensive.
Credit Cards: AE, MC, V.
Special Features: No smoking; no pets; inquire about children.

A stunning array of art and antiques in the richly detailed architectural setting of a 19th-century mansion, with a fireplace around just about every corner, a billiards room, a paneled library, a music room, and 3 acres of secluded gardens and fields: the description of a romantic country manor house in a Victorian novel. Actually, the Taggart House is right on Main Street in Stockbridge, where the resident owners have transformed fiction into reality. For farther escape, though, canoe and kayak are available on the contiguous Housatonic River.

Throughout the downstairs living rooms and the upstairs bedrooms are a variety of fabulous faux effects painted on walls and ceilings, including bois and tortoiseshell finishes. In the butler's pantry, trompe l'oeil painting merges a real garden scene with an illusory one. The abundance of imaginative details also includes fabrics and wallpaper with William Morris designs, and a birch-bark canoe suspended from a frescoed ceiling over the billiards table. The cavernous music room has hosted chamber concerts from Bach to Gershwin—and an 18-foot Christmas tree. Four bedrooms feature rich and restful color themes, fireplaces, and luxurious antique beds; each room's private bath is equally sumptuous, with antique furnishings, heated towel racks, and even bath salts. Morning brings gourmet breakfasts, and there are some self-serve options, too. Afternoon tea can be provided as well as early-evening wine and cheese, if requested.

### WEST STOCKBRIDGE

#### THE CARD LAKE COUNTRY INN

Owners: Ed and Lisa Robbins.
413-232-0272; fax: 413-232-0294.
www.cardlakeinn.com.
29 Main St., Box 38, W. Stockbridge, MA 01266.
Price: Moderate to Expensive.
Credit Cards: MC, V.
Special Features: No pets, no smoking.

The inn offers 14 guest rooms featuring brass and iron beds. All have private baths and air-conditioning. Village shops across street are artsy-craftsy. Guests may want to ask for a room at the back of the inn to avoid traffic noise. Restaurant and tavern (open July–October) on the premises.

#### SHAKER MILL INN

Owners: Lori Bashour and Michael Lee.
413-232-4600; fax 413-232-4601.
www.shakermillinn.com.
2 Oak St. Box 61, W. Stockbridge, MA 01266.
On Rte. 102.
Price: Expensive to Very Expensive.
Credit Cards: AE, D, MC, V.
Special Features: Children and pets welcome.

The inn offers nine enormous modern, deluxe rooms, some with patio or balcony, with queen-sized beds and complete with small kitchens and living rooms. The Berkshire Suite has two full bedrooms, two full baths, a large fully equipped kitchen, and a living room; three TVs, laundry facilities, and just about anything else anyone might want. All accommodations are in a converted barn. Continental breakfast is served.

Yoga (Phoenix Rising) offered next door (see chapter 6, "Body & Spirit.")

#### THE WILLIAMSVILLE INN

Owners: Kandy and Erhard Wendt.
413-274-6118; fax: 413-274-3539.
www.williamsvilleinn.com
Rte. 41 (289 Gt. Barrington Rd.), W. Stockbridge, MA 01266.
Closed: Nov. 1–Nov. 20.
Price: Expensive to Very Expensive.
Credit Cards: AE, MC, V.
Features: Tennis, swimming pool; quality restaurant on premises; no smoking; no pets.

The Wendts have wrought major change in the stately inn since they purchased it in 2002. The entire interior has been redone, maintaining the charm of the 1797 building but, through judicious paint selection and upscale furniture, rendering the rooms pleasant and open. Kandy, who has a background in décor, says: "You should feel as though a room is hugging you." There are nine rooms and a two-room suite in the main house, which has central air-conditioning. Two cottages are available and four rooms in the renovated barn. All rooms have private baths. Three rooms have California king-sized beds; the rest are amply spacious.

The lovely stone terrace and walls in the rear are new, together with their gardens and a kind of sculpture park. The inn's 10 acres beckon the traveler to pause and recreate: tennis, swimming, and a childrens' playground. For a more passive form of recreation, Tanglewood is only 15 minutes away. A breakfast buffet is included. The inn is available for weddings and other special events, with a capacity of 250. The restaurant, with Erhard the chef, serves dinner. He also teaches culinary school.

TYRINGHAM

### COBBLEVIEW B&B

Owners: Lynn Bertelli and Alan Wilcox.
413-243-2463, 800-467-4136; fax 413-243-1299.
www.cobbleviewbandb.com.
123 Main Rd., Tyringham, MA 01264.
Across from Town Hall.
Price: Expensive to Very Expensive.
Credit Cards: None.
Special Features: Hiking and cross-country skiing; no smoking; no pets; call ahead about children under 12.

This attractive B&B, is set smack in one of the most scenic landscapes in the commonwealth. Its six refurbished rooms—whose décor could be defined as "elegant country"—include a loft that holds four and a studio with bedroom, bath, and kitchen. All rooms have private baths and air-conditioning. For breakfast, Lynn serves a continental buffet, always including something she's baked fresh, to be eaten at the huge dining-room table or on the deck. The 6 acres of land have come alive with gardens.

## INNS AND B&BS CENTRAL COUNTY

DALTON

### THE DALTON HOUSE

Hosts: Gary and Bernice Turetsky.
413-684-3854; fax 413-684-0203.
www.thedaltonhouse.com.
955 Main St., Dalton, MA 01226.
Price: Moderate to Expensive.
Credit Cards: AE, MC, V.
Special Features: Pool; no smoking; no pets; children over 10.

Set in a small New England village, this inn offers 11 rooms in the main house and carriage house. All have private baths, telephones, and televisions. The house has been partially furnished with antiques. Summer guests enjoy air-conditioning, a pool, an extensively landscaped lawn and flower gardens, and a picnic area. Breakfast is served, with blueberry pancakes when in-season.

HANCOCK

### HANCOCK INN

Owners: Joe and Gail Mullady.
413-738-5873; fax 413-738-5758.
www.thehancockinn.com.
102 Main St., Hancock, MA 01237.
On Rte. 43 between Williamstown and Stephentown, NY.
Price: Moderate.
Credit Cards: D, MC, V.
Special Features: No smoking.

This cozy Victorian inn is set in a village that seems unaware of the 21st century's arrival. A tastefully furnished family-run establishment, the inn has the charm of a delightful, forgotten keepsake discovered one day in grandmother's attic. Six comfortable rooms, all with private baths and air-conditioning. A full breakfast is included.

HINSDALE

### MAPLEWOOD B&B

Innkeepers: Charlotte and Bob Baillargeon.
413-655-8167.
www.maplewoodbandb.com.
435 Maple St., P.O. Box 477, Hinsdale, MA 01235.
On Rte. 143.
Price: Moderate.
Credit Cards: None.
Special Features: No smoking; no pets.

Country setting, country style. Set on 6 acres with a small pond, this antiques-filled house has two rooms with private baths and a two-bedroom suite with private bath. Guests have a common room, with library, dining room, and separate entrance. Full breakfast might feature fresh trout or corn pancakes with fresh, locally made maple syrup; special diets can be accommodated.

LANESBOROUGH

### THE TUCKERED TURKEY

Owners: Dan and Marianne Sullivan.
413-442-0260.
30 Old Cheshire Rd., P.O. Box 638, Lanesborough, MA 01237.
From Rte. 7, turn E. on Summer St., then N. on Old Cheshire Rd.
Price: Moderate.
Credit Cards: None.
Special Features: No smoking; no pets.

A restored 19th-century Colonial farmhouse set on 4 acres with spacious views. Three antiques-furnished rooms share baths. Guests are welcome to bring their children to play with the owner's children. Full breakfast served.

LENOX

### THE APPLE TREE INN

Owners: Sharon Walker and Joel Catalano.
413-637-1477; fax 413-637-2528.
www.appletree-inn.com.
10 Richmond Mtn. Rd., P.O. Box 699, Lenox, MA 01240.
Just S.of Tanglewood main gate.
Price: Expensive to Very Expensive.
Credit Cards: AE, D, MC, V.
Special Features: Pool; tennis; no pets.

Magically set, the Apple Tree Inn is indisputably the lodging that lies closest to the main gate of Tanglewood. The 13 guest rooms in the main house are down-comforter dainty, some with antique brass beds and fireplaces, all with private baths. The Lodge, with 21 additional rooms—bringing the total number of units to 34—is less charming, though the rooms are convenient and clean.

The Apple Tree would be worth a visit for the views alone: a magnificent Berkshire panorama from the south-facing rooms, from poolside, or from the gazebo, which serves as a restaurant. There is also dining on the deck. The downstairs parlor is thoughtfully appointed and very comfortable; the bar has rich wood paneling, stained-glass windows, and a huge hearth. A crowning touch is the landscaping, boasting hundreds of varieties of roses set among apple trees—truly a visual feast throughout late spring and summer. Continental breakfast included.

### BIRCHWOOD INN

Owner: Ellen Chenaux.
413-637-2600, 800-524-1646.
www.birchwood-inn.com.
7 Hubbard St., Box 2020, Lenox, MA 01240.

Corner of Main St.
Price: Expensive to Very Expensive.
Credit Cards: AE, D, MC, V.
Special Features: No smoking; pets for fee; children over 12.

The oldest house in Lenox, this elegant 1767 mansion high on the hill overlooking a storybook town (within walking distance) continues renovations. Eleven rooms in the main house, all with private baths, and two rooms in the carriage house. Wireless Internet connection. All rooms are air-conditioned. A magnificent library extends along one side of the house, with books, magazines, and games galore. The wicker-furnished front porch is a popular spot in summer. A full gourmet breakfast is included. Tea is served (weather permitting) on the porch; and sometimes a midnight snack.

**BLANTYRE**

Manager: Katja Henke.
413-637-3556; fax 413-637-4282.
www.blantyre.com.
16 Blantyre Rd., Lenox, MA 01240.
Off Rte. 20, 3 mi. N. of MassPike Exit 2.
Price: Very Expensive.
Credit Cards: AE, DC, MC, V.
Handicap Access: Limited.
Special Features: Pool; tennis; croquet; luxury spa; no pets; children over 12.

Regally set amid over 100 conscientiously groomed acres of lawns, trees, and hedges, Blantyre offers its guests attentive and even ingenious service, great natural and architectural beauty, palatial furnishings, and magnificent vistas. Built by New York City businessman Robert Paterson in 1902 as a replica of his wife's ancestral home in the Scottish village of Blantyre—east of Glasgow—Blantyre went through several hands in the mid-20th century and fell into disrepair. In 1980 Jack and Jane Fitzpatrick bought the property (which has now passed to their daughter Ann), restored it to its present excellent condition: a baronial yet hospitable place—massive but comfortable, grand yet delicately appointed.

A member of the prestigious Relais & Châteaux, Blantyre has also been awarded five stars in *Mobil Travel Guide*. The five original suite-sized bedrooms—with four-poster beds, fireplaces, and magnificent bathrooms—are the true "jewels" in Blantyre's crown. Three other rooms are on the same floor, created in the "nanny's wing" on a different scale—smaller but just as elegant. Twelve more rooms are neatly tucked away in the original carriage house. There are also three cottages on the grounds: cozy, endearingly whimsical, and brilliantly situated.

In addition to its superb accommodations, Blantyre has a magnificent gourmet dining room, which AAA recognized with four diamonds. The hotel maintains four Har-Tru tennis courts and two tournament-sized bent-grass croquet courts. The spa includes a sauna, hot tub, steam room, treatments rooms and fitness center. Nearby is a lovely, landscaped swimming pool. Tanglewood is a mere 3 miles to the west. Conferences and small meetings are welcome. (The grounds and buildings are *not* open to the public for casual viewing.)

**BROOK FARM INN**

Owners/Innkeepers: Linda and Phil Halpern.
413-637-3013, 800-285-7638.
www.brookfarm.com.
15 Hawthorne St., Lenox, MA 01240.
Just off Old Stockbridge Rd.
Price: Expensive to Very Expensive.
Credit Cards: AE, D, MC, V.
Special Features: Heated pool; no smoking; no pets; children 15 and over.

The Halperns bought this inn in March 2001. Twelve antiques-furnished rooms—all with private baths, air-conditioning, and telephones—are offered in this large Victorian home, close to many Berkshire attractions. Several of the rooms have been renovated, with special attention lavished on the two large rooms at the front of the house, both with four-posters, sitting areas, and new bathrooms. A third-floor room offers a queen-sized bed and two twins. The new carriage house offers two, two-room suites; the downstairs one is handicapped accessible. The suites contain fireplaces, TV, DVD and other amenities. A unique attraction to this inn: Each day has it own poem, displayed in the 1,400-volume library and supplemented by 75 poets on tape. Occasional readings and storytellings (Linda is a storyteller) take place, accompanied by tea and scones. A buffet breakfast and afternoon tea are served daily to guests.

### CHESAPEAKE INN

Owner: John Sporck.
413-637-3429, 800-966-3429.
http://members.aol.com/cinnlenox.
210 West St., Lenox, MA 01240.
Closed: Call to inquire Nov.–May.
Price: Very Expensive.
Credit Cards: AE, MC, V.
Special Features: 75-foot lap pool; no smoking; no pets; children 12 and over.

We might as well say right off that, in John's words, the Chesapeake Inn is only "1,038" steps from Tanglewood—and a mile from Lenox. No need to to drive. The four guest rooms, named for Chesapeake Bay area sites, all have private baths and central air-conditioning. The furnishings are elegant but not fussy, set on lovely hardwood floors. All queen beds; one room with an additional Murphy bed. Wireless Internet available. Breakfast is literally to order. Dining room décor features table waterfall backed by a candle.

When we visited, John was about to plant a hedge to create a bit more seclusion from the Tanglewood traffic that goes by his door. The grounds are well maintained; some of the plants and flowers find their way into window boxes and indoors. Those who need more than Tanglewood to soothe their souls can work out their aggressions in the heated lap pool.

### CLIFFWOOD INN

Owners: Scottie and Joy Farrelly.
413-637-3330, 800-789-3331; fax 413-637-0221.
www.cliffwood.com.
25 Cliffwood St., Lenox, MA 01240.
Just off Main St. in the village.
Price: Expensive to Very Expensive.
Credit Cards: None.
Special Features: Indoor and outdoor pools; putting green; no smoking; no pets; children over 11.

This special inn, on a quiet, residential street, was built for a French diplomat in 1889. The elegant public rooms have tall ceilings, polished inlaid hardwood floors, and grand fireplaces. The seven guest rooms have private baths and air-conditioning; six come with their own fireplaces. The inn features an outdoor pool, an indoor countercurrent pool, and a putting green. The spacious veranda overlooks the gardens, pool, and putting green. We move in winter to the warming fire in the oval dining room, with its ornate wood-carved fireplace mantel. Wine, hors d'oeuvres, and friendly conversation are served in the early evening; coffee and juice in the morning.

### CORNELL INN

Owners: Billie and Doug McLoughlin.
413-637-0562, 800-637-0562; fax 413-737-0927.
www.cornellinn.com.
203 Main St., Lenox, MA 01240.
Rte. 7A just N. of center of town.
Price: Expensive to Very Expensive.
Credit Cards: AE, CB, D, DC, MC, V.
Handicap Access: Two rooms.
Special Features: Pub; no smoking; no pets; children 13 and over.

Written in the guest book at the Cornell Inn: "Charming home. The pancakes were delicious." The home began life in 1888 as a large, well-built Victorian, and the owners keep making all the right improvements. Each of the 10 bedrooms in the main house has its own bath and is furnished with brass or four-poster beds; several have fireplaces. Eight additional rooms are in the converted carriage house and 10 in the adjacent 227-year-old McDonald House. The McDonald House rooms have fireplaces and whirlpool tubs. Phone, color TV in all rooms. Extended continental breakfast; full breakfast Sunday.

### B&B AT THE EGMONTS

Owners: Nina and Steve Egmont.
413-637-9807, 800-866-EGMONTS.
www.egmonts.net
123 Walker St., P.O. Box 45, Lenox, MA 01240.
Closed Nov.–May.
Price: Expensive.
Credit Cards: None.
Special Features: No smoking; no pets; children 12 and over.

The Egmonts offer three rooms, all with private baths, in their elegant, contemporary home. Set back from Walker Street and among trees and bushes, the the house is quiet. While most furnishings are antique, the eye-catcher is an enormous array of bookcases in the second-floor hall, containing an extensive collection of French and American literature. The largest room contains a king-sized bed, walk-in closet, and Jacuzzi plus shower. Breakfast is pretty much what guests want, although the order should recognize that Nina is an accomplished baker.

### THE GABLES INN

Owners: Frank and Mary Newton.
413-637-3416, 800-382-9401; fax 413-637-3416.
www.gableslenox.com.
81 Walker St., Lenox, MA 01240.
On Rte. 183 in center of village.
Price: Expensive to Very Expensive.
Credit Cards: D, MC, V.
Special Features: Pool; tennis; no pets; children over 12.

This charming, handsome 1885 home is where Edith Wharton summered while her "cottage," the Mount, was being built. Visitors can sleep in her room or in that of her husband, Teddy. He stayed there until 1928, long after she'd taken off. Frank Newton discusses the Whartons knowledgeably. The inn is fully air-conditioned, with TV and VCR. The 17 bedrooms all have private baths; 9 have fireplaces. Full breakfast. A sister inn, called the Summer White House, is at 17 Main Street, Lenox.

### GARDEN GABLES INN

Owners: Mario and Lynn Mekinda.
413-637-0193.
www.lenoxinn.com.
135 Main St., P.O. Box 52, Lenox, MA 01240.
Price: Expensive to Very Expensive.
Credit Cards: AE, D, MC, V.
Special Features: Pool; no pets; children over 12.

The Mekinda family has brought new life to this inn since purchasing it in 1987. All 18 rooms include air-conditioning and private baths (three have whirlpools), all have telephones and answering machines, eight have fireplaces; some have private porches, and some have TVs. The 5 acres of landscaped grounds include the largest outdoor pool in Berkshire County. Walking distance to shops and restaurants—even to Tanglewood for the hardy. The breakfast buffets are special.

### GATEWAYS INN

Owners: Fabrizio and Rosemary Chiariello.
413-637-2532, 888-492-9466; fax 413-637-1432.

www.gatewaysinn.com.
51 Walker St., Lenox, MA 01240.
Just off Main St.
Price: Expensive to Very Expensive.
Credit Cards: AE, DC, MC, V.
Special Features: Restaurant; no smoking; no pets; call about children.

Built in 1912 by Harley Procter of Procter and Gamble, this Berkshire "cottage" continues to receive extensive upgrading. Up a graceful, skylighted mahogany staircase from an award-winning restaurant are 12 spacious, elegant rooms, each with bath, 8 with fireplaces, a four-poster here, a canopy bed there, and peace and quiet everywhere. A guest library has everything from a computer terminal to old-fashioned games. Arthur Fiedler, who stayed here when performing at Tanglewood, gave his name to the lovely Fiedler Suite. Television, data port, and telephone in each room; air-conditioned throughout; a Jacuzzi in the suite and in one other room.

### HAMPTON TERRACE

Owners: Stan and Susan Rosen.
413-637-1773 (phone/fax), 800-203-0656.
www.hamptonterrace.com.
91 Walker St., Lenox, MA 01240.
Price: Expensive to Very Expensive.
Credit Cards: AE, D, DC, MC, V.
Special Features: Pool; no pets; children 10 and over.

The Rosens have thoroughly renovated and refurbished this lovely property, which consists of the Main House and the Carriage House, both dating from 1897.The Main House, renovated in 2001, has five rooms with private baths and air-conditioning; some rooms have fireplaces, some have spa tubs or claw-foot tubs. Period furnishings preserve the 19th-century flavor. The Carriage House, refurbished in 2000, features six additional rooms with king- or queen-sized beds, private baths, fireplaces, Jacuzzis, air-conditioning, and television/VCRs—but likewise has vintage furniture, drapes, and decorations. Three new, king suites face a new pool. A full breakfast is served.

### HARRISON HOUSE

Owner: Andrew Fishbein.
413-637-1746; fax 413-637-9957.
www.harrison-house.com.
174 Main St., Lenox, MA 01240.
Across from Kennedy Park.
Price: Expensive to Very Expensive.
Credit Cards: AE, D, MC, V.
Handicap Access: Limited.
Special Features: No pets.

A charming country inn offering seven elegant guest rooms and splendid public areas is at home in an attractive Victorian, at the crest of Main Street. It has a wraparound porch and a handsome sitting/breakfast room overlooking the back lawn. The bedrooms are air-conditioned, each with a private bath and period fixtures and décor. There are fireplaces—many with the original Victorian tiles—in every room as well as cable TV. Duvets and cutwork linens add a romantic touch. The Norman Rockwell suite has a canopy bed, a sitting room with sofa bed, and an especially splendid bathroom. Full buffet breakfast and afternoon refreshments served.

### THE KEMBLE INN

Owners/Innkeepers: Richard and Linda Reardon.
413-637-4113, 800-353-4113.
www.kembleinn.com.
2 Kemble St., Lenox, MA 01240.
On Rte. 7A.
Price: Expensive to Very Expensive.
Credit Cards: MC, V.
Handicap Access: Yes.
Special Features: No smoking; no pets; children 12 and over.

This luxury bed-and-breakfast inn in Lenox is named for the actress Fanny

*The Kemble Inn, seen from Trinity Church, Lenox* Judith Monachina

Kemble, who once lived on the street named for her. It occupies yet another Berkshire "cottage"—this one the Georgian mansion built in 1881 by President Chester A. Arthur's secretary of state, Frederick T. Frelinghuysen. Richard Reardon, a contractor, supervised the complete renovation of the house, which included adding several bathrooms. Each of the 14 guest rooms, all named for Berkshire authors, has a private bath and air-conditioning. The furnishings throughout the house are period reproductions. The master suite has a bedroom with fireplace and a bathroom with Jacuzzi—and another fireplace. The most impressive features inside the inn are the elegant and spacious common spaces on the ground floor—foyer, reception room, dining room—all with magnificent Adams-style paneling. Also magnificent are the views of the mountains to the back and historic Trinity Church to the front. Continental breakfast is included in the summer.

**ROOKWOOD INN**

Owner/Innkeeper: Amy Lindner-Lesser.
413-637-9750, 800-223-9750; fax 413-637-1352.
www.rookwoodinn.com.
11 Old Stockbridge Rd., P.O. Box 1717, Lenox, MA 01240.
Just off Main St. in center of town.
Price: Expensive to Very Expensive.
Credit Cards: AE, D, DC, MC, V.
Handicap Access: Limited.
Special Features: No smoking; ask about pets; children welcome.

The Lessers purchased the inn in the fall of 1996. This grand 1825 Victorian lady sits on a quiet street behind the Town Hall. All 21 rooms and the two-room suite have private baths; 11 include fireplaces. The two-level turret room is a marvelous secluded aerie, and the 3 rooms in the back of the house can be considered small suites. *New York* Magazine and Target stores have named Rookwood as a top B&B in New England.

A gourmet chef prepares innovative and low-fat breakfasts. Special dietary needs can be accommodated. Children are welcome as guests, and babysitting can be arranged.

### SEVEN HILLS INN

Owners: Roberto Flores and Patty Eder.
413-637-0060, 800-869-6518.
www.sevenhillsinn.com.
40 Plunkett St., Lenox, MA 01240.
Just beyond the Mount.
Price: Expensive to Very Expensive.
Credit cards: AE, MC, V.
Handicapped Access: Yes.
Special Features: Fireplaces in many rooms; pool; pets accepted.

This Berkshire cottage formerly belonged to Emily Spencer, who maintained it as a summer house on 27 well-landscaped acres. Brother and sister, Roberto and Patty kept the lovely main building largely intact, gutted and redid the Terrace House to make it more useful as an inn, and more recently added a carriage house. All 58 rooms have private baths. Each comfortable and welcoming room is imaginatively decorated in a different style, and all look out on the wooded scene that surrounds Edith Wharton's home, the Mount. Patty kept much of the original furnishings and traveled to auctions to pick up the rest.

While the tone is less formal than at Wheatleigh or Blantyre, the inn aims at conferences and weddings. As well as the attractive dining room on the first floor of the main building, public spaces include a banquet room and other functions and a bar from which music wafts on summer evenings. A continental breakfast is included.

### STONOVER FARM

Owners: Tom and Suky Werman.
413-637-9100; fax 413-637-1717.
www.stonoverfarm.com.
169 Undermountain Rd., Lenox, MA 01240.
Price: Very Expensive.
Credit Cards: AE, MC, V.
Special Features: On a scenic road 0.7 mi. from Tanglewood.

Tom Werman, returning to Massachusetts after a career as a record producer in Los Angeles, opened his refurbished 1890s stone farmhouse on 10.5 acres, a stone's throw from Tanglewood, in 2002, by hosting Linda Ronstadt. He has created four three-room suites in the main house as well as a four-room cottage. He serves wine and cheese in the afternoons and a full breakfast, "cooked to order."

Luxurious, elegant, all details attended to, plus all the hi-tech electronics anyone could desire, Stonover is a platinum disk of a B&B, selected as "Hideaway of the Year" in 2004 by *Andrew Harper's Hideaway Report.*

### THE VILLAGE INN

Owners: Billy and Pat Soto.
413-637-0020, 800-253-0917; fax 413-637-9756.
www.villageinn-lenox.com.
16 Church St., P.O. Box 1810, Lenox, MA 01240.
Off Walker St. in center of town.
Price: Expensive to Very Expensive.
Credit Cards: MC, V.
Handicap Access: Yes.
Special Features: No smoking; no pets; children over 6.

This old, highly respected hostelry remains a warm and friendly space under new owners. Their pride in restoration and furnishings is evident. Of the 32 guest rooms, all with private baths and telephones, 6 have fireplaces. The suite has a kitchenette. The smoking ban includes the public rooms.

The inn was built in 1771 as a farmhouse; 4 years later, its original owner started to

*The Italianate entrance to Wheatleigh* Judith Monachina

put up weary travelers arriving by horse-drawn coach. By 1815 he had sold his surrounding land, presumably to continue exclusively an innkeeper.

Full breakfasts are served in-season on the sunny porch. A full-scale restaurant as well as a downstairs tavern (See chapter 4, "Dining").

### WALKER HOUSE INN

Innkeepers: Peggy and Richard Houdek.
413-637-1271, 800-235-3098; fax 413-637-2387.
www.walkerhouse.com.
64 Walker St., Lenox, MA 01240.
On Rte. 183.
Price: Moderate to Very Expensive.
Credit Cards: None.
Handicap Access: Limited.
Special Features: No smoking; well-mannered pets with prior approval.

Attractive, well-furnished 1804-vintage Federal house operated for over 25 years by the same two friendly people. The 3 acres of garden and woods behind the house are gorgeous. Eight rooms all have private baths; five have fireplaces. The décor in each is an impression of the composer for whom the room is named; the Houdaks will explain. Sitting rooms offer an impressive collection of music and books, and a 12-foot video screen enhances the Library Theatre—wonderful for watching opera, films, and sporting events. Generous continental breakfast. Within walking distance of Tanglewood, Lenox shops, and restaurants.

### WHEATLEIGH

Owners: Susan and Linfield Simon.
Manager: François Thomas.
413-637-0610; fax 413-637-4507.
www.wheatleigh.com.
Hawthorne Rd., P.O. Box 824, Lenox, MA 01240.
From Rte. 183 in Lenox, left on Hawthorne Rd. to "Wheatleigh" sign.
Price: Very Expensive.
Credit Cards: AE, DC, MC, V.
Special Features: Pool; tennis; fitness room; no pets; children over 9.

Wheatleigh is pure romance. An estate built for heiress Georgie Bruce Cook, wife of "Count" Carlos de Heredia, it encourages flights of imagination. The grounds and setting captivate. From the broad terrace, the manicured lawns slope down to a grassy stairway and then to a fountain. Straight ahead is a view of the Stockbridge Bowl with the Berkshire hills in the distance. The heated pool is hidden away in a knoll surrounded by trees, and the tennis court is off in another direction.

Owners Linfield and Susan Simon have preserved the expansive luxury of the interior space and decorative details in this turn-of-the-20th-century mansion. The approach is by way of a winding driveway, then through an enclosed courtyard with a circular drive—reminiscent of a 16th-century private palazzo in the hills outside Florence. Once you're inside, the Great Hall is impressive with its magnificent Tiffany windows lining the grand staircase, antique furnishings, and original brass chandelier. The dark-wooded Conservatory with its cooling breezes is perfect for summer dining.

The 19 guest rooms, recently renovated, are baronial in size. Nine have working fireplaces. All have television, VCR, high-speed Internet connections and personal portable telephones. The bathrooms are splendid, several with original fixtures. Breakfast does not come with the room, but Wheatleigh contains an award-winning prix-fixe restaurant, whose food is complemented by an award-winning wine list. The premises are available for business meetings, weddings, and parties.

### WHISTLER'S INN

Managers: Richard, Joan, and Lisa Mears.
413-637-0975; fax 413-637-2190.
www.whistlersinnlenox.com.
5 Greenwood St., Lenox, MA 01240.
Corner Rte.7A.
Price: Expensive to Very Expensive.
Credit Cards: AE, D, MC, V.
Special Features: No pets.

This charming, much-admired inn created within a 7-acre 1820s English Tudor summer estate was featured on the Travel Channel among the world's most haunted houses. Cultivated, accommodating hosts (Richard is an author; Joan is an artist; Lisa an artist and writer) put us at ease. The inn is furnished with antiques, chandeliers, and Persian rugs, resulting in an old-world Victorian atmosphere. The 14 bedrooms, all with private baths, are quaint and cozy. A seasonal suite features an African motif. The interior is full of pleasant surprises, including an extensive library. From the stone-walled terrace you can walk among seven gardens and woodland—or wind through the kudzu maze. Full breakfast is provided.

PITTSFIELD

### THADDEUS CLAPP HOUSE

Innkeeper: Becky Smith.
413-499-6840, 888-499-6840; fax 413-499-6942.
www.clapphouse.com.
74 Wendell Ave., Pittsfield, MA 01201.
S. of Berkshire Athenaeum.
Price: Moderate to Very Expensive.
Credit Cards: AE, D, MC, V.
Handicap Accessible: Yes

This recently renovated Victorian house has eight suites (one wheelchair-friendly), which include all communications media, catering to both the business traveler and recreational tourist. The wood furnishings are Victorian, the upholstered pieces more contemporary. A large front porch provides a view of passing events. Clapp House is close to the Berkshire Museum, downtown restaurants, and the shuttered Colonial Theater—which is due to reopen in all its glory.

### WHITE HORSE INN

Innkeepers: Joe and Linda Kalisz.
413-442-2512; fax 413-443-0490.
www.whitehorsebb.com.
378 South St., Pittsfield, MA 01201.
On Rte. 7/20, W. side, 2 mi. N. of

*The White Horse Inn, Pittsfield* Judith Monachina

"Pittsfield" sign; 1 mi. S. of town center.
Price: Moderate to Expensive.
Credit Cards: All major.
Special Features: No smoking; no pets.

An attractive 1907 Colonial Revival—set back from the busy main street, south of the center of Pittsfield—offers eight rooms with private baths, air-conditioning, phones, and TV (and fax and wireless connections). The rooms have been redecorated with charming linens and wallpapers. Guests may use a kitchenette and a small sitting room on the second floor. A full breakfast is served in the dining room, where guests are seated at individual tables, or on the deck in summer. Perennial gardens and a picnic table complete the picture.

RICHMOND

### BERKSHIRE HILLS COUNTRY INN

Owner: Ann Meyer.
413-698-3379.
673 Dean Hill Rd., Richmond, MA 01254.
Near "W. Stockbridge" sign on Rte. 41; turn on Baker St., then Dean.
Closed: Nov.–May.
Price: Inexpensive.
Credit Cards: None.
Special Features: No smoking; no pets; children over 17.

Enjoy a great view of the Berkshires from this 147-acre hilltop property. "It's really marvelous," Ann says. Three comfortable rooms share a bath. Another has a private bath. Continental breakfast served. Tanglewood and Hancock Shaker Village are just a hop, skimp, and a jump . . . such as the resident chicken and sheep might make.

### ECHEZEAUX, A COUNTRY BED & BREAKFAST

Proprietors: Ronald Barron and Ina Wilhelm.
413-698-2802; 617-965-3957; winter: 617-965-3957.
180 Cheever Rd., Richmond, MA 01254.
N. on Swamp Rd. 2.25 mi. from W. Stockbridge, then right on Cheever.
Closed: Labor Day–last weekend in June.
Price: Moderate.
Credit Cards: None.
Special Features: Pool; no smoking; no pets.

Delightful country retreat, owned by a member of the Boston Symphony Orchestra and frequently rented to other BSO members, this house often fills the surrounding hills with music. Just 2 miles from the front gate of Tanglewood, the main house has three antiques-furnished rooms that share a bath. A fourth room in a separate building is available for weekends or weekly rental. An elegant continental breakfast is served.

## INNS AND B&BS NORTH COUNTY

ADAMS

### BASCOM LODGE

Managed: Nature's Classroom.
413-743-1591.
Summit Road, Adams, MA 01220.
From Rte. 7 take N. Main St., Lanesborough, to Rockwell Rd.; from Rte. 2,

N. Adams, Notch Rd.; to the summit of Mt. Greylock.
Open: Mid-May—Mid-Oct.
Price: Inexpensive.
Credit Cards: MC, V.
Handicap Access: Yes.
Special Features: Rustic lodge; extraordinary view.

Bascom Lodge atop Mount Greylock reveals a marvel of dramatic beauty. Operated by Nature's Classroom and owned by the Massachusetts Department of Conservation and Recreation, the lodge at the 3,491-foot summit of the state's highest peak was built of stone and wood by the commonwealth and Civilian Conservation Corps during the Depression. Generations of hikers, birders, and canny travelers have celebrated the accommodations, returning often.

The stone fireplace and hand-cut oak beams cultivate a sense of adventure, which the magnificent hills and trails confirm. This is lodging for the hearty—or at least the sporting. Although linens are supplied, travelers might want to bring a sleeping bag or an extra blanket. The guest rooms are private or dormitory-style, with bathrooms down the hall. Breakfast and dinner are served family-style at a set time. Reservations are required for rooms or meals.

### CHESHIRE

#### HARBOUR HOUSE INN

Owners: Eva and Samuel Amuso.
413-743-8959.
www.harbourhouseinn.com.
725 N. State Rd., Cheshire, MA 01225.
On Rte. 8.
Price: Moderate to Expensive.
Credit Cards: AE, D, MC, V.
Special Features: No smoking; full breakfast.

The main farmhouse for Rolling Acres Farm was converted to a B&B in 1998, with six guest rooms, four with private baths and one with working fireplace. A third-floor two-room suite overlooks Mount Greylock. The rooms, which are artfully decorated with curtains, wall coverings, and canopies, all have names, such as Field of Dreams for the bridal room, Country Sunshine, and Garden View—a family-sized room. Guests have the use of a spacious common room, music room, and formal dining room, where a full breakfast is served.

The house has a colorful history, from its 18th-century origins through massive 1903 additions, having served as a tavern, a stagecoach stop, and possibly a stop on the Underground Railway—for which it is named. Set on an eminence among sweeping fields, its views of Mount Greylock and the Hoosac Valley are immense.

### NORTH ADAMS

#### BLACKINTON MANOR

Hosts: Paul and Laura Maciones.
413-663-5795, 800-795-8613.
www.blackinton-manor.com.
1391 Massachusetts Ave., N. Adams, MA 01247.
One block off Rte. 2, minutes from Williamstown.
Price: Expensive.
Credit Cards: MC, V.
Special Features: Pool; chamber music; hiking; no smoking; no pets; children over 8.

This handsome Federal-style mansion is available to guests "as a country escape in the Berkshires." Reopened in 1993 after a complete renovation, the 1849 house is notable for its Italianate features—including intricate wrought-iron balconies, floor-to-ceiling pocket windows, and a spacious bay window. Now, under new owners, the five bedrooms, all with private baths, have furnishings, fabrics, and wallpaper appropriate to the period, but all are comfortably air-conditioned. A full, hot, gourmet breakfast is served in the formal dining room or, in summer, on the screened porch.

### JAE'S INN

Owner: Jae H. Chung.
413-663-6933; fax 413-664-0105.
www.jaesinn.com.
1111 S. State St., Box 193, N. Adams, MA 01247.
Rte. 8, 2 mi. S. of N. Adams City Hall.
Price: Expensive.
Credit Cards: AE, CB, D, DC, MC, V.
Special features: Spa and restaurant on property; pets for fee.

Jae Inn's owner, who also owns the Miss Adams Diner in Adams, Le Jardin in Williamstown, and a restaurant chain in the Boston area, invested $500,000 to turn the Twin Sisters into the upscale Jae's Inn, including 11 country guest rooms, a 45-seat restaurant and bar, health club and spa, tennis court, basketball court, and heated swimming pool. All the rooms have private baths and Jacuzzis; air-conditioning and flat screen TV/DVD. Three "courtyard" rooms offer direct access to tennis and pool. Complimentary toiletries and a continental breakfast.

The spa offers "a full range of spa treatment and beauty services."

### THE PORCHES INN

Manager: Olivier Glattfelder.
413-664-0400; fax 413-664-0401.
www.porches.com.
231 River St., N. Adams, MA 01247.
Across from MASS MoCA.
Price: Expensive to Very Expensive.
Credit Cards: AE, DC, MC, V.
Special Features: Packages include MoCA admission.

This 52-room all-convenience inn—including DVD players, hot tub, heated lap pool, fitness center, sauna, cordless telephones, and high-speed Internet access—results from the miraculous transformation of six refurbished Victorian-era row houses. Untransformed row houses and small businesses flank the inn, whose rooms and suites are a synthesis of retro and contemporary design, described as "industrial-granny chic"—including long verandas, bold inside/outside spaces, and striking, colorful interiors. Named one of the hottest new inns nationwide; also named one of the coolest hotels in the world by *Condé Nast* (UK).

A European-style breakfast is offered in the dining room or delivered to guests' rooms or eponymous porches. Cocktails are available. Management is under the same careful eyes as the Red Lion Inn in Stockbridge.

## WILLIAMSTOWN

### BUXTON BROOK FARM

Innkeeper: Nancy B. Alden.
413-458-3621.
www.buxtonbrookfarm.com.
91 Northwest Hill Rd., Williamstown, MA 01267.
Between W. end of Main and Bulkley sts.
Price: Expensive.
Credit Cards: AE, D, MC, V.
Special Features: No smoking; no pets; no small children.

Situated on 70 country acres adjacent to the 2,500-acre Hopkins Memorial Forest, Buxton Brook Farm is one of the most gracious B&Bs in these pages. The spacious Federal-style house has three rooms with three baths, which can be arranged in several different ways to accommodate the numbers of a party. The rooms are somewhat smaller in the former servants' wing. The furnishings and appointments, although related to individuals in the family, are of the 1820s—tasteful without being fussy.

Common space on the first floor focuses on three fireplaces and a woodstove. The grounds include a pool. Nancy serves a homemade breakfast, either in the stylish dining room or on the terrace in summer. Buxton Brook Farm is within 2 scenic miles of the Williamstown Theatre Festival, the

Clark Art Institute, and the Williams College Museum of Art. Miles of the best hiking and cross-country skiing trails in town are out the back door.

### 1896 HOUSE COUNTRY INN & MOTELS

Owners: Sue Morell and Denise Richer.
413-458-1896, 888-999-1896.
www.1896house.com.
910 Cold Spring Rd., Williamstown, MA 01267.
On Rte. 7/2.
Price: Moderate to Very Expensive.
Credit Cards: AE, D, DC, MC, V.
Handicap Access: Yes.
Special Features: Pond, brooks; pool; restaurant on premises.

The buildings that constitute the 1896 House now include Barnside, a country inn with six luxury suites located in the large barn that also accommodates the '6 House Pub; 14 rooms at the Pondside Motel, including an apartment and a small "Sweetheart" room; and 16 rooms at the Brookside Motel. (These are all within a few hundred feet of one another along U.S. Routes 7 & 2.) Owners Sue and Denise have excellent taste in décor and a keen eye for upkeep so that each unit of this extensive property, ranging in amenities from suites to Pondside, has its own charms and is immaculately cared for. Each of the suites has a historical decorating theme (all appear on the Web site). TVs are stowed in handsome furniture, bathrooms have Jacuzzis, and one suite has its own kitchen. A European-style continental buffet breakfast is served in a breakfast room. The motel units, too, have their own distinctive personalities and accessories. Breakfast is also served. A pool is available to all guests. Adirondack chairs grace the grounds.

### GUEST HOUSE AT FIELD FARM

Innkeeper: Bob Chok.
413-458-3135; fax 413-458-3144.
www.guesthouseatfieldfarm.org.
554 Sloan Rd., Williamstown, MA 01267.
From jct. of Rtes. 43 and 7, 1 mi. on right.
Price: Expensive to Very Expensive.
Credit Cards: AE, D, MC, V.
Special Features: Pool; hiking/skiing trails; no pets.

A property of the Trustees of Reservations, Field Farm comprises 254 acres, excellent for hiking and cross-country skiing, and a house built in 1948 in the American Modern style (for comparison, see the Frelinghuysen-Morris House in chapter 5, "Arts & Pleasures"). Five guest rooms all have private baths, two have working fireplaces, and three have sundecks. A swimming pool and tennis courts are available. Country living, with views of Mount Greylock and the Taconic Range, just minutes from the attractions of Williamstown, with a full breakfast.

### THE HOUSE ON MAIN STREET

Innkeepers: Timothy Hamilton and Donna Riley
413-458-303, 800-519-4667; fax 413-458-2254.
www.houseonmainstreet.com
1120 Main St., Williamstown, MA 01267.
W. of the Williams Inn.
Price: Moderate.
Credit Cards: D, MC, V.
Handicap Access: Limited.
Special Features: No smoking; no pets; children welcome.

Known as the Victorian Tourist and Antiques House in former times, this bed & breakfast has been receiving guests since the 1930s. In 1991 Bud and Phyllis Riley bought the B&B, changing it from a seasonal to a year-round concern. In July 2000 their daughter, Donna Riley, and son-in-law, Timothy Hamilton, moved from Manhattan to carry on the family tradition of innkeeping.

This home was constructed in the 18th century, with a major Victorian addition in

1860. The six guest rooms are light and spacious, with accents of antique furnishings, pretty country prints, and braided rugs. Some have private baths; some shared. The 21st century is represented by high-speed Internet access.

A healthful and hearty breakfast—seasonal fruits; various organic cereals with low-fat milk, or soy or rice beverages; french toast, or light whole wheat pancakes—is served in the country kitchen. The innkeepers are happy to provide vegetarian, vegan, or other dietary changes, as requested by health-conscious patrons. Guests can enjoy the fireplace in the parlor, or the wicker-furnished screened porch in warmer months. The innkeepers are well versed in the attractions of Williamstown, all within walking distance.

### LE JARDIN

Owner: Jae H. Chung.
413-458-8032.
777 Cold Spring Rd., Williamstown 01267.
On Rte. 7/2 just south of town.
Price: Expensive to Very Expensive.
Credit cards: All major.
Special Features: Restaurant below;
No pets.

Just south of the Field park in Williamstown, on a wooded hillside above Hemlock Brook, the newly refurbished Le Jardin offers four cozy rooms and a two-room suite, four with fireplace, all air-conditioned; the suite with a Jacuzzi. The inn resides in a large, comfortable farmhouse with a well-regarded restaurant of the same name.

### THE ORCHARDS HOTEL

Owner: Sayed M. Saleh.
413-458-9611, 800-225-1517; fax 413-458-1917.
www.orchardshotel.com.
222 Adams Rd., Williamstown, MA 01267.
On Rte. 2, E. of town center.
Price: Expensive to Very Expensive.
Credit Cards: AE, CB, DC, MC, V.
Handicap Access: Yes.
Special Features: Pool; exercise center with sauna, environmental chamber, and whirlpool; no pets; private conference and meeting rooms.

This small luxury hotel—a member of the Leading Hotels of the World—is reminiscent of an English country inn. Antique furnishings, complimentary afternoon tea, and 47 enormous guest rooms—newly renovated and featuring four-poster beds with down pillows—are just a few of the amenities. Many rooms have gas fireplaces and bay windows. The Orchards's award-winning restaurant, the Yasmin, features a menu that reflects New England's heritage and the chef's distinctive international talents. In summer alfresco patio dining is available overlooking the pond in the nicely landscaped inner courtyard. Chocolate chip cookies are a regular bedtime treat.

### RIVER BEND FARM

Owners: David and Judy Loomis.
413-458-3121.
www.riverbendfarmbb.com.
643 Simonds Rd., Williamstown, MA 01267.
On Rte. 7, 1 mi. N. of town green.
Price: Moderate.
Credit Cards: None.
Closed: Nov.–Mar.
Special Features: Restored 1770 tavern.

A stay at River Bend Farm, an authentic 1770 tavern listed on the National Register of Historic Places and featured on PBS's *This Old House*, comes as close to an 18th-century lodging experience as one can have—but with heat and running water. Colonel Benjamin Simonds built the house as a tavern. Thanks to painstaking work by the Loomises, original features are intact: wide-pine floorboards, magnificent paneling, corner cupboards, and a central chimney containing five separate fireplaces, three ovens, and an attic smoking chamber. Furnishings, accessories, and fabrics used throughout the house are from the period or appropriate to it. Four guest rooms share two very large bathrooms (one was the buttery of the house, and its walls are lined with crocks, paddles, and other implements). Breakfast (homemade breads, jams, and granola, with River Bend's own honey) is served in the keeping room at the back of the house, and the former taproom is a guest parlor. In summer, lawn furniture and a hammock are placed among the perennial and herb gardens, which feature a variety of 18th-century plants.

### STEEP ACRES FARM

Owners: Mary and Marvin Gangemi, Daniel Gangemi.
413-458-3774.
520 White Oaks Rd., Williamstown, MA 01267.
From Rte. 7, E. on Sand Springs Rd., N. on White Oaks Rd.
Price: Inexpensive to Expensive.
Credit Cards: None.
Special Features: Pond for swimming, boating, and fishing; hiking trails; no smoking; no pets; children 5 and over.

Two miles from the center of Williamstown, Steep Acres offers country lodging up a long, gravel drive. The 1900 stone-and-shingle house sits on a hilltop on the Vermont state line, overlooking Mount Greylock. The property's 50 acres include a 1.5-acre pond for canoeing, trout fishing, and swimming (there is a diving board and raft), plus trails for hiking and cross-country skiing. A patio off the sunporch—great for summer breakfasts or reading—seems to be perched at the top of the world. The house features an attractive décor combining late-Victorian oak, wicker, and handsome fabrics. Two of four possible guest rooms available, depending on the preference of the party; three baths. Next door, in a contemporary house, the Birches at Steep Acres offers three more rooms—twin, queen, and king with Jacuzzi and fireplace. A full gourmet breakfast and afternoon refreshments are included.

### WILLIAMS INN

Owners: Carl and Marilyn Faulkner.
413-458-9371, 800-828-0138.
www.williamsinn.com.
Main St., Williamstown, MA 01267.
On the green, jct. Rtes. 7 and 2.
Price: Expensive to Very Expensive.
Credit Cards: All major.
Handicap Access: Yes.
Special Features: Indoor pool, sauna, whirlpool; full-service dining room; banquet facilities; no pets.

The generous Faulkners are much respected for making their inn a hub of town activities.The Williams Inn and its staff please a great many North County travelers—and take the hassle of being an interstate bus stop, as well. Vast and modern, the facility offers 125 rooms, each with a telephone and TV. Sunday brunch is highly regarded. The Faulkners are energetic about organizing special events, such as horse-drawn wagon rides. On Friday evenings a guitarist provides entertainment in the Tavern; on Saturday evenings there is jazz. Nearby are two of America's fine art museums and the renowned Williamstown Theatre Festival. There is no charge for children under 14 in parents' room.

### THE WILLIAMSTOWN BED AND BREAKFAST

Owners: Kim Rozell and Lucinda Edmonds.
413-458-9202.
www.williamstownbandb.com.
30 Cold Spring Rd., Williamstown, MA 01267.
Rte. 7 just S. of town library.

Price: Moderate.
Credit Cards: None.
Special Features: No smoking; no pets; children over 12.

Open for business since 1989, the Williamstown Bed and Breakfast credits its success to a central in-town location and a high proportion of returning guests. This spacious and airy Victorian has been completely renovated, including central air-conditioning, and is tastefully furnished with a mixture of antiques and comfortable sofas and chairs. Each of the four guest rooms has its own bath and is individually decorated in period oak, maple, or mahogany furniture. Guests have exclusive use of the living room, dining room, and broad front porch. Lingering around the table after one of the inn's popular breakfasts—featuring homemade breads, muffins, scones, and always a hot entrée—is standard operating procedure at Williamstown B&B. Summer guests enjoy the perennial gardens and hammocks for lazy afternoons.

## INNS AND B&BS OUTSIDE THE COUNTY

SALISBURY, CONNECTICUT

### THE WHITE HART INN

Owners: Scott and Roxanne Bok.
Manager: Kendra Tobin.
860-435-0030, 800-832-0041; fax 860-435-0040.
www.whitehartinn.com.
The Village Green, Box 545, Salisbury, CT 06068.
Jct. of Rtes. 41 and 44 in center of town.
Price: Expensive to Very Expensive.
Credit Cards: All major.
Handicap Access: Yes.
Special Features: Pets in some rooms; children welcome; senior discount weekdays.

The oldest portions of the inn were built prior to 1810, when records indicate that the farmhouse was converted to a tavern. The public spaces display an air of country elegance and comfort. Twenty-three charming guest rooms plus three suites all offer private baths, air-conditioning, phones, and cable TV. Meals are not included in the rate, but breakfast, lunch, and dinner are served on the premises.

AVERILL PARK, NEW YORK

### LAPERLA AT GREGORY HOUSE

Owners: Alfonso and Anna Maria Acampora.
518-674-3774; fax 518-674-8916.
www.gregoryhouse.com.
Box 401, Averill Park, NY 12018.
On Rte. 43.
Price: Moderate.
Credit Cards: D, MC, V.
Handicap Access: Limited.
Special Features: Pool; no smoking; no pets.

LaPerla at Gregory House has a clean, sophisticated country look. Twelve guest rooms, all with air-conditioning, television, Internet access, and private baths, have stenciled walls and attractive country furnishings. A continental breakfast is served to guests, and the cozy bar and the restaurant are open for dinner Wednesday through Monday. Averill Park is convenient to Williamstown attractions and North County ski areas as well as to the Saratoga Performing Arts Center.

BERLIN, NEW YORK

### THE SEDGWICK INN

Innkeepers: Chet and Diane Niedzwiecki.
518-658-2334; fax 518-658-3998.
www.sedgwickinn.com.
17971 State Rte. 22, P.O. Box 250, Berlin, NY 12022.
Price: Moderate to Expensive.
Credit Cards: AE, D, MC, V.

Special Features: Jacuzzi; pets and children in annex only.

A 1791 house with restaurant and small motel unit (the Annex) attached, set on 12 acres in the country. Privately owned and operated, this quaint, well-kept property offers 11 comfortable rooms and proximity to Berkshire attractions. Rooms in the main house are preferred.

HILLSDALE, NEW YORK

### SWISS HÜTTE COUNTRY INN

Managers: Gert and Cindy Alper.
518-325-3333; 413-528-6200.
www.swisshutte.com.
P.O. Box 357, Hillsdale, NY 12529.
Rte. 23, 2 mi. E. of Hillsdale on MA–NY border.
Price: Moderate.
Credit Cards: MC, V.
Handicap Access: Limited.
Special Features: Pool; tennis.

Located at the entrance to the popular South County ski area Catamount, this property boasts several tennis courts, a pool, lovely gardens, and, of course, an inviting downhill slope in its front yard. Fourteen comfortable, well-furnished rooms are split between the original wooden chalet and a newer building. An award-winning restaurant completes the picture. A modified American plan is available. Breakfast is not included with the basic room rate.

NEW LEBANON, NEW YORK

### CHURCHILL HOUSE BED & BREAKFAST

Owners: Stephen and Laura Lappier.
518-766-5852, 800-532-2702.
www.churchillhousebb.com.
228 Churchill Rd., New Lebanon, NY 12125.
Rte. 22, 0.25 mi. S. of Rte. 20.
Price: Expensive.
Credit Cards: AE, D, MC, V.
Special Features: Hiking trails; no smoking; no pets; children over 6 welcome.

Churchill House was built in 1830 for the Reverend Silas Churchill and remained in the Churchill family until 1965. The Greek Revival house and 18 acres of land have changed hands several times since. Churchill House has four guest rooms with private baths; two can have an additional bed in the room. There is air-conditioning and cable TV, and one room has a private phone line. A charming room under the eaves has stenciled morning glories. Each room has bathrobes, and the beds are mounded high with comforters. The living room and wraparound front porch with views of the Taconic Hills are for the guests' use. A full breakfast is served on weekends, a continental breakfast on weekdays. Away from the madding crowds but handy to all Berkshire attractions.

### SHAKER MEADOWS BED AND BREAKFAST

Owners: Jean and Sean Cowhig.
518-794-9385; fax 518-794-9381.
www.shakermeadows.com.
14209 Rte. 22, Canaan, NY 12029.
Price: Inexpensive to Expensive.
Credit Cards: AE, D, MC, V.
Special Features: 50 acres for hiking; function room; children welcome; rentals by the week accepted.

Guests have their choice of three rooms with private baths plus two small rooms in the 1821 farmhouse, or three suites in the creamery that was renovated in 1993. The common area in the farmhouse has full kitchen facilities but, thankfully, no phones or TV. The suites, which can sleep four to six each, have king- or queen-sized beds, kitchens, private decks or lawn space, phones, TVs, VCRs. Room rent includes beach privileges at nearby Quechee Lake. The property was the Palmer House B&B until 1999 and, before that, Sleepy Hollow Dairy, which processed the produce of local cows.

A breakfast room serves all the guests a hot meal—guaranteed tasty, as both Jean and Sean have extensive experience in lodging and cooking. The function room accommodates 50 for parties or meetings. Tents on the adjacent lawn can increase the number of guests to 150, with food provided by the owners or a caterer. Twelve miles to Tanglewood and 12 miles to Jiminy Peak.

STEPHENTOWN, NEW YORK

**MILL HOUSE INN**

Innkeepers: Mike Ostroskey and Rochelle Goodrich.
413-738-5348, 800-563-8645; fax 518-733-6025.
www.themillhouseinn.com.
Mailing Address: Box 1079, Hancock, MA 01237.
On Rte 43, Stephentown, NY.
Price: Moderate to Expensive.
Credit Cards: AE, D, MC, V.
Special Features: Pool; no smoking.

Old-world touches in a former sawmill enhance this cozy, well-regarded country inn, with refurbishing ongoing. Furnished with antiques, the rooms are warm and whimsical. A living room with fireplace offers warm comfort. Seven rooms and five suites, several with fireplaces of their own, all have private baths, air-conditioning, wireless Internet, and telephones. Set on 3 peaceful, rural acres with formal gardens, stone walls, garden paths, and a pool, it's the perfect romantic escape—a touch of country with a European flair. Afternoon tea and a full breakfast.

## HOTELS & RESORTS

**Bucksteep Manor** (413-623-5535, 800-645-BUCK; www.bucksteep manor.com; 885 Washington Mtn. Rd., Washington, MA 01223; off Rte. 8 N. from Becket) Price: Moderate. Credit Cards: AE, MC, V. Handicap Access: Limited. Special Features: X-C ski center; pool; no pets; children welcome.

Deep in the Washington woods, a cross-country skier's paradise. Of the eight rooms in the manor, all share baths and are comfortably furnished. Fourteen rooms in the lodge have private baths. In the summer nine cabins plus campground ($20 for adults) increase the number of accommodations and add to the rustic feeling of the property. Hiking, biking, and birding opportunities abound. Pool and tennis. Great dancing. Rock, country, bluegrass, and reggae concerts in the barn and on the lawn on summer weekends. Good vibes, funky buildings, and a mellow, laid-back feeling predominate.

**Cranwell Resort Spa and Golf Club** (413-637-1364, 800-272-6935; www.cranwell.com; 55 Lee Rd., Lenox, MA 01240; Rte. 20, S. of Lenox center, 3.5 mi. from MassPike Exit 2) Price: Expensive to Very Expensive. Credit Cards: AE, D, DC, MC, V. Handicap Access: Yes. Special Features: Pool; tennis; golf; spa; no pets. Restaurant, member Berkshire Grown.

Cranwell is a 380-acre estate high on a hill with one of the finest views of the Berkshire Hills. The 1893 Tudor Mansion is surrounded by lawns, gardens, and a par-71 championship golf course. Guest rooms are in the Mansion, Beecher's Cottage, the Carriage House, and Founder's Cottage; and in a group of one-bedroom cottages (totaling 105 units). The most luxurious bedrooms in the Mansion are spacious and individually decorated in the Victorian style, with private marble baths. In the various outbuildings, accommodations are slightly simpler and more contemporary, but some have the advantages of wet bar, refrigerator, and/or galley kitchens. Four dining rooms, including Sloane's Tavern, and numerous conference rooms complete the full-service offerings of this property. (See also under "Spas and Wellness Centers" chapter 6.)

**Crowne Plaza Hotel** (413-499-2000; www.crowneplaza.com; Berkshire Common, One West St., Pittsfield, MA 01201; off Park Square) Price: Expensive to Very Expensive. Credit Cards: All major. Handicap Access: 8 units. Special Features: Exercise room; indoor pool; sauna; Jacuzzi.

The Crowne Plaza crowns downtown Pittsfield—a big hotel with all the comforts. Located within striking distance of central, north, and south Berkshire, it is a good choice for travelers who prefer modern amenities over rustic charm.

Children appreciate the Sony Play Stations (video games) in each room, and the television channels are beyond counting. Rooms, rugs, and drapes are fancy; the beds spacious and comfortable. Rockwell's, the formal dining room, remains under renovation as of this writing. Other amenities include Dewey's, the lounge adjacent to the indoor pool, and Muddy McGee's, a sports bar. From a grand ballroom to small meeting rooms, the Crowne Plaza is prepared for business needs.

**Eastover Resort and Conference Center** (413-637-0625, 800-822-2386; www.eastover.com.; 430 East St., Lenox, MA 01240; from Rte. 7 in Lenox, take Housatonic St. E., then L. onto East St. for a little over 1 mi.) Price: Moderate. Credit Cards: AE, D, MC, V. Special Features: Indoor and outdoor pools; tennis; exercise room; sauna; driving range; miniature golf; horseback riding; X-C skiing; toboggan run; no pets.

Eastover is a picturesque, amiable place, admirably free of pretension. Another of the celebrated Lenox "cottages," this grand Gilded Age house is obviously living out of character but seems to be thriving. The sprawling grounds present tennis, swimming, biking, volleyball, horseback riding, and all sorts of winter activities, including cross-country skiing, and the longest toboggan run in New England.

Inspired by the remarkable spirit of the late founder, George Bisacca, the staff is up for anything as long as it's fun. To add to the festivities, there is dancing to live music during happy hour and again later in the evening. No liquor license here, so it's BYOB, but the band can play into the wee morning hours. Special weekends are organized for couples, singles, and families. Prospective guests should call ahead. While wandering the grounds, guests may catch a glimpse of the American bison, geese, and other pets. The founder's collection of Civil War artifacts and the museum in the Heritage Room will fascinate boys of all ages. The 165 guest rooms are large in the main house and of various sorts elsewhere.

**Holiday Inn Berkshires** (413-663-6500, 800-465-4329; www.holidayinnberkshires.com; 40 Main St., N. Adams, MA 01247) Price: Moderate. Credit Cards: All major. Handicap Access: Yes. Special Features: Indoor pool; sauna and steam room; Jacuzzi; full fitness center; no pets.

The 86 air-conditioned rooms—all with private baths, color TV, and telephones—are large and decorated in soft tones of red and blue. The Steeples, a full-service restaurant, serves breakfast, lunch, and dinner. Conference and meeting facilities are available, tours are welcome, and the gymnasium is available to local membership as well as guests.

**Jiminy Peak, The Mountain Resort** (413-738-5500, 800-882-8859 outside Mass.; www.jiminypeak.com. bet. Rtes. 7 and 43, 10 mi. N. of Pittsfield). Price: Very Expensive. Credit Cards: AE, D, DC, MC, V. Handicap Access: Yes. Special Features: Heated pool; tennis; health club; trout fishing; Alpine Slide; Giant Swing; Zip Line; mountain biking; downhill skiing; no pets.

This full-service resort has it all. In the Country Inn, each of the 105 suites features a kitchenette, a living room with queen-sized sofa bed, a bath with powder room, and a master bedroom with king-sized bed (or twins). A new lodge is under construction. Most of the units can be rented for 1 night on weekdays or 2 nights on weekends. There are also two- and three-bedroom condominiums for rent. Add to that the Founders' Grille, Christiansen's Tavern, and two cafeterias during ski season; tennis, swimming, trout fishing, an Alpine Slide for summer, and—best of all—great downhill skiing. One of the Berkshire's most complete resorts. Conference facilities are available. Meals are not included. Several package plans.

## MOTELS

### SOUTH COUNTY

**Barrington Court Travelodge** (413-528-2340; 400 Stockbridge Rd., Gt. Barrington, MA 01230; on Rte. 7, N. of town) Price: Expensive to Very Expensive. AE, D, MC, V. Handicap access. 30 motel units with refrigerators; 4 suites with kitchenettes, Jacuzzi; pool.

**Best Value Inn** (413-243-0501, 800-329-7466; Rte. 102, 980 Pleasant St., Box 426, Lee, MA 01238; between Stockbridge and Lee) Price: Moderate to Expensive. AE, D, DC, MC, V. 26 units convenient to Tanglewood, Berkshire Theatre Festival, Jacob's Pillow, and other South County attractions. Cable TV, AC.

**Briarcliff Inn** (413-528-3000; 506 Stockbridge Rd., Gt. Barrington, MA 01230; on Rte 7, N. of town) Price: Inexpensive to Moderate. AE, D, DC, MC, V. 16 units. Spacious landscaped grounds with view of Monument Mountain.

**Comfort Inn & Suites** (413-644-3200; 249 Stockbridge Rd., Gt. Barrington, MA 01230) Price: Expensive to Very Expensive. AE, D, MC, V. Handicapped access. 40 rooms. 20 suites. Indoor pool, Jacuzzi, fitness room.

**Days Inn, Gt. Barrington** (413-528-3150; 372 Main St., Gt. Barrington 01230) Price: Moderate to Expensive. AE, CB, D, DC, MC, V. Handicapped access. 62 units.

**Holiday Inn Express Hotel & Suites** (413-528-1810; 415 Stockbridge Rd., Gt. Barrington, MA 01230; on Rte. 7, N. of town) Price: Inexpensive to Very Expensive. AE, D, DC, MC, V. 58 units, including 20 suites. Cable TV, AC. Pool, exercise room. Continental breakfast.

**Lantern House Motel** (413-528-2350, 800-959-2350; 256 Stockbridge Rd., Box 97, Gt. Barrington, MA 01230; Rte. 7, 1 mi. N. of town) Price: Moderate. (3-night weekend min. in summer). D, MC, V. 14 rooms. Refrigerators, cable TV, pool.

**Laurel Hill Motel** (413-243-0813; 200 Laurel St., Box 285, Lee, MA 01238; on Rte. 20) Price: Moderate to Expensive. AE, D, DC, MC, V. 23 units, 2 efficiencies. Pool, view.

**Monument Mountain Motel** (413-528-3272; 249 Stockbridge Rd., Gt. Barrington, MA 01230; Rte. 7, N. of town) Price: Moderate to Expensive. AE, D, DC, MC, V. Cable TV, heated pool, lit tennis courts, picnic tables, 20 acres bordering Housatonic River, flower gardens.

**Mountain View Motel** (413-528-0250; 304 State Rd., Gt. Barrington, MA 01230; Rte. 23E., E. of town) Price: Moderate to Expensive. AE, D, MC, V. 17 units. Cable TV; pets allowed; 1 mi. to Butternut.

**Pilgrim Inn** (413-243-1328; 165 Housatonic St., Lee, MA 01238; Rte. 20, E. of town) Price: Expensive. AE, D, DC, MC, V. 34 units. Cable TV, pool.

**Pleasant Valley Motel** (413-232-8511; Rte. 102, W. Stockbridge, MA 01266; sandwiched between Exit 1, Mass Pike &

Rte. 102) Price: Inexpensive to Expensive. AE, D, MC, V. Handicap access. Cable TV, pool. Continental breakfast included on summer weekends.

**Sunset Motel** (413-243-0302; 150 Housatonic St., Rte. 20, Lee, MA 01238) Price: Inexpensive to Expensive. AE, CB, D, DC, MC, V. 22 units with AC, cable TV, pool. Convenient to MassPike Exit 2.

**Super 8 Motel** (413-243-0143; 170 Housatonic St., Lee, MA 01238; Rte. 20, just off MassPike) Price: Inexpensive to Moderate. AE, D, DC, MC, V. Handicap access. 49 rooms, including nonsmoking. Free coffee and paper. Cable TV.

### Central County

**Berkshire Inn** (413-443-3000; 150 W. Housatonic St., Pittsfield, MA 01201; Rte. 20, W. of town) Price: Moderate to Expensive. AE, MC, V. 38 units, 9 with refrigerators; cable TV, AC. Pool. Continental breakfast.

**Colonial Motor Lodge** (413-442-2633; Housatonic St., Pittsfield, MA 01201; Rte. 20 , W. of town) Price: Inexpensive to Moderate. AE, D, MC, V. 24 units. Cable TV, AC, phones.

**Comfort Inn** (413-443-4714; 1055 South St., Pittsfield, MA 01201; on Rte. 7/20) Price: Moderate to Very Expensive. AE, D, DC, MC, V. 58 units. Cable TV, AC, exercise room; discount pass to Berkshire West. Pool. Deluxe continental breakfast.

**Days Inn of Lenox** (413-637-3560; 194 Pittsfield Rd., Lenox 01240) Price: Inexpensive to Expensive. Breakfast included. AE, D, DC, MC, V. 52 units.

**Econo Lodge** (413-637-4244; 130 Pittsfield Rd., Lenox 01240) Price: Expensive. Breakfast included. AE, D, DC, MC, V. 120 units.

**Heart of the Berkshires Motel** (413-443-1255; 970 W. Housatonic St., Pittsfield, MA 01201; Rte. 20, W. of town) Price: Inexpensive to Moderate. AE, MC, V. 17 units. Cable TV, AC.

**Howard Johnson Motel** (413-442-4000, 800-446-4656; 462 Pittsfield Rd., Lenox, MA 01240; Rte. 7/20, N. of town) Price: Moderate to Very Expensive. AE, D, MC, V. 44 units, some with Jacuzzis. Cable TV, AC. Pool.

**Lampost Motel** (413-443-2979; Box 335, Lanesborough, MA 01237; Rte. 7, N. of Pittsfield) Price: Inexpensive to Moderate. AE, D, MC, V. 10 units, all with efficiency kitchens. Cable TV. Pool available.

**Lanesborough Mountain Motel** (413-442-6717; Rte. 7, Box 335, Lanesborough, MA 01237) Price: Inexpensive to Moderate (special midweek rates). AE, D, MC, V. 10 rooms.

**Lenox Inn** (413-499-0324; Rte. 7/20, Box 713, Lenox, MA 01240; N. of town) Price: Moderate to Expensive. AE, D, MC, V. 17 units. Cable TV, AC. Pool.

**Mayflower Motor Inn** (413-443-4468; 474 Pittsfield–Lenox Rd., P.O. Box 116, Lenox, MA 01240; Rte. 7/20, N. of town) Price: Inexpensive to Expensive. AE, D, MC, V. 20 rooms. Cable TV. Pool, views.

**Mt. View Motel** (413-442-1009; 499 S. Main St., Lanesborough, MA 01237) Price: Moderate to Expensive. AE, D, MC, V. 13 rooms in motel; 3 efficiency cottages available year-round. Cable TV.

**Pittsfield Travelodge** (413-443-5661, 800-578-7878; 16 Cheshire Rd., Pittsfield, MA 01201; jct. of Rtes. 8 and 9) Price: Inexpensive to Expensive. AE, D, DC, MC, V. Handicap access. 47 units. Cable TV.

**Quality Inn** (413-637-4244; 130 Pittsfield Rd., Rte. 7, Lenox, MA 01240) Price: Inexpensive to Very Expensive. AE, D, DC, JCB, MC, V. 120 rooms. Cable TV, AC, refrigerators, in-room coffee. Outdoor pool and tennis courts. Continental breakfast included. Cocktail lounge, banquet facilities.

**Ramada Inn & Suites** (413-442-8714; 1350 W. Housatonic St., Pittsfield, MA 01201; Rte. 20, W. of town) Price: Moderate to Very Expensive. AE, D, DC, MC, V. 59 units; 10 two-bedroom suites, 9 executive suites.

**Shamrock Village Inn** (413-684-0860; 645 Main St., Dalton, MA 01226) Price: Moderate. AE, D, MC, V. 15 units. Cable TV, restaurant.

**Super Eight Motel** (413-637-3560, 800-800-8000; 194 Pittsfield Rd., Lenox, MA 01240; Rte. 7 /20, N. of town) Price: Expensive. AE, D, DC, MC, V. 59 units. Cable TV. Pool.

**Wagon Wheel Motel** (413-445-4532; 484 Pittsfield Rd., P.O. Box 808, Lenox, MA 01240; Rte. 7 /20, 3 mi. N. of town) Price: Inexpensive to Expensive. AE, D, MC, V. 18 units, 2 Jacuzzi rooms. Cable TV, refrigerators in rooms.

**The Weathervane Motel** (413-443-3230; 475 S. Main St., Lanesborough, MA 01237; Rte. 7, S. of town) Price: Moderate. AE, CB, D, MC, V. 17 units.

**Yankee Inn** (413-499-3700, 800-835-2364; 461 Pittsfield Rd., Lenox, MA 01240; Rte. 7/20, near Pittsfield line) Price: Moderate to Very Expensive. AE, D, DC, MC, V. Handicap access. 106 units; 22 rooms with fireplaces; some rooms with Jacuzzis. Cable TV. Indoor pool; spa; manicured grounds. Three-night minimum in summer.

### NORTH COUNTY

**Berkshire Hills Motel** (413-458-3950; 1146 Cold Spring Rd., Williamstown, MA 01267; on Rte. 7/2, 2 mi. S. of town) Price: Moderate to Expensive. AE, D, MC, V. 21 rooms. King-sized beds available. Cable TV. No smoking. Heated pool, landscaped grounds. Cold breakfast buffet.

**Carriage House Motel** (413-458-5359; P.O. Box 925, Lanesborough, MA 01237; on Rte. 7) Price: Inexpensive. AE, CB, D, DC, MC, V. Partial handicap access. 14 units. Pool.

**Chimney Mirror Motel** (413-458-5202; 295 Main St., Williamstown, MA 01267; Rte. 2, E. of town) Price: Moderate. AE, MC, V. 18 units. Cable TV. Continental breakfast included on summer weekends.

**Cozy Corner Motel** (413-458-8006; 784 Sand Springs Rd., Williamstown, MA 01267; at Rte. 7, N. of town center) Price: Moderate. AE, D, MC, V. 12 units across from convenience store at gateway to Vermont.

**Econo Lodge Springs Motor Inn** (413-458-5945; Rte. 7, New Ashford, MA 01237) Price: Moderate to Expensive. AE, D, DC, MC, V. 40 motel rooms; 2 small chalets with fireplaces. Cable TV, in-room coffee. Pool, tennis court.

**Four Acres Motel** (413-458-8158; 213 Main St., Williamstown, MA 01267; Rte. 2) Price: Moderate to Expensive. AE, D, DC, MC, V. Handicap access. 31 units. Cable TV. Garden area with pool. Continental breakfast.

**Green Valley Motel** (413-458-3864; 1214 Simonds Rd., Williamstown, MA 01267; Rte. 7N) Price: Moderate. AE, MC, V. 18 units. Cable TV. Pool. Continental breakfast.

**Jericho Valley Inn** (413-458-9511, 800-537-4246; 2541 Hancock Rd., Williamstown, MA 01267; Rte. 43) Price: Moderate. AE, MC, V. 25 units; suites, cottages available. Satellite TV. Heated pool. 350 mountain acres with spectacular views, fireplace lounge. Pets allowed in cottages.

**Maple Terrace Motel** (413-458-9677; www.mapleterracehotel; 555 Main St., Williamstown, MA 01267; Rte. 2, 0.5 mi. from Williams College) Price: Moderate. AE, D, DC, MC, V. 17 units, 2 efficiencies. Cable TV, VCR in all rooms. Heated pool; mountain views.

**New Ashford Motor Inn** (413-458-8041; 259 Rte. 7, New Ashford, MA 01237; 1 mi. N. of Brodie Mtn.) Price: Inexpensive to Moderate. AE, D, MC, V. 16 units, Direct TV, air-conditioning, telephones.

**Northside Motel** (413-458-8107; 45 N. St., Rte. 7, Williamstown, MA 01267; N. of Williams Inn) Price: Inexpensive. AE, D, MC, V. Handicap access. 32 units. Cable TV; pool. Coffee shop for breakfast.

**Villager Motel** (413-458-4046; 953 Simonds Rd., Williamstown, MA 01267; Rte. 7, N. of town) Price: Inexpensive. AE, MC, V. 13 rooms. Cable TV, AC. Expanded continental breakfast.

**Wigwam & Western Summit Cottages** (413-663-3205; 2850 Mohawk Trail, P.O. Box 7, N. Adams, MA 01247; Rte. 2, E and above town) Price: Inexpensive to Moderate. AE, D, MC, V. Five cottages. TV. Porch with fantastic view of Mount Greylock. Gift shop. Open late May–mid-Oct.

**The Willows Motel** (413-458-5768; 480 Main St., Williamstown, MA 01267; Rte. 2, E. of town) Price: Inexpensive to Moderate. AE, MC, V. 17 rooms. Cable TV. Heated pool.

*One of the newer additions to Railroad St. in Great Barrington, Pearl's has one of the best views of the street.*
Judith Monachina

# 4

# Dining

## *Pleasing the Palate*

**Some of the county's** showiest restaurants are found in the "cottages" of the Gilded Age: at Orleton, now called the Gateways, and at Blantyre and Wheatleigh. Yet a great table is set as well in more humble Berkshire settings, such as pre-Revolutionary farmhouses, old mills, and inns.

The fare is no longer just American, with a dash of the continental, but has become abundant in many other cuisines, including Japanese, Chinese, Indian, Swiss, Vietnamese, even Finnish.

The number of restaurants in the county is vast: more than 225—nearly 40 in Great Barrington alone!—and they keep popping up. To cover all of them would require a book twice this size. Diners should be guided by what we suggest but follow their own hunches, as well. (We would be pleased to hear of discoveries for a future edition.) We have grouped the best of the breakfast/lunch eateries in a section of their own (pages 115–117). There are dozens of specialty food suppliers, too, engaging alternatives to supermarkets.

We have concentrated on those establishments that we've found most interesting and most successful. A dining experience has many dimensions. The food, of course, is primary, but we have also based our judgments on factors such as the range of the menu, the décor and ambiance of the restaurant, the quality of service, and value for price. We tend to be skeptical of chains. We also note that a restaurant participates in the Berkshire Grown Restaurant Certification Program, which restaurateurs are invited to join if they "pledge to buy and utilize locally grown food and food products to the extent that they are able, thus supporting local farmers and food producers who preserve and sustain the beauty and the bounty of the Berkshire region." Patrons who dine at Berkshire Grown restaurants enjoy their fine meals knowing that they are supporting the local agricultural way of life. Berkshire Grown also hosts a wonderful opportunity to sample local produce as skillfully prepared by local chefs at the Beautiful Bountiful Berkshires tasting in the early autumn.

Restaurants are organized first by section of the county, then alphabetically by town, then by name. Food purveyors are grouped alphabetically by type, then by name of establishment. Every entry appears in the general index, too. While the information is as up-to-date as we can make it, it is still wise to call ahead.

We designate each restaurant with a price code, signifying the approximate cost of a meal, including appetizer, entrée, and dessert, but *not* cocktails, wine, tax, or tip. Restaurants with a prix-fixe menu are noted accordingly.

For further gustatory experiences, sample "A Taste of the Berkshires" or "Taste of Williamstown" or any of several other town-sponsored annual extravaganzas that celebrate the bounty of our region.

**Dining Price Codes**

| | |
|---|---|
| Inexpensive | Up to $15 |
| Expensive | $30 to $50 |
| Moderate | $15 to $30 |
| Very Expensive | $50 or more |

**Credit Cards**

AE — American Express
CB — Carte Blanche
D — Discover

**Meals:**

B — Breakfast
L — Lunch
SB — Sunday brunch
D — Dinner

## RESTAURANTS IN SOUTH COUNTY

EGREMONT / NORTH EGREMONT

### ELM COURT INN

413-528-0325.
www.elmcourtinn.com.
227 Rte. 71, N. Egremont, MA 01252.
Closed: Mon. and Tues. in winter; Mon., July–Aug.
Price: Expensive.
Cuisine: Continental.
Serving: D.
Credit Cards: AE, MC, V.
Reservations: Recommended.
Special Features: Fireplaces.

Elm Court's hosts Glee Bieri and her chef husband, Urs Bieri—a former executive chef at the United Nations—maintain the Swiss tradition in Berkshire County. The staff in the dining room is knowledgeable and friendly. Our servers knew the ingredients and tastes of the dishes, and could recommend with aplomb. With a fire crackling on a cool evening, the comfort level is high and relaxing.

The wine list includes a good variety and the concise menu is filled with choices hard to make. We remember an Asian duck salad that was rich with delicious slivers of well-prepared duck in a brown sauce. The flavorful escargot compelled us to mop up the butter sauce with chunks of rustic bread. The crisp baby-spinach salad was large enough to share. The veal Suisse comes in a generous portion with wild mushrooms. The flame-seared tuna, although rich and meaty as a beefsteak, came in rare, tender slices, beautifully served. Family-style side dishes of buttery brussels sprouts and sweet baby carrots were hearty and crisp. Roesti potatoes, a specialty of the house, accompanied our entrées.

Our just desserts? Apple tart and pecan Kahlúa pie, a perfect ending to an excellent meal.

SOUTH EGREMONT

### THE EGREMONT INN

413-528-2111.
www.egremontinn.com.
10 Old Sheffield Rd., S. Egremont, MA 01252.
Off Rte. 23 in center of village.
Closed: Mon. and Tues.
Price: Moderate to Expensive.
Cuisine: American and Continental.
Serving: D.
Credit Cards: AE, MC, V.
Special Features: Fireplaces; live entertainment Thurs. and Sat.

Proprietors Steve and Karen Waller have created a charming dining experience at their inn. One or the other greets all visitors, welcoming them to what is indeed the Wallers' home.

The appetizers are generous and tasty. The salad is wonderfully textured with many flavors and ingredients. The sauce on the side of the crabcakes is worth repeated visits. The steak was tender and the salmon luxurious.

Steve asked us if we wanted to see the short or the long wine list. The complete one runs perhaps 50 pages, with wines from all over the world. *Wine Spectator* has cited the Egremont Inn for its cellar. Desserts are rich and fabulous. We had a chocolate mousse that defied description. Specialties include Berkshire products and excellent coffee.

## JOHN ANDREW'S

413-528-3469.
www.jarestaurant.com.
Rte. 23, S. Egremont, MA 01252.
2.5 mi. W. of village.
Closed: Wed.
Price: Moderate to Expensive.
Cuisine: American.
Serving: D.
Credit Cards: MC, V.
Reservations: Recommended (necessary in summer).
Special Features: Glassed-in back porch, fireplace, outdoor deck and terrace in-season; member, Berkshire Grown.

John Andrew's Restaurant continues to stand in the first rank of restaurants in the Berkshires and is certainly one of the best bargains in that category. The subtly decorated dining rooms are perfectly in tune with the excellent, understated New American cuisine. Service is attentive, professional, and discreet. The delicious breads are fresh baked on premises. The grilled, roasted, and braised entrées emphasize marvelous natural flavors, enhanced with perfectly executed vegetable accompaniments. The wine list has been chosen with sufficient care and taste to bring John Andrew's a *Wine Spectator* magazine Award of Excellence.

Proprietors Susan and Danny Smith are true professionals and excellent hosts. Susan creates an enviable combination of efficiency and serenity in the dining rooms, while Danny is the hands-on executive chef.

## OLD MILL

413-528-1421.
Rte. 23, S. Egremont, MA 01252.
Center of village.
Closed: Mon. in winter.
Price: Moderate to Expensive.
Cuisine: American and Continental.
Serving: D.
Credit Cards: AE, DC, MC, V.
Reservations: For parties of five or more.
Special Features: Private dining room; fireplace; member, Berkshire Grown.

An understated interior of warm, glowing antique walls and floors gives this renovated 1797 gristmill a particularly welcoming air. The colonial atmosphere creates the feeling of stepping back in time. Owner Terry Moore has presided here for over a quarter century, making the Old Mill if not actually colonial, certainly a venerable institution among Berkshire restaurants. It is also an enduring favorite among residents and second-home owners who wouldn't think of stopping anywhere else on Friday night after escaping New York. The unobtrusive, pleasant, timely service contributes greatly to the soothing atmosphere.

The regular menu is an eclectic blend of generally Continental offerings, always supplemented with several specials of the day, both appetizers and entrées, conveniently described in a supplemental note rather than recited by the waitperson. Maine crabcakes and the house-cured gravlax are delicious regular appetizers. Grilled fish, chops and steaks, pan-seared calf's liver, several vegetarian dishes, and other offerings provide a fine range of entrées. The wine list is extensive, mostly French, American, and Italian, with offerings from $18 to $75. Desserts tend toward the rich and sinful—for example, Grand Marnier chocolate mousse in a chocolate cake crust. Delicious! Always welcoming, reliable but not predictable, the Old Mill continues to reward its loyal following and new arrivals, too.

GREAT BARRINGTON

### AEGEAN BREEZE

413-528-4001.
327 Stockbridge Rd., Gt. Barrington, MA 01230.
Price: Moderate to Expensive.
Cuisine: Greek.
Serving: L, D.
Credit Cards: All major.
Handicap Access: Yes.
Reservations: Recommended.

A recent entrant to the burgeoning Great Barrington restaurant scene, proprietor George Camie and manager Jennifer Dousmanis offer a light and pleasant atmosphere as evocative of Greek-island dining as one can imagine on Route 7. The staff is young, well trained, quietly attentive, and good. The kitchen produces classic Greek specialties from *mezes*—"more than just appetizers"—to dessert. An assortment of the generously proportioned hot and cold *mezedes* can be combined into a delicious tasting meal if desired. But the crowning glory of the cuisine is the *thalasina* (from the sea) offerings, four marvelous grilled or broiled whole-fish entrées and a dozen other fish and shellfish specialties. Grilled lamb shish kebab and moussaka, too, of course, plus excellent steaks and chops. Aegean Breeze has deservedly become very popular, so potential diners should be sure to call ahead and plan to enjoy a great meal.

### BARRINGTON BREWERY & RESTAURANT

413-528-8282.
www.barringtonbrewery.com.
420 Stockbridge Rd., Gt. Barrington, MA 01230.
At Jenifer House Commons.
Price: Inexpensive to Moderate.
Cuisine: American.
Serving: L, D.
Credit Cards: AE, D, MC, V.
Special Features: Outdoor patio in summer; pool tables and dartboard; member, Berkshire Grown.

Sizzling streaks and burgers, sandwiches, and salads may seem like the backbone of the extensive Barrington Brewery & Restaurant menu, but a closer look reveals the real star: That's right, beer. Barrington brews its own on the premises, including a very good Black Bear Stout and Barrington Brown Ale. But beer isn't found only in pint-sized glasses here: beer-battered fries, onion rings, and mozzarella sticks; a cheddar ale soup; even a steak and stout—sliced sirloin marinated in stout, open faced on garlic bread. Vegetarians don't fare badly here, either: vegetarian burgers, nachos, salads, and soups, of course, but also veggie pockets, tortellini salad, and more.

The atmosphere is cozy and lively, with some large tables that always seem filled with groups and families. Small tables and tucked-away booths are also available.

A special kids' menu includes the standards: PB&J, pizza, grilled cheese, burgers, and spaghetti (with butter or red sauce). This is a real kid-friendly place: The back page of the menu is games and crossword puzzles.

### BIZEN

413-528-4343.
17 Railroad St., Gt. Barrington, MA 01230.
Price: Moderate to Expensive.
Cuisine: Japanese.
Serving: L, D.
Credit Cards: AE, D, MC, V.
Handicap Access: Yes.
Reservations: Encouraged.
Special Features: Sushi bar; Japanese grill; private room available; tatami booth; full bar.

*Japanese greeting in the entryway at Bizen on Railroad St. in Gt. Barrington.* Judith Monachina

Bizen was the first of the fine sushi bars that Great Barrington now enjoys. New York City–based second-home owners and numerous sophisticated locals keep them all deservedly busy, but Bizen still stands first. Proprietor Michael Marcus learned the classic Japanese arts of both sushi making and fine pottery (*bizen*) in Japan. He brings intensity, creativity, and high standards to both. Bizen is furnished with ceramic tableware all from Michael's own Joyous Spring Pottery. It complements the authentic-seeming décor, which especially features a traditional tatami booth for the cross-legged set. The tables are close together and the ambiance somewhat bustling. Michael has recently opened a *kaiseki* room, with a tea ceremony from Kyoto. There is a full bar and a Japanese grill. The menu covers the full array of traditional Japanese cuisine, from sushi and sashimi by the piece, to varied and delicious hand rolls, excellent cooked and grilled dishes, soups, and salads.

### CASTLE STREET CAFÉ

413-528-5244; fax 413-528-8863.
www.castlestreetcafe.
10 Castle St., Gt. Barrington, MA 01230.
Closed: Tues.
Price: Moderate to Expensive.
Cuisine: Continental–Contemporary American
Serving: D.
Credit Cards: All major.
Special Features: Wine by the glass; live jazz; member, Berkshire Grown.

Michael Ballon's Castle Street Café continues to charm, fully deserving its legion of loyal followers as well as its new devotees. Michael whets our appetites by offering some of his recipes on WAMC's Round Table. The bistro atmosphere of exposed brick walls, frequently changing hangings of contemporary paintings, white-linen tablecloths, and fresh flowers never fails to please the eye. The eclectic menu is always a mixture of classic favorites such as steak au poivre made from New England Heritage Breed beef, grilled cornish game hen, and ever-changing new dishes. Michael proudly features—and prepares himself—locally grown and produced foods, from goat cheese to french bread to fresh produce. The *Wine Spectator* award-winning wine list features many moderately priced French and American wines that complement the fine food without breaking the bank. The veteran and accomplished waitstaff know their business and do it to perfection. One always feels welcome—well attended to but perfectly undisturbed.

The adjoining Celestial Bar and Jazz Club does not obtrude on the dining-only crowd. Offering jazz (soloists weeknights, combos on weekends) and a lighter menu 6 nights a week, it provides a welcome atmosphere for both the pure jazz aficionado and the more casual diner.

### THE EAST

413-528-8850.
305 Stockbridge Rd., Gt. Barrington, MA 01230.
Open: Daily.

Price: Moderate
Cuisine: Chinese and Japanese.
Serving: L, D.
Credit Cards: AE, MC, V.
Reservations: Recommended for weekend dinners.

The East serves Chinese food from Hunan, Szechwan, and Canton, and makes fresh sushi, sashimi, and other Japanese dishes. The tuna maki is fresh and tasty—we watched the chef roll the maki, standing before his work area to see how efficiently he moved—with a varied texture of fish and rice. Other specialty fillings are cucumber, salmon, octopus, eel, and avocet; not to mention the sweetened squash maki and sea urchin sushi. The crispy tofu, under the vegetarian menu, is quite good.

Although Chinese selections can be pedestrian, here they are served with generosity and attention. Substitutions are cheerfully made, such as tofu for chicken and bok choy for broccoli. The long list of chef's specialties should keep diners happy for years.

Luncheon specialties, served from 11 to 3, are in large portions but smaller than the dinner servings. We recommend the roast pork with Chinese vegetables. The vegetables are crisp, the pork not too salty.

### HELSINKI TEA ROOM

(See under "Nightlife" in chapter 5)

### KOI

413-528-5678.
302 State Rd., Gt. Barrington, MA 01230.
Rte. 23 east toward Butternut Basin.
Price: Moderate.
Cuisine: Chinese.
Serving: L, D.
Credit Cards: AE, MC, V.

For those wondering about the name, paintings of the overblown goldfish grace the entryway. Fancy, red leatherette seating to the left; simpler décor to the right, in the room also available for banquets, in what was formerly a Panda. This recent addition to the Barrington scene must vie for its share of the market with The East, above. Both offer similar items, although Koi seems willing to make a broader appeal to Westerners with such entrées as rib-eye steak, basil delight, portobello mushrooms, and salmon filet. Still, the word is out and people are finding their way along State Route 23 to it.

### PEARL'S

413-528-7767.
www.pearlsrestaurant.com.
47 Railroad St., Gt. Barrington, MA 01230.
Price: Expensive.
Cuisine: Continental.
Serving: L (Fri. & Sat.), D, SB.
Credit Cards: AE, MC, V.
Handicap Access: Yes.
Reservations: Recommended (no reservations in bar).
Special Features: Handsome dine-in bar; member, Berkshire Grown.

Another bit of New York City sophistication come to the Berkshires, Pearl's is handsome in a contemporary vein, elegant without demanding formal wear of its patrons, and a significant addition to the upscale end of the local dining scene. Having begun with a special tilt toward steaks and chops, Pearl's now also features game dishes in a generally Continental cuisine. Its few critics assert that the décor is a bit superior to the food, and some remark on the New York City air of the prices, but it is a success and a well-deserved one. *Wine Spectator* has blessed its wine list. The handsome bar—its glass wall making it seemingly open to a lively vista down Railroad Street—offers excellent (and reasonably priced) drinks and a more casual setting to enjoy a light repast or full dinner—without a reservation.

### SHIRO RESTAURANT

413-528-1898.
105 Stockbridge Rd., Gt. Barrington, MA 01230.
Open 7 days.
Price: Moderate.
Cuisine: Japanese.
Serving: L (except Sun.), D.
Credit Cards: AE, MC, V.

Shiro is a Japanese culinary experience and eating there avoids the frustration of trying to park in downtown Great Barrington. Shiro, north of the intersection of Routes 7 and 23, is a compact haven of muted greens and tans in a space emanating tempting aromas that lure us in as soon as we open the stocky wooden doors. From the inside, it is hard to believe that this used to house Burger King!

The simple, immaculate wooden tables each nestle against a wall, affording a sense of privacy. An efficient waitperson seats us and shortly thereafter greets us with a plush, hot towel—a soothing courtesy. Our questions are patiently and thoroughly answered, and we are encouraged to try something unusual, rather than the more standard (but delicious!) tempura and teriyaki dishes. The wine list includes an excellent array of sake, of course, and a mix of domestic and imported wines (carefully selected to complement the menu).

Shiro offers all the usual types of sushi, but we opted to try the special crispy, spicy, whitefish roll: Large, with delicate cooked whitefish wrapped with rice and seaweed and topped with a spicy, caviar-filled mayonnaise (we could have done with less of the topping, but it was an interesting balance of cool and spicy). We tried the seafood kushiyaki combo: grilled shrimp, scallop, salmon, and vegetables on skewers. It was perfect. This dish is served on a bed of braised onions in a tantalizing sauce, with mung bean sprouts, broccoli, and green peppers. Shiro also has a hibachi area where the whole family will enjoy watching the chef exhibit his flair for chopping and flipping the food atop tiny bursts of fire.

### SPENCER'S RESTAURANT AT THE THORNEWOOD INN

413-528-3828, 800-854-1008.
www.thornewood.com.
453 Stockbridge Rd., Gt. Barrington, MA 01230.
Jct. Rtes. 7 and 183.
Open: Thurs.–Sun. (summer); weekends (winter).
Price: Moderate to Expensive.
Cuisine: Country Continental.
Serving: D, SB (seasonal).
Credit Cards: AE, D, MC, V.
Reservations: Preferred.
Special Features: View from terrace.

Spencer's Restaurant in the Dutch Colonial Thornewood Inn currently welcomes diners in the formal, candlelit room with dance floor, and in the pub-like atmosphere of the library, as well as the newly opened porch dining area. On Saturday evenings and during summer's Sunday brunch, innkeeper David Thorne leads his trio in mellow jazz and blues selections.

Dinner is gracefully placed on crisp white table linens. Chef Terry Thorne presents a brief, creative menu, with much thought given to how subtle flavors relate. Although three salads were offered, we began with cheddar, bacon, and chive tomato soup and bruschetta with brie over a beefsteak tomato. A rack of lamb served with rosemary, garlic, and walnuts was delicious both inside and out. The duck was tasty in a sauce of plum and molasses. Both were accompanied by mashed potatoes, green beans, and baby carrots, artfully arranged. An Australian white wine and an Australian red brought out the flavor of the food and the thoughts of the diners. The smooth lemon tart, contrasting sweet and sour, had a delightful crumb shell.

Dreams of the evening, overlooking Taft Farm, included sampling other delightful offerings such as the fish of the day or vegetable pie with a french-bread crust or salmon stuffed with scallop mousse. And, of course, others of those fresh homemade desserts prepared on the premises.

### 20 RAILROAD STREET

413-528-9345.
20 Railroad St., Gt. Barrington, MA 01230.
Price: Inexpensive.
Cuisine: American.
Serving: L, D, SB.
Credit Cards: MC, V.
Handicap Access: Yes.
Special Features: Open late.

20 Railroad Street is the restaurant granddaddy of the Railroad Street revival. In the warm high-ceilinged brick dining room, always convivial, we shared dining space with jovial families, couples young and old, as well as softball teams and ski patrol squadrons. We heard about divorces and deals, patients and quarterbacks. In story or in person, most of southern Berkshire has been in 20 Railroad. The 28-foot-long mahogany bar and back bar, built in New York City in 1883, arrived in Great Barrington in 1919. It served as one of the area's speakeasies during Prohibition, referred to as "Mahogany Ridge" by those who explained to their spouses just where they were hunting.

But good food is what makes 20 Railroad chug along. For lunch, dinner, or whenever, 20 Railroad's starters, salads, sandwiches, and burgers are legendary. Unusual starters include the Plowman's Snack, a combination of brie, *soprassata* sausage, and french bread. Pocket sandwiches are outstanding, with the vegetarian side pocket being among our favorites. The restaurant also nurtures a whole Rueben family (available in halves), with ham (Mama Rueben), turkey (Rebecca Rueben), and roast beef (Rolland Rueben). More than a dozen different burgers and an equal number of sandwiches fill out Railroad Street's printed menu.

### UNION BAR AND GRILL

413-528-6228.
293 Main St., Gt. Barrington, MA 01230.
Open: Daily.
Price: Moderate to Expensive
Cuisine: New American.
Serving: L Sat.; SB; D daily.
Credit Cards: MC, V.
Handicap Access: Yes.
Reservations: Only for parties of 10 or more.
Special Features: 40-foot bar; kids' menu; food served to 11 PM winter, 12 PM summer.

Gianfranco Sorrentino has kept up the high standards that Union began with. Lunch is served on Saturday, brunch on Sunday, and dinner 7 nights of the week year-round in the new industrial-chic setting. A good kids' menu for the early set and a lively bar scene and dining until midnight combine to make the Union one of the most popular bistros in all of Berkshire County.

The menu changes often, keeping a few regulars like the grilled flank steak sandwich with grilled red onion, smoked gouda, and an Asian barbecue sauce on flatbread. Steaks and hamburgers served with excellent fries satisfy the meat-and-potatoes crowd, while a variety of seafood appetizers and entrées appeal to subtler tastes. Desserts are delicious, and they all cost $7. The apple tart specialty is made from a homemade flaky, crisp, buttery, golden puff pastry round topped with micro-thin sliced apples and a dollop of homemade vanilla-y! ice cream.

The Union is a great place for a leisurely weekend lunch, a sophisticated dinner, or a late-night supper or bite. The food is consistently good and innovative.

### VERDURA CUCINA RUSTICA

413-528-8969.
44 Railroad St., Gt. Barrington, MA 01230.
Closed: Wed.
Price: Expensive.
Cuisine: Italian.
Serving: D.
Credit Cards: MC, V.
Reservations: Recommended.
Special Features: Member, Berkshire Grown.

*Creative* is the key word for Verdura's operation. The atmosphere is self-consciously sophisticated; with low lighting, comfortable tables, and a large tree growing out of the corner of the bar, it strives for the feeling of an upscale city restaurant. Food is intended to excite the palate; no substitutions is the policy—allowing the chef to put together his combinations of flavors. Verdura makes extensive use of local products.

The menu, although brief, is varied, with good choices for vegetarians. Desserts are creative as well.

Verdura has added the slightly less formal, adjacent, **Dué Enoteca** (413-664-9166; 42 Railroad St., Gt. Barrington, MA 01230), where *primi, secondi,* and *contorni* may be had for about $35.

### VIVIANI'S

413-528-3843.
177 Main St., Gt. Barrington, MA 01230.
N. end of Main.
Open: Wed.–Sun.
Price: Moderate.
Cuisine: Italian.
Serving: D daily, L Sat. and Sun.
Credit Cards: MC, V.
Reservations: Recommended.

Italian dining in Gt. Barrington? Not really—until now. Owner-chef Nancy Pecorelli has established it with Viviani's, a small and bustling trattoria in a very modest storefront setting. At the "wrong" end of Main Street, it is the real thing, worth the few blocks' trip. Parking is a breeze compared to Railroad Street. The décor is simple and attractive, featuring a wall full of fascinating period family pictures that seem familiar even if not sprigs of one's own family tree. While there are only about a dozen tables in the main-floor dining room, Viviani's offers full bar service: An all-Italian wine list with about 18 well-chosen and well-described offerings, many available by the glass. Complimentary special appetizers are offered with pre-dinner drinks. The menu has a full range of regular plus daily special antipasti, pastas, *primi e secondi* entrées and desserts, all prepared to order by Nancy herself and served by a small but attentive and well-trained staff.

## HOUSATONIC

### JACKS GRILL

413-274-1000.
www.jacksgrill.com.
1063 Main St., Housatonic, MA 01236.
Closed: Halloween to Mother's Day.
Price: Moderate.
Cuisine: American.
Credit Cards: AE, MC, V.
Reservations: Suggested.
Special Features: Kids' menu; electric train overhead; member, Berkshire Grown

Jacks Grill. No apostrophe, no *e*. "Honest Food; Satisfaction Guaranteed," is Jacks' motto. And Jacks delivers. With well-made drinks, user-friendly wines, and Jacks' regular daily specials—from corned beef and cabbage (Tuesday) to roast pork, corn bread, and applesauce (Sunday)—satisfaction is the theme, and it is pervasive. The menu selections, the setting in a former hardware store in an old mill town, and the décor (the original store shelves are full of endlessly varied collections of stuff, and an operating electric train hangs from the ceiling) all say "comfort," loud and clear. Families are welcome, of course. There is a nice selection of kids' choices on the menu to satisfy the younger set while parents enjoy more adult fare; however, some adults may prefer to avoid kids' night.

The Fitzpatrick family knows hospitality. The food is seriously well prepared. Guinness and Harp are on tap. Every wine on the very serviceable wine list is available by the glass or the bottle. The waitstaffers are eager and attentive. It's a great, simple evening out—and at a painless price, as well.

LEE

### BOMBAY BAR & GRILL

413-243-6731.
435 Laurel St., Lee, MA 01238.
At the Black Swan Inn.
Closed: Mon.
Price: Moderate.
Cuisine: Indian
Serving: L, D, SB.
Credit Cards: All major.
Special Feature: Pool and lakeside.

One of five restaurants in a northeast chain, Bombay Bar & Grill pays little attention to décor. Why bother, when the focus is on the adjacent swimming pool and lovely Laurel Lake beyond? The bar looks serious, however, and the food is a geographical as well as culinary tour of the subcontinent. A clay oven produces the tandoori entrées, including chicken kebab and fish tikka. The luncheon buffets and "Maharaja Sunday Brunches" sound like especially good deals.

### CORK N' HEARTH

413-243-0535.
635 Laurel St., Lee, MA 01238.
Rte. 20, on Laurel Lake N. of Lee.
Closed: Mon.
Price: Moderate.
Cuisine: New England contemporary.
Serving: D.
Credit Cards: AE, MC, V.
Special Features: Fireside ambiance; view of lake.

Owner-chef Christopher Ryan maintains the charm and warm hospitality of Cork N' Hearth, on the shores of lovely Laurel Lake. While the restaurant is not overflowing with ambiance, amenities include antique quilts on the walls, a profusion of flowers and plants, and attentive waitstaff.

The food is dependably good, from an extensive menu or prepared to order.

### CHEZ NOUS

413-243 6397.
150 Main St., Lee, MA 01238.
Closed: March.
Price: Expensive.
Serving: D Wed.–Sun.
Cuisine: French bistro.
Credit Cards: AE, MC, V.
Reservations: Required in summer, suggested other seasons.
Special Features: Catering; member, Berkshire Grown.

Frank Tessier, co-chef at Ketchup to Caviar, and his wife, Rachel Portnoy, who began the Cakewalk Bakery, have taken over and renamed the former establishment, changing its accent from American to French. Tiny lights lace together a twisted vine, while watercolor paintings adorn the walls. All in all it is less formal than K2C. Chez Nous is divided into three dining rooms, so the atmosphere is intimate throughout. Summer dining begins at 5 PM to accommodate the Tanglewood, Jacob's Pillow, and theater audiences.

Tessier, a Breton native, worked at Le Gavroche, a two-star Michelin restaurant in London. Varieties of french bread are featured. The wine list offers perhaps the best selection of moderately priced, well-described wines we've encountered anywhere. Wines from France, California, Chile, New Zealand, and South Africa, among others, are thoughtfully selected to complement every meal and taste. Not inexpensive, but excellent values throughout. Desserts are rich and succulent. Enjoy!

### JOE'S DINER

413-243-9756.
85 Center St., Lee, MA 01238.
Corner Center (Rte. 20) and Main sts.
Closed: Sun.
Price: Inexpensive.
Cuisine: American.
Serving: B, L, D.

Joe's: the little diner that time forgot but history honors, where things are just as they were. Still bustling with the vigor of the 1940s, Joe's stocks packets of Red Man Chewing Tobacco right next to buckets of lifetime-guarantee combs; artichokes are practically free, and a real New York egg cream runs only a few cents more. A politician wouldn't think of breezing through Berkshire without a photo op and a plate of meat loaf at Joe's.

But the secret of success is that Joe Sorrentino and his family serve good food. This ex-army cook will happily serve "breakfast at dinner or dinner at breakfast." Joe creates a special each day. "We'll go through a whole hip of beef every Monday, 120 pounds of corned beef every Thursday," says Joe. Those serious about taking in one of Joe's specials (like a roast beef dinner with vegetable, potato, and bread) had better arrive early. On corned beef night we recently and watched the last of the 120 pounds disappear quickly, leaving disappointed latecomers. Not for long. They soon wrapped their tongues around something even better that they just hadn't thought of.

### SALMON RUN FISH HOUSE

413-243-3900.
78 Main St., Lee, MA 01238.
Price: Inexpensive to Moderate.
Cuisine: Seafood.
Serving: L, D.
Credit Cards: D, MC, V.
Reservations: Recommended for four or more.
Special Features: Private dining room for up to 40; monthly seasonal specials; kids' menu.

Opened in 1999 by Dawn and Paul Face, Salmon Run has made itself a well-loved member of the Lee family in a short time. Occupying a storefront on Main Street, it may be short on elaborate décor but conveys both its nautical theme and a friendly air.

The menu offers a wide range of seafood and other (buffalo wings!) appetizers. Otherwise, except for a few token main-course offerings for meat eaters, Salmon Run is a fish house. The house specialty is (surprise!) salmon—offered six different ways—or the Salmon Sampler of three of the options. Other fish and shellfish offerings are available, singly or in numerous combinations. Overstuffed, mostly seafood, sandwiches are served all day. There is a full-service bar and a fairly brief beer and wine list.

For very good food, a welcoming atmosphere, and generous servings, Salmon Run is a great spot for a full meal on a moderate budget.

## SOUTH LEE

### THE SWEET BASIL GRILLE

413-243-1114.
1575 Pleasant St., S. Lee, 01260.
Rte. 102.
Closed: Mon. in winter.
Price: Moderate.
Cuisine: Italian.
Serving: L (summer), D year-round.
Credit Cards: AE, DC, MC, V.
Reservations: Recommended.
Owners Rick and Lynn Penna make certain that the service is friendly and

knowledgeable in spite of numerous trips up and down the stairs, the prices reasonable, and the food tasty. Sweet Basil, settled in a comfortable house in South Lee near the Stockbridge border, is dependable and occasionally outstanding.

The house wines—from a specific Italian community and available by the glass, half carafe, or carafe—are a pleasant accompaniment to an enjoyable evening.

New Marlborough

### THE HILLSIDE

413-528-3123.
Rte. 57, New Marlborough, MA 01230.
Closed: Mon. year-round; Mon. and Tues. in winter.
Price: Moderate.
Cuisine: Continental.
Credit Cards: AE, MC, V.
Serving: Sun. L 12–2; D.
Reservations: Recommended.
Special Features: Catering for parties up to 75 people.

The Hillside, 33 years of age, continues to excel in traditional Continental cuisine. No "nouvelle" dishes for owner-chef Giuseppe (Joe) Chighine. He knows how to cook classical dishes, and what a pleasure they are.

A modest but satisfactory wine list is available. Among the possible entrées, a marvelous french onion soup and an avocado stuffed with real crabmeat. A fresh green salad accompanied the entrées, with a choice of dressing: Roquefort (creamy and delicious), Russian, Italian, or French. When a fine chef offers five different veal dishes, they are a sure bet. Veal *piccatta*, anyone?

Crème caramel? Coconut cream pie? Good things come in Cs. Espresso, cappuccino, and a wide selection of international coffees are available. Well-prepared food, good service, and an attractive setting put the Hillside on our "to repeat" list.

### OLD INN ON THE GREEN

413-229-7924.
www.oldinn.com.
Mail: Star Route 70, New Marlborough, MA 01230.
Rte. 57, on the Green, 6 mi. E. of Rte. 23.
Closed: Mon.–Wed.; open 6 days in summer.
Price: Weekday: Moderate to Expensive; Saturdays: Very Expensive, prix fixe.
Cuisine: Innovative American.
Serving: D.
Credit Cards: AE, MC, V.
Reservations: Required.
Special Features: Intimate candlelit dining; outdoor patio dining in summer; member, Berkshire Grown.

We can almost hear the stagecoach coming as we sit in the candlelit dining room. It can't possibly be more romantic. Clippety-clop to a 240-year-old inn. Nothing outdated about the food, however.

Peter Platt, a Williams College graduate and formerly chef at Wheatleigh, came to the inn as chef. As of 2005, the inn having separated from Gedney Farm, he and Meredith Kennard, his wife, own the inn. Platt is one of Berkshire County's finest chefs. He describes his cuisine as "innovative American with French technique." We tend to agree with *Zagat 27*: Given the quality of the food, the atmosphere in the restaurant, and the garden terrace dining, the Old Inn on the Green is Berkshire's finest dining experience. *Food and Wine* magazine listed this inn as one of America's 50 best hotel restaurants. AAA gives it four diamonds. Its wine cellar has made the *Wine Spectator* list. Much of the food is grown locally, as Platt is on the board of Berkshire Grown.

Although Gedney Farm is now now separate, the Old Inn contains five guest rooms, while nearby Thayer House has six; prices in the very expensive range. Midweek, however, it is possible to enjoy 2 nights and a dinner at a bargain rate; à la carte dinners on Wednesday and Thursday evening also offer less expensive options.

SANDISFIELD

### NEW BOSTON INN

413-258-4477.
www.newbostoninn.com.
Rte. 57, Sandisfield, MA 01255.
At Rte. 8.
Price: Inexpensive to Moderate.
Cuisine: American.
Serving: L, D; SB June–Sept.
Credit Cards: AE, MC, V.

Reservations: Recommended for dinner.
Proudly situated at a crossroad somewhat removed, the New Boston Inn is cheerful, accommodating, and friendly. This 1737 landmark with seven rooms up steep stairs is the oldest continually operating inn in the county. The several dining rooms have been carefully restored, the walls still stenciled. Some of the original wide boards remain in the bar.

The staff is knowledgeable about the cuisine and the area, local people congregate, and the atmosphere is homey and familial. The food is comforting, not surprising: burgers, fries, Philly steak sandwiches, fresh fish dishes, and pasta are made to order. When asked about the potato salad, the server brought out a generous sample to try before deciding. It was delicious. We said yes. Desserts change with the season and the whims of the competent chef.

SHEFFIELD

### STAGECOACH TAVERN

413-229-8585.
854 S. Undermountain Rd., Sheffield, MA 01257.
Rte. 41, N. of Lakeville, CT.
Closed: Mon. and Tues.
Price: Moderate.
Cuisine: American.
Serving: D.
Credit Cards: MC, V.
Reservations: Recommended.
Special Features: Candlelit dining; catering for groups and wedding receptions; member, Berkshire Grown.

The owners of Race Brooks Lodge purchased the adjacent restaurant in 2002 and have recently imported the talent behind John Andrew's Restaurant in Egremont, Dan and Susan Smith, to manage it. *They* brought their pastry chef, Susan Gidden, to run the kitchen, serving simpler fare than at JA but nevertheless good quality. The picturesque building is redolent of serving food and spirits since 1829. Diners may eat at rustic tables in the bar or in the more formal dining room. Conditions can be a bit noisy. The menu is short but engaging; the food is good. Seafood abounds in appetizers and entrées. Duck, beef, and pasta make appearances. Given Gidden's background, it is no surprise that the desserts excel.

Among the varieties of wine, nearly a dozen are offered by the glass, a fine way of accommodating the abstemious—or those who wish to mix and match.

Don't be put off by the sign that recently still read "Stagecoach Hill Inn."

STOCKBRIDGE

### GLENDALE RIVER GRILLE

413-298-4711; fax 413-298-4711.
www.ggrille.com.
14 Glendale Rd., Glendale, MA 01229.
Rte. 183.
Serving: D daily except Wed.
Open: 5–9:30 weekdays, 5–11 weekends.
Price: Moderate to Expensive
Cuisine: Eclectic.
Credit Cards: AE, D, MC, V.
Reservations: Appreciated.
Special Features: Custom catering; "Tuesdays" tavern section.

Veteran Berkshire restaurateur Al Weinman presides over "the hottest (800 degrees) grill in Glendale," and produces from it excellent steaks, chops, fish, and fowl, all with their own delicious juices sealed in. On the banks of the Housatonic just down the road from the Norman Rockwell Museum, the Glendale River Grille is a fine example of the classic (and disappearing) country highway steak house. The grilled offerings are accompanied by choices of a dozen or so excellent sauces and condiments, all homemade and delicious. The balance of the menu offers Continental selections, including several hearty and tasty vegetarian entrées. The lamb specialties feature delicious local Berkshire lamb. The simple and moderately priced wine list is predominantly American and has a good selection of the increasingly appreciated wines of the eastern United States. Al has redesigned the tavern section as "Tuesdays" (a nod to the legendary Mundays that once occupied these premises) for those in search of well-made potables and lighter fare.

### MICHAEL'S RESTAURANT & PUB

413-298-3530.
5 Elm St., Stockbridge, MA 01262.
Price: Inexpensive to moderate.
Cuisine: American.
Open: Daily.
Serving: L, D.
Credit Cards: All major.

Michael's has a lively pub with karaoke every Friday night. The restaurant is separated from it, so that diners can find some peace and quite. Not too much, though, because Michael's is a happening place. Lunch is served from 11:30; dinner from 4:30 or 5, depending on what you read. There is also a late-night menu and a pub menu. The lunches feature sandwiches, wraps, and burgers. The dinners are somewhat more adventuresome and international. Décor is no nonsense: this is a busy place.

### ONCE UPON A TABLE

413-298-3870.
36 Main St., P.O. Box 1428, Stockbridge, MA 01262.
The Mews.
Price: Moderate to Expensive.
Cuisine: American.
Serving: L daily, D Wed.–Mon.
Credit Cards: AE, MC, V.
Reservations: Recommended.

Once Upon a Table fits nicely—and literally—between the Red Lion Inn and the Stockbridge General Store or the Elm Street Market in the Stockbridge dining scene. Small, secluded in the Mews, informal and attractive, it offers tasty full lunches and dinners, well served in a pleasant setting. Neither as formal as the Red Lion nor as casual as the above-mentioned diners, it fills its niche very well, as attested by its frequently full tables and very good reputation. Mussels in white wine broth are a tasty specialty appetizer, which can do as a lighter main course, as well. Another five or six appetizers, three salad options, and a half-dozen entrées—somewhat lighter at lunch, more substantial at dinner—provide choices for all. Moderately priced wines by the glass or bottle further enhance a pleasant, low-key dining experience.

### THE RED LION INN

413-298-5545.
www.redlioninn.com.
30 Main St., Stockbridge, MA 01262.
Rte. 7.
Price: Expensive.
Cuisine: Traditional American.
Serving: B, L, D.
Credit Cards: AE, DC, MC, V.
Reservations: Recommended.
Handicap Access: Yes.
Special Features: Member, Berkshire Grown.

The Red Lion Inn is almost everyone's idea of a classic New England inn. Not surpris-

*Early fall brings rare quiet moments to the courtyard at the Red Lion Inn, where lunch and dinner are served, weather permitting.* Judith Monachina

ing, as that is just what it has been since 1773 (or thereabouts; local historians differ on the exact date). A hotbed of pre-Revolutionary fever then, it has been the focal point of the Stockbridge community ever since. Owned and operated by the Fitzpatrick family since 1968, the inn has grown and evolved with the times. Many things about the inn seem changeless—the wonderful collections of antiques, the festive holiday decorations, the 19th-century wire-cage elevator, the enormous and eclectic artwork. The cuisine, on the other hand, has kept up with the times. The classic favorites remain, from Red Lion clam chowder to carved native turkey to old-fashioned apple pie, but there are numerous contemporary New American–style selections, as well, designed to tempt the palate of the more demanding diner. To complement the newer menu selections, the inn has developed one of the most extensive and interesting wine lists in the region and has earned a *Wine Spectator* magazine Award of Excellence for its efforts.

Both the handsome 19th-century main dining room and the adjoining Widow Bingham's Tavern offer the full menu. During the balmy days of summer (late spring and early autumn, too), so do the back porch and courtyard. Jackets are required at dinner in the dining room. The tavern, which has a wonderful rustic air, the porch, and the courtyard are informal. A prime, and famous, place for cocktails or tea is the sweeping front porch, complete with wicker rocking chairs. The Lion's Den, in the basement of the inn, is a lion of a different color. Live music, a menu running to soups and sandwiches, and a busy bar make this one of the livelier nightspots in this quiet community. The Red Lion Inn is, deservedly, a very busy and popular place, especially during the summer months and the autumn leaf-peeping season; reservations are always a good idea—and a day or two in advance during those times.

WEST STOCKBRIDGE

## ROUGE

413-232-4111.
3 Center St., W. Stockbridge, MA 01266.
Open: Wed.–Sun.
Price: Moderate.
Cuisine: French.
Serving: D.
Credit Cards: MC, V.
Reservations: For parties of four or more.
Special Feature: Member, Berkshire Grown.

William and Maggie Merelle have put their hearts and souls into their intimate restaurant in West Stockbridge. Colorful, with pretty place settings and a bar that William crafted himself, this French bistro is a delightful addition to the small village that hosts more than its fair share of good food and pretty views. Rouge is tucked into a side street, somehow making it feel like a surprise, a secret find.

We sampled the torte vegetarian, sautéed salmon encrusted with pistachios and plantains, and New York strip steak. Everything was delicious, pleasantly presented and served. This spot is delightful.

## TRUC ORIENT EXPRESS

413-232-4204.
3 Harris St., W. Stockbridge, MA 01266.
One block off Main St. (Rte. 102), over the Williams River.
Closed: Tues., Sept.–May.
Price: Moderate to Expensive.
Cuisine: Vietnamese.
Serving: L, D.
Credit Cards: AE, DC, MC, V.
Reservations: Recommended.
Special Features: Vegetarian dishes; outdoor dining; Vietnamese gift shop.

Truc was earning converts to Vietnamese cuisine long before one could find it in every major city in the USA. This West Stockbridge fixture and favorite, set behind Main Street and the Williams River, was founded in 1979 by the husband-and-wife team of Luy

*Rouge, a French restaurant and bistro in W. Stockbridge, decorates for Halloween.* Judith Monachina

Nguyen and Drai Duong. The family has been beguiling Berkshire residents and visitors ever since with the flavors of classic Vietnamese fare tailored to American tastes, a complex and sophisticated blend of sweet and sour, mellow and piquant.

Special shrimp rolls, a crisp-fried, rice-paper pocket filled with crabmeat, pork, shrimp, and cabbage; and jumbo battered honeycomb shrimp, coated in cellophane noodles, quick-fried, and served with a thick soy-peanut sauce, are favorite appetizers. Barbecued pork on rice noodles—very flavorful, well marinated, and tender—is an excellent entrée, as is the deep-fried whole flounder in a sweet-sour sauce with chilies. Also recommended is the Happy Pancake (a rice-flour crêpe studded with lots of meat and fresh vegetables). Vegetarian offerings abound throughout the menu, as well. At lunch, everything is at least one-third off the evening price.

The interior is light and spacious, with wide wooden floorboards, a plant-filled balcony, Vietnamese art on the walls, and attractive bamboo curtains, all signs of the owner's dedication to a quality dining experience. The adjoining shop has been very handsomely expanded to become an attraction in its own right, filled with imported Asian gifts and decorative items.

### WILLIAMSVILLE INN

413-274-6118.
Rte. 41, W. Stockbridge, MA 01266.
Gt. Barrington end of Rte. 41.
Closed: Nov. 1–Nov. 20.
Price: Expensive.
Cuisine: German.
Serving: D.
Credit Cards: AE, MC, V.
Reservations: Required.
Special Feature: Culinary school; member, Berkshire Grown.

Welcome to the only German restaurant in Berkshire County, and a good one it is. Erhard Wendt, master chef and culinary instructor, offers a practicum to a select, small class Sunday from 11 AM to 3 PM. While these range through international cuisines, the restaurant bears a decidedly German accent—albeit toned down a bit to accommodate health-conscious Americans. A recent menu included herring salad in cream as an appetizer; braised Rheinish beef-sauerbraten with cabbage and dumplings, and Wiener schnitzel with sauce tartar for main courses; and Bavarian-style warm apple strudel for dessert, along with many other choices. A feature of the airy and inviting dining room is that diners can see the inner workings of the kitchen.

## RESTAURANTS IN CENTRAL COUNTY

BECKET

### DREAM AWAY LODGE

(See under "Nightlife" in chapter 5)

HANCOCK

### POWDER HOUNDS RESTAURANT AND TAVERN

413-738-5660.
137 Brodie Mountain Rd., Hancock, MA 01237.
Price: Moderate.
Closed: Tues.
Cuisine: American.
Serving: D.
Credit Cards: AE, MC, V.
Special Feature: Entire menu available to go.

Located at the foot of Jiminy Peak ski area and in the midst of burgeoning Hancock condominiums, Powder Hounds—named for the dogs Fred and Lisa Kruger keep out back—is a bar and grill in an American roadhouse building. Still, the chef has aspirations, preparing dishes of interest and presenting them with a flair. Our meat loaf, nestled beside sculptured scoops of mashed potatoes, was covered with wild mushrooms. The string beans were cooked the right amount and fresh—as were the carefully arranged, different textures of lettuce and tomatoes in the house salad. A peach pie, while not made in-house, provided decorative and tasty nuts around the shell. Several varieties of beer are on tap.

LENOX

### BLANTYRE

413-637-3556; fax 413-637-4282.
www.blantyre.com.
16 Blantyre Rd., Lenox, MA 01240.
Off Rte. 20, NW of Lee.
Closed: Early Nov.–early May.
Price: Very Expensive (prix fixe).
Cuisine: French, Country House.
Serving: D (jacket and tie required).
Credit Cards: AE, MC, V.
Reservations: Required.
Handicap Access: Yes.
Special Features: Fireplaces; private dining room; excellent wine cellar; member, Berkshire Grown.

Blantyre, a member of Relais & Châteaux, is one of the very best dining venues in the region, some say *the* best. Built as one of the grandest and most impressive of the Berkshire "cottages" of the Gilded Age, Blantyre was rescued and restored inside and out over two decades by the Fitzpatrick family. It has been developed to a high state of period excellence and offers a true taste of the life of its original time.

Before dinner, drinks are offered in the parlor from a handsome rolling bar. Champagne seems almost obligatory in these surroundings. Chef de cuisine Christopher Brooks generally offers six entrées, plus a veggie option and a five-course tasting menu, prix fixe. The cuisine is characterized as "country house"—utilizing contemporary French techniques to combine local, regional, and New England products. Offerings change seasonally. The food is exquisite—absolutely worth the lofty price—and the wine list is what one would expect from such an establishment, a *Wine Spectator* Award of Excellence winner, of course. The inn has also been awarded five stars from Mobil, and it received the Hideaway Report Grand Award. Desserts are varied, generally rich, and worth the extra indulgence. Blantyre is the perfect setting for one of those "memorable occasion" celebrations. Though as many as a half-dozen restaurants may have their adherents for "the best dining in the Berkshires," Blantyre and neighboring Wheatleigh stand alone in their combination of superlative dining with truly regal surroundings.

### BISTRO ZINC

413-637-8800.
www.bistrozinc.com.
56 Church St., Lenox, MA 01240.
Price: Moderate to Expensive.
Cuisine: French Bistro.
Serving: L, D.
Credit Cards: AE, MC, V.
Reservations: Recommended for dinner (necessary in summer).
Special Features: Smoking permitted in separate bar area; member, Berkshire Grown.

Bistro Zinc is a popular favorite for both lunch and dinner in the southern Berkshire dining scene. Both the dining room and the commodious separate bar/dining room convey a welcoming atmosphere. The dining room features perimeter banquettes and closely ranked tables in true bistro manner. It is separated from the handsome, more open, bar/dining area by a glass wall, permitting everyone to see everything but allowing the nonsmokers in the dining room to breathe undisturbed by the exhalations of the tobacco slaves in the bar.

The dinner menu is classic bistro: mussels marinière, charcuterie; a number of delicious green salads; 10 different grilled,

*A serious discussion over lunch at the Church Street Café in Lenox* Judith Monachina

roasted, or sautéed entrées; and desserts from selected cheeses to tarte tatin. The wine list is almost all French, moderately priced, and very well chosen. The lunch menu is a bit simpler and lighter, and one of the good dining bargains of the Berkshires. As a nice additional touch—not in the bistro tradition—Zinc offers a short but very good kids' menu, complete with kids' drinks and classic birthday cake with ice cream for dessert (adults can order it, too). Everything is served—pleasantly and efficiently—in both dining rooms.

### CAFÉ LUCIA

413-637-2640.
90 Church St., Lenox, MA 01240.
Closed: Sun. and Mon.
Price: Expensive.
Cuisine: Italian.
Serving: D.
Credit Cards: AE, CB, DC, MC, V.
Reservations: Recommended.
Special Features: Outdoor dining; member, Berkshire Grown.

Café owners Jim and Nadine Lucie preside over this sophisticated but informal restaurant, where Ken Almgren serves as chef. The many regular clients expect and get their popular dishes of Italian pasta and osso buco. Lucia has a fine wine cellar, with an excellent selection of half bottles. Aside from the stately mansions of Blantyre and Wheatleigh, no better meal is served in Lenox. Enough said.

### CHURCH STREET CAFÉ

413-637-2745; fax 413-637-2050.
65 Church St., Lenox, MA 01240.
Closed: Sun. and Mon., Oct.–May.
Price: Moderate.
Cuisine: American, Regional Eclectic.
Serving: L, D.
Credit Cards: MC, V.
Reservations: Recommended.
Special Features: Outdoor dining; member, Berkshire Grown.

We walk by the Church Street Café in summer to catch the smells wafting over the lively diners on the spacious, shaded deck. In fall we are drawn into one of the three bright dining rooms warmed with desert hues, local art, and, of course, those good smells. The mood is informal, the menu interesting, and the food delicious. The seasonal fall menu featured a luscious, velvety butternut squash soup, sweetened with apple and finished with a hint of cheddar. A luncheon delight was early-autumn chicken stew, richly flavored with roasted chicken breast and garlic, butternut squash, greens, mushrooms, and sage. A favorite of midday diners is "The Real Deal"—a pulled-pork sandwich with homemade barbecue sauce or North Carolina spicy vinegar, with excellent coleslaw and homemade fries.

Dinner entrées range from a classic coq au vin to autumn yam and roasted-onion ravioli with wild mushrooms, glazed shallots, and sautéed greens to seared Japanese sea bass with shrimp raviolis, dashi broth, and steamed greens—and on to a grilled dry-aged top sirloin steak with mashed potatoes and crispy fried onions.

The wine list is equally interesting. Dessert could be a meal by itself. How about a pumpkin marble brownie sundae with walnut toffee and cinnamon ice cream? Or perhaps a mocha ice cream torte with dark-chocolate sauce? A nice selection of local farmhouse cheeses could also provide a proper ending to a meal well prepared and beautifully presented.

### GATEWAYS INN

413-637-2532.
www.gatewaysinn.com.
51 Walker St., Lenox, MA 01240.
Closed: Mon. off-season.
Price: Expensive.
Cuisine: American.
Serving: B, L (weekends), D.
Credit Cards: AE, CB, D, DC, MC, V.
Reservations: Recommended.
Special Features: Vegetarian dishes; outdoor dining; private dining room; member, Berkshire Grown.

Pearly praise and glittering awards don't always guarantee a good meal. So it is fair to wonder if the Gateways Inn could possibly live up to the accolades it has received from *Gourmet*, *Wine Spectator*, and other salivating critics. However, with its graceful service and menu stocked full of knockouts, whether in the Main Dining Room or the Rockwell Room, Gateways more than justifies the acclaim.

Tucked in the front of soap magnate Harley Procter's Victorian cottage, the restaurant blends classic appointments with bright flourishes. Chef Frederic Boyarm achieves a similar balance, serving up bass, salmon, lamb, steak; as well as Tomato Three Ways and pasta. He aims at an American cuisine with "an Italian undertone." Desserts, including a homey apple-cherry crisp, were a fitting end to a meal that balanced sophistication with elegant simplicity. La Terrazza bar and lounge serves lunch, light meals, desserts, cocktails.

Despite the linen, silver, fine china, and tuxedo-clad waitstaff, Gateways betrays nary a bit of stiffness. The meal comes with a healthy dollop of small-town charm: Portions are generous and the servers warm and attentive. The result is a meal that delivers that rare combination of class and country comfort.

### LENOX 218

413-637-4218; fax 413-232-4205.
www.lenox218.com.
218 Main St., Lenox, MA 01240.
Rte. 7A.
Price: Moderate.
Cuisine: Northern Italian, American.
Serving: L, D.
Credit Cards: AE, D, DC, MC, V.
Handicap Access: Yes.

From the crackling fire, sleek bar, framed prints, spacious room, comfortable chairs, and art deco décor, Lenox 218 is a feast for the eyes as well as the palate. The breads and warm muffins, served in a basket, were so irresistibly light and flavorful, they could have been meals in themselves. Wines are varied; service and presentation are attentive and gracious.

Recent entrées by chef Jimmy DeMayo included delectable salmon fillets with red roasted pepper sauce, chicken parmigiana with penne pasta, and an interesting assortment of veal, chicken, duck, and fish. Several vegetarian selections are available as well.

Desserts such as the toll house nut pie with chocolate sauce and ice cream and deep dish fruit pies are delectable. Lenox 218 meets expectations. Mobil: three stars; AAA: three diamonds.

### PANDA HOUSE

413-499-0660.
506 Pittsfield–Lenox Rd., Lenox, MA 01240.
On Rte. 7/20, N. of town.
Price: Inexpensive to Moderate.
Cuisine: Chinese.
Serving: L, D.
Credit Cards: AE, D, MC, V.

This Panda House, not affiliated with other Pandas in the area, is the best Chinese restaurant in the Berkshires. The décor at Panda House may be lackluster, but its Szechuan, Mandarin, and Hunan food is not!

We suggest trying scallion cakes, should they be offered as a special—light, crispy, and not too greasy pan-fried scallion-filled pancakes dipped in a garlic and ginger sauce. Sheer perfection. We also tried the house-special vegetable crêpes, delicate and airy bean-curd crêpes wrapped around an earthy mixture of matchstick vegetables, including shiitake mushrooms, jicama, and bamboo shoots. The hot and sour seafood soup—another favorite of ours—was chock-full of lobster, shrimp, scallops, an assortment of Chinese mushrooms, crisp sweet snow peas, and silken tofu. The soup goes down smoothly and left us with the perfect afterbite of heat.

All the old-time favorites are offered here. The chow mein is full of taste and not the pasty, bland concoction one encounters elsewhere. The sweet and sour chicken is, indeed, quite sweet, but the tender morsels are lightly fried to perfection. For seafood, the crispy sesame shrimp offers giant prawns dredged in lotus flower, fried (not overcooked), and finished with a delicate, pleasingly sweet, and very light sesame sauce, all surrounded by steamed broccoli. Also flanked by fresh broccoli, the chef's special jumbo shrimp is topped with a fluffy secret sauce that betrays its origins in orange.

The host is cheerful, the service is friendly and good, and the kitchen puts out meals in a timely fashion—no worries about being late for Tanglewood. There are also plenty of choices for vegetarians. Take-out is always an excellent option.

### SPIGALINA

413-637-4455.
www.spigalina.com.
80 Main St., Lenox, MA 01240.
Closed: Late winter.
Price: Moderate.
Cuisine: Mediterranean.
Serving: D (Fri.–Sun.).
Credit Cards: All major.
Special Features: Member, Berkshire Grown.

With its Main Street Lenox location and a spacious porch overlooking the main drag, Spigalina is easy to find and a perfect vantage point in Lenox. The restaurant is a series of connected rooms. The exposed beams, tile floor, and ochre walls create a pleasant Mediterranean feeling throughout, while fashionable tourists carrying Prada and Gucci bags add to a European ambiance.

The restaurant also promotes its menu as "cuisine reflecting the flavors of the sunny Mediterranean;" it succeeds in offering fresh flavors in some eclectic and exciting combinations. A delicious salad of local goat cheese wrapped in a bird's nest of shredded phyllo-like dough on a bed of spring greens with dried cranberries and nuts was memorable. Monkfish—which seems nearly impossible to find in the Berkshires—was wonderfully prepared, sweet and spicy, on a bed of orzo and fennel. Other entrées included local free-range chicken, osso buco, pancetta- wrapped tenderloin, and a number of pastas. For dessert we recommend the *panna cotta,* slightly sweet, melt-in-the-mouth creamy, loaded with vanilla, and topped with fruit.

The wine list is long and well balanced. A fine selection of sherries and ports is also available.

### TRATTORIA IL VESUVIO

413-637-4904.
242 Pittsfield Rd., Lenox, MA 01240.
Rte. 7/20.
Closed: Mon. in winter.
Price: Moderate to Expensive.
Cuisine: Italian.
Serving: D.
Credit Cards: AE, D, MC, V.
Special Features: Member, Berkshire Grown.

Trattoria Il Vesuvio, in a handsomely refurbished barn on the Pittsfield–Lenox Rd., raised the bar considerably for Italian cuisine in the Berkshires; cheers for Anna Arace's wood-fired brick oven. It is slightly tricky to find if driving north on Route 7, being partially obscured by earthen bank and foliage on a long downgrade, but well worth looking for. Its high ceilings, wood beams, and warm wood walls create a comfortable, country atmosphere, while friendly staff and the savory aromas of northern Italian cooking at its finest further conspire to make the diner welcome.

The menu offerings are the usual for a good Italian restaurant: several excellent antipasti, a dozen pasta offerings (some available as half orders for a first course), and an array of fish, fowl, and meat main courses. Two items constitute house trademarks: delicious, chewy, homemade bread, baked fresh every day by Anna's mother; and the *arrosto di vitello,* a rolled breast of veal, stuffed with prosciutto and spinach and slow-roasted for several hours until wonderfully tender and flavorful. There are many other excellent options. The *frutti di mare*—a delectable combination of seafood in a pinot grigio garlic-tomato broth—begs for a refill of grandma's bread to get every last drop of the fine fish broth. Entrées come with a choice of pasta, creamy and corny homemade polenta, or mashed potatoes. For dessert, the homemade *tiramisù* is as good as one will find anywhere.

### THE VILLAGE INN

413-637-0020, 800-253-0917.
www.villageinn-lenox.com.
16 Church St., Lenox, MA 01240.
Open: Sat. and Sun. only, winter and spring.
Closed: Mon. for dinner, summer and fall.
Price: Moderate.
Cuisine: American.
Serving: B, SB, D.
Credit Cards: AE, DC, MC, V.
Reservations: Recommended.
Special Features: English tea Sat. afternoon.

Nestled in the quaint heart of Lenox, the Village Inn offers classic American fare in colonial quarters. Built in 1771, the inn certainly has a cozy charm. Meals are served either in a simply appointed dining room or the warmly lighted, glass-enclosed porch.

However, chef John Gosselin doesn't get bogged down by history. He enlivens his roster of regional dishes with modest modern twists and bold flavors, changing the menu frequently. Not too long ago, broiled Maine crabcakes were served speckled with chives, while a salad of poached pear and mixed baby field greens was sparked by tangy stilton cheese and spiced pecans. The chicken smothered in pecans was a bit dry, but the overall effect was tasty. Beef tournedos and Shaker-style pot roast were also available.

Friendly service and an extensive wine list help mitigate any shortcomings, although the small dessert menu, including a perfunctory blueberry torte, ended the meal on a flat note.

### WHEATLEIGH

413-637-0610.
www.wheatleigh.com.
Hawthorne Rd., Lenox, MA 01240.
Price: Very Expensive (prix fixe).
Cuisine: Contemporary French.
Serving: L (guests only winter), D.
Credit Cards: AE, DC, MC, V.
Reservations: Required.
Special Features: Fireplaces; private dining room; member, Berkshire Grown. The Library has limited menu, somewhat more moderate pricing.

Proprietors Linfield and Susan Simon are uncompromising perfectionists. Wheatleigh is the product of their 30-year drive for excellence. A complete renovation of the interior by distinguished architects Calvin Tsao and Zack McKown has been universally praised for its elegant but unobtrusive blending of the Beaux-Arts architecture of the building with clean, modern effects. The reactions of rapturous critics, and much else, can be viewed on Wheatleigh's informative Web site.

*Elegance at Wheatleigh* | Judith Monachina

Executive chef Bryce Whittlesey has sustained the restaurant's well-deserved reputation as one of the finest anywhere. Wheatleigh competes on the world, not merely the U.S. or Berkshire, dining scene. The prix-fixe menu changes nightly, but the structure is constant. Dinner is served in four courses, supplemented with several delicious small entremets between courses. There are generally three choices for each course. The cuisine evokes the best of classic French, with a Mexican grace note. Not given to heavy sauces, it relies on the development of natural flavors and is full of imaginative and varied choices. The service is faultless and literally Continental, as the young staff are all European, trained in the rigorous schools of restaurant service there. The wine list has earned Wheatleigh a *Wine Spectator* Award of Excellence every year since 1989—perhaps the longest run for that prestigious honor of any Berkshire restaurant. The wine selections are varied, running toward the finer and more expensive that such food deserves.

For those days and evenings when something less opulent appeals, Wheatleigh has created the Library. Offering a simpler but still beautifully prepared three-course à la carte menu for lunch and dinner with the same array of wines and faultless service, the Library is one of the area's best fine dining options—not inexpensive but a wonderful value.

PITTSFIELD

### ASTERS

413-499-2075.
1015 South St., Pittsfield, MA 01201.
East side of Rte. 7/20, S. of downtown Pittsfield.
Price: Moderate.
Serving: SB, D.
Cuisine: American.
Credit Cards: AE, MC, V.

Joe and Lynn Toole of Lee, owners of several lodgings, acquired the old South Mountain Grille, which had slid down hill, practically into the Housatonic River. They got architect Judd Brown to redesign the interior, creating a raw bar, a wine room, and a jazz bar. In the new, dark and homey atmosphere they hung an exhibit of the late photographer Bill Tague's iconic Berkshire images. They changed the name closer to a previous one and presented, Asters: Steaks and Raw Bar. The menu is straightforward: seafood, steaks, burgers, salads, pastas, chicken. A major improvement!

### DAKOTA

413-499-7900; fax 413-499-8610.
www.dakotarestaurant.com.
1035 South St., Pittsfield, MA 01201
On Rte. 7/20.
Price: Moderate.
Cuisine: American.
Serving: D, SB.
Credit Cards: AE, DC, MC, V.
Reservations: Strongly recommended.
Special Features: Fireplaces; member, Berkshire Grown.

With its pine walls, raised fieldstone fireplaces, mounted deer and moose heads, and overhanging birch-bark canoes, the Dakota successfully communicates the feeling of a grand hunting lodge. In addition, the restaurant fills its odd spaces and some of its walls with Native American artifacts, all of museum quality. (Some, in fact, come from Andy Warhol's collection.) Spacious and comfortable, well managed and conceived, the Dakota is one of the county's most popular restaurants.

With good reason. The restaurant usually operates with clockwork precision, serving an array of steak and seafood dishes that are simply prepared—mesquite-grilled, broiled, or baked—and simply presented. We chose from sirloin steak, pork and lamb chops, prime rib, shrimp, salmon, scallops, and chicken teriyaki, among others. A lobster tank up front offers lobster lovers their pick, with the day's price per pound clearly posted above. The copious salad bar features fresh greens, bean and grain salads, and a variety of marinated vegetables.

All meals come with huge slabs of good, freshly baked whole-grain bread and unlimited salad bar privileges. The wine list offers two dozen popular varieties. Desserts are unabashedly rich and sure to please any chocolate lover (we recommend the chocolate falling cake). In all, with its relaxed atmosphere, moderate prices, and all-you-can-eat Sunday brunch—which includes delicious omelets made to order with an array of ingredients—it's easy to see why the Dakota remains a Berkshire roadside favorite.

### ELIZABETH'S BORDERLAND CAFÉ

413-448-8244.
1264 East St., Pittsfield, MA 01201.
Across from "the G.E."
Price: Inexpensive.
Credit Cards: None.
Special Features: Specialty pizzas; Member, Berkshire Grown.

Elizabeth's Borderland Café has added space upstairs yet remains just as good as ever, which is good news to those who like pizza, pasta, and enormous salads. Elizabeth's still stands like a tiny beacon across from the enormous sprawl of the old GE complex. (If heading out from Pittsfield, drivers need to stay on East Street, without being beguiled onto the new bridge.) Elizabeth's accepts "American money, personal checks, and IOUs" but no credit cards. The sentiments expressed on the menu are free.

We started with smooth tomato soup, enlivened by a bit of spice. The salads are superior—for example, the insulata mista is chunked with delicious feta cheese, studded with old-world olives, striped with roasted pepper, crowned with slices of kiwi, and supported by a bed of the freshest, youngest, most tender baby salad greens from the heart of the lettuce. The bread is also among the best available hereabouts.

The baked *cavatappi* alfredo was in the family of, but several generations removed from, macaroni and cheese: cream, parmesan, mozzarella, and sweet peas under a lovely crust. The pasta cacciatore, this time with a bit of chicken in the sauce, just slides down the gullet until we can't believe how much we ate. We did draw the line at desserts, though, either cheesecake or a chocolate confection.

Chef Tom presides with his accustomed verve. While not obnoxious, he enjoys interaction—especially with those who reveal it is their first visit and choose to sit downstairs.

## HOUSE OF INDIA

413-443-3262.
122 North St., Pittsfield, MA 01201.
Open: Daily.
Price: Inexpensive.
Cuisine: Indian.
Serving: L, D.
Credit Cards: MC, V.

Sitting in the window of this storefront restaurant in Pittsfield, we feel we may have left the Berkshires. A decidedly urban environment replaces the usual bucolic scenery and beautiful vistas. For elegant or romantic ambiance, other restaurants are a better choice; for a really good meal at a really good price, the House of India is a really good place to dine.

The service is attentive without being fawning, the beer is cold, and, most important, the food is perfectly spiced. We are constantly amazed at how the chef reads our minds when it comes to the level of spiciness. At House of India, medium is indeed medium, just hot enough to make us appreciate a bite of cooling *raita* but not so hot that we must dive for the water pitcher.

While we love to watch the action on North Street, for those not in a mood to speculate on Pittsfield's peculiar blend of characters, takeout is available.

*House of India, North St., Pittsfield* Judith Monachina

### KIM'S DRAGON RESTAURANT

413-442-5594.
1231 W. Housatonic St., Pittsfield, MA 01201.
Rte. 20.
Closed: Mon.
Price: Moderate.
Cuisine: Vietnamese.
Serving: D.
Credit Cards: MC, V.
Reservations: Not accepted.

To meet the East, it may be necessary to go west—to Kim Van Huynh's restaurant, nearly as far west on Housatonic Street as Hancock Shaker Village. Offering a variety of delicious Vietnamese and other far-Eastern cuisine, fragrant with lemongrass and filled with delicious contrasts, Dragon is a great place to initiate a novice into the wonderful world of this French-inspired fare. The menu is in English, with clear descriptions of each dish. Portions are generous: A doggie bag will yield not just lunch for the next day but probably dinner as well.

We began with the requisite spring rolls, offered both vegetarian and not, and a truly mellow lemongrass soup, full of vegetables and chicken. Our favorite entrées include exquisite fried fish; pad Thai (either vegetarian or shrimp), which is loaded with crispy vegetables; vegetable curry, a surprisingly spicy mélange of vegetables in red curry sauce; and Shaken Beef served on a bed of watercress and tomatoes.

Elegance, no—the tables are covered in plastic cloths—just great food. Kim urges that we allow an hour to eat since he is preparing food to order. Just relax, enjoy some Vietnamese beer, and savor the flavors of this one-of-a-kind cuisine.

### TRATTORIA RUSTICA

413-499-1192.
75 North St., Pittsfield, MA 01201.
Entrance on McKay St.
Closed: Tues.
Price: Moderate.
Cuisine: Italian.
Serving: D.
Credit Cards: Major.
Reservations: Recommended on weekends.

Who knew that the basement of the Central Block had been fashioned into a *cave*—stone and brick walls, with lanterns and candles. Not the casual passerby because signs are scarce, and the doors at 75 North are locked at night (enter from McKay Street). Here chef-owner Davidé Manzo, having built his wonderful wood-fired oven, serves food prepared with a vast assortment of herbs and inspiring skill. Each thinly sliced zucchini, carrot, and eggplant in the appetizer we shared carried its delicate freight of seasoning, individual and unforgettable. The *basciale*, a pasta entrée, mated with mushrooms, leeks, and prosciutto before our eyes, while the *pollo a la rustica*, tender chicken apparently raised on a tasty assortment of cheeses, was equally salubrious. Out of the oven in its own dish, by itself it took the chill of a windy evening off the entire corner of one of two dining areas. While the menu carried ample variety, the young waitress recited a dozen specials that were not only enticing but a good test of her Italian. She passed with aplomb.

The homemade bread dipped in olive oil, a fine assortment of desserts—some made on the premises and some imported from Italy—and an intriguing wine list of Italian extraction, including ample selections by the glass for those who want to explore—all of these are features of a new and intriguing restaurant in, of all places, downtown Pittsfield. Summer brings an opportunity for alfresco dining in an adjacent courtyard.

## RESTAURANTS IN NORTH COUNTY

### ADAMS

**HARRINGTON'S RESTAURANT & INN**
413-749-3637.
17 Commercial St., Adams, MA 01220.
Rte. 8.
Closed: Wed.
Price: Moderate.
Cuisine: "American with a French twist."
Serving: D.
Credit Cards: AE, D, MC, V.
Reservations: Requested.
Special Features: Handicapped accessible; accommodations; member, Berkshire Grown.

Eric Harrington, owner of Harrington's in Lanesborough, an Adams native, and graduate of the culinary arts departments of McCann's and Berkshire Community College, picked up the former Silvia Inn at a bank sale. This gracious building, a former mill owner's home, later a nursing home in Adams, has a staircase that is worthy of Scarlett O'Hara, and several fireplaces are large enough to hide a 10-year-old. Eric installed a new bar and redid the kitchen for restaurant efficiency.

The menu, primarily steaks, chops, fish, the requisite pasta and a rack of lamb, contains no surprises but should be dependable. Although Eric is reluctant to say the words, he seems to be aiming on Rte. 8 at an upscale version of what is more a pub on Rte. 7.

### NEW ASHFORD

**MILL ON THE FLOSS**
413-458-9123.
342 Rte. 7, New Ashford, MA 01267.
Closed: Mon.
Price: Moderate to Expensive.
Cuisine: French.
Serving: D.
Credit Cards: AE, MC, V.
Reservations: Recommended.

The Mill on the Floss provides elegant dining and service in an informal French country style. An open kitchen adorned with hanging copper pots over a country-tile counter is part of the cozy atmosphere also created by massive exposed beams, a large stone fireplace, and blue-and-white patterned rustic china. In winter, a table by the fire fits a romantic event.

Suzanne, daughter of the late chef-owner Maurice Champang, maintains a classic French menu that delights regular diners who love coq au vin and braised sweetbreads in beurre noir. Specialties change with the seasons. Other staples include a starter of richly flavored onion soup baked with lusciously browned swiss and parmesan cheeses on top of a delicate crabcake adorned with a dijon mayonnaise (also an entrée). Several lightly dressed salads of the freshest greens provide additional appetizers. For dinner a sumptuously delicious duck à l'orange with a darkly glazed crackling skin was one choice; another, tournedos of beef tenderloin, perfectly cooked and lovingly arranged.

The extensive wine list includes selections from France, Italy, and California. The dessert cart beckoned with *le gâteau de la maison*, a densely delicious chocolate cake; tasty apples bursting from puff pastry in the deep-dish apple pie; and creamy crème caramel. Still, the simple sundae of intense coffee ice cream with wonderfully gooey butterscotch sauce attracted us.

### NORTH ADAMS

**CAFE LATINO**
413-662-2004.
1111 MASS MoCA Way, N. Adams, MA 01247.
Building 11, MASS MoCA.
Serving: L, D.
Open: Daily.

Price: Moderate.
Credit cards: All major.
Cuisine: Nuevo Latino.
Reservations: Recommended.
Handicap Access: Yes.

Nancy Thomas, the successful restaurateur behind Williamstown's Mezze Bistro and Bar, opened Eleven in this space on August 31, 2001, just 2 weeks after the original Mezze burned. Almost 4 years later it was time to convert cuisines, with the aid of Peruvian chef Omar Montoya. The new décor is softer, less MoCA-like, including a backlit bar that was a feature at the original Mezze. Drinks here include South American mixtures; wines from Argentina, Chile, and Spain; and a remarkable Sararnac root beer soda on tap.

Appetizers, such as the clam calamari and the quesadilla plate, are generous in size and appealing. The Latino Plate calls, however, to get a sense of the culinary geography. The entrées include meat, fish, and vegetarian, all with distinctive sauces. The desserts are tasty, rich, and somewhat exotic.

### GIDEON'S FINE DINING

413-664-9449; fax 413-664-9669.
www.gideonsrestaurant.com.
34 Holden St., N. Adams, MA 01247.
Closed: Mon.
Price: Expensive.
Cuisine: Eclectic.
Serving: D.
Credit Cards: AE, MC, V.
Reservations: Suggested.
Special Features: Lunch and late-night eatery on Eagle St.

Bill Gideon, owner-chef with 27 years' experience in the restaurant business, almost took a job in Stockbridge when he came across a restaurant for sale in North Adams. Gideon's, with its suave and understated décor, now has elegant dining for 70 in the main room and a private room to boot. Gideon talks about the "dining experience," which includes watching the food in preparation in the open kitchen. It hasn't taken long to catch on and is now the place to go in North Adams. Chef Gideon describes his cuisine as a little Italian, such as *pappardelle* pasta, and inspired by many other regions as well: Asian roasted sea bass, Vermont apple chicken, even "untraditional veal oscar," sautéed veal with chunks of Maine lobster. Gideon's aims and achieves a touch of class. A note: The door is not on Holden St., but around the corner, opening onto a parking lot.

**Gideon's Luncheon and Nightery** (413-664-0404; 23 Eagle St., North Adams, MA 01247), although on a different street, is also owned by Bill Gideon. Open Tuesday–Saturday from 11 AM into the evening, it features *panini*, pasta, and salads, and a bar with live entertainment.

### GRAMERCY BISTRO

413-663-5300.
24 Marshall St., N. Adams, MA 01247.
Across from MASS MoCA parking lot.
Closed: Tues.
Price: Moderate.
Cuisine: International.
Serving: SB, D.
Credit Cards: AE, MC, V.
Reservations: Suggested.
Special Feature: Member, Berkshire Grown.

"Gramercy"—that is, "Thank you very much," for providing an unadorned, short-menu bistro with interesting choices and an extensive wine list. One soup, three salads, a few small-helping dishes that might be called meals, and eight or so entrées, ranging from vegetarian to fish to beef and lamb. The basics, with interesting treatments. The house salad was sprinkled with bachelor's buttons. The vegetable with the entrées was spinach. Herbs informed all flavors. Yes, a predictable New York cheesecake for dessert but also apple brown betty—resurrected from our childhood and served with panache.

### JAE'S INN

413-664-0100.
www.jaesinn.com.
1111 S. State St., N. Adams, MA 01247.
Price: Moderate
Cuisine: Asian.
Serving: L, D.
Credit Cards: AE, CB, D, DC, MC, V.

Jae H. Chung invites us to "Eat at Jae's . . . live forever." Fair enough. His is an upscale, pleasant establishment open both to the residents of the inn and the public. Although the menu has a special Korean section, the cuisine is broader than that. The sushi bar tempts the somewhat adventurous, while his lunch boxes are a convenience to those whose adventures may be outside the restaurant. His menu lists a wide range of Asian dishes and some more conventionally Western fare, such as Maine crab and lobster cake, and filet mignon.

A native of northern Berkshire, Jae established a handful of his cafés in the Boston area before returning to make his mark at home. This he has accomplished by converting the former Twin Sisters into an upscale inn and spa, Jae's Inn; and by purchasing and upgrading the Miss Adams Diner in the eponymous town and Le Jardin in Williamstown. Of the food at Jae's, he says that it is similar to and of the same high standards as the food served at his acclaimed Boston-area cafés. So, whether we tuck into Paradise Chicken or the grilled chicken teriyaki, we know that it has been tested and approved.

### MILAN AT 55 MAIN

413-664-9995.
55 Main St., N. Adams, MA 01247.
Closed: Tues.
Price: Moderate.
Cuisine: Italian.
Serving: L, D.
Credit Cards: AE, MC, V.
Reservations: Recommended.

Having taken the old 55 Main restaurant and softened the ambiance with pastel colors, chef Jack Carlow has created a decidedly upscale venue that nevertheless appeals to local residents. It is another sign of the North Adams renaissance, and, like the other new restaurants, it will have to compete for its market share until either the clientele increases or restaurants fall by the wayside.

On a recent visit, warm bread arrived early on, with oil and a tasty garlic dip. The menu carries almost as many insalata dishes as entrées. They enjoyed a variety of textures, and we enjoyed them. Pasta, meat (mostly veal), and a couple of fish dishes are all tastefully prepared and well presented, based on our own and what we could see on other tables. A well-flavored veal *picatta* rested on polenta. The nicely prepared beans, carrots, and asparagus were stacked like a snake fence. We shared three good desserts, of which the key lime cheesecake was most distinctive. The wine selection was varied but not extensive. The waitstaff were anxious to please and helpful, even on an unexpectedly busy evening.

WILLIAMSTOWN

### HOBSON'S CHOICE

413-458-9101.
159 Water St., Williamstown, MA 01267.
Rte. 43.
Price: Moderate.
Serving: D.
Credit Cards: MC, V.
Reservations: Recommended.

Locals know making Hobson's Choice is a good one in Williamstown for a quiet drink, dinner, or a late-evening snack. Dark wooden booths line the walls of the restaurant, creating a sense of intimacy. Hobson's is a comfortable place to linger—especially with the expansion, which now provides an entrance door that doesn't blow cold air on diners.

With owner Dan Campbell playfully holding court from the open kitchen behind the salad bar—one of the tastiest in northern Berkshire—the patron is likely to get a meal custom-cooked just the way she likes it. We were delighted with the Chicken Santa Fe, nicely presented with fresh asparagus and seasoned just so. Hobson's offers a wide variety of chicken (grilled, blackened, barbecued, teriyaki, and Santa Fe–style), beef, fish, pasta, and vegetarian specialties, all flavorfully prepared. It makes its own soups; an onion soup gratiné is especially good. The desserts are also excellent, especially the mud pie.

A comfortable, well-stocked bar includes a nice selection of imported beers and ales, plus a modest wine list. Espresso and cappuccino provide warmth and cheer for the abstemious.

### LE JARDIN

413-458-8032.
777 Cold Spring Rd., Williamstown, MA 01267.
Price: Expensive.
Cuisine: French.
Serving: L, D, SB.
Credit Cards: All major.
Reservations: Encouraged.

Jae H. Chung, owner of well-regarded restaurants in the Boston area, has returned to his northern Berkshire home in a big way, investing half-a-million in Jae's Inn in North Adams, buying and now running the Miss Adams Diner and, most recently, with other partners including the former owner, putting $1.5 million into Le Jardin, which had declined in recent years. The restaurant, now including six guest rooms, has been completely redone.

In spite of extensive rehabilitation to the building, however, the menu remains unapologetically French without being overly burdened by diet consciousness. Chef Walter Hayn still serves up escargots, oysters, onion soup, pâté, and all the sauces that define Gallic high living, without much of the Orient showing yet, anyway. We enjoyed a fine brunch—not as elaborate a production as that of the Williams Inn, say, but nevertheless satisfying: an emphasis on eggs benedict and other breakfast items. Dinner showed the same careful preparation and attention to detail. Why not? Frogs legs Provençale, anyone?

### MEZZE

413-458-0123.
16 Water St., Williamstown, MA 01267.
Rte. 43, jct. Rte. 2 (Main St.).
Price: Expensive.
Cuisine: Fusion.
Serving: D.
Credit Cards: AE, MC, V.
Reservations: Recommended.
Special Features: In former general store; member, Berkshire Grown.

It was a sad day in Williamstown when Nancy Thomas's original Mezze suffered a devastating fire in August 2000. Thomas had established a restaurant known for great food and great hospitality. While Mezze loyalists were thrilled that Thomas opened a new restaurant, then called Eleven at MASS MoCA, just 10 days later, they were doubly happy when their old favorite reopened in May 2002, just up the hill from its original Water Street location.

The new Mezze is bigger, but the food, warm greeting, and chic ambiance are welcome holdovers. Thomas and chef Todd Clements emphasize the freshest ingredients and buy locally so that their vegetables glow. Even sophisticated diners find new ingredients and new combinations on the Mezze menu. A peekytoe crab appetizer was beautifully presented as a tower, with layers of tomato, crab, and avocado; while another fish starter was a very tasty *hamachi* (yellowtail) with jicama. Entrées range from tenderloin to goat cheese stuffed ravioli; or a tasting dish is available, with a morsel of everything on the menu. Desserts are equally sophisticated. The Brillat Savarin (a salty, creamy cheese) with candied pecans and honeyed grapes was worthy of the high recommendation it received from the staff.

The wine list, filled with interesting varieties and excellent values, is large enough to offer diversity but not overwhelming. A surprising number of wines are available by the half bottle.

In the summer Mezze caters to Williamstown Theatre Festival patrons; we can nearly always count on a seat after they have left for an 8 PM curtain.

### MICHAEL'S RESTAURANT

413-458-2114.
460 Main St., Williamstown 01267
Price: Inexpensive.
Cuisine: Greek & American.
Serving: D.
Reservations: None.
Special Feature: Takeout.

No longer a pizzeria, Michael's aims to fill a niche as a modestly priced, family, Greek restaurant, where folks can decide late in the afternoon, Let's go out tonight, without having to worry about dressing up or reservations. Regulars can count on the flavorful and intriguing Greek salads and, at least as a Thursday-night special, Greek chicken. Of course the pasta is plentiful and the garlic bread tasty. Those in the know also know to order *galatoboureko,* a sumptuous pudding-cake, for dessert. Diners will also be warmly greeted by Michael Nikitas himself and his sister, Cindy, who is in charge in the front of the house.

Newcomers will also be made to feel at home. They should rejoice in the ambiance of an old A&W, which it was. In fact, root beer remains on the menu.

### YASMIN'S AT THE ORCHARDS

413-458-9611.
222 Adams Rd., Williamstown, MA 01267.
Price: Moderate to Expensive.
Cuisine: Eclectic.
Serving: B, SB, L, D.
Credit Cards: AE, DC, MC, V.
Reservations: Recommended.
Special Features: Table settings and linens; member, Berkshire Grown.

Sayed Saleh's Orchards is a place to dine for a special night out. The physical setting is elegant and uncrowded. After a walk in the attractive, quiet garden, it's almost hard to go back indoors for dinner. Yet we look forward to the food—and to chatting with the international young people who serve it. Our server recently was from Bosnia.

For starters we had *lomi-lomi* (raw tuna) and mint-pickled eggplant, both delicious. For those with a light appetite, either could have been a meal. Since mixed greens were included on the plates, we chose not to order separate, additional salads. Both appetizers were original in composition and presentation. As main courses we had the Vermont free-range chicken supreme with open-faced ravioli, morels, and sugar snap peas and the yellowtail snapper with a mango-asparagus confit coriande. Chef Swen Boehm matches individual accompaniments to each main course and does not overwhelm the diner with volume. For a finish, we highly recommend the lemon tart.

Prices are on the high side for dinner; however, the wine list includes some good, reasonably priced bottles, as well as domestics and imports that span the globe. Wines by the glass are priced no higher than we have found at most restaurants. Diners with a Williams College connection might want to try a selection from the list of vineyards operated by Williams graduates.

The Orchards is an elegant gem set in north Berkshire County, having won the Five Star Diamond Award from the american Academy of Hospitality Sciences.

*Pappa Charlie's is a popular spot for students and others in Williamstown.* Judith Monachina

### PAPPA CHARLIE'S DELI SANDWICH SHOP

413-458-5969.
28 Spring St., Williamstown, MA 01267.
Price: Inexpensive.
Cuisine: American.
Serving: B, L, D.
Special Features: Open late.

Pappa Charlie's reigns supreme as a people's place and local hangout, convenient to Images Cinema and the Williams College gymnasium. It serves sandwiches, chili, and mulled cider. The delicious overstuffed sandwiches—and elaborately adorned, well-stuffed bagels—are mostly named for actors at the Williamstown Theatre Festival, politicians, and other well-known local folks. Any-one for a bite of Blythe Danner? Richard Chamberlain? Kate Burton? James Naughton— or a taste of Zonker Harris for that matter? Or how about an Avocado Smoothie—bagel of choice, spread of cream cheese, slices of avocado—all zapped in the steamer? The philosophical issue is whether the dishes are a commentary on the named.

The fresh cider, root beer that traces its roots to the A&W where Charlie Nikitas began, exotic fruit juice combos like strawberry-banana OJ—these are the potable Pappa. The cooler holds one of North County's better arrays of domestic and imported cheeses. The ambiance is created by the friendly service and plain wooden booths. The benches in the small park to the north are a fine alternative; however, the basement has all the charm of a middle-school lunchroom.

### TACONIC RESTAURANT

413-458-9499.
1161 Cold Spring Rd., Williamstown, MA 01267.
Jct. Rtes. 7 and 2.
Price: Moderate.
Cuisine: New England.
Serving: SB, D.
Credit Cards: AE, D, MC, V.
Reservations: Recommended.
Special Features: Caters.

Deborah and James Guiden's restaurant provides gracious space for banquets and wedding receptions, and good food for the wayfarer. The menu, which features a half-dozen veal dishes, revels in its New England environment, serving locally grown produce (Jimmy Guiden's brother farms). Dependable, fun, not exotic: a place to get a good baked potato with sour cream and string beans still crunchy. The main dining room provides an uninspiring view of the Route 7 traffic, but there's a large fireplace to ward off a cool evening. The restaurant attracts local people, drive-bys, and groups.

The soup du jour recently was a savory cream of mushroom. The Original Vermont Chicken was a playful concoction with cinnamon apples and a maple brown sauce. Among the other desserts, the Taconic Pie is an extraordinary confection that tests even a chocolate lover's capacity. The Taconic carries an adequate variety of wines and beer.

### THAI GARDEN

413-458-0004; fax 413-458-2220.
27 Spring St., Williamstown, MA 01267.
Price: Inexpensive.
Cuisine: Thai.
Serving: L, D.
Credit Cards: All major.
Special Features: Takeout.

Aside from the protective Buddha behind the counter and the food served to the guests, Thai Garden makes no attempt to reproduce Thai culture: The décor is solidly in the American diner tradition. The helpful menu, in English, signals the degree of heat of a dish by one, two, or three chili peppers in the margin. The only chili trifecta is the Drunken Squid.

Our pad Thai—rice noodles, chicken, and shrimp with peanut sauce—was a large helping of tastiness, while the Thai pepper beef (one chili) luxuriated in "the chef's special sauce." Owner Bob Khun explains that, although Thai food is known for its heat, the goal is harmony. We will come back another time to learn how the sweet coconut milk dishes, for example, bring out the more delicate ingredients.

Some Thai desserts, beer, and wine are available.

### WATER STREET GRILL

413-458-2175.
123 Water St., Williamstown, MA 01267.
Rte. 43.
Price: Inexpensive to Moderate.
Cuisine: Contemporary American.
Serving: L, D.
Credit Cards: AE, D, MC, V.
Reservations: Recommended.
Handicap Access: Yes.
Special Features: Tavern; expanded menu in Grill, with fireplace.

The owners of the Freight Yard Pub in North Adams also own Water Street Grill as an upscale outlet. The Tavern side is more like the Freight Yard, with nachos, fajitas, burgers, and seafood; open lunch and dinner. (A buffet is a lunch option.) In the Grill (open dinner only) we enjoyed Absolut (vodka) Chicken and the special, sirloin tips with mushrooms. The house chardonnay was above average. The house salad offered a great variety of dressings, and the bread sticks received a bonus for being served warm. Our waitperson seemed interested without hovering. All in all, a fine night out for the price.

One caution—or maybe it's an enticement: Overly lively acoustics in this all-wood room can turn innocent diners into eavesdroppers.

## RESTAURANTS OUTSIDE THE COUNTY

HILLSDALE, NEW YORK

### AUBERGINE

518-325-3412.
www.aubergine.com.
Mail: P.O. Box 387, Hillsdale, NY 12529.
Jct. Rtes. 22 and 23.
Closed: Mon. and Tues.
Price: Moderate to Very Expensive.
Cuisine: American with a French twist.
Serving: D.
Credit Cards: AE, MC, V.

Reservations: Recommended.
Special Features: Vegetarian dishes; member, Berkshire Grown.

Chef-owner David Lawson and his wife, Stacy, preside over Aubergine, offering fine food and lodging in a venue long renowned for both. Trained at London's legendary Gavroche, David is both a classic hands-on executive chef and a charming and affable host who offers "French-inspired country cooking" and hospitality to a devoted clientele. Aubergine is housed in a handsome 1783 Dutch Colonial mansion in Hillsdale, New York, just outside Berkshire County proper but close enough for easy access—and well worth the trip. The atmosphere is not terribly formal; "high casual" is the suggested standard for attire, although most of the clients seem inclined to put on at least a jacket if not a tie out of respect for the food, the fine wine, and the warm atmosphere that the Lawsons offer.

Like many of Berkshire's finest restaurants, Aubergine incorporates the best of locally produced foods into its menu. Selections are largely in the traditional French vein, imaginatively adapted by David to incorporate more cosmopolitan and contemporary elements, a couscous, a polenta, gnocchi, or shiitake mushrooms. The wine list draws on a cellar that has been there for many years and is one of the deepest and best in the region, featuring mostly fine French and California offerings. Desserts are rich and worth the calories. David's classic soufflés are a signature feature of the restaurant. They must (and should) be ordered at the outset of the meal and are themselves worth the visit.

### SWISS HÜTTE

413-528-6200, 518-325-3333; fax 413-528-6201.
www.swisshutte.com.
Rte. 23, Hillsdale, NY 12529.
On Mass. line.
Price: Expensive.
Cuisine: Continental.
Serving: D.
Credit Cards: MC, V.
Reservations: Recommended.
Special Features: View of ski slopes; seasonal outdoor dining; member, Berkshire Grown.

We turn sharply back toward Massachusetts at the Catamount ski slopes to dine in something like a chalet, with a lovely deck for warm weather. Swiss Hütte is a comfortable, friendly spot that seems to attract an older clientele—regulars, perhaps. The staff is especially well trained and gracious, good at judging just how far we want to take the discussion of wine—not far—or desserts—at length. Precision and reliability describe Swiss Hütte.

Chef Gert Alper's french onion soup was perfect, down to the cheese cooked to the ceramic pot. His chicken liver pâté was also tasty, including the small onions that accompanied it. About the salad course that followed, let it be said that we got our money's worth in paying $1.50 extra for blue cheese. The pork chops, smothered in delectable toasted-onion flakes, while resting sublimely on Granny Smith apple slices, dreamed of earlier days feasting on apple drops. The halibut, beautifully served on a bed of spinach, delicate tomatoes, and herbs, was tasty and moist—and good for weight watchers. All dishes at the Hütte are beautifully presented.

Management brought in a bard to recite the dessert menu, an extended paean to pleasure. We chose crème brûlée, done to perfection, and a *tiramisù* with the added touch of a thin layer of chocolate icing.

## NEW LEBANON, NEW YORK

### THE PILLARS CARRIAGE HOUSE RESTAURANT

518-794-8007; fax 518-766-5141.
860 Rte. 20, New Lebanon, NY 12125.

Price: Moderate.
Cuisine: Continental.
Serving: D.
Closed: Mon. and Tues.
Credit Cards: AE, MC, V.
Reservations: Recommended.

The Pillars is a Lebanon Valley institution. Owned and operated by Paul and Patti Bock since 1987, it occupies the former carriage house of the 1834 Abner Haight estate and evokes a strong sense of continuity with the past.

This is a restaurant for a special occasion. From the entrance, flanked by stone pillars, the driveway leads through landscaped grounds decorated with whimsical sculpture and small trees glowing with miniature white lights. The entry hall—with a wood floor, high ceiling, elaborate moldings, and impressive staircase—feels like an inn, which the building was in the 1970s. The many small dining rooms, floral padded-fabric wall coverings, and scent of polished wood create an ambiance of genteel civility. The decoration at Christmas is elaborate, with cheerful figures of carolers grouped in the hall and marching up the stairs.

Dinner begins with a variety of unusual breads, followed by hot popovers served with the first course. The wine cellar, well suited to the menu, stocks New York wines, varietals, and other regionals. Each dish is imaginatively presented and impeccably prepared. The menu blends continental tradition and international fusion. Oysters Mornay, tournedos charlemagne, frogs legs Provençale or fines herbs, veal oscar, and chateaubriand maison for two—carved tableside—share the page with grilled sea bass—in a sauce of miso, sake, and *nurin*, with wasabi and sweet soy—and shrimp fritters in honey and horseradish. Accompaniments, which on a recent occasion included zucchini Provençale and potato croquettes with applesauce, are served family-style.

Desserts here are a frequent subject of local legends and longings. The chef displays his special creations of spun sugar and chocolate in the entry, including a piano, molded in dark chocolate with white-chocolate keys, its top propped up to reveal a creamy, slightly tart raspberry mousse filling—something to think about while enjoying the rest of the meal.

The news that one year (in November) the Pillars was booked for the next eight weekends prompts us all to call *well* ahead for reservations.

## Breakfast & Lunch

Of the many Berkshire eateries designed to gladden morning and noon, we have selected a handful. As is appropriate, almost all are on the inexpensive end of the scale.

**Blueberries** (405 Stockbridge Rd., Gt. Barrington, MA 01230) Open from 7 AM to 2 PM except Tuesdays, Blueberries offers all-American breakfasts, including bakery treats, with plenty of cholesterol options: bacon, ham, sausage, home fries, and, of course, eggs.

**Brewhaha!** (413-664-2020; 20 Marshall St., N. Adams, MA 01247) Brewhaha! presents a menu of coffees, muffins, wraps, soups, grilled sandwiches, and desserts that is changeable to "maintain the brouhaha in Brewhaha!" At this coffee bar and café, within walking distance of MASS MoCA, small groups munch *panini* while singles sip coffee as they work their laptops. Others dash in for a take-out latte and bagel. Chef-owner Barry Garton wraps fluffy eggs, ham, cheese, and tomato in a large tortilla as his wife, Nancy, bakes fresh, tasty muffins. Member, Berkshire Grown (closed Wednesday).

**Caffe Pomo d'Oro** (413-232-4616; 6 Depot St., W. Stockbridge, MA 01266) A bit more upscale (and expensive) than others in this section, Caffe is dining proof that good things come in small packages: eight small tables in a portion of an old train station. Tough to find a seat on a Sunday morning (closed Tuesday and Wednesday in winter).

**Carol's** (413-637-8948; 8 Franklin St., Lenox, MA 01240) Serving in what was formerly an elder services center, Carol's offers scant ambiance but good and popular down-home food, especially including Carol's own homemade seven-grain and sourdough breads baked daily and offered for breakfast toast and sandwich wrappers. Breakfast is served all day, highlighted by imaginative pancake and omelet options and justly famous home fries. Lunch features big and tasty sandwiches, plus a good number of hearty vegetarian selections.

**Chef's Hat** (413-458-5120; 905 Simonds Rd., Williamstown, MA 01267; Rte. 7, N. of town center) Packed every lunch, serving breakfast early enough for hunters, the Chef's Hat has a formula that clearly works. From truck drivers to Williams College academics, it has a true, eclectic clientele. At booths, tables, and counter, Chef's Hat serves solid, reliable, inexpensive breakfast and luncheon foods to regulars and even outsiders, without making them feel conspicuous.

**Court Square Breakfast & Deli** (413-442-9896; 95 East St., Pittsfield, MA 01201) Lawyers, judges, and politicians in the county seat mostly turn up at the Court Square for breakfast. And it's a good breakfast, too: eggs, french toast, omelets—just about anything these folks need before sitting through a long day of weighty matters. They may get to be a bit more weighty, too, but satisfied.

**Elm Street Market** (413-298-3040; 4 Elm St., Stockbridge, MA 01262) Now owned by the Red Lion Inn, ESM continues to offer a classic lunch counter, much favored by Stockbridge locals. It serves a tasty chili and two good soups daily. The sandwiches are as filled as a hungry person wants them to be, including the hearty special.

**Juice n' Java** (413-243-3131, 60 Main St., Lee, MA 01238; 413-499-6130, 216 Elm St., Pittsfield, MA 01201; and 413-684-5080, 661 Main St., Dalton, MA 01226) Coffee, juices, plus salads and sandwiches to eat in or take out.

**Linda's Cafe** (413-663-8003; 178 Union St., N. Adams, MA 01247) Attentive service by Linda herself seems to bring out the best in her country cooking. Large breakfasts the way they ought to be. Warning, though: The regulars are very faithful, leaving scant room for newcomers Sunday mornings.

**Main Street Café** (413-298-5465; 40 Main St., Stockbridge, MA 01262) Theresa offers a full and diverse breakfast menu, from ham and eggs to breakfast burritos, and an extensive selection of luncheon choices. The roomy, rustic dining area with a large window onto Main Street is a pleasant setting for tasty fare. Member, Berkshire Grown.

**Martin's** (413-528-5455; 49 Railroad St., Gt. Barrington, MA 01230) Martin's is bright and light, serving breakfast from 7 AM to 3 PM, daily. Omelets are varied and outstanding. Pancakes come standard plus the daily special, such as pumpkin. For lunch, burger styles include the Berkshire Cheeseburger (mushrooms, onion, tomatoes, and peppers), sandwiches, salads, soups, and specials. Beer plus the usual. Crayons at every table so that

**Dog Houses**

JACK'S HOT DOGS
(413-664-9006; 12 Eagle St., N. Adams, MA 01247) Jack's Hot Dogs holds its historic position as the place to get hot dogs in North County, lunch or supper. Continuing a 70-year family tradition, owner Jeff Levanos and manager Maria Carmain provide a continuous flow of hot dogs, plain and fancy, with rapid-fire conversation accompanying the bustle behind the counter. Whether pressed against the wall waiting for an order to go or wedged on one of the 12 stools along the counter munching hot dogs and fries, customers are experiencing a lively bit of history.

TEO'S HOT DOGS
(413-447-9592; 1410 East St., Pittsfield, MA 01201) Teo's is an institution and a local tradition—and home, lunch or supper, to the tastiest miniature (4-inch) hot dogs smothered in chili sauce we've ever eaten. Friendly controversy rages as to who invented the sauce and when. We don't care; it is enough to know that Teo's is at its present home. We drop by for "the works" (chili sauce, chopped onions, and mustard), washing them down with Genesee Cream Ale or Rolling Rock on tap. Then we stop at the take-out window for a bagful for the crowd at home, who love 'em.

artists can illustrate on their placemats, with true talent ending up on the wall. Member, Berkshire Grown.

**Sweet Pea and Petunia** (413-528-7786; 325 Stockbridge Rd., Gt. Barrington, MA 01230) Baked goods, sandwiches, and wraps made to order; quiche; breakfast and lunch. Thursday, Friday, and Saturday, 5–10 PM, it becomes *La Cocina de Oaxaca*, serving authentic Mexican food made from scratch.

## DINING IN

From the freshest sweet corn at the farm stand, raced from purchase to pot, to the latest imported gourmet specialty appearing by candlelight on a Tanglewood picnic blanket, Berkshire supplies food that ranges from pure and simple to sophisticated and innovative. The food and beverage purveyors listed below are sources for baked goods, coffee and ice cream, produce and other farm products, picnic provisions, and health and gourmet food. The surprising array of unique food specialties created and produced in the Berkshires is listed at the end of the chapter.

### Bakeries

European pastries, New York bagels, French baguettes, and grandma's pies: Breads and baked goods from Berkshire bakeries offer the staff of life and all its variations. Many of these bakeries also provide dining areas.

**Berkshire Mountain Bakery** (413-274-3412; 367 Park St., Housatonic, MA 01236) Member, Berkshire Grown. Excellent bread, especially the sourdough.

**Cakewalk Bakery & Café** (413-243-2806; 56 Main St., Lee, MA 01238) For a gourmet sweet or a light lunch, Lee rejoices in stepping out to this beat.

**Daily Bread** (413-528-9610, 17 Railroad St., Gt. Barrington, MA 01230; and 413-298-0272, 31 Main St., Stockbridge, MA 01262; also 413-499-3441, 75 North St., Pittsfield, MA 01201) Give us our daily bread: real crusty sourdough french baguettes fresh out of the oven plus almond crescent cookies, hazelnut torte, sticky buns, and other necessities of life (closed Sunday).

**Bagels**

All bagels are not created equal; nevertheless distinctions seem to be based primarily on individual taste. Here are some of the area purveyors: **Berkshire Bagels** (413-637-1500; 18 Franklin St., Lenox, MA 01240), **Bagel Smith** (413-243-4041; 33 Park St., Lee, MA 01238), **Bagels Too** (413-499-0119; 166 North St., Pittsfield, MA 01201), and **Gt. Barrington Bagel Co.** (413-528-9055; 777 S. Main St., Gt. Barrington, MA 01230).

**Homer's Variety** (413-637-3066; 27 Housatonic St., Lenox, MA 01240) Arthur (Tony) Schwartz opened Homer's in the old Lenox Variety store in 2004 with a large machine that cranks out doughnuts the traditional way, not the fried cakes of you-know-whom.

## Coffee Specialists

**Barrington Coffee Roasting Co., Inc.** (413-528-0998; 955 S. Main St., Gt. Barrington, MA 01230) Coffees from all over the world, available at the touch of a faucet.

**Berkshire Bistro** (413-442-4226; 44 West St., Pittsfield, MA 01201) Offers coffee (Seattle's best) and light breakfast fare Monday–Friday from 7 AM; Saturday from 9 AM. Lunch is the main meal served Monday–Saturday, plus specialty sandwiches and desserts until 9 PM. Take-out service and gourmet coffees to serve at home.

**Berkshire Coffee Roasting Company** (413-528-5505; 286 Main St., Gt. Barrington, MA 01230) A top choice for exceptional coffee in an unpretentiously funky setting, conducive to the related activities of conversation, relaxing, people-watching, reading, or admiring the latest art exhibit on the walls. Choose from a selection of coffee flavors plus cappuccino, espresso, hot chocolate, cookies, muffins, and biscotti (try the chocolate-covered variety). Bags of coffee beans are for sale. The popular coffee take-out setup thoughtfully provides raised lids for preserving the foam on the cappuccino.

*Roasting their own beans and serving a loyal clientele, the Berkshire Coffee Roasting Company is a popular Main St. spot in Gt. Barrington for locals and tourists.*
Judith Monachina

**Cup and Saucer Cafe** (413-663-7543; 67 Main St., N. Adams, MA 01247) The old Appalachian Bean was a pleasant spot for a quick sip or leisurely drink; the chairs in and tables out provided for ideal people-watching. Newly reopened under new owners; we'll see.

*A sunny spot in front of the Cup and Saucer in N. Adams* Judith Monachina

**Tunnel City Coffee** (413-458-5010; 100 Spring St., Williamstown, MA 01267) A new name and a new location farther down Spring Street. More space, but nothing else has changed in Williamstown's favorite hangout. More than 60 varieties of specialty coffees are roasted on the premises here (and there are 25 varieties of loose teas). Cappuccino, latte, or espresso can be accompanied by baked goodies in a café atmosphere—or takeout.

## Farm, Orchard & Produce Markets

Fresh tomatoes right off the vine, crisp and juicy apples, enormous heads of organically grown lettuce—bounty from Berkshire fields and hills is available at area produce markets, farm and orchard outlets, seasonal farm stands, and farmer's markets, where area growers truck in their harvests to a central outdoor location 1 or 2 days a week. Homegrown is potent, as in the restaurants that have enrolled in the Berkshire Grown program. Sources of non-Berkshire produce throughout the county—for those occasions when only kiwi fruit or bok choy will do—are listed, as well.

The **Berkshire County Extension Service** (413-448-8285; 44 Bank Row, Pittsfield, MA 01201) and **Berkshire Grown** (413-528-0041; 22 Railroad St., Gt. Barrington, MA 01230) can provide up-to-date information on seasonal farm stands and farmer's markets.

**Bartlett's Orchard** (413-698-2559; Swamp Rd., Richmond, MA 01254) "Buy 'em where they grow 'em." Apple varieties throughout the season include Empire, Macs, Delicious (Red and Golden), Cortland, Northern Spy, Macoun, Ida Red, Jonagold, and more. Each variety is labeled with a description of its distinct flavor and best use. Bartlett's own cider is all natural and preservative free. The shop also stocks an array of apple products and other country-gourmet condiments and preserves; the bakery offers doughnuts, turnovers, and pies.

**Burgner's Farm Products** (413-445-4704; Dalton Division Rd., Pittsfield, MA 01201) No longer a turkey farm, alas, Burgner's at its farm stand still provides fresh produce, especially its corn in-season, plus other fruits and vegetables from local farms and farther afield. Eggs, chicken, and turkey products are a specialty.

**Chenail's Farmstand** (413-458-4910; Luce Rd., Williamstown, MA 01267) Not easy to find since corn huskers must follow Luce Road partway up to Mt. Greylock, but the corn and other vegetables Chenail's puts out are tastefully fresher than those at stands not on the farm. The farm stand should not be confused with **Chenail's Farm Fresh Products**

(413-458-4737; 903 Simonds Rd., Williamstown, MA 01267; Rte. 7), which offers corn, plants, crafts, and seasonal decorations.

**Corn Crib** (413-528-4947; Rte. 7, Sheffield, MA 01257) Farm-raised produce plus that of other local farmers—fresh fruit, veggies, plants, perennials. **Carol's Cookery** has home-made pastries, soup, and bread; **Dolls & Dwellings** offers dolls, supplies, dollhouses, miniatures, dried flowers.

**Green River Produce & Stables** (413-458-2470; 2478 Green River Rd., Williamstown, MA 01267; at the Five Corners) Lovely farm stand with attractively displayed local produce, pick-your-own strawberries, and apple trees coming along. Opportunity to pet young farm animals, and other specialties.

**Guido's Fresh Marketplace** (413-442-9909; 1020 South St., Pittsfield, MA 01201; Rte. 7; also 413-528-9255; 760 S. Main St., Gt. Barrington, MA 01230) A fine place to buy vegetables and fruit in the county, with local produce in-season and a multicultural array of standards and exotics from all over the world year-round—baby carrots, cilantro, radicchio, endive, fresh herbs, oriental vegetables, tropical fruits, mushrooms. A true marketplace ambiance with distinct Guido touches: The signs posted at the carefully arranged but overflowing produce bins are polite and informative, and help carrying bags out to the car is available. Also at Guido's Pittsfield are **Berger's Bakery and Deli**, **Masse's Seafood**, **Mazzeo's Meat Center**, and **Pasta Prima** (described in the appropriate categories below) plus all sorts of cooking supplies, health foods, earth-conscious cosmetics, gourmet items, candles, baskets, Guido's T-shirts. Also at Guido's Gt. Barrington, **Masse's** (including sushi), **Mazzeo's**, **Bella Flora** florist, and **The Kitchen Store.** Member, Berkshire Grown.

**Farmer's Markets**

Farmer's markets, where local growers set up temporarily to offer this week's freshest harvest, have sprung up throughout the county. Held from June to the first frost, for the markets' days, times, and locations check a newspaper or the extension service (413-448-8285). In **Pittsfield,** the Allendale Shopping Center hosts a market on Wednesday and Saturday mornings, and downtown Pittsfield sets up an open-air market on Columbus Avenue on Friday. In **Great Barrington,** the Farmer's Market is Saturday from 8:30 AM to 12:30 PM in the yard of the old train station, with vegetables plus local cheeses and hand-crafted products related to farming. In **Lee,** Friday 12–6, next to the post office, find fresh seafood (Vic's), herbs, veggies, flowers, and more. In **Williamstown,** on Saturday morning July through September, local farmers set up in the parking lot at the foot of Spring Street.

**Jaeschke's Brothers Farms** (413-743-3896; West Rd., Adams, MA 01220) Do-it-yourselfers can pick apples and pears at the orchard after the pro pickers have been through, or pick up apples and cider any time. The farm store is in Pittsfield, 736 Crane Ave., near Allendale (413-443-7180).

**Lakeview Orchard** (413-448-6009; 94 Old Cheshire Rd., Lanesborough, MA 01237) Grows apples and sells an array of fresh fruit, even doughnuts.

**Taft Farms** (413-528-1515, 800-528-1015; Rte. 183 & Division St., Gt. Barrington, MA 01230) Taft Farms's own delicious produce in-season, including potatoes, tomatoes, peppers, broccoli, cucumbers, and their famous just-picked sweet corn. It's all grown accord-

**Picking Your Own Fruit**

A berry- or apple-picking expedition is a great way to enjoy the Berkshire countryside, while gathering the makings for a special dessert, muffin, or pancake breakfast. Blueberries in particular are available wild throughout these hills, but few natives will reveal their special picking spots. Call ahead at the following farms and orchards for picking conditions.

Blueberries abound at **Blueberry Hill Farm,** which offers 320 acres for family picking from late July until frost (East St., 7 miles up the Mount Washington ridge; call 413-528-1479 for a recorded message about the status of picking). At **Strawberry Acres** (413-655-2672; off Rte. 8, Hinsdale) there are blueberries and Christmas trees, too. Three acres of strawberries are at **Crooked Row Farm** (413-698-2608; Dublin Rd., Richmond, MA 01254). Strawberries can also be picked at **Ioka Valley Farm** (413-738-5915; 3475 Hancock Rd., Hancock, MA 01237; Rte. 43) and **Green River Produce** (413-458-3112; 2480 Green River Rd., Williamstown, MA 01267). Apples at **Windy Hill Farm** (413-298-3217; Rte. 7, Gt. Barrington, MA 01230) are waiting to be picked in-season; there's also a garden shop and nursery (open Apr.–Oct.).

ing to the Integrated Pest Management system, which minimizes or eliminates the use of pesticides. Taft also offers fruit and vegetables from other climes, such as radicchio, kiwi fruit, or pomegranates. Pasture-raised chicken, baked goods, jams and jellies, cider, Taft salsa, and seafood from the fish market (Thurs.–Sat.); flowers and plants from the greenhouse, too.

*Taft Farms in Gt. Barrington draws customers to its fresh produce.* Judith Monachina

## Gourmet & Deli Markets & Caterers

The small grocery markets and specialty food shops and caterers of the Berkshires will please the palates of just about everyone, from the classicist to the experimenter. These markets and food specialists combine the latest culinary styles with ethnic traditions and personal service, and also magnificently maintain the celebrated Berkshire custom of the gourmet picnic. There's an old-time country store or two thrown in, too.

**Berger's Specialty Foods** (413-442-1898; 1020 South St., Pittsfield, MA 01201; at Guido's) Some assert that the best baguettes to be found in the Berkshires are here; others avoid the controversy by

**Maple Sugar and Syrup**

Maple sugaring and syrup making is a Berkshire tradition. Watch the process, or participate at the following places during the season (usually March), or just pick up some of the final product at any time of year. Williams College's **Hopkins Forest** (413-458-3080; Northwest Hill Rd., Williamstown, MA 01267) usually demonstrates sugaring off. **Sunset Farm Maple Products** (413-243-3229; Tyringham Rd., Tyringham, MA 01264) has an open sugarhouse. **Turner Farms Maple Syrup** (413-528-9956; Phillips Rd., S. Egremont, MA 01258): The sugar shack operation is open to the public; groups of 15 or more should make appointment for a tour. Other sources of local maple products include **Gould Farm's Roadside Store and Café** (413-528-2633; Rte., 23, Monterey, MA 01245); **Holiday Farm** (413-684-0444; Rte. 9, Windsor, MA 01270); and **Mill Brook Sugar House** (413-637-0474; 317 New Lenox Rd., Lenox, MA 01240).

*Turner Farms Maple Syrup in Egremont* Judith Monachina

selecting from the abundant variety of cheeses, crackers, condiments, pasta and other salads, and gourmet items from far and wide. Berger's also caters and does gift baskets.

**Berkshire Catering, Inc.** (413-488-9900; 182 Lebanon Mountain Rd., Hancock, MA 01237).

**Caffe Pomo d'Oro** (413-232-4616; 6 Depot St., W. Stockbridge, MA 01266). Gourmet provisions and a café in a sunny room in West Stockbridge's small-scale downtown. Cheese and deli items, bread, imported gourmet foods, even their own gourmet vinegar. Catering. Member, Berkshire Grown.

**Cariddi Catering** (413-663-5785; 117 Church St., N. Adams, MA 01247).

**Cheesecake Charlie's** (413-528-7790; 271 Main St., Gt. Barrington, MA 01230) Toasted Almond, Creamsicle, Piña Colada, Peppermint Patty—these are only a few of the cheesecake flavors that you can get here. Available in different sizes, and the store ships, too.

Breakfast, lunch, dinner, or a break for a cappuccino or a healthy, refreshing blast from the well-stocked juice bar. Member, Berkshire Grown.

**Chez Vous Catering** (413-298-4278; Box 1162, Stockbridge, MA 01262) Elegant food beautifully presented, including Oriental Roast Beef, Madeira Chicken, lentil-salad plates, and desserts.

**County Catering** (413-684-3725; 20 Orchard Rd., Dalton, MA 01226).

**Gorham & Norton** (413-528-0900; 278 Main St., Gt. Barrington, MA 01230) This authentically old-fashioned market has up-to-the-minute good things: groceries, gourmet items, imported cheese, an excellent wine selection.

**Helen's Place** (413-458-1360; 60 Spring St., Williamstown, MA 01267) Specialty food, restaurant, some catering, takeout—with a juice bar, fresh fish, poultry, Helen's is ready for almost anything.

**Hickory Bill's Bar-B-Que** (413-663-6665; 20 Holden St., N. Adams, MA 01247) Bill offers the best ribs for the best price in Berkshire.

**Kate Baldwin** (413-698-2885; 630 Dublin Rd., Richmond, MA 01254) Those in the know, know that Kate provides for some of the best catered events. Member, Berkshire Grown.

**La Bruschetta** (413-232-7141; 1 Harris St., W. Stockbridge, MA 01262) Offers gourmet catering.

**The Marketplace** (413-528-5775; 760 S. Main St., Gt. Barrington, MA 01230; at Guido's) Take out a complete fine restaurant meal, lunch or dinner. A variety of salads, hot and cold, fish, cold cuts, and more are also take-out ready. All explained and served up with enthusiasm and panache.

**Picnic Provisions**

The Berkshires are ideal picnic territory, whether the context for alfresco dining is a hike, an all-day canoe trip, or the prelude to an outdoor performance at the Mount or Tanglewood. The picnic may start with turkey and end with ice cream, but the picnic specialists listed here also offer many other options. And, of course, the picnickers can provision the picnic themselves at any of the markets and gourmet shops described above.

**Cheesecake Charlie's** makes a special New England Clambake Picnic for Two, which includes lobster, mussels, clams, shrimp, corn on the cob, melon, and bread. **Moore Fine Food** (see under "Gourmet & Deli Markets & Caterers") will provide an unforgettable picnic. **Perfect Picnics** (413-637-315; 72 Church St., Lenox, MA 01240) offers gourmet dishes and will deliver to Tanglewood. **The Marketplace** (see under "Gourmet & Deli Markets & Caterers") will customize a gourmet picnic, with 24 hours' notice. **The Red Lion Inn** (413-298-5545; 30 Main St., Stockbridge, MA 01262) offers pick-up picnics, too. **Samel's Deli and Catering** (see under "Gourmet & Deli Markets & Caterers") has boxed meals ideal for portable dining. **The Store at Five Corners** (see under "Gourmet & Deli Markets & Caterers") will pack a picnic from its deli.

**Monterey General Store** (413-528-4437; Rte. 23, Monterey, MA 01245) Not necessarily a gourmet shop but an established oasis in southeastern Berkshire, this old-time general store stocks fresh vegetables, cold cuts, preserves, and locally made maple syrup. It offers fresh-baked goods daily. With a lunch room in the back and a front porch for people-watching, this spot is a perennial gathering place.

**Moore Fine Food** (413-637-0336; P.O. Box 85,Lenox, MA 01240; also 413-528-4500; 148 Main St., Gt. Barrington, MA 01230) Some say the best in the county for catering; she also does elegant takeout. Member, Berkshire Grown.

**Samel's Deli and Catering** (413-442-5927; 115 Elm St., Pittsfield, MA 01201) Bread, chicken, wine, cheese, pepperoni, legendary pickles, and much more in the deli and gourmet line. It delivers in the Pittsfield area.

**Store at Five Corners** (413-458-3176; 6 New Ashford Rd., Williamstown, MA 01267; jct. Rtes. 7 and 43) Upscale country store, with well-chosen wine and beer selections, juices and waters, imported and domestic cheeses, fresh-baked breads and treats. Also homemade fudge, picnic and gift baskets, gifts, fresh produce, deli items such as sandwiches and salads, fancy preserves, gourmet coffee and ice cream, and various international offerings. Breakfast and light fare on the deck or inside. It will ship and cater.

**A Place for Pasta**

**Pasta Prima** (413-499-7478, 1020 South St., Pittsfield, MA 01201; at Guido's; also 413-528-3755, 740 Main St., Gt. Barrington, MA 01230) Fresh pasta made on the premises. Cut to order or purchased in sheets for cutting at home. Selection of other pastas of the dried variety, sauces, and parmesan and romano cheese for grating.

Other area restaurants or markets with catering services include the **Castle Street Cafe**, **Harry's Supermarket**, **Michael's Restaurant**, **The Silver Screen**, and the **Sweet Basil Grille.**

## Health/Natural-Food Stores

**Berkshire Co-op Market** (413-528-9697; 37 Rosseter St., Gt. Barrington, MA 01230) Open to the public, but co-op members get a 2 percent discount. Ingredients for healthy eating and living, including organic produce, much of it grown locally, and baked goods, macrobiotic foods, bulk pasta, beans, grains, and herbal remedies. Member, Berkshire Grown.

**Clearwater Natural Foods** (413-637-2721; 11 Housatonic St., Lenox, MA 01240) Fresh bread, sandwiches, a wide range of groceries, including macrobiotic and allergy-free selections; organic produce, non-dairy and dairy ice cream. Look for monthly specials. Member, Berkshire Grown.

**Locke, Stock, and Barrel** (413-528-0800; 265 Stockbridge Rd., Gt. Barrington, MA 01230; Rte. 7) Where health food meets gourmet food, artfully and abundantly arranged: a large selection of cheeses, plus cold cuts, fish, honey, teas, yogurt, juices, fresh tofu, flours, grains, rices, and soy and tamari sauces. There's a wall-length case of frozen health foods, and vitamins, mineral supplements, and natural cosmetics.

**Sprout House** (413-528-5200; 284 Main St., P.O. Box 1100, Gt. Barrington, MA 01230) Steve Meyerowitz, the "Sproutman," has sprouting kits and books, indoor vegetable kits, and organic seeds; via mail order and wholesale.

**Sunflowers Natural Foods** (413-243-1775; 42 Park St., Lee, MA 01238) Organic and natural items include bread, coffee, fat-free snacks, and natural personal-care items; products are available here that are wheat-free, gluten-free, sugar-free. Vitamins, books, health video club.

**Wild Oats Community Market** (413-458-8060; 320 Main St., Williamstown, MA 01267; Rte. 2) Bigger and better quarters, more variety; the same organic and local produce, whole foods, gourmet and specialty items, vitamins, and natural cosmetics, along with food and health books and magazines. Members get discounts, but the public is welcome. Member, Berkshire Grown.

## Ice Cream

Berkshire-made ice cream, plus that of those two guys from Vermont, can be found in strategic locations throughout the county. Reliably delicious, Massachusetts' own **Friendly's** ice cream, in cones, containers, and sundaes, is also available at one of the many Friendly's restaurants in the county.

**Ben & Jerry's Ice Cream** (413-448-2250; 179 South St., Pittsfield, MA 01201; also 50 Water St., Lee, MA 01238) Vermont's famous ice cream, in cones, cakes, sundaes, and containers; also frozen yogurt. Worth standing in line for.

**Berkshire Ice Cream** (413-232-4111; 4 Albany Rd., W. Stockbridge, MA 01266) High Lawn Jersey cows produce the county's own premium ice cream, sold in specialty shops.

**Pizza**

Pizza cravings will be easily satisfied anywhere throughout Berkshire County, but all pizzas are not created equal. Top choices or choices of toppings) include the following:

**Babalouie's Sour Dough Pizza Co.** (413-528-8100; 286 Main St., Gt. Barrington, MA 01230) offers Italian-style pizzas (thin-crust, organic sourdough, or wheat-free crusts), cooked in a wood-fired oven with super fresh toppings and a full menu, too (member, Berkshire Grown). **The Village Oven** (413-232-7269; 30 Main St., W. Stockbridge, MA 01266) and **La Bruschetta** (413-232-7141; 1 Harris St., W. Stockbridge, MA 01266) make certain residents along the New York border get their share of pizzas, subs, pasta, *panini*, salad, and homemade desserts. **Manhattan Pizza Company** (413-528-2550; 490 Main St., Gt. Barrington, MA 01230) Pizzas here are big, flat, oozing, and delicious. They reheat well and are available by the slice. The **East Side Café** (413-447-9405; 278 Newell St., Pittsfield, MA 01201), essentially a bar, makes pizza only on Thursday–Sunday evenings from 5 PM on; it's small, thin, crisp, and tasty. **Elizabeth's Borderland Café** on East St., Pittsfield (see under "Restaurants in Central County") offers signature "white pies" with abundant toppings and fresh, innovative ingredients. The unbeatable taste of a wood-fired brick-oven pizza is somewhere **Over the Rainbow** (413-445-6836; 109 First St., Pittsfield, MA 01201); generous toppings and imaginative combinations include chicken pesto, spinach and broccoli, or the Primavera—eggplant, black olives, broccoli, and more. Take out or eat in and watch the flames in the oven. **Pasta's Wood-Fired Pizzas** (413-499-5562; 660 Cheshire Rd., Lanesborough, MA 01237) likewise offers the wood-fired flavor. **Hot Tomatoes** (413-458-2722; 100 Water St., Williamstown, MA 01267) may be the best in town for those who prefer the thinner crust.

**Jilly's Ice Cream** (413-499-2961; 119 Elm St., Pittsfield, MA 01201) We can enjoy our ice cream, working it off at Jilly's miniature golf.

**Lickety Split** (413-458-1818; 69 Spring St., Williamstown, MA 01267) With Herrell's Famous Ice Cream from Northampton, Lickety Split is a great day or evening stop; hot soup in winter. Also serves light fare at MASS MoCA. Member, Berkshire Grown.

**Rita Marie's Ice Cream** (413-448-2742; 685 S. Main St., Lanesborough, MA 01237) Rita Marie's is the colorful shack across from the north end of Pontoosuc Lake.

**South County (SoCo)** (413-637-0371, 38 Housatonic St., Lenox, MA 01240; also 413-528-6645, 5 Railroad St., Gt. Barrington, MA 01230) The same Tony Schwartz who brings us

**Berkshire Food and Beverage Specialties**

Nurtured by Berkshire soil or created by Berkshire entrepreneurs, this select group of food and beverage specialties includes condiments and sauces, breads and other baked goods, sweets and sweeteners, and dairy products, spring water, and soft drinks. Some are world famous; all are locally treasured. There's no individual retail outlet for many of these products, but look for them at **Guido's, Bartlett's, The Store at Five Corners,** and most other gourmet shops, farm and produce markets, and many supermarkets.

BEVERAGES

**Berkshire Mountain Spring Water** (413-229-2086, 800-244-3212; 214 Norfolk Rd., Southfield, MA 01259) Bottled daily at the spring, it's sodium-, bacteria-, and additive-free. Or try **Sand Springs** Spring Water Co. (413-458-3412; 160 Sand Springs Rd., Williamstown, MA 01267) The American Indians liked it, why not you? Have either delivered, or buy it in supermarkets. **Gilly's Hot Vanilla** (413-637-1515) was created by Lenox resident Joanne Deutch as a hot-chocolate alternative; just add hot water to the vanilla-flavored powder. And there's no caffeine. Buy it by the bag locally, or have a cup at many local eateries. Squeeze beverages originated in Adams and are still available here.

BREAD & BAKED GOODS

Look for some goods made locally but not sold retail, such as the products of **Berkshire Mountain Bakery**. Its traditional sourdough breads should be sought out at area natural-food stores. The peasant bread and the raisin bread are particular favorites; try their crisp biscotti, too. **Pittsfield Rye Bakery** produces the alternative to wheat. **Nejaime's** lavasch is deliciously addictive: a Mideast specialty, lavasch is a crusty, crackerlike bread. Nejaime's is made with a variety of flavorings, all good.

CONDIMENTS & SAUCES

**Berkshire Berries** (413-23-5779; Rte. 20, Becket, MA 01223), purveyors of jam, jelly, syrup, and honey, sold at numerous local and regional locations, including New York City's Greenmarket.

DAIRY PRODUCTS

Monterey Chèvre is made from the milk of goats at **Rawson Brook Farm** (413-528-2138; Box 426, New Marlboro Rd., Monterey, MA 01245) and from acid starter from France. It's sold deliciously

Homer's doughnuts purchased the regional assets of Bev's Homemade Ice Cream in the spring of 2005 and continues to make it daily on the same premises. Traditional to exotic flavors; ice-cream sodas and sundaes, malteds, and egg creams, plus coffee and baked treats.

**Sugar Llama** (413-662-2990; 15 Eagle St., N. Adams, 01247) SoCo ice cream (see page 126), candies, sandwiches; open 8 AM–10 PM except Sundays 9–5.

**Utter Delight** (413-644-9100; 684 Main St., Gt. Barrington, MA 01230) Featuring several brands.

plain, flavored with chives and garlic, or with a particularly tasty combination of wild thyme and olive oil. It is sold younger than imported chèvre and has a milder, more delicate flavor. Milk (with the cream on top) and light or heavy cream from **High Lawn Farm** (413-242-0672) is available at many grocery stores or can still be delivered to the door. The Jersey cows on the farm on Lenox Road in Lee are the source. Berkshire Blue Cheese has gained a national reputation for cheese made from High Lawn's herd.

DESSERTS, SWEETS & SWEETENERS

**Charles H. Baldwin & Sons** (413-232-7785; Depot St., W. Stockbridge, MA 01266) offers "since 1888, the best in vanilla." This manufacturer of flavoring extracts and maple table syrup uses only the best—the Bourbon Vanilla Bean from Madagascar—for their Pure Vanilla Extract. It's made in a copper percolator (the "still") and aged in 100-year-old oak barrels, which can be seen in the small and fascinating retail outlet in a former carriage shop. Inhale essence of vanilla and admire the ranks of extract bottles—including lemon, orange, mint, and more—on the old-fashioned counter. Also available is **Baldwin's Table Syrup,** a blend of maple and cane sugar syrup from a recipe created in the 1920s.

**Catherine's Chocolate Shop** (413-528-2510; 260 Stockbridge Rd., Gt. Barrington, MA 01230) makes candies on the premises from century-old family recipes. These smooth and flavorful concoctions include chocolate truffles, a variety of hand-dipped candies, fudges, brittles, and barks. The nonpareils are, in fact, unequaled. Buy 'em by the piece, the pound, or in a boxed gift assortment. A strong contender in chocolate is **Chocolate Springs Cafe,** in the Lenox Shops (413-637-9820; 55 Pittsfield–Lenox Rd., Lenox 01240). Chocolate from France, with treats made in-house—plus other desserts too tasty to mention. **David Rawson's honey** from Richmond is pretty close to nectar for the gods, who get it in 1-pound jars at Bartlett's Orchards (see "Farm, Orchard & Produce Markets").

AND . . .

The **Delftree Corporation** (413-664-4907; 234 Union St., N. Adams, MA 01247) grows shiitake mushrooms on hardwood logs in a 19th-century textile mill building in North Adams. Shipped all over the world, they are available here.

## Meat, Fish, and Poultry Markets

**Burgner's Poultry Farm** (413-445-4704; Dalton Division Rd., Pittsfield, MA 01201) Burgner's sells turkeys and chickens; order them uncooked, roasted, or stuffed and roasted, in all sizes. Burgner's turkey potpies are local favorites. The farm store also carries eggs, produce, and store-made bakery items and fresh homemade potato salad and coleslaw.

**Masse's Seafood** (413-528-4913, 760 S. Main St., Gt. Barrington, MA 01230; also 413-499-3474, 1020 South St., Pittsfield, MA 01201; at Guido's) A variety of fresh and frozen former denizens of the sea.

**Mazzeo's Meat Center** (413-528-4488, 760 S. Main St., Gt. Barrington, MA 01230; also 413-442-2222, 1020 South St., Pittsfield, MA 01201). Meat concessions at both Guido's. Carnivores need seek no further.

**Otis Poultry Farm** (413-269-4438; Rte. 8, Otis, MA 01253) "custom laid eggs" says the sign—eggs and chickens, geese, ducks, and capons, too. Their excellent frozen chicken and turkey pies are a staple of well-stocked Berkshire refrigerators. Various homemade goodies join sheepskin gloves and slippers and so forth in the country store.

Additional options for meat and fish include **Harry's Supermarket** (413-442-9084, 290 Wahconah St., Pittsfield, MA 01201; also 413-443-7247, 37 Elm St., Pittsfield, MA 01201), **Vic's Seafood** at the Lee Farmer's Market, Fri. 12–6. **The Other Brother Darryl's** (413-269-4235, 800-6FLOPPIN; Rte. 8, Otis, MA 01253) and **Other Brother Darryl's Too** (413-528-8088; 760 S. Main St., Gt. Barrington, MA 01230; at Guido's). They offer wholesale seafood to retail customers and promise "still-floppin'" freshness.

## Wine & Liquor

**Domaney's Discount Liquors** (413-528-0024; 66 Main St., Gt. Barrington, MA 01230) An excellent selection, and Ed is knowledgeable.

**Gorham and Norton** (413-528-0900; 278 Main St., Gt. Barrington, MA 01230)

**Liquor Mart** (413-663-3910; State Rd., Adams, MA 01220).

**Liquors Inc.** (413-443-4466; 485 Dalton Ave., Pittsfield, MA 01201) The biggest and best for discount wine, beer, and spirits.

**Locke, Stock & Barrel** (413-528-0800; 265 Stockbridge Rd., Gt. Barrington, MA 01230; Rte. 7) A great wine selection.

**Nejaime's Wine & Liquor** (413-448-2274; 598 Pittsfield–Lenox Rd., Lenox, MA 01240), **Nejaime's Stockbridge Wine Cellar** (413-298-3454; 3 Elm St., Stockbridge, MA 01262), and **Lenox Wine Cellar and Cheese Shop** (413-637-2221; 33 Church St, Lenox, MA 01240.) In addition to wines, beers, and spirits, they offer gourmet and deli items, and helpful, knowledgeable assistance.

**Queensborough Spirits** (413-232-8522; 20 Main St., W. Stockbridge) Beer, liquor, and wine.

**South Egremont Spirit Shoppe** (413-528-1490; 71 Main St., S. Egremont, MA 01258; Rte. 23) "The wine shop of The Berkshires." Also a good selection of cigars.

**Spirit Shop and Deli Station** (413-458-3704; 280 Cole Ave., Williamstown, MA 01267) Beer, liquor, wine, and a deli.

**Trotta's Discount Liquors** (529-3490; 490 Main St., Gt. Barrington, MA 01230; near jct. Rtes. 7 and 23) Beer, liquor, wine, and fine cigars.

**Val's Pipe & Package Store** (413-743-0962; 5 Columbia St., Adams, MA 01220) Beer, liquor, wine, groceries, milk, and lottery tickets.

**West's Package & Variety Stores** (413-663-6081; 367 State Rd., N. Adams, MA 01247) and **West's Wines & Spirits** (513-458-5948; 52 Spring St., Williamstown, MA 01267) Bob West is an authority on wine.

**Whitney's Beverage Shop** (413-663-8881; 144 American Legion Dr., N. Adams, MA 01247).

*Two young women await one of the biggest treats in a Berkshire summer: Inside Out at Jacob's Pillow.*

Judith Monachina

# 5

# Arts & Pleasures

## *What to See, What to Do*

**Glorifying God's grandeur** by gracefully combining Art and Nature—this was the goal of the Stockbridge Laurel Hill Society, as expressed in 1853. Such thinking joined a new appreciation of the natural setting with a well-developed Berkshire cultural awareness that had roots in colonial times when the earliest schools, churches, and newspapers were the centers of cultural activity. By the early 19th century, artists came to Berkshire to absorb the beauty and teach its appreciation. By the midcentury, the tradition of a Berkshire cultural bounty had taken hold.

The county's artistic abundance is out of proportion to its size and population. In music, dance, theater, and other art forms, Berkshire has long had a cultural calendar of astonishing excellence and variety—especially for a mountainous area once thought of as remote. There are good reasons for this legacy. Summers in the crowded eastern cities were not only unpleasant but frequently unhealthy. Improvements in transportation opened this area, while other scenic spots some might now find more dramatic were still inaccessible. By the mid-1800s a few families of taste, talent, and money were setting the tone of cultural sophistication still found here today.

Of the intelligentsia that developed around Stockbridge and Lenox in the early 19th century, no single family was more dynamic than the convivial and civic-minded Sedgwicks of Stockbridge. Novelist Catherine Sedgwick shares honors with poet William Cullen Bryant as Berkshire's—and America's—first native-born published writers in their fields. The Sedgwick house and family still grace Stockbridge today.

Other writers like Herman Melville and Nathaniel Hawthorne cross-fertilized their fiction in Berkshire in the 1850s, along with the popular Oliver Wendell Holmes, the doctor-poet who returned to his roots by summering in Pittsfield. Henry David Thoreau beheld a transcendental sunrise on the summit of Mount Greylock. Edith Wharton moved here, creating the kind of opulent European lifestyle that she skewered in her fiction. Williams College was becoming a scientific and literary center. The list of famous artistic residents is lengthy and impressive. Our bibliography (in chapter 9, "Information") cites several engaging books that tell the story.

When the Berkshires became the "inland Newport" during the late-19th-century Gilded Age, culture rode into Berkshire along with big money: architectural indulgences, furnishings and paintings, musical instruments and people to play them, chefs importing their foreign cuisines, and landscape gardeners. We are the beneficiaries of much

*Public sculpture in front of the Congregational Church, Gt. Barrington* Judith Monachina

inherited culture. Many of the family estates here have become cultural centers, such as Tanglewood for music and the Mount for literature. And yet as if to remind us that beauty need not be ornate or expensive, the Shaker Village at Hancock is also a Berkshire cultural legacy of remarkable value and vitality.

Furthermore, Berkshire families have been patrons of the arts and the landscape. For example; the Crane family of the Crane Paper Company of Dalton started the Berkshire Museum; Francine and Sterling Clark created the Art Institute in Williamstown; and the Tappan family gave Tanglewood to the Boston Symphony Orchestra. We owe them our thanks.

Some of the many of the artists drawn to the Berkshires lived here seasonally, like Wharton; others, year-round like Norman Rockwell. Thousands more have come just to perform or exhibit. Berkshire has left its mark on each. When asked what the Berkshires and Tanglewood mean to him, Seiji Ozawa, former music director of the Boston Symphony Orchestra, replied: "Tanglewood has an absolutely special connotation for me. It was the first place I ever saw in America, since I came to Tanglewood as a student in 1960 at the invitation of Charles Munch. For me and the orchestra, Tanglewood represents an opportunity to appreciate both the beauty of the Berkshires and of the music we make here."

Art combines with nature, from the fine woodwork in colonist John Ashley's study at Ashley Falls to the nation's four founding documents in Williams College's Chapin Library; from dioramas and an Egyptian mummy at the Berkshire Museum in Pittsfield to beautiful flowers and shrubs at the Berkshire Botanical Garden in Stockbridge. In performance halls, museums, libraries, theaters, nightclubs, and historic homes, Berkshire is rich in art and the pleasures it brings.

The following descriptions provide many ideas of where to go and what to do in Berkshire, but they cannot say what's currently playing or showing. Tanglewood issues its summer schedule around March 15; other arts organizations soon follow. For the larger seasonal schedules, such Jacob's Pillow, the museums, theaters, and other concert series, it's best to write, call, or check their Web sites for information. (We provide contact information.) That information helps to customize a personal Berkshire festival. Sold-out performances are not uncommon. Area newspapers provide information on cultural events as they happen. Especially comprehensive is the *Berkshire Eagle's* Thursday magazine supplement, *Berkshires Week*.

## Architecture

Those who enjoy roaming through New England in search of handsome buildings will find Berkshire County an inexhaustible delight. They will find styles popular in North America from colonial times to the present. Few counties anywhere can claim this much architectural variety.

Berkshire is justly famous for the scores of mansions built during the opulent Gilded Age. Under "Historic Homes" in this chapter, in chapters 3, "*Lodging*," and chapter 4,"*Dining*," and elsewhere in this book, we describe several of the best-surviving examples of these great "cottages," as they were called. Yet the saga of the sumptuous cottages isn't half the Berkshire building history.

Humbler examples include one-room schoolhouses or steepled churches, icons of America's simpler past. Still performing as designed in some Berkshire towns, adapted to alternative uses in others, these white-clapboard structures are often handsome and always charming. Some of the best are the ones in Alford, Lenox, Lee, New Ashford, and Washington. A beautiful circa-1800 stone church can be found in Lanesborough.

Many Berkshire villages seem architectural set pieces, so artfully coordinated are their building styles and locations. The villages of Alford, New Marlborough, Stockbridge, and Williamstown have this look. Conspicuously absent is neon and plastic commercial clutter. Feelings of space and grace predominate. Yet also in each town arises the clear sense of the heart of a community where religion (churches), education (schoolhouses), government (town hall), domestic life (private homes), and the honor due the dead (cemeteries) all naturally fit together. People who live in cities or suburbs will find the centralization of Berkshire villages intriguing as well as architecturally beautiful. New Marlborough bears all of this out with its archetypal village green surrounded in part by the Colonial-style **Old Inn on the Green** (1760), a fine Federal-style house (1824), and the Greek Revival–style **Congregational Church** (1839).

Farms have long formed the Berkshire landscape. Almost any country road leads past splendid examples of old farmhouses with numerous outbuildings. Some of the barns date to times earlier than the homes. Good rides for farm viewing include Routes 57 (New Marlborough); 41 (south from South Egremont or north from West Stockbridge); and 7 (north from Lanesborough). Dramatic Tudor-style barns from the Gilded Age are still in use at High Lawn Farm (on Summer Street off Route 7, Lee), but the most famous barn in Berkshire is the round stone barn at **Hancock Shaker Village,** described under "Museums" in this chapter.

### South County

South County towns have many impressive buildings, among them several interesting industrial sites. Rising above them all is the Fox Paper Company's **Rising Paper Mill**

*The Congregational Church, Lee, boasts the tallest wooden steeple in the country.* Judith Monachina (circa 1875; Route 183 in Housatonic), with its handsome mansard slate roof. A similar mansard slate roof style is pushed to artful extremes on campus buildings at **Simon's Rock College of Bard** (on Alford Road, Great Barrington).

The village of Lee boasts the tallest wood-framed steeple in the county atop its **Congregational Church**. In South Lee **Merrill Tavern** (Route 102), a Federal-period building still functioning as an inn, is exquisitely maintained by the Society for the Preservation of New England Antiquities.

Sheffield, architecturally lovely and filled with antiques shops, appropriately prided itself on having preserved the **oldest covered bridge in Massachusetts** (1837) until it burned in 1994. The Massachusetts Highway Department has erected a duplicate. Otis, a Berkshire hill town, is graced with **St. Paul's Church** (1829), a fine example of the Gothic Revival style.

Stockbridge dazzles. Architect Stanford White's turn-of-the-20th-century work appears in impressive diversity here: A casino (now the **Berkshire Theatre Festival**; at Route 102 and Yale Hill Road); a mansion (**Naumkeag**; on Prospect Hill Road); a former railroad station on Route 7 south of the village; and a church (**St. Paul's Episcopal**; center of town). Two other Stockbridge churches well worth a look are the redbrick **Congregational Church** (Main Street, next to Town Hall) and the chapel at the **Marian Fathers Seminary** (on Eden Hill, off Prospect Hill Road). Whereas the interior of the Congregational Church has a powerful beauty in its plainness, the Marian fathers' chapel is beautiful for its finely crafted stone, woodwork, painting, and fabrics—much of it done by transplanted European artists. We describe the **Mission House**, a Colonial "Historic Home," later in this chapter.

Three outlying sites in Stockbridge are worth a drive. The district originally called Curtisville, now known as Interlaken (Route 183, north of Route 102), boasts several strikingly pretty 18th- and 19th-century homes and a remarkable former tavern-inn, as well as **Citizens Hall**, with its Victorian-period, Second Empire–style exterior details. Another building of note in rural Stockbridge is at Tanglewood's Lions' Gate (Hawthorne Street, off Route 183), where the replica of Nathaniel Hawthorne's "**Little Red House**" overlooks Stockbridge Bowl and the distant mountains. The estate known as **Linwood** has opened to the public as the site of the **Norman Rockwell Museum**, a Robert A. M. Stern–designed New England town hall upscale. Charles E. Butler's unpolished marble cottage, **Linwood** (1859), remains the architectural highlight of this delightful Berkshire hilltop.

Finally, in South County, a ride out on the Tyringham Road (off Route 102, south of Lee) and then upland on Jerusalem Road will lead to "**Jerusalem**," the remnants of a Shaker settlement dating from 1792. Five buildings remain, none open. Jerusalem Road begins in tiny Tyringham Village. Along the Tyringham Valley Road is the **Gingerbread House**, a thatched-roof English cottage built by sculptor Henry Kitson in the late 1800s and known currently as **Santarella**; see "Galleries" in this chapter.

### Central County

Central County abounds with notable architecture. In Dalton, a ride along Main Street (Route 9) provides views of the **Crane Paper Mills** (the Old Stone Mill, dating to 1844, is open as a museum in season) and several Crane family estates. In addition to other fine papers, Crane manufactures U.S. currency paper in these venerable mills. In 1816 Zenas Crane, the company founder, built a dignified Federal-style house, which still stands. There are also three 19th-century Richardsonian Romanesque churches on Main Street in Dalton proper.

*The wide porch of the Curtis Hotel—now used for elderly housing—recalls a more leisurely era.* Judith Monachina

In the hill town of Hinsdale on Route 8 are some architectural surprises, vestiges of more prosperous, populous times when various mills were alive and well in the Berkshire highlands. The oldest (1798) Federal-style church in Berkshire is here. A Greek Revival town hall was built in 1848. The public library is in the high Gothic–style, designed in 1868 by architect Leopold Eidlitz, who did St. George's Church in New York City and the New York State Capitol in Albany.

*The simplicity of Shaker design draws thousands each year to the Hancock Shaker Village.* Judith Monachina

The only stone early–Gothic Revival church in the county is **St. Luke's Chapel**, in Lanesborough (on Route 7). Like many other buildings cited in this book, St. Luke's is on the National Register of Historic Places.

Equal to any other village in Berkshire as an impressive architectural set piece is stately Lenox—especially the historic center of the village, including the **Lenox Academy** (Federal style, 1803), the irresistibly photogenic **Church on the Hill** (1805), and the **Lenox Library** (1815; see "Libraries" in this chapter). All three buildings are on Main Street (Route 7A). The **Curtis Hotel**, dominating the center of town, has been restored and converted to an apartment complex. From the Gilded Age to recent times, the Curtis was one of Berkshire's most fashionable addresses for travelers. Not far from Lenox village, on Route 20 heading toward Lee, is **Cranwell**, once a Jesuit-run school, now a resort, golf club, and condominium complex (see chapter 3, "Lodging").

Pittsfield's architectural record is distinguished although problematic. Preservation and restoration nowadays receive good attention, as a walk around Park Square reveals. Several new buildings integrate quite well with the ornate elegance of the old Venetian Gothic Athenaeum, the two churches, the bank buildings, and the courthouse—all dating from the 19th century.

The former *Berkshire Eagle* newspaper building (on Eagle Street, off North Street) is a fine example of the art deco style, set on a triangle like a miniature of Chicago's Flatiron Building. Another important business structure in Pittsfield is the General Electric Plastics House, a handsome and interesting experimental display house in the Plastics Division's world headquarters complex. The address? "Plastics Avenue," of course (between Merrill Road and Dalton Avenue).

### North County

North County provides stark contrasts in architecture and variety in the stories that buildings tell about social history. The cities of Adams and North Adams owe their expansion to past industrial times. However, revitalization proceeds, the most spectacular being the conversion of the idle Sprague Electric plant (formerly textile mills) into a mammoth museum of contemporary art (visual and performing), **MASS MoCA**. Although urban renewal hit the downtowns unkindly, Adams and North Adams have recently beautified their main streets. In North Adams, **Western Gateway Heritage State Park** celebrates a 19th-century architectural and engineering wonder, the **Hoosac Tunnel**. (See "Museums" in this chapter.) The spires of North Adams's many churches are a pretty sight as one descends into the city from the east on Route 2. In Adams, suffragettes will want to pass the **Susan B. Anthony Birthplace** (1814; a private home near the corner of East Road and

East Street) and the **Quaker Meeting House** (1782; near the end of Friends Street), another National Register of Historic Places building.

Williamstown contains homes from Colonial to contemporary, a college that has been adding buildings nearly since the country began, quaint shops, and two masterfully designed art museums (the **Clark Art Institute** and the **Williams College Museum of Art**, both described under "Museums"). **West College** (1790), **Griffin Hall** (1828), the oldest (1838) extant college observatory in the U.S., and the 1802 **President's House** at Williams College are alone worth touring the campus (via a large map in front of the main administration building, Hopkins Hall, or guided by brochure maps available at the information booth). The much photographed **First Congregational Church** (1869) is the replica of a Colonial one that burned in Old Lyme, Connecticut. The **Williamstown Public Library**, which houses the local history museum, faces the **1753 House**, built with authentic methods and materials for the town's bicentennial on Field Park.

In Berkshire, a proud history still stands.

## Arts Classes

The world is turning interactive. Art in Berkshire is part of the trend. Not content with simply looking at fine art and craftswork in the multitude of galleries and museums in the county, many residents and visitors want to create art, as well. Opportunities grow apace. The Berkshire Museum, the Norman Rockwell Museum, the YMCAs (call for their schedules), and several local institutions have made art education the mainspring of their business.

### IS183—ART SCHOOL OF THE BERKSHIRES

413-298-5252.
www.is183.org.
13 Willard Hill Rd., P.O. Box 1400, Stockbridge, MA 01262.

Founded in 1992 by eminent hand weaver and visionary Sam Kasten, IS183 has developed into a full-scale, studio-based year-round school of arts. Located in historic Citizens Hall, on Hill Road just off Route 183 (via Trask Lane) in Interlaken Village, it has something for everyone with artistic inclinations. IS183 offers programs for children, teens, and adults, including single classes, semester courses, half-day to weekend workshops, and lectures in painting, drawing, ceramics, printmaking, sculpture, metal jewelry, and textiles of several sorts. Faculty members are drawn from the local artistic community or are visiting teachers and lecturers. On Lights & Socks Day in December, faculty art can be previewed for sale; continental breakfast and champagne are served, and discounts are offered for enrollment in winter programs.

## Cinema

### IMAGES CINEMA

413-458-5612.
www.imagescinema.org.
50 Spring St., P.O. Box 283, Williamstown, MA 01267.

Eclectic, exciting films—independent first-run flicks as well as the best from camp to classic—are the order of the evening in the only year-round, single-screen, independent movie house in the county. Its survival as North County's most dynamic movie house is a wonder. In 1989, when it was threatened with closure, local actor and late resident Christopher Reeve pulled together support to keep the theater open. In 1998, it became a nonprofit organization under the leadership of energetic managers and support from the community at large. Today, Images lives on in refurbished modernity. Memberships, printed or e-mailed schedules, and special programs.

### LITTLE CINEMA

413-443-7171.
www.berkshiremuseum.org.
At the Berkshire Museum.
39 South St., Pittsfield, MA 01201.

This is *the* great little film program in Berkshire, featuring state-of-the-art projection and sound. Films are shown in the summer, with special showings during the year. Fine independent and foreign films, downstairs in the Berkshire Museum auditorium.

### THE WILLIAMSTOWN FILM FESTIVAL

Cinephiles should keep their eyes open for the Williamstown Film Festival, begun in a preliminary way in June 1999, now growing and appearing in October. Each festival has honored one of Hollywood's more honorable. Call 413-458-2700.

## Other Cinema

South County

**Simon's Rock College of Bard** (413-528-0771; www.simons-rock.edu; 84 Alford Rd., Gt. Barrington, MA 01230). Occasional classics and fun films, open to the public.

**Triplex Cinema** (413-528-8885 info; 413-528-8886 office; fax 413-528-8889; www.thetriplex.com; 70 Railroad St., Gt. Barrington; mail: P.O. Box 508, S. Egremont, MA 01258) An art venue as well as cinema with surround sound.

Central County

**Hoyts Berkshire Cinema 10** (413-499-2558; Berkshire Mall, 123 Old State Rd., Lanesborough, MA 01237; off Rte. 8) Dolby stereo, action, adventure, drama, comedy, popcorn.

North County

**Hoyts North Adams Cinemas** (413-663-5873; Curran Hwy., N. Adams, MA 01247; Rte. 8) North County's multiplex, with six screens.

Outside the County

**Crandell Theatre** (518-392-3331; www.crandelltheatre.com; 46–48 Main St., Chatham, NY 12037) One screen in a pleasant, old-fashioned movie house showing first-run films with the cheapest popcorn around.

**Hollywood Drive-In** (518-283-4425; www.hollywooddrivein.com; Averill Park Rd., Averill Park, NY 12018; Rte. 66) Berkshire families are increasingly making the journey over the mountains to this traditional drive-in for an inexpensive evening's entertainment.

**Movie House** (518-7893408; Main St., Millerton, NY 12546) The best first-run films, three screens, espresso, and other refinements.

## DANCE

### ALBANY BERKSHIRE BALLET

413-445-5382, 800-476-6964.
www.berkshireballet.org.
Mail: 51 North St., Pittsfield, MA 01201.
Performances at various theaters.
Season: Year-round.
Tickets: Discounts for seniors, children, and groups.

The Albany Berkshire Ballet includes a school and professional performances, given in numerous sites in New York State, Berkshire County, and the Northeast. Lavish productions of *Cinderella* and *Giselle* have highlighted past seasons. Fall and winter concerts are capped with the traditional *Nutcracker,* staged at Berkshire Community College and throughout New England in November and December.

### JACOB'S PILLOW DANCE FESTIVAL

413-243-9919.
www.jacobspillow.org.
358 George Carter Rd., Becket, MA 01223.
Off Rte. 20, 8 mi. E. of Lee.
Season: Summer; Tues.–Sun.
Tickets: Variety of prices for different events.
Special Features: Gift shop; snack bar.

Founded in 1933, Jacob's Pillow is America's first and oldest summer dance festival. The Pillow keeps step with the times, presenting the best in classical, modern, postmodern, jazz, and ethnic dance. Its schedule of offerings creates a Who's Who of contemporary dance, featuring over the years Merce Cunningham, Dame Margot Fonteyn, Peter Martins, Alicia Markova, Twyla Tharp, Alexander Gudunov, Martha Graham, Paul Taylor, Alvin Ailey, Phildanceco, the Pilobolus troupe, Jane Comfort and Co., among many others.

High on a hillside in Becket is the farm that famed dancer Ted Shawn bought after successfully touring with his wife, Ruth St. Denis, and the Denishawn troupe in the 1920s. Here Shawn worked to establish dance as a legitimate profession for men, founding a world-class dance-performance center and a school for dance. The school continues to flourish along with the festival, honoring its founder's heartfelt philosophy that the best dancers in the world make the most inspirational dance instructors. In addition to performing here, some of the Pillow's visiting dance luminaries stay on to teach master classes in the compound's rustic studios.

A visit is more memorable for those who drive to the Pillow early to stroll among those studios where works are in progress; dancers are in development. Through a window, lithe

*The Paul Taylor II company, part of Jacob Pillow's "Inside/Out" series, draws an overflow crowd on a rain-threatened night. In good weather, this series is held outdoors prior to main-stage productions.* Judith Monachina

figures create choreography. Down at the Pillow's rustic outdoor theater, "Inside/Out," all forms from experimental dance to ballet are rehearsed and performed—for free. And after savoring that dance hors d'oeuvre, strollers might wish to sup at the Pillow. Happily, here, too, there are several lovely options: the Pillow Café, feasting under a brightly colored tent; or the picnic area, possibly glimpsing a dancer who will be performing later in the Ted Shawn Theatre. The Pillow's Studio/Theatre adds a separate 10-week schedule of new and emerging, offbeat companies, complementing the Ted Shawn Theatre's exciting dance schedule.

**OLGA DUNN DANCE COMPANY, INC.**

413-528-9674.
321 Main St., P.O. Box 157, Gt. Barrington, MA 01230.
Season: Year-round.
Tickets: Prices vary.

Since its founding in 1977, the Olga Dunn Dance Company has enjoyed such success that it spawned the Junior Company and the Olga Dunn Dance Ensemble. Performing a free mix of exuberant and witty jazz, modern, and ballet, frequently with live musicians, the company has also toured area schools, exposing children to the creativity of dance and the excitement of movement. Annual performances at its own studio, at the Berkshire Museum, and at other theaters in the tristate area are highlights of the dance year. As Marge Champion—famed dancer and Berkshire resident—put it: "The Olga Dunn Dance Company has become the radiating center of our experience in appreciating and participating in the art of the dance."

## Other Dance

With Jacob's Pillow bringing the world's best dancers to the Berkshires, it's not surprising that quality dance troupes would spring up here and there throughout the county.

### SOUTH COUNTY

In South County, Great Barrington leads the dance. Many of the most innovative performances take place at the Simon's Rock's **Art Center Theater**, known as "the **ARC**," on Alford Road (413-528-0771), which has been offering student/faculty dance programs in December and May. These feature original music and choreography by members of the school's dance program. **Laurie McLoed** is an award-winning dancer, choreographer, and filmmaker who with her company, **Victory Girl Productions** (413-298-3006; P.O. Box 141, Stockbridge, MA 01262), presents innovative works at such places as Jacob's Pillows and MASS MoCA. She recently produced a film of dance—underwater. Modern dancer and choreographer **Dawn Lane** is the program director and choreographer for the Community Access to the Arts (414-528-5485; 40 Railroad St., Gt. Barrington, MA 01230). **Community Access** is a nonprofit organization that brings visual performing arts experiences to the disabled community. There is also a flourishing country and contra dance network in the Berkshires. Check newspapers and bulletin boards for listings.

### CENTRAL COUNTY

**Susan Dibble** (413-637-1199; www.shakespeare.org) is resident choreographer for Shakespeare & Co. She also leads **Dibble Dance**, presenting one or two weekends of dance at Shakespeare & Co.

### NORTH COUNTY

The **Berkshire Dance Theater** (413-743-4645; 34 Commercial St., Adams, MA 01220) provides instruction and performances for aspiring dancers. **Massachusetts College of Liberal Arts**'s dance program appears to be taking form. The Fine and Performing Arts number is 413-662-5255. The **Williams College Dance Department** (413-597-2410), now located in the **'62 Center for Theatre and Dance**, sponsors an ongoing, energetic series with student and faculty choreography, and visiting notables. **Chen & Dancers**, a Chinese company, has been the artists-in-residence; the **Chuck Davis African Dance Collective** has also been seen and heard in Williamstown. Exciting **Kusika**, the college's own African dance company, which accompanies itself with drumming, often performs with the spirited **Zambezi Marimba Band**, usually inviting the audience to join in. **MASS MoCA** (413-664-4481; 87 Marshall St., N. Adams, MA 01247) presents numerous dance companies.

## GALLERIES

Since the arrival in Berkshire of nationally recognized early-20th-century sculptors Daniel Chester French (who sculpted *The Minute Man* at Concord) and Sir Henry Hudson Kitson (who created *The Minute Man* at Lexington), the county has been home to an increasing number of talented visual artists.

Much of the art on display in local galleries reflects the uplifting reality of the Berkshire landscape. Many artists focus on the undulating hills and their ever-changing light. Local galleries also show other themes and styles, from traditional still-life sketches to intriguing mixed-media works. Some galleries show Berkshire artists exclusively; others bring in works from artists the world over. Some are open regularly only in warm weather, so it's wise to call ahead. *The Artful Mind* is an attractive, free publication dedicated to the arts and art scene in the Berkshires and neighboring areas of New York and Connecticut. It is a wonderful monthly source for information on what's happening.

## South County

### Great Barrington

**Asian Arts** (413-528-5091; 199 Stockbridge Rd., Gt. Barrington, MA 01230; Rte. 7) Imported Asian furniture and art.

**Berkshire Art Gallery** (413-528-2690; Jenifer House Commons, Stockbridge Rd., Gt. Barrington, MA 01230; Rte. 7) 19th- and 20th-century and current Berkshire paintings; some sculpture.

**Birdhouse** (413-528-0984; 280 Main St., Gt. Barrington, MA 01230) Contemporary American folk art and crafts. Open daily 10:30 AM–5:30 PM.

**Habitat Galleries** (413-528-9123, winter 561-241-4544; www.habitatgalleries.com; 117 State Rd., Gt. Barrington, MA 01330) The oldest gallery in the U.S. to carry contemporary glasswork; national and international artists. Changing exhibitions. Seasonal at this location.

**Kaolin & Co. Pottery** (413-528-1531; www.kaolinpottery.com; 80 Rte. 71, Gt. Barrington, MA 01230; next to Gt. Barrington airport) Wheel-thrown and hand-built ceramics, including sculptures of animals. Home furnishings to conversation pieces.

**Mill River Studio** (413-528-9433; 8 Railroad St., Gt. Barrington, MA 01230) Posters, hand-colored engravings, historic maps, and custom framing.

**Sanford Smith Fine Art** (413-528-6777; 13 Railroad St., Gt. Barrington, MA 01230) Modern masters and contemporary art; oils, watercolors, photography, works on paper; Jill Bokor Jewelry representing 12 contemporary artists.

**SKH Gallery** (413 528-3300; 46 Castle St., Gt. Barrington, MA 01230; at the railroad station, top of Castle St.) Fine art and handmade objects spanning contemporary abstract and representational art as the textile work of world-renowned weaver Sam Kasten.

**Simon's Rock College of Bard** (413-528-7209; www.simons-rock.edu; 84 Alford Rd., Gt. Barrington, MA 01230) Changing exhibits at various venues on campus.

### Housatonic

There are a variety of artists operating studios in this quaint mill village. Watch out for periodic open studios. A number of artists maintain public galleries with varied hours of operation.

**Tokonoma Gallery & Framing Studio** (413-274-1166; 402 Park St., Housatonic, MA 01236) A diverse collection of fine art and functional, decorative, contemporary crafts. The gallery presents works of such regional artists as Terry Wise along with internationally recognized artists. Also offers a framing service.

*A beautiful barn in Tyringham, converted to the Naoussa Gallery.* Judith Monachina

LEE

**Myles Bradford Collection** (413 243-1010; 40 Main St., Lee, MA 01238) A little bit of the Southwest in the Berkshires, along with changing exhibits of artists from near and far. Jewelry, pottery, oils, watercolors, and collectibles providing "presents of mind."

MONTEREY

**Hayloft Gallery and Studio** (413-528-1806; Monterey Stage Rd., Box 11, Gt. Barrington, MA 01230; jct. Rtes. 23 and 57, 4 mi. E. of Gt. Barrington) Berkshire prints and watercolors, including popular townscapes, by local artist Leonard Webber.

SHEFFIELD

**Butler Sculpture Park** (413-229-8924; 481 Shunpike Rd., Sheffield, MA 01257) An outdoor exhibit space for monumental sculpture. Open daily May–Oct., 11 AM–5 PM, winter by appointment.

**Loring Gallery** (413-229-0110; www.loringgallery.com; P.O. Box 938, Sheffield, MA 01257; Rte. 7, diagonally across the road from Bradford's auction house) Fine art, sculpture, and turn-of-the-last-century posters. 11 AM–5PM, closed Tues.

SOUTH LEE

**House of Earth Studio Ge-raj Gallery** (413-243-1575; P.O. Box 145, S. Lee, MA 01260; 1240 Pleasant St., Rte. 102 E. of town center) Contemporary oil, acrylic, and watercolor landscapes in a garage beside a rammed-earth studio.

Stockbridge

**Holsten Galleries** (413-298-3044; www.holstengalleries.com; 3 Elm St., Stockbridge, MA 01262) Contemporary glass art, including stunning glass pieces by Dale Chihuly. Daily 11 AM–5 PM.

**IS183** (413 298-5252; 13 Willard Hill Rd., Stockbridge, MA 01262) Interlaken School just off Rte. 183 offers classes, shows, a kids' summer camp, and weekend workshops in all art media. It also has a studio at MASS MoCA in North Adams.

**Image Gallery** (413-298-5500; Main St., P.O. Box 111, Stockbridge, MA 01262) Modern arts and photography—usually by gallery owner and master photographer Clemens Kalischer.

**Origins Gallery** (413-298-0002; 36 Main St., Stockbridge, MA 01262; the Mews) Tribal and folk art of Africa and Asia, collected by Albert Gordon.

Tyringham

**Naoussa Gallery** (413 243-1812; 8 Main Rd., Tyringham, MA 01264) Featuring Berkshire and regional artists including Peggy Braun, Paula Shaun, and Michael Flower, working in a variety of media.

West Stockbridge

**All Fired Up Gallery—Berkshire Center for Contemporary Glass** (413-232-4662; 6 Harris St., P.O. Box 377, W. Stockbridge, MA 01266) Handblown contemporary glass, workshops, demonstrations.

**Artifacts** (413-232-9900; 5 Center St., W. Stockbridge, MA 01266) They specialize in architectural objects and related artworks, including miniatures, wooden items, and intaglio.

**Hotchkiss Mobiles Gallery and Studio** (413-232-0200, 866-4-HOTART; fax 413-232-0210; www.artmobiles.com; 8 Center St., P.O. Box 373, W. Stockbridge, MA 01266) Original and colorful mobiles for moving art, both indoors and out. Museum quality at reasonable prices. Another gallery in Lenox.

**Train Station Gallery** (413 232-7930; 6 Depot St., W. Stockbridge, MA 01266) Bright, open display space in a restored train station featuring a selection of art in various media, from a variety of artists including Bruce MacDonald.

**Waterside** (413-232-7997; 30 Main St., W. Stockbridge, MA 01266) Striking graphics, ceramics, jewelry, and sculpture. Some powerful pieces in many different media.

## Central County

Becket

**Becket Arts Center** (413-623-6635; www.hidden-hills.com/becketartscenter; Brooker Hill Rd. and Rte. 8, Becket, MA 01223; Rte. 8) Local shows and programs.

Hancock

**Beaver Pond** (413-738-5895; 2993 Hancock Rd., Rte. 43, Williamstown, MA 01267; Rte. 43) Paintings by owner Richard Heyer and others; Open daily noon–5 PM except Tues.

HINSDALE

**John Stritch** (413-655-8804; 526 Maple St., Hinsdale, MA 01235) A gallery showcasing paintings, prints, and the Tanglewood poster collection by Berkshire artist John Stritch. Studio and sculpture garden open weekend afternoons.

LANESBOROUGH

**Stone School Gallery** (413-442-0996; www.oldstoneschool.com; 732 N. Main St., Lanesborough, MA 01237) Photographer Cheryl Sacks exhibits her work and that of others.

LENOX

**B. J. Faulkner** (413-637-2958; www.bjfaulkner.com; 48 Main St., Lenox, MA 01240) Highlighting the watercolors, oils, and reproductions of the artist-owner's Berkshire scenes, musical themes, and European dreams.

**Charles Steinhacker Editions** (800-244-9120; 4 Housatonic St., Lenox, MA 01240) Steinhacker's photographs (some taken while he was a photographer for *National Geographic*) are showcased in this tiny shop, which also sells "the world's best imported chocolate."

**Concepts of Art** (413-637-4845; fax 413-637-2723; www.lenoxjudaica.com; Route 7A, Lenox, MA 01240) Crafts—including glass, jewelry, pottery, and wood—concentrating on Judaica.

**Ferrin Gallery** (413 637-4414; www.ferringallery.com; 69 Church St., Lenox, MA 01240) Group shows of well-known artists and sculptors in a stunning new gallery just opened after 20 years in Northampton. Well-deserved reputation for offering the best in ceramic sculpture and studio pottery.

**Hand of Man—A Craft Gallery** (413 637-0632; 5 Walker St., Curtis Shops, Lenox, MA 01240; in the Curtis Bldg.) A wide range of crafts, photographs, and paintings.

**Hoadley Gallery: Contemporary Crafts** (413 637-2814; www.hoadleygallery.com; 21 Church St., Lenox, MA 01240) Pottery by Tom Hoadley is one of this store's specialties. Functional and decorative objects in all media, including a collection of wearable art.

**Inspired Planet** (413-637-2836; www.inspiredplanet.com; 36 Pittsfield Rd., Lenox, MA 01240; at Brushwood Farms on Rte. 7) Photographs by the owner; paintings, furniture, and artifacts from Asia, Africa, and the Americas.

**Lenox Artisans Gallery** (413 637-9539; 25 Pittsfield Rd., Lenox, MA 01240; Rte. 7) Eclectic collection of art in a variety of media. The playful sculpture on the front lawn sets a whimsical tone.

**Lenox Gallery of Fine Art** (413-637-2276; 69 Church St., Lenox, MA 01240) Two floors of paintings, watercolors, drawings, and sculpture by major Berkshire artists, including Stephen Filmus. Open daily year-round.

**Liliana Gallery** (413 637-6964; 38 Church St., Lenox, MA 01240) A shop featuring fine art and custom framing.

**Lydia Mongiardo Collection** (413- 637-0809; 51 Church Street; Lenox, MA 01240) Elegant contemporary furniture and screens by Nicholas Mongiardo—sculpture, paintings, jewelry, pottery, fabrics, objets d'art by other internationally known artists.

**Michael Charles Cabinetmakers** (413-637-3483; www.michaelcharles.com; 53 Church St., Lenox, MA 01240) Gallery of handmade custom furniture using hardwood and traditional 19th-century joinery.

**Wit Gallery** (413 637-8808; www.thewitgallery.com; 27 Church St., Lenox, MA 01240) An acronym for "wonders in time," this gallery offers larger than life sculptures and also features watercolors and oil paintings, all by well-known artists. Open daily from 10 AM.

### Pittsfield

**Berkshire Community College, Koussevitzky Arts Center** (413-499-4660; www.cc.berkshire.org; 1350 West St., Pittsfield, MA 01201) Changing exhibitions, 9–5 weekdays.

**Lichtenstein Center for the Arts** (formerly Berkshire Artisans) (413-499-9348; www.berkshireweb.com/artisans; 28 Renne Ave., Pittsfield, MA 01201; 1 block E. of lower North St.) Exhibitions and workshops at the city's nonprofit community arts center.

## North County

### Adams

**TOPIA Arts Center** (413- 743-9600; www.topiaarts.org; 27 Park Street, Rte. 8, Adams, MA 01220) Performing arts and education center in development offering live performances of world music, theater, and dance; multidisciplinary performance classes offered.

### North Adams

**Contemporary Artists Center** (413-663-9555; www.thecac.org; 189 Beaver St., N. Adams, MA 01247) A not-for-profit artists' studio facility in the historic brick and stone Beaver Mill, with five unique galleries featuring regional and international and CAC artists-in-residence exhibits. Visit their Web site for more information on their schedule of shows and events.

**Dark Ride** (413-664-9550; www.darkrideproject.org; 189 Beaver St., N. Adams, MA 01247) Visitors can take a 10-minute ride on the *Sensory Integrator* into creative space or view the galleries. Open Sat. and Sun. 11 AM–5 PM in summer in fall. Admission fees.

**Everything Art** (413-662-3556; 51 Main St., N. Adams, MA 01247) Fine art, (including works by Danny O recently featured in a show at Chesterwood) gifts, artists' supplies, and custom framing.

### Williamstown

**1/2 Dozen or So** (413-458-9582; Mount Greylock Regional High School, 1781 Cold Spring Rd., Williamstown, MA 01267) Changing exhibitions open during school hours.

**Harrison Gallery** (413 458-1700; www.theharrisongallery.com; 39 Spring St., Williamstown, MA 01267) Wonderful gallery featuring contemporary landscape work from locals and other well-known painters, potters, and graphic artists. New shows every month.

**LiAsia Gallery** (413 458-1600; www.liasiagallery.com; 31 Spring St., Williamstown, MA 01267) A gallery showcasing beautiful Asian handcrafts and antiques, from priceless Ming pieces to utilitarian country furniture and folk art.

**Plum** (413-458-3389; www.plumgallery.com; 112 Water St., Williamstown, MA 01267). Exhibiting the work of painter Mary Natilizia, photographer Nicholas Whitman, and many others. Open year-round.

**Wilson Wilde** (413-458-8277; Spencer Studio Building, Williams College, Williamstown, MA 01267) Changing student exhibits.

## HISTORIC HOMES

### ARROWHEAD

413-442-1793.
www.mobydick.org.
780 Holmes Rd., Pittsfield, MA 01201.
About 1.5 mi. E. of Rte. 7
Open: Memorial Day Weekend–Columbus Day, hourly tours 10–4; winter by appointment.
Admission: Adults $10, students 16–25 with ID $5, children 6–15 $3, children 5 and under free.
Special Features: Gift shop.

In 1850, seeking to escape what he later called "the Babylonish brick-kiln of New York," Herman Melville gave in to his yearning "to feel the grass" and moved with his family to the Berkshires. By the time he came here, Melville had already published two tales of his South Sea adventures, *Typee* and *Omoo*, and he had earned a reputation as a man "who had lived among cannibals." Longing to be known as a great writer and fresh from a new "close acquaintance" with the "divine" writings of Shakespeare, here he took off on the grand literary whale hunt that was to become *Moby-Dick*.

Arrowhead is home to the Berkshire Historical Society, which offers excellent guided tours through the house. The second-floor study is where Melville wrote his great novel, looking northward at the Mount Greylock range, its rolling form reminiscent of a giant whale. He dedicated his next novel, *Pierre*, to "Greylock's most excellent majesty." The implements of the writer's trade and duplicates of many important books in his library are here.

The other thoroughly "Melville" room is the dining room, dominated by a grand stone hearth. His brother inscribed the mantle with the opening of Melville's story, *I and My Chimney*. The house contains 19th-century period furnishings, fine arts, and textiles with Berkshire origins, several pieces of which belonged to Melville. The Ammi Phillips folk-art portraits are of particular interest. Outside, the piazza is the site of another story. The grounds include an extensive herb garden and a vintage cutting garden. Arrowhead is also a lovely picnic spot.

The barn behind the house is the site of cultural programs such as literary readings and historical talks. A video about Berkshire literary figures and artists takes 20 minutes. Those hungry for more Melville can visit The Melville Room at the Berkshire Athenaeum on Wendell Avenue, also in Pittsfield. (See the Berkshire Athenaeum entry under "Libraries" in this chapter.)

### ASHINTULLY GARDENS

413-298-3239.
Sodom Rd., Tyringham, MA 01264.

Follow signs from Main Rd. toward W. Otis.
Open: Mid-June—Mid-Sept., Wed. & Sat., 1–5 PM.
Admission: Self-guided tours, free; group tours of 15 or more, $15.

*Ashintully* is Gaelic for "Brow of the Hill" and, indeed, the grassy terraces, fountains, statuary, and ponds descend gracefully from the pillars that remain of the marble palace, a mansion completed in 1912. A property of The Trustees for Reservations, a statewide group that has done well by Berkshire County.

### THE BIDWELL HOUSE

413-528-6888.
www.bidwellhousemuseum.org.
Art School Rd., Monterey, MA 01245.
2.5 mi. from town of Monterey (turn left).
Season: Memorial Day–Oct. 15, Tues.–Sun., holidays 11–4.
Admission: Adults $5, seniors/students with ID $4, children under 18 $1.

Located at the end of the traveled section of Art School Road, Bidwell is one of Berkshire's oldest homes, dating to 1750 and listed on the National Register. Because the center of town moved on, Bidwell is now surrounded by 196 acres of pristine Monterey woodland, looking much as it might have back in the 18th century. Two designers from New York discovered the abandoned former home of the Reverend Adonijah Bidwell in the 1960s, brought it back to fine condition, and left instruction in their wills that it continue as a museum.

An active slate of lectures, workshops, and hikes (in the fall along historical Royal Hemlock Road) takes place.

### COLONEL ASHLEY HOUSE

413-298-8146.
www.thetrustees.org.
Mail: P.O. Box 792, Stockbridge, MA 01262.
Cooper Hill Rd., Ashley Falls, off Route 7A.
Season: Memorial Day Weekend–Columbus Day, Sat.–Sun. 10–5.
Admission: Adults $5, children 6–12 $3.

In his military role as a colonel and as a political radical, John Ashley was destined to become as prominent a citizen as Berkshire would produce in the Revolution. He began his Berkshire life as a surveyor, trudging through the woods and swamps of Sheffield and mapping the wilderness with compass and chain.

Ashley loved what he saw. By 1735 he had built a handsome home on the west bank of the Housatonic River, now the oldest extant house in Berkshire County. Framed of well-seasoned oak with chestnut rafters, it was the finest house in Sheffield. Woodworkers from across the colony came to carve paneling and to fashion the gracefully curved staircase. The craftsmanship of Ashley's study, with its broad fireplace and sunburst cupboard, inspires confidence. It was here that Ashley met with a group of his neighbors in early 1773 to draft the Sheffield Declaration, stating to the world that all people were "equal, free and independent." They asserted their independence from Britain some 3 years before Thomas Jefferson and associates did so in Philadelphia. One of his slaves, Mumbet, overhearing the conversations, thought she should be free, too. Lawyer Theodore Sedgwick won her case.

The house was rescued, moved a quarter mile, restored, and turned over to The Trustees of Reservations. TTOR has seen to it that the Ashley House, listed on the National Register, lives on telling the history of the Ashley Family. An herb garden flourishes outside while colonial furnishings, redware, and the original wood paneling survive inside. A visit can complement viewing the extraordinary flowers at Bartholemew's Cobble or antiques hunting in the Sheffield-Ashley Falls area.

**The Sheffield Declaration, 1773**

RESOLVED that Mankind in a State of Nature are equal, free and independent of each Other, and have a right to the undisturbed Enjoyment of their lives, their Liberty and Property.

RESOLVED that it is a well known and undoubted privilege of the British Constitution that every Subject hath . . . a Right to the free and uncontrolled injoyment and Improvement of his estate or property. . . .

RESOLVED that the late acts of the parlement of Great Breton expres porpos of Rating and regulating the colecting a Revenew in the Colonies: are unconstitutional as thereby the Just earning of our labours and Industry without Any Regard to our own consent are by mere power ravished from us. . . .

### THE WILLIAM CULLEN BRYANT HOMESTEAD

413-634-2244.
www.thetrustees.org.
207 Bryant Rd., Cummington, MA 01026.
Off Rte. 9 on Rte. 112 in Cummington.
Open: Grounds open daily year-round sunrise–sunset; tours: late June–Labor Day, Fri.–Sun. plus Mon. holidays 1–5.
Admission: Adults $5, children 6–12 $2.50.

William Cullen Bryant was born in 1794 in a small gambrel-roofed cabin of rough-hewn lumber, 2 miles from the frontier village of Cummington, on a farm of 465 acres. He stayed at Williams College only 8 months, shortly thereafter taking up the law. From 1816 on, Cullen, as he was called, practiced law in Great Barrington, where he wrote approximately 30 well-respected poems on such local themes as Monument Mountain's Indian legend, the Green River, and native waterfowl. With the influence of Catherine Sedgwick's brothers, Bryant became coeditor of the *New York Review* and *Athenaeum Magazine*, then editor at the *New York Evening Post* (one of America's oldest and most influential newspapers), and ultimately America's first popular and widely respected native-born poet.

Bryant returned to and added substantially to his Cummington homestead; today it has 23 rooms. Visitors should read the poems first to capture the tour's fine points. Well managed by The Trustees of Reservations; National Historic Landmark; interpretive trail.

### CHESTERWOOD

413-298-3579.
www.chesterwood.org.
Mail: P.O. Box 827, Stockbridge, MA 01262.
Off Rte. 183, Glendale.
Season: May–Oct., daily 10–5.
Admission: Adults $10, seniors $9, college students $9, youths 6–18 $5, children 5 and under free.
Special Features: Gift shop.

At the age of 25 Daniel Chester French was commissioned by his hometown of Concord, Massachusetts, to create his first public monument, *The Minute Man.* Its lifelike pose and exquisite sense of surface modeling won the artist national acclaim, and the statue became an American icon.

Years and scores of sculptures later, French sought a permanent country home to augment the New York City studio he maintained. In 1896 he and his wife, Mary, were shown the old Warner Farm and Boys School in the Glendale section of Stockbridge. After taking in the magnificent vista southward, toward Monument Mountain, French pronounced it "the best dry view" he had ever seen and promptly arranged to buy the property. Thereafter, he and Mary spent half of each year in New York City, half at Chesterwood. Glendale "is heaven," he said. "New York is—well, New York."

In Glendale he built a grand residence, studio, and garden complex, which are an enduring and eloquent tableau of his artistry. Here he created his masterpiece, *Abraham Lincoln,* the statue that sits in the Lincoln Memorial in Washington. "What I wanted to convey," said French, "was the mental and physical strength of the great President." Visitors are invited to handle sculpting tools in his studio. Centerpieces are his marble *Andromeda,* a surprisingly erotic work; and the "railway" to move his works-in-progress out into the revealing daylight.

French designed magnificent gardens, maintained today after his fashion by the property's managers, the National Trust for Historic Preservation. The grounds host special exhibits during the season.

*Through the glass doors at Daniel Chester French's studio at Chesterwood* | Judith Monachina

## HARRISON HOUSE

80 Third St., Pittsfield, MA 01201.

Harrison House is not yet rehabilitated or open to the public as this book goes to press. It was the home of the Reverend Samuel Harrison, chaplain to the Massachusetts 54th Regiment, the first all-black infantry to fight in the Civil War, and pastor of the Second Congregational Church in Pittsfield. He was active in the American abolitionist movement. His former homestead is on its way to becoming the Harrison House Museum, an archive and research center on African American history in New England. It as anticipated to become a site along a proposed African American Heritage Trail.

## THE MERWIN HOUSE

413-298-4703.
www.spnea.org.
14 W. Main St., P.O. Box 72, Stockbridge, MA 01262.
Center of town.

Season: One day in June and 1 day in Dec., 11 AM–4 PM; private tours by reservation.
Admission: Fee.

"Tranquility," a bit of 19th-century Berkshire refinement stopped in time, is the former home of Mrs. Vipont Merwin. This charming brick mansion, built about 1825, is filled with antiques (mostly Victorian); both furnishings and collectibles reflect global travel and domestic dignity. Merwin House is maintained as a property of the Society for the Preservation of New England Antiquities. For Stockbridge strollers, evening views through the multipaned front windows give an inviting glimpse of an elegant world gone by.

## THE MISSION HOUSE

413-298-3239.
www.thetrustees.org.
Box 792, Stockbridge, MA 01262.
Corner Main & Sergeant sts.
Season: Memorial Day Weekend–Columbus Day, daily 10–5.
Admission: Adults $6, children 6–12 $3.

In 1735, an earnest minister from Yale College came to the Berkshire wilderness to pastor to the Mahican Indians. John Sergeant learned the Indian language in which he preached two sermons every Sunday. In the springtime, he went out with the Indians to tap the maples, writing the first account in English of this sugar production method. He talked with the Indians in the back of his simple log cabin. Under Sergeant's leadership, the Stockbridge Mission flourished.

To please his wife, Abigail, the Reverend Sergeant built what is now called Mission House, high on Prospect Hill. The tall and ornate Connecticut doorway, with beautiful panels, was carved in Westfield, Massachusetts, and dragged by oxen 50 miles over rugged terrain to Stockbridge. This front door and the front rooms were Abigail's domain; in the back, a separate entry and long corridor allowed the Indians access to Sergeant's study.

When he died in 1749, the days of the Stockbridge Mission were numbered, too, although eminent theologian Jonathan Edwards succeeded him. By 1785 the Indians had been displaced from Stockbridge, driven out for the most part by land speculators.

In 1927 Mabel Choate—the art collector and philanthropist who was heir to Naumkeag—acquired the Mission House. She moved it to its present Main Street location, near the site of John Sergeant's first log cabin. Boston landscape architect Fletcher Steele, who had designed the gardens at Naumkeag, planted an orderly, symmetrical 18th-century herb, flower, and fruit garden beside the restored and relocated Mission House. Today apple and quince trees; herbs such as lamb's ear, rue, and southern wood; bright flowers; a grape arbor; and a "salet garden" filled with garden greens greet visitors.

The Trustees of Reservations maintains Mission House, which is a National Historic Landmark. Tours of the house capture the 18th century's furnishings and kitchen implements, and the feeling of humble domesticity that gathered around the dominant central hearth. An adjoining museum focuses on Native Americans.

## THE MOUNT

413-637-1899, 888-637-1902.
www.edithwharton.org.
2 Plunkett St., Box 974, Lenox, MA 01240.

*The Mount, as seen from the gardens* Judith Monachina

*The birches at Naumkeag* Judith Monachina

Near southern jct. of Rtes. 7 and 7A.
Open: May–Oct. 9–5; grounds 9–6.
Admission: Adults $18, students $9, children under 12 free.
Special Features: Book/gift shop; refreshments.

It is amazing what a difference a few million dollars make. With federal money and matching funds, the building has been repaired. Even more spectacular is the restoration of the grounds.

In February 1901 the writer and heiress Edith Wharton arrived at the Curtis Hotel in Lenox for a week in the country. She had summered in the area for the preceding 2 years and now, having found the "watering place trivialities of Newport" all but intolerable, sought a new site on which to realize the design principles incorporated in her book *The Decoration of Houses.* The Georgian Revival house she built was modeled on Christopher Wren's Belton House in Lincolnshire, England. At first Wharton retained as architect her associate, Ogden Codman. When his design fees grew exorbitant, she called on Francis L. V. Hoppin to complete the job.

Wharton supervised creation of the gardens, orchards, and buildings while finishing her novel *Disintegration,* writing as always in bed and tossing the pages on the floor for the staff to assemble. The Mount, elegant throughout, boasts marble floors and fireplaces, and originally required 12 resident servants. Besides the 14 horses in their stables, the Whartons owned one of the earliest motorcars, a convenience that thrilled the visiting Henry James. In the fall of 1904, James and Wharton motored through Berkshire's autumnal splendor every day, enjoying social afternoons and evenings with visiting sophisticates.

"The Mount was to give me country cares and joys," she wrote, "long happy rides, and drives through the wooded lanes of that loveliest region, the companionship of a few dear friends, and the freedom from trivial obligations which was necessary if I was to go on with my writing. The Mount was my first real home . . . and its blessed influence still lives in me."

Happily, its blessed influence lives on for all of us as the Mount's physical and spiritual restoration continue. The National Trust for Historic Preservation bought the Mount to save it from commercial exploitation; the house is run today by Edith Wharton Restoration, Inc.

### NAUMKEAG

413-298-8146.
www.thetrustees.org.
5 Prospect Hill Rd., Box 792, Stockbridge, MA 01262.
Season: Memorial Day weekend–Columbus Day, daily 10–5.
Admission: House and garden: adults $10, children 6–12 $3; garden only: adults $8, children 6–12 $3.
Special Features: Gift shop.

During the Gilded Age of the late 19th century, men and women of power played out their fantasies in Berkshire, dotting the hillsides with dream houses. A most livable example is the mansion of illustrious lawyer Joseph Choate, the summer "cottage" that the Choate family came to call *Naumkeag* (a Native American name for Salem, where Choate was born). Here Choate found both a retreat from New York City life as well as an enclave of great legal minds in Supreme Court justices Field, Brewer, and Brown, all Stockbridge contemporaries.

Choate bought the property from David Dudley Field in 1884 and began construction. By the autumn of 1886, the 44-room, shingled, gabled, and dormered Norman-style house was complete, with architectural design by McKim, Mead & White and imaginative gardens by the landscaping pioneer Nathaniel Barrett.

The house eventually came into the hands of Choate's daughter, Mable, who maintained it while adding extensively to the gardens under the direction of landscape architect Fletcher Steele. The Fountain Steps, framed by birches; the Afternoon Garden, an outdoor room; farther southward, the Chinese Pagoda and Linden Walk; uphill, in the brick-walled Chinese Garden, mosses and stone Buddhas gathered with carved lions and dogs, all shaded by ginkos; to the north, the topiary of the Evergreen Garden and the fragrance and color of the Rose Garden—all reflect decades of inspired and distinctive garden design.

Now held by The Trustees of Reservations, Naumkeag still includes its gardens, furnishings, and an extraordinary porcelain collection, much of it from the Far East. The tours are excellent.

### SEARLES CASTLE

413-528-9800.
389 Main St., Gt. Barrington, MA 01230.

When Mark Hopkins, a founder and treasurer of the Central Pacific Railroad, died, his widow, Mary, consoled herself with the creation of a grand home in Great Barrington. Stanford White designed this 40-room castle, which was constructed between 1882 and 1887 of locally cut blue dolomite stone. Upon its completion, Mary Hopkins married her interior decorator, Edward Searles, a man 20 years her junior. Searles had spared no expense on the castle's interior. Many of the major rooms feature massive carved wood or marble fireplaces, each one unique. More than 100 of the world's best artisans and craftsmen were brought on site to work with oak carvings, marble statues, atriums, columns, and pillars. The bills totaled $2.5 million.

The castle now serves as the home of the John Dewey Academy, a residential therapeutic prep school. In 1982 Searles Castle was added to the National Register of Historic Places. Usually closed to the public, the building and grounds are visible to pedestrians walking

**Touring the Berkshire Mansions**

For those who yearn to step back into Berkshire's Gilded Age, visits to Naumkeag, the Mount, and Tanglewood, described in this chapter, will make an excellent start. In the chapters 3 and 4, "Lodging" and "Dining," other Gilded Age mansions are noted for their original beauty or their contemporary adaptations. In addition, local historical societies and garden clubs arrange visits to some of the best mansions, normally off-limits because they remain private homes.

Many Gilded Age "cottages" are visible from the road and are well worth a look. Their owners' privacy should be respected, of course. Carole Owens's book *The Berkshire Cottages* (which is available at most bookstores) tells their stories in lively detail, bringing to life the business magnates, robber barons, philanthropists, architects and designers, artists in residence, and squadrons of domestic servants. Maps to guide the way are included.

along Main Street. Several times a year—for the Antiquarian Book Fair, for the Stockbridge Chamber Concerts, and for other special events—Searles Castle is open to the public and well worth a visit.

### VENTFORT HALL

413-637-3206.
www.gildedage.org.
104 Walker St., P.O. Box 2424, Lenox, MA 01240.
Open: Memorial Day Weekend–Columbus Day, daily 10–3; winter by appointment.
Admission: Adults $9, children $4.
Special Features: Gift shop.

This Berkshire cottage's Elizabethan Revival style was already out of date when George and Sarah Morgan built their summer home in 1893, but it is enjoyable today to imagine the kind of life it led to. For those who need a more visual stimulus, Ventfort served as the set for the orphanage in the 1999 movie *The Cider House Rules*. Unlike the other cottages open for our inspection, Ventfort aims to be a museum of the Gilded Age, not solely an example of period architecture.

Sarah, sister to J. Pierpont Morgan, kept her last name by marrying a cousin. Their Boston architects, Rotch & Tilden, designed four other homes nearby in Lenox—all different from this one. Ventfort Hall was placed on the site of a home originally built and named by Ogden Haggerty; "Strong Wind" was for 4 years home to the Whitneys, who gave the land for October Mountain State Forest. But it paled in comparison to the new Morgan home of "15 bedrooms, 13 bathrooms, and 17 fireplaces." Built perhaps too quickly, the brickwork has sadly decomposed.

Sarah Morgan died soon after Ventfort Hall was completed, and the building passed through a number of owners, both private and institutional, until a proposed nursing home threatened "structurecide" by wrecking ball in 1990. Local residents in 1997 joined to form the Ventfort Hall Association and, with a loan from the National Trust for Historic Preservation, purchased the building and the remaining 11.7 acres of grounds. Further state grants and private funds supported the daunting preservation work—on the interior, with the skilled assistance of joiner Michael Costerisan, who meticulously pieced together tattered paneling. With none of the original furnishings available, transforming Ventfort into a period museum will require a lot more money and a lot more time.

## Libraries

### BERKSHIRE ATHENAEUM

413-499-9480.
www.berkshire.net/PittsfieldLibrary.
1 Wendell Ave., Pittsfield, MA 01201.
Open: Sept.–June, Mon.–Thurs. 9–9, Fri. 9–5, Sat. 10–5; July and Aug., Mon., Wed., Fri. 9–5, Tues., Thurs. 9–9, Sat. 10–5. Closed holidays.

The former Berkshire Athenaeum is a 19th-century specimen of the Venetian Gothic style, constructed next to the courthouse on Pittsfield's handsome Park Square. Built of Berkshire deep-blue dolomite (a limestone) from Great Barrington, along with red sandstone from Longmeadow, Massachusetts, and red granite from Missouri, this Athenaeum, once Berkshire's central library, now serves Pittsfield's courts and registry of deeds. The new Athenaeum is a three-level brick and glass facility featuring a tall and airy reading room with natural clerestory lighting. An outdoor reading terrace serves adults and another, children.

There is an outstanding dance collection, a Local Authors' Room, and a Local History Room. The jewel of the Athenaeum is its Herman Melville Room: a trove of Melville memorabilia, from carved scrimshaw depicting the terror of the Great White Whale to first editions of the author's works. Here are *Moby-Dick* in Japanese; autographed letters from Melville; photos of his Pittsfield farm, Arrowhead (described under "Historic Homes," in this chapter), and the desk on which he wrote his last, haunting work, *Billy Budd, Sailor*.

### CHAPIN LIBRARY OF RARE BOOKS

413-597-2462.
www.williams.edu./resources/chapin.
P.O. Box 426, Williamstown, MA 01267.
On the 2nd floor of Stetson Hall, Williams College.
Open: Mon.–Fri. 10–12 and 1–5 except holidays. Open July 4. Call for summer hours.

Chapin Library has one of the most well rounded collections of rare books and manuscripts anywhere. On permanent display are the four founding documents of this country: the Declaration of Independence, originally owned by a member of the Continental Congress; the Articles of Confederation and Perpetual Union; the Constitution of the United States, annotated by George Mason; and two copies of the Bill of Rights. The library also owns General Greene's handwritten order for boats to cross the Delaware, and on loan is George Washington's copy of the Federalist Papers. Every July Fourth, actors from the Williamstown Theatre Festival read the Declaration and the British Reply.

In 1923 Alfred Clark Chapin—Williams class of 1869 and mayor of Brooklyn—presented his alma mater with his magnificent library of first editions and manuscripts, specializing in historic literary and artistic masterworks. Other alumni have subsequently given their collections.

Among others, the literary holdings are a Shakespeare First Folio and first editions of Pope, Swift, Fielding, Defoe, Richardson, Sterne, Johnson, Scott, Byron, Burns, Browning, Keats, Shelley, Thackeray, and Dickens. There is also a fine T. S. Eliot collection. Representing American literature are first editions by such writers as Crane, Melville, Whitman, and Faulkner. Scientific endeavor is represented by Tycho Brahe's *Astronomia* (1602), Harvey's *Anatomical Exercitations* (1653), Darwin's *Origin of Species* (1859), and a double elephant folio of Audubon's *Birds of America*.

### LENOX LIBRARY

413-637-0197.
www.lenoxlib.org.
18 Main St., Lenox, MA 01240.
Open: Summer, Mon.–Sat. 10–5; rest of year, Tues.–Sat. 10–5; Thurs. until 8.

Built in 1815 as the Berkshire County Courthouse, when Lenox was still the "shire town," this classic Greek Revival building became the Lenox Library Association in 1873. It is listed on the National Register of Historic Places. Readers there can enjoy the main reading room, with its lofty illuminated ceiling and its amazing array of periodicals, or the outdoor reading park. This is old-world reading at its best. A solid collection of about 75,000 volumes plus a music room are available to the public. There is a closed collection of historical memorabilia, too, including the sled from the incident on which Edith Wharton based her novella *Ethan Frome*.

Recent renovations have increased space for young people and computers, and uncovered the domed ceiling that arched over the original courtroom.

*Historic Lenox Library has recently undergone a splendid restoration.* Judith Monachina

### MILNE PUBLIC LIBRARY AND HOUSE OF LOCAL HISTORY

413-458-5369, 413-458-2160 (HLH).
www.milnelibrary.org.
1095 Main St., Williamstown, MA 01267.
Open: Mon.–Wed. and Fri. 10–5, Thurs. 10–8, Sat. 10–1.

Williamstown is proud that a treasured resource has a roomy home—a former school with ample parking. With strong holdings of children's books, fiction, local history, videos, and popular music, the public library complements the Sawyer Library (below). Comfortable areas for reading and a helpful staff. The House of Local History shares the library's roof, having room enough to display much of its holdings, including a major exhibit, From Wilderness to Williamstown. Both the library and HLH offer frequent programs.

### NORTH ADAMS PUBLIC LIBRARY

413-662-3133.
www.naplibrary.com.
74 Church St., N. Adams, MA 01247.
Open: Mon., Tues., Thurs. 9–8; Wed., Fri. 9–5; Sat., 9–1.

Sanford Blackinton build a marvelous mansion in 1867. Although the first mayor of North Adams, Albert C. Houghton, purchased it and donated it to the city for a library in 1896, no fundamental changes were made to the building until 2004, when it was totally refurbished and added to, to create a modern library that nevertheless meticulously maintains the aura of the original. As Librarian Marcia Gross puts it, the library "is the community's living room." Private citizens who raised over $1 million of the $4.3 million are honored in the brick walkways and a stained-glass window. Furthermore this green building manufactures much of its electricity through solar panels on the roof and is largely heated and cooled through geothermal wells, so that its utility costs are minimal. An elegant setting for an up-to-date, working library.

### SAWYER LIBRARY

413-597-2501.
www.williams.edu/library.
55 Sawyer Library Dr., Williamstown, MA 01267.
Center of Williams College campus.
Open: Daily—except weekends and holidays when Williams is not in session.

At 900,000-plus volumes, 1,600 periodicals in paper, 10,000-plus electronic texts, 500,000 micro texts, 29,000 sound recordings, including the Paul Whiteman Collection, 9,000 videos, and 430,000 federal documents, the Sawyer is a research resource unmatched within the county. Here we find a wide array of the latest periodicals, shelves of newly released books, and a library staff as helpful as they come. The public may use the facility, the stacks are open, and Sawyer is a pleasant place in which to work. The Schow Science Library is state of the art; all titles are included in Francis, the online catalog. The Williams Library belongs to the Boston Library Consortium. College plans call for a new library, just over the horizon.

### SIMON'S ROCK LIBRARY

413-528-7370.
http://library.simons-rock.edu.
Simon's Rock College of Bard.
84 Alford Rd., Gt. Barrington, MA 01230.
Open: Hours vary.

The Simon's Rock Library is one of the best in South County, the staff always attentive to one's research needs. The college it serves may be small, but this library's holdings are exceedingly well chosen. It is open to visitors and to all Berkshire County residents for obtaining a library card. This is a library of half a dozen rooms on two floors in three interconnected pagoda-style buildings—all in a sylvan setting. With large skylights, the reading rooms are highly recommended for naturally lit, wet-weather browsing. And fascinating art exhibits almost always grace the library's skylighted gallery.

### STOCKBRIDGE LIBRARY AND HISTORICAL ROOM

413-298-5501.
Mail: P.O. Box 119, Stockbridge, MA 01262.
Main St. (Rte. 7).
Open: Mon.–Fri. 9–5, Sat. 9–4; Mon. and Fri. eve. 7–9; closed Sun.; the Historical Room, Tues.–Fri. 9–5, Sat. 9–4.

Parts of the Stockbridge Library date to 1864, and the reading room is one the most felicitous anywhere—tall, stately, and obviously from another era. The children's collection is also first-rate.

*A pleasant and well-maintained garden lies behind the library in Stockbridge.* Judith Monachina

Called *W-nahk-ta-kook* (Great Meadow) by the Mahican Indians who settled there, the town of Stockbridge was incorporated by the English in 1739. The colonial charter made the town Indian property, a mission, and thereafter it was known as Indian Town. The history of this great meadow and its town is displayed and explained in the Stockbridge Historical Room, a small museum in the basement of the library. Here are Indian artifacts, photos from the mid-1800s onward, memorabilia from many famous residents and visitors to the village, and other intriguing historical bits that illuminate Stockbridge present.

## MUSEUMS

### THE BERKSHIRE MUSEUM

413-443-7171; fax 413-443-2135.
www.berkshiremuseum.org.
39 South St., Pittsfield, MA 01201.
Open: Mon–Sat. 10–5, Sun. 12–5.
Admission: Adults $7.50, children 3–18 $4.50, students over 18 with ID and seniors $6, children under 3 and guests on their birthdays, free.
Special Features: Gift shop.

Three museums in one, the Berkshire Museum presents strong collections of art, science, and regional history as well as an exciting calendar of lectures, films, concerts, classes, and field trips.

Founded in 1903 by Dalton papermaker and philanthropist Zenas Crane, the museum shows Hudson River school paintings, the Proctor Shell Collection, and the Cohn Collection of Minerals. Also, changing exhibits, such as the Power of Place landscapes summer 2005, are featured throughout year. The collections are far-ranging: 19th-century glass made in the towns of Berkshire and Cheshire and pre-Christian glass bottles from Egypt; exhibits of shells and aquatic life, fossils, mushrooms, reptiles, and amphibians. The Bird Room has a special section on Berkshire birds; the owl exhibit especially captivates. The Berkshire Backyard presents native mammal specimens. A collection of beautiful dioramas by Louis Paul Jonas Sr. shows the animals of the world in one-tenth scale. An aquarium holds more than 100 species, featuring a hands-on exhibit for children called Touch of the Sea.

That the museum is committed to families and community is demonstrated by exhibits and numerous programs. The life-sized stegosaurus (named Wally) on the museum's front lawn is a community landmark. The Museum Theater, a 300-seat facility, is site for lectures, plays, concerts, and the Little Cinema's admirable program of feature films.

Upstairs, works of Copley, Stuart, and Peale represent American portraiture. The Hudson River school appears in works by Cole, Inness, and others. A European gallery is devoted to the work of such English portrait painters as West and Reynolds, plus European works by masters spanning the 15th to 18th centuries. In the museum's center is the lofty and skylighted Ellen Crane Memorial Room, devoted to American and European sculpture from the 19th and 20th centuries. An ancient civilizations gallery includes "Pa-hat," the ever-popular Egyptian mummy, who lies resplendent amid a first-rate collection of ancient reliefs and artifacts.

### BERKSHIRE SCENIC RAILWAY MUSEUM

413-637-2210.
www.berkshirescenicrailroad.org.
10 Willow Creek Rd., P.O. Box 2195, Lenox, MA 01240.

One and a half miles E. of jct. of Rte. 7/20, 5 miles N. of Lee exit off the MassPike.
Open: Memorial Day–Oct., on weekends and holidays, 10–4.
Tickets: Adults $13, seniors $11, children under 14 $8.
Special Features: Museum; gift shop.

Freed by a major state grant in 2002 and an agreement to use the Housatonic Railroad's tracks, the Berkshire Scenic Railroad runs again. For the first time in more than a decade, visitors can take a scenic train ride (two daily, both narrated by a uniformed conductor) along the Housatonic River between Lenox and Stockbridge—a 20-mile round-trip in 1920s-vintage Erie Lackawanna passenger coaches, on occasion a caboose, pulled and pushed by a GE diesel locomotive. Afterward, passengers can blow the whistle or ring the bell, check out the model trains in the 1902 Lenox train station, admire Woods Pond, and visit a refurbished 1920s-vintage Baltimore and Ohio Railroad coach fitted out as a home for a Gateway to the Gilded Age exhibit—interpreting the turn-of-the-20th-century era of fabulous summer cottages in the Berkshires.

### STERLING AND FRANCINE CLARK ART INSTITUTE

413-458-2303, 413-458-9545.
www.clarkart.edu.
225 South St., Williamstown, MA 01267.
One mi. S. of jct. of Rtes. 7 and 2.
Open: Tues.–Sun. 10–5; July and Aug., daily 10–5; closed Thanksgiving, Christmas, New Year's Day.
Admission: June through Oct., adults $10, students and children under 18 free; Nov. through May, free.
Special Features: Gift shop; café.

Sterling Clark acquired his first Renoir in 1916. By the time he was finished collecting, he owned 36. He and his French wife, Francine, bought what they liked. Thus the basis of this fine collection reflects their personal taste. Included with impressionists are galleries filled with 19th-century American classics—by Winslow Homer, John Singer Sargent, and Frederic Remington—and a small but impressive collection of old masters. Traveling exhibits of Renoir, Degas, Millet, Painting Quickly in France, and Jacques-Louis David: Empire to Exile have attracted large summer crowds. The Clark originated the Vienna Project that united several Berkshire cultural entities in a common theme during the summer of 2002.

The Clark celebrated its 50th anniversary in 2005. The original 1950s building is elegant and efficient, a white Vermont-marble neoclassical structure whose interior is finished in Italian marble, plaster, and natural-finish oak. The large 1973 red-granite addition houses more galleries and a serious art library. Substantial remodeling in 1996 added more galleries, storage, and a café. A new campus, entryway, and home for the art conservation laboratory are planned. The museum shop includes an extensive collection of art books.

For most visitors, the centerpiece of the museum's collection is its gathering of French impressionists, the Clarks' greatest artistic love. Among the standouts, besides Renoir, are works by Monet and Degas, the latter in both his racehorse and ballet dancer series. Almost every gallery has some form of natural light; many galleries offer not only splendid art on the walls but also peaceful views of the Berkshire Hills.

The Clark is more than a painting gallery, however. As we walk among its colorful masterworks and their accompanying drawings and prints, we also see some of the collection's antique furniture and silver, masterpieces of craftsmanship. A piano as artwork may be the Clark's most controversial recent acquisition.

An important art education center, as well, the Clark offers a broad spectrum of lectures open to the public, serving as classroom to a graduate program in art history run jointly with Williams College. The Clark also offers major events in connection with its exhibits, chamber music, video film programs, folk music, children's programs, and popular outdoor band concerts in the summer.

### FRELINGHUYSEN-MORRIS HOUSE & STUDIO

413-637-0166; fax 413-637-9790.
www.frelinghuysen.org.
92 Hawthorne St., Lenox, MA 01240.
Open: June 28–Labor Day, Thurs.–Sun. 10–4; Labor Day–Columbus Day, Thurs.–Sat. 10–4.
Admission: Adults $10, children $3.
Special Features: Limited items for sale.

Anyone interested in art, architecture, or art history might be intrigued by one of the hourly tours of the home and studio of George L. K. Morris and his wife, Suzy Frelinghuysen, artists and advocates of the avant-garde. On exhibit are his and her framed works and murals, along with a smattering of Matisse, Degas, Picasso, Braque, Leger, and Gris. A large earth mother by Gaston Lachaise reclines among the trees on the wooded 46 acres that stretch between Hawthorne Street and Route 183, adjacent to Tanglewood.

*The avant-garde stairway at the Frelinghuysen-Morris House* Judith Monachina

Morris built his studio on the grounds in 1930, then added the Le Corbusier–style home in 1940—to the chagrin of Berkshire's traditionally housed residents. Morris, descended from a signer of the Declaration of Independence, died in an automobile accident in 1975. Frelinghuysen, from a line of Dutch Reform clergymen, college presidents, and politicians, survived the accident, living until 1988.

## HANCOCK SHAKER VILLAGE

413-443-0188.
www.hancockshakervillage.org.
Mail: P.O. Box 927, Pittsfield, MA 01202.
Jct. of Rtes. 20 and 41, 6 mi. W. of Pittsfield.
Open: Memorial Day weekend–Columbus Day, daily 9:30–5; rest of year, Guided Tour Season, 10–3; closed Thanksgiving, Christmas, New Year's Day; call ahead in winter.
Admission: Adults $15 summer/fall, $12.50 winter/spring; children under 18 free.
Special Features: Museum shops, seasonal café; walking-tour brochures available in English, French, German, Spanish, Japanese, and Braille.

The United Society of Believers in Christ's Second Appearing, later called Shakers, were founded in England in 1747 as a small group of religious nonconformists. Ann Lee, a young woman with strong religious convictions, became their spiritual leader. In 1774, a small group joined "Mother Ann" in sailing for the New World. They landed in New York, near Albany, where they later formed the Shaker community of Niskeyuna.

Shaker religion was also a way of life. Members joined into distinct communities isolated from the outside world. Men and women held equal status in daily life and leadership positions, but the genders were separated to support the Shaker commitment to celibacy. Communities were organized into families. Members gave public confession of their sins. Ritual dancing gave rise to their name, originally derisive but later adopted by the sect.

A community was established in 1790 at Hancock. Given the spiritual name of the City of Peace, it prospered for more than 150 years. Residents sought heavenly perfection, resulting in products that came to be known for their beauty. Design of clothing, furniture, implements, and buildings was strictly functional, without addition of deliberate ornamentation. "'Tis a gift to be simple . . ." goes an old Shaker hymn, and such simplicity was a primary aim of both inner and outer life. "Beauty rests on utility," said their credo. Of great beauty, then, is Hancock's symbol, the stunning Round Stone Barn. As splendid as the structure is to the eye, how much more splendid is it that with such an efficient architecture, one farmhand at the center could easily and quickly feed an entire herd of cattle.

When the sect was at its peak, in the mid-19th century, Hancock was one of 18 Shaker communities from Maine to Kentucky and had a population of about 300 members. The agricultural base of the village was augmented by cottage industries, offering such items as cooperware, flat brooms, agricultural seeds, and dairy products to sell to the World's People. But as religious ferment ceased, the Shaker population at Hancock declined steadily until 1960, when the last of the Hancock Shakers moved away.

Since then the village and its 1,200 acres of meadows and woodlands have been a living museum to accommodate visitors who want a taste of the Shaker ways. The City of Peace now acts as center of re-created Shaker activities, including workshops, candlelit dinners, and evening tours. The second weekend in July features the Americana artists and crafts show.

Visitors can tour 20 original Shaker buildings to see Shaker furniture and tools, some of them attended by craftspeople working in the Shaker way: the chair maker, the blacksmith, basket makers, spinners, and weavers. Hancock's workshops teach how to create Shaker chair seats, oval boxes, natural herb wreaths, and a variety of other crafts. From the gardens, both herbal and vegetable, and from any of the village workers, visitors absorb the power of Shaker simplicity.

Always a destination for families, the replica of a circa 1820 schoolhouse—complete with a teacher, in-season—the discovery room, and the Center for Shaker Studies, make the museum even more appealing. With a new parking lot and entrance, together with space for rotating exhibits and programs, the village, its original residents departed, nevertheless continues into the future.

For a fee, the village offers its facilities for special events such as weddings.

### MASSACHUSETTS MUSEUM OF CONTEMPORARY ART (MASS MoCA)

413-664-4481; fax 413-663-8548.
www.massmoca.org.
87 Marshall St., N. Adams, MA 01247.
Open: June 1–Oct. 31, daily 10–6; Nov. 1–May 30, Wed.–Mon. 11–5; closed Thanksgiving, Christmas, New Year's Day.
Admission: Adults $10, seniors and students over 16 with ID $8, children 6–16 $4.
Special Features: Museum shop; performances.

For 12 years the idea of a big museum in an old mill and director Joe Thompson hung on by their fingernails—until the Massachusetts Museum of Contemporary Art, or MASS MoCA as it is universally known, opened as a critical and public success in the summer of 1999. People in numbers beyond expectation streamed into the "supercollider for the best of

*David Cole installed his* Knitting Machine *at MASS MoCA in 2005. It knitted the flag.* Argen Noordeman

today's visual, performing, and new media arts," as Thompson defines his 13-acre, 27-building factory campus. "Until now," he explains, "large complex art forms—exotic multimedia productions, for example, or monumental installations—have been without a public forum that is striking, properly scaled, and technically wired for cross-disciplinary collaborations."

Although not everyone may take to the artworks—gigantic to minimalist by Rauschenberg, Rosenquist, Flavin, Nauman, and Morris—everyone has responded to the gorgeous retrofitting of hangarlike spaces once a textile mill and more recently given over to the manufacture of capacitors. However, it was probably the accompanying variety of special events that made the opening summer and fall such a public success: "Swing Shift Dance Parties," "Film Factory" with outside projection, dance performances by the Paul Taylor Dance Company and others, concerts, and a musical, Quark Victory, put on by the Williamstown Theatre Festival. With the assistance of Jacob's Pillow, the Clark Art Institute, and WTF, this kind of aggressive programming continues.

North Adams, done up in banners and flowers, new streetlights, and new signage, looks—improbably as it may seem—like a city being lifted up and uplifted by art. The city itself, with MASS MoCA at its heart, may be the ultimate "large complex art form" on view to thousands of visitors from around the world. As the museum changes and evolves, we shall see what they shall see.

## NORMAN ROCKWELL MUSEUM

413-298-4100, 800-742-9450; fax 413-298-4142.
www.nrm.org.
Mail: P.O. Box 308, Stockbridge, MA 01262.
On Rte. 183, 0.6 mi. S. of Rte. 102.
Open: May–Oct., daily 10–5; Nov.–April, Mon.–Fri. 10–4, Sat., Sun., holidays, 10–5.
Closed Thanksgiving, Christmas, New Year's Day.
Admission: Adults $12.50, students over 18 with ID $7, children 18 and under free with adult.
Special Features: Gift shop; Terrace Café open seasonally.

Norman Rockwell is coming to be seen more as artist than illustrator; the display of his life's work at the Norman Rockwell Museum resonates. A visit to this grand monument to his talent and insight is worth the crush of bus passengers—or go off-season.

Set on a gracious knoll overlooking the Housatonic River in the Glendale section of Stockbridge, the $4.4-million building designed by Robert A. M. Stern has a New England town hall look to it, with slate gables, clapboard siding, and fieldstone terraces. Inside, spacious, well-lit galleries show permanent exhibits of Rockwell's paintings, while changing exhibits feature Rockwell and other illustrators, notably *New Yorker* covers in the summer of 2005.

At the core is the skylighted gallery where Rockwell's *Four Freedoms* hang on permanent display. Created during the Second World War, they depict what the U.S. was fighting to uphold: *Freedom of Speech; Freedom from Fear; Freedom of Worship; Freedom from Want.* These four archetypal American images constitute a shrine to America's progressive image of itself.

Rockwell's 47-year relationship with the *Saturday Evening Post* is well known; in 1963 it ended, and he signed on with *Look* and *McCall's*. His palette and his cast of characters broadened. Where once he depicted white boys running from a prohibited swimming hole, now federal marshals lead a young black girl to school in Little Rock. From lovers and gossips, he moved on to Peace Corps volunteers and astronauts on the moon.

Outside stands Rockwell's studio, a 19th-century carriage house with a bucolic view of the Housatonic. Inside the studio, which was moved from Stockbridge village to its present site in 1986, we understand the light in which he loved to paint, the curious assemblage of props with which he liked to surround himself, and the modest space he felt was his "best studio yet." The studio is open May through October.

The Rockwell Museum offers a variety of community-oriented programs beyond its public exhibitions, including lectures, performances, special events, and art classes.

### WESTERN GATEWAY HERITAGE STATE PARK

413-663-6312.
115 State St., Bldg. 4, N. Adams, MA 01247-3852.
In freight-yard district.
Open: Daily 10–5; closed Thanksgiving, Christmas, New Year's Day.
Admission: Free; donations accepted.
Special Features: Shops, history museum, and restaurant part of complex.

Berkshire County, nestled between long ridges, had always been separated from the rest of Massachusetts. In 1851, engineers and construction workers began an assault, drilling and blasting a 4.75-mile-long tunnel through the northeastern ridge. This Hoosac Tunnel was the first major tunneling work in the United States. New methods were devised over the 20-year construction, at a cost of over $20 million and more than 195 lives. The building of the tunnel and related railroad development made North Adams the largest city in Berkshire in 1900. "We hold the Western Gateway," says the North Adams seal. At the turn of the 20th century, more than half of Boston's freight came through the tunnel.

Western Gateway Heritage State Park now celebrates the former Boston and Maine Freight House and the Hoosac Tunnel, both of which are on the National Register of Historic Places. Inside, films, slide shows, and written histories of the railway and tunnel are presented. Outside are shops, the restored freight yard, the Freight Yard Pub restaurant, and the church-spired charm of North Adams.

Heritage State Park is also home to the **North Adams Museum of History & Science** (413-664-4700; www.northadams.com/history; Building 5-A), open Thursday through Sunday from 10 to 4, at no charge. An old-fashioned museum of 25 exhibits, discovery room, and three working train models chronicle the history of and achievements related to North Adams and northern Berkshire.

### WILLIAMS COLLEGE MUSEUM OF ART

413-597-2429.
www.wcma.org.
Main St., Williamstown, MA 01267.
Rte. 2, across from Gothic chapel.
Open: Tues.–Sat. 10–5, Sun. 1–5, inc. Memorial Day, Labor Day, Columbus Day; closed Thanksgiving, Christmas, New Year's Day.
Admission: Free.
Special Features: Gift shop.

One of the finest college art museums in the country, the Williams College Museum of Art is housed in a 19th-century structure that has been strikingly revisited. Behind the original 1846 building, with its neoclassical octagonal rotunda, is an addition designed by Charles Moore that opened in 1983. Combining wit and sophistication, Moore created a versatile, multileveled exhibition space in both old and new buildings, retaining the brick wall of the former as the stunning backdrop for a multilevel stairwell. His design for the building's rear facade is a continuation of his lighthearted approach, featuring his "ironic columns"—their nonfunctionality revealed by the gap near the top. Now the eyes have it in front—as a result of a searching and striking piece commissioned of Louise Bourgeois.

Inside, the museum's permanent collection contains some 11,000 objects. Complementing the neighboring Clark Art Institute's collection of 19th-century European art, WCMA emphasizes early art, 20th-century art, and the art of Asia and other non-Western civilizations. Thanks to a $32 million gift by the widow of American impressionist Charles Prendergast, what was once a small, regional museum now houses the finest collection by both Charles and his talented brother, Maurice, and is the leading center in the world for study of the Prendergasts' work.

A lively education program includes school events and other events for children. Several times a year WCMA hosts popular free "family days," when children can try a range of art projects thematically linked to the collection, guided by enthusiastic Williams students.

Frequent loan exhibitions focus on a wide range of provocative subjects; in the summer of 2002 such an exhibit was influences on Adolf Hitler. Moving Pictures, which detailed the influence of early film on American art and vice versa, took up nearly the entire museum in the summer of 2005. Visitors should expect to be engaged, not soothed.

### Other Museums

Besides delving into fine art and rare books, the many museums in Williamstown lead in still other directions. For example, *out* to the **Hopkins Forest Museum** (413-597-2346; **Hopkins Memorial Forest**, the **Rosenberg Center**, and **Buxton Garden**; Northwest Hill Rd.) and such seasonal events as fall harvesting and maple sugaring, while the museum itself exhibits old photographs, farm machinery, and tools. Or *up* to the stars at the 19th-century fieldstone **Hopkins Observatory** (413-597-2188; Main St.) via the projected shows at the **Milham Planetarium** (evenings Tues. and Thurs. summer; Fri. during school year), and out and up to the real pulsars and quasars through the telescopes at Williams College.

**Bennington Museum** (802-447-1571), 15 miles north of Williamstown on Route 7, west on Route 9 in Vermont; and **Historic Deerfield, Inc.** (413-774-5581), east on Route 2 and south on Route 5, are fine day-trip destinations.

## Music

### ASTON MAGNA

413-528-3595, 800-875-7156.
www.astonmagna.org.
323 Main St., P.O. Box 28, Gt. Barrington, MA 01230.
Performances: Daniel Art Center, Simonds Rock College, 84 Alford Rd., Gt. Barrington.

*The Berkshire Choral Festival sings, with soloists Leslie Jones and Jane Jennings.* Stephan G. Donaldson

Season: July and Aug.
Tickets: Call for prices.

Of historic preservation in the Berkshires, none is more artistic than the renaissance of baroque, classical, and early romantic chamber music by Aston Magna. Offering unique cross-disciplinary educational programs for professional musicians and superb concerts in the summer and at other times, Aston Magna has specialized in 17th-, 18th-, and early-19th-century music, always played on period instruments or reproductions. In recent summers, Mozart, Haydn, Bach, Handel, Vivaldi, Monteverdi, and Corelli have been played as in their own time, with festival artistic director and virtuoso violinist Daniel Stepner leading a distinguished roster of singers and instrumentalists. Participants study the temperament and cultural milieu of the age and then make music that is imbued with the period's sensibility.

**BERKSHIRE CHORAL FESTIVAL**

Box office 413-229-1999, administration 413-229-8526; fax 413-229-0109.
www.chorus.org.
Mail: 245 N. Undermountain Rd., Sheffield, MA 01257.

Performances: Concert Shed, Berkshire School, Rte. 41, Sheffield.
Season: July and Aug.
Tickets: Required.

An experiment in mixing amateur, semipro, and professional singers into a chorus culminated in a single concert. Success there has led the Berkshire Choral Festival more than 20 years later to evolve into a summer-long, professional-quality chorus—changing with each performance—that can be counted on for stirring moments, as in a recent Mass in B-minor.

Each summer now brings a five-concert Berkshire celebration featuring 200 adult, amateur voices from all over the world, powerful soloists and conductors, and the Springfield Symphony, at one of the loveliest preparatory schools in New England, The Berkshire School. These performances are also given at other venues around the world.

### BERKSHIRE OPERA COMPANY

Box office 413-442-0099, administration 443-442-9955; fax 413-442-5995.
www.berkshireopera.org.
297 North St., Pittsfield, MA 01201.
Performances: Venues to be announced.
Season: July and Aug.
Tickets: Required.

In over a decade, originally under founder-director Rex Hearn, the Berkshire Opera has grown stronger than ever. This talented group has won praise from both audiences and serious critics alike for its renditions of chamber opera.

There are discoveries to be made here. Among them was Stockbridge resident Maureen O. Flynn, whom Hearn initially heard singing at the First Congregational Church in Lee and who has since gone from the Berkshire Opera to the Metropolitan and a brilliant international career.

Under Artistic Director Joel Revzen, in the summer of 2005 BOC presented original language versions of Handel's *Rinaldo* and Donizetti's *L'Elisir d'Amore* at the Mahaiwe Theater in Great Barrington, the Koussevitzky Arts Center in Pittsfield, and Chapin Hall in Williamstown. The productions fill a needed role in the rich summer life of the region by offering artfully prepared chamber operas.

### SOUTH MOUNTAIN CONCERTS

413-442-2106.
www.southmountainconcerts.org.
Mail: P.O. Box 23, Pittsfield, MA 01202.
On Rte. 7/20 about 1 mi. S. of Pittsfield Country Club.
Season: Sept.–Oct.
Tickets: Prices vary.

South Mountain's Colonial-style Temple of Music, built in 1918 and the gift of Mrs. Elizabeth Sprague Coolidge, was intended to house the concerts of the Berkshire String Quartet. The acoustically splendid 450-seat auditorium, listed on the National Register of Historic Places, is set gracefully on its wooded South Mountain slope.

Distinguished performers have always made South Mountain a special place. In recent years string quartets have led the fare—the Guarneri, the Juilliard, the Emerson, and the

Tokyo string quartets have been regular performers. Usually one concert each season features another combination, such as the Kalichstein-Laredo-Robinson Trio.

With a devoted subscription membership, South Mountain Concerts almost always sell out. Nonsubscribers should call early for seats. Fortunately, every seat is good because of the acoustics.

Unlike Tanglewood, where watching the stars or basking in the sunshine may substitute for close listening to the music, South Mountain's more limited season and number of concerts are designed for the serious music lover.

## TANGLEWOOD

Tickets/information 413-637-5165; concert line 413-637-1666; administration 413-637-1600.
www.bso.org.
297 West St., Lenox, MA 01240.
On Rte. 183.
Off-season: 617-266-1492; 301 Massachusetts Ave., Boston, MA 02115.
Season: June–Sept.
Tickets: Vary.
Special Features: Gift shops; restaurant.

Tanglewood remains *the* summer music festival in New England, an incomparable facility for all the world's musicians and music lovers. Whether you picnic on the lawn or sit closer to the Boston Symphony Orchestra in the Shed, hearing music at Tanglewood is an unparalleled experience. The powerful positive feeling among musicians, students, and concertgoers alike, and the sheer fun of seeing and hearing great music made in the great outdoors, make Tanglewood the quintessential Berkshire entertainment—even if some people start repacking their picnic baskets during the Chorale in Beethoven's *Ninth*.

Tanglewood began as the Berkshire Music Festival in the summer of 1934. Members of the New York Philharmonic were bused from Manhattan to the mountains and lodged in the area's hotels for the concert series. A rousing success, it was repeated the following summer. But then the New York orchestra withdrew. As a result, Serge Koussevitzky, the Russian-born conductor of the Boston Symphony Orchestra, was wooed and won. The BSO signed on for a series of three concerts on a single August weekend in 1936.

The popularity of this series was immense, with nearly 15,000 people attending. That fall the Tappan family gave their Tanglewood estate on the Stockbridge-Lenox border to the BSO as a permanent summer home in the Berkshires. For the first two summers, concerts were held in a large canvas tent, but during one 1937 program, a torrential thunderstorm drowned out Wagner's "The Ride of the Valkyries," and dampened instruments, musicians, and audience alike. During intermission, an impromptu fund-raising drive raised pledges totaling $30,000 for the creation of a permanent "music pavilion." By the following summer, through the combined efforts of the distinguished architect Eliel Saarinen and Stockbridge engineer Joseph Franz, the Shed was a reality.

Sensing the opportunity and the ideal setting, Koussevitzky and the BSO added the Berkshire Music Center for advanced musicians in 1940, the only such school run by a major symphony orchestra. For the school's opening ceremony, Randall Thompson composed his haunting *Alleluia* for unaccompanied chorus, a work that made such a lasting impression that it has been performed as the school's opening music ever since.

Each summer the Tanglewood Music Center Orchestra is re-created from that year's crop of students; for their weekly concerts, this impressive group is usually led by a student conductor, but sometimes by the likes of Kurt Masur, Zubin Mehta, or André Previn. So significant is this Tanglewood education that upwards of 20 percent of the members of America's major orchestras count themselves among Tanglewood Music Center alumni. Leonard Bernstein was a graduate, as are Seiji Ozawa and Mr. Mehta.

The $10 million arched Seiji Ozawa Hall opened in the summer of 1994. Accommodating 1,200 inside and an additional 700 on nearby lawns, the new hall has sides that open, giving it flexibility and versatility as well as excellent acoustics. The hall is located on the Highwood section of Tanglewood, now designated as the Leonard Bernstein campus. With the departure of Maestro Ozawa, James Levine now directs the BSO.

The Music Festival has evolved into a performance center of major proportions, with an annual attendance of some 300,000 visitors. Pianists Emanuel Ax

*Tanglewood parades in its sylvan setting.* Michael Lutch

**Where to Sit at Tanglewood**

Those planning to picnic at Tanglewood before a performance given in the Shed should arrive an hour or so in advance of concert time. Besides allowing time to eat before listening, arriving early affords a greater choice of spaces on the lawn, an important factor in hearing the music clearly. Although Tanglewood's amplification system is excellent and facilitates good listening from almost any lawn position, places about 25 yards beyond the Shed-mounted speakers provide the best lawn listening.

Inside the Shed, the last series of back rows are good only for saying we were there, allowing only the most distant orchestra views and suffering greatly from much-diminished sound. (In fact, at the optimum sites on the lawn, the sound is far superior.) Those who can afford to indulge should buy their way forward into the good seats, where the sound is rich, sometimes robust and sometimes delicate, and where you can really see classical music in the making. (Food is not allowed in the Shed, however.)

Seiji Ozawa Hall has its own lawn with seating for several hundred.

All attendees should allow time for a walk in Tanglewood's beautifully groomed boxwood gardens. As the sun sets on a clear day, the hills range in three states.

**Festivals-within-the-Festival at Tanglewood**
Not content to satisfy the classical music lover, Tanglewood offers minifestivals and series featuring contemporary, jazz, and popular music.

Recent offerings in the Contemporary Music Festival have been an appropriately eclectic mix, including a performance by puppets. When our free spirits are being kept too staid by our classicism, we require a dose of Tanglewood's contemporary music.

Artistry of an even jazzier sort is showcased during Tanglewood's annual Jazz Festival, with the likes of Branford Marsalis, Dave Brubeck, and the New Black Eagle Jazz Band; and songs of a slightly different sort are featured during Tanglewood's Popular Artist Series, frequently including the always-popular James Taylor and a live broadcast of NPR's *A Prairie Home Companion*.

and Peter Serkin, violinist Itzhak Perlman, cellist Yo-Yo Ma, and the Juilliard String Quartet return regularly. In addition to the regular BSO concerts, Tanglewood presents weekly chamber music concerts in the smaller sheds, Prelude Concerts on Friday nights, open rehearsals on Saturday mornings, the annual Festival of Contemporary Music, the annual Jazz Festival, and almost daily concerts by gifted young musicians at the Music Center. Some student concerts are free. The Boston Pops comes to play, as well.

A favorite of each season is "Tanglewood on Parade," an amazingly varied musical day lasting some 10 hours, climaxing with booming cannon shots and fireworks. But whatever the scale of the offerings, an evening at Tanglewood marks a high point in any summer.

## Other Music

### South County

The **Berkshire Bach Society** (413-528-9277; P.O. Box 553, S. Egremont, MA 01258) offers a fine series of concerts and lectures at various area churches, schools, and colleges. **Simon's Rock College of Bard** (413-528-0771; Alford Rd., Gt. Barrington, MA 01230) is one of the liveliest promoters of professional music in South County. **Close Encounters with Music** (518-392-6677, 800-843-0778; P.O. Box 34, Gt. Barrington, MA 01230) offers beautiful music and intriguing commentary by artistic director Yehuda Hanani and guests at Gt. Barrington's St. James Church and elsewhere during the winter season. The **Curtisville Consortium** (413-698-2618; P.O. Box 140, W. Stockbridge, MA 01266) takes its name from the hamlet of Interlaken in Stockbridge, which was originally settled as Curtisville. The consortium is a group of Boston Symphony Orchestra musicians and guest artists who present a 5-week-long series of concerts each summer at the Trinity Church in Lenox. **Stockbridge Chamber Concerts** (888-528-7728; P.O. Box 164, Stockbridge, MA 01262) offers a summer series in Searles Castle.

### Central County

Chamber music can also be enjoyed at the **Richmond Performance Series** (413-698-2002; P.O. Box 199, Richmond, MA 01254). Each of these concerts—performed at the Richmond Congregational Church, Route 41, and other venues—features professional symphony orchestra veterans making intimate music in special settings. **Berkshire Com-**

*The Town Hall in Lenox has been the site of numerous cultural events throughout the years.* Judith Monachina

**munity College** (413-499-4660; www.ccberkshire.org; 1350 West St., Pittsfield, MA 01201) offers concerts year-round. The **Berkshire Lyric Theatre** (413-499-0258; www.berkshirelyric.org; P.O. Box 347, Pittsfield, MA 01201) plays at Lenox Town Hall and in Central and South County churches. The **Berkshire Concert Choir** (413-443-4758; P.O. Box 174, Richmond, MA 01254), under the direction of John Cheney, presents sacred and secular music in two concerts each year, one in December and one in May.

### North County

**Williams College** alone offers enough music to keep anyone humming, with four classical Thompson visiting performances, a world-music series, and performances by Williams faculty. The **Berkshire Symphony**, part professional and part student, and **Williams Choral Society**, both under the auspices of the Williams Department of Music, generally present three concerts apiece during the academic year. The student **Jazz Ensemble**, **Kusika**, the **Zambezi Marimba Band**, and close harmony groups too numerous to name provide musical saturation of high quality. The **Griffin Hall** series presents harpsichord and organ music. (Concert manager's office: 413-597-2736; 24-hour Concertline: 413-597-3146; Griffin Hall Concerts: 413-597-2428.) In summer, the **Taubman Piano Festival** brings rising young virtuosi to town to perform at Chapin Hall, Williams College.

Elsewhere in Williamstown, the **Clark Art Institute** (413-458-2303; www.clark art.edu; 225 South St., Williamstown, MA 01267) presents free band music outdoors in summer and a variety of concerts indoors, including those of the **Williamstown Chamber Concerts** (413-458-8273; P.O. Box 287, Williamstown, MA 01267), which continues its winning ways. **The Northern Berkshire Chorale**, a citizens' group under the direction of Judith Reichert, offers a concert spring and fall. Over in North Adams, **Massachusetts College of Liberal Arts** (413-662-5000) sponsors the **Smith House Concert Series** (413-662-5201), usually professional musicians with local connections.

### OUTSIDE THE COUNTY

Just east of the county, in the Berkshire hill town of Charlemont (Rte. 2, Franklin County), the **Mohawk Trail Concerts** (413-625-9511, 888-MTC-MUSE; www.mohawktrail.org; P.O. Box 75, Shelburne Falls, MA 01370) presents a season of informal classical concerts at the Federated Church. In South Worthington, the Schrade family presents its summer **Sevenars Music Festival** (413-238-5854) at the Academy on Rte. 112.

Over the state line, in New Lebanon, New York, are the **Tannery Pond Concerts** (tickets 888-846-5848, information 888-820-1696; P.O. Box 446, New Lebanon, NY 12125). Tannery's season comprises five or six chamber or song recitals between May and October. In adjacent Spencertown, New York, the **Spencertown Academy** (518-392-3693; P.O. Box 80, Spencertown, NY 12165) puts on concerts that are diverse, compelling, and held in a remarkable elderly former school building that is now a center for the arts.

Two well-regarded chamber music festivals in northwestern Connecticut enrich the greater Berkshire area. One is the **Norfolk Chamber Music Festival** (860-542-3000; fax 860-542-3004; www.yale.edu/norfolk; Ellen Battell Stoeckell Estate, Rtes. 44 & 272; P.O. Box 545, Norfolk, CT 06058; off-season 203-432-1966; P.O. Box 208246, New Haven, CT 06520). Norfolk presents visiting virtuosi, such as the Tokyo String Quartet and the Vermeer Quartet, mid-June through mid-August, as a byproduct of the Yale Summer School of Music.

In nearby Falls Village is **Music Mountain** (860-824-7126; www.musicmoun tain.org; P.O. Box 738, Lakeville, CT 06039; Music Mountain Rd., off Rte. 7 opposite Housatonic Valley High School). Here the Manhattan String Quartet and visiting artists perform mid-June through Labor Day. Founded in 1930 by Chicago Symphony Orchestra concertmaster Jacques Gordon, Music Mountain is the oldest continuing chamber music festival in America.

## NIGHTLIFE

Although the Berkshires may be better known as home to great theater, visual art, and classical music, there is a long-standing tradition of popular nightlife in these parts, including top national and regional performing talent in jazz, folk, rock, and cabaret.

While new venues are always popping up and older ones occasionally falling by the wayside, several well-established nightclubs and restaurants offer after-hours entertainment.

### SOUTH COUNTY

Starting in Great Barrington, **Club Helsinki** (413-528-3394; 284 Main St., Gt. Barrington, MA 01230) has in the last few years become the shining star of the Berkshire live-music scene, presenting an eclectic array of regional and nationally known performers in an intimate, funky, L-shaped den of brickwork and art deco objects. The list of artists who have packed the 100-seat club ranges from avant-garde guitarist Marc Ribot to jazz singer Mose Allison to Texas country legend Guy Clark to folksinger Michelle Shocked. Reggae, blues, and funk bands often play the club—which boasts a terrific selection of imported vodkas and a bar menu of specialties from the adjoining restaurant, Helsinki Café. The club periodically presents marquee artists like Doc Watson, Pete Seeger, and the Blind Boys of Alabama at other venues in the Berkshires, including the Berkshire Music Hall and First United Methodist Church in Pittsfield.

A few blocks from Helsinki, the Castle Street Café's **Celestial Bar** (413-528-5244; 10 Castle St., Gt. Barrington, MA 01230) is a traditional-style piano bar with featured performers, including pianists, guitar-and-vocal trios, and the occasional swing or bluegrass group, on weekend nights year-round. Also in Great Barrington, late-night dancing to DJ music often takes place on weekends at **Union Bar and Grill** (413-528-6228; 293 Main St., Gt. Barrington, MA 01230) and just south of downtown at **Bogies Restaurant and Pub** (413-528-5959; 935 S. Main St., Gt. Barrington, MA 01230). Over in South Egremont, the **Egremont Inn** (413-528-2111; 10 Old Sheffield Rd., S. Egremont, MA 01258, just off Rte. 23) also reliably presents the best in local jazz on weekends.

From late spring through foliage season, the **Guthrie Center** (413-528-1955; 4 Van Deusenville Rd., Gt. Barrington, MA 01230) presents weekend concerts featuring regional and national folk and bluegrass talent, including Dar Williams, Christine Lavin, and Oscar Brand. Located at the historic Trinity Church—best known as the location for the antics immortalized in "Alice's Restaurant," the song and movie—the Guthrie Center also is home base to folksinger Arlo Guthrie, who lives nearby and frequently performs there.

In Stockbridge, the subterranean **Lion's Den** at the Red Lion Inn (413-298-5545; 30 Main St., Stockbridge, MA 01262) is a cozy, coffeehouse-style nightclub featuring nightly entertainment—and no cover charge—drawn from the region's top talent, including the ever popular David Grover. Around the corner, **Michael's** (413-298-3530; Elm St., Stockbridge, MA 01262) attracts a dancing crowd on weekends.

As its name indicates, the **Berkshire Blues Café** (413-243-0062; Rte. 102, Lee, MA 01238) specializes in presenting local blues-based bands and singers.

For years, the **Dream Away Lodge** (413-623-8725; 1342 County Rd., Becket, MA 01223) has attracted the bohemian after-hours crowd from Tanglewood and Jacob's Pillow. After a period of hibernation, the rambling, way-off-the-beaten-path roadhouse, which has played host to everyone from Bob Dylan to Liberace, is under new management that has revived the traditional Wednesday-night hootenanny and hosts folk-based performers on weekends. Food's pretty good, too.

### Central County

In Pittsfield, the **Berkshire Museum** (413-443-7171; 39 South St., Pittsfield, MA 01201; Rte. 7), presents concerts in its 300-seat auditorium by nationally known singer-songwriters like Lucy Kaplansky, John Gorka, and Cheryl Wheeler. The **Common Grounds Coffee House** (499-0866; 55 Fenn St., Pittsfield, MA 01201) presents troubadour-style folksingers at the First United Methodist Church on a monthly basis. Under new management, Mexican restaurant **La Cocina** (413-499-6363; 140 Wahconah St., Pittsfield, MA 01201) is ground-zero for the regional neo-hippie, jam-band set, while over in Dalton, the region's best Top 40 cover bands entertain crowds at **The Depot** (413-684-1730; 450 W. Housatonic St., Dalton, MA 01226).

### North County

Sleepy North County has awoken over the last few years, in large part due to the opening of **MASS MoCA** (413-662-2111; 87 Marshall St., N. Adams, MA 01237) in North Adams, which has become a key venue for nightlife, hosting monthly dance parties featuring live bands playing swing, polka, salsa, African, zydeco, and blues. MASS MoCA also typically presents several big-name concerts each year—Patti Smith, Dr. John, They Might Be Giants, Suzanne Vega, Nanci Griffith, and Rosanne Cash are just a handful of the acts who have performed in the museum's state-of-the-art black-box theater or outdoor concert courtyard.

With the opening of **Gideon's Luncheon and Nightery** (413-664-0404; 23 Eagle St., N. Adams, MA 01237), North Adams finally has a legitimate nightclub to call its own, featuring stand-up comedy, jazz, blues, singer-songwriters, and more on Tuesday through Saturday nights. The **Railway Café** (413-664-6393; 59 Summer St., N. Adams, MA 01237) is a monthly folk venue at St. John's Episcopal Church, hosting top New England singer-songwriters like Cliff Eberhardt.

Over in Williamstown, the **Clark** (413-458-2303; 225 South St., Williamstown, MA 01267) presents occasional concerts by traditional and progressive folk musicians from around the world.

When the **Williamstown Theatre Festival** is up and running during the summer months, top stars of stage and screen occasionally ham it up at the **WTF Cabaret** (413-597-3400) on the Williams College campus. On Friday nights, pianist Howie Levitz accompanies guitarist Jim Bayliss in the tavern at the **Williams Inn** (413-458-9371; 1090 Main St., Williamstown, MA 01267), and the Walt Lehmann Jazz Band keeps the legacy of the late bandleader and clarinetist alive on Saturday nights. Fans of piano jazz should also check out the cozy confines of Yasmin's Lounge at **The Orchards** (413-458-9611; Adams Rd., Williamstown, MA 01267), where Bill Perault tickles the ivories most Friday and Saturday nights.

### OUTSIDE THE COUNTY

Berkshirites think nothing of hopping in the car and driving an hour to nearby Northampton for a fix of that college town's eclectic musical menu at one of several venues, including the recently restored **Calvin Theatre** to see the likes of Lyle Lovett or Sonny Rollins; **Pearl Street** for hot rock, reggae, or hip-hop acts; or the venerable **Iron Horse Music Hall**, where the best in folk, jazz, country, and alternative music can be heard most any night of the year. Call the Northampton Box office (800-THE-TICK) for schedules or reservations at any of these venues.

**Festival Frenzy**

Music moves outdoors in the summertime, when the Berkshire Hills come alive with the sounds of folk, bluegrass, and roots music. Just a short drive over the New York State line gets you to two of the best summer music festivals in the nation. The venerable **Grey Fox Bluegrass Festival** (888-946-8495; www.greyfoxbluegrass.com) has taken place at the Rothvoss Farm in Ancramdale, New York, for over 20 years. It's a must-stop on the summer bluegrass circuit for fans as well as top performers, including Sam Bush, Tony Trischka, Ralph Stanley, Peter Rowan, Bill Keith, and Alison Krauss. The **Falcon Ridge Folk Festival** (877-844-7742; www.falconridgefolk.com) at the Long Hill Farm in Hillsdale, New York, rivals the Newport (Rhode Island) Folk Festival for crowds and top contemporary folk acts, including Ani DiFranco, Richard Thompson, Janis Ian, Greg Brown, and Patty Larkin.

## Theater

### BARRINGTON STAGE COMPANY

413-499-5446.
www.barringtonstageco.org.
Berkshire Music Hall, 30 Union St., Pittsfield, MA 01201.
Season: Year-round.
Tickets: Various prices; students half price.

Spelling Bee *began at Barrington Stage Company and then moved to Broadway.* Joe Schuyler

Julianne Boyd, artistic director of the Barrington Stage Company, is a whiz at detecting the enduring in what might seem the old soft shoe, e.g., the 2002 production that took *South Pacific* into the 21st century. Or consider what really got BSC under way in 1995: *Lady Day at Emerson's Bar & Grill,* starring Gail Nelson as blues singer Billie Holiday, playing to sellouts at restaurants. In between, *Mac and Mabel* had a highly successful run on the main stage, while *St. Nicholas* and *Grease* flourished on Stage II. Perhaps the greatest hit so far, however, has been 2004's *The 27th Annual Putnam County Spelling Bee,* which enjoyed a considerable success on Broadway after its opening in Berkshire County. Barrington runs KidsAct, training 10-to-17-year-olds, summer and fall, and has opened StudioSpace for intimate productions.

In 2005 BSC purchased the old Berkshire Music Hall and adjoining administrative building, allowing it to move from summer use of a high school stage in Sheffield to year-round occupancy in a former theater and movie house in Pittsfield.

### BERKSHIRE THEATRE FESTIVAL

Box office 413-298-5576; administration 413-298-5536.
www.berkshiretheatre.org.
6 E. Main St., P.O. Box 797, Stockbridge, MA 01262.
On Rte. 102.
Season: Summer.
Tickets: Vary.
Special Features: Gift shop.

In 1887 architect Stanford White completed his design for the Stockbridge Casino Company, created for the "establishment and maintenance of a place for a reading room, library and social meeting." Forty years later, when the structure had fallen into disuse, Mabel Choate, daughter of Ambassador Joseph H. Choate of Stockbridge, gave the casino to the Three Arts Society. That group, in turn, moved it to its present site at the foot of Yale Hill, renting it to Alexander Kirkland and F. Cowles Strickland, who opened the Berkshire Playhouse in 1928.

Since that time, the playhouse—later renamed Berkshire Theatre Festival—has been in the forefront of American summer theater. Major works by nearly every American playwright of note have been performed here, including Lillian Hellmann, Tennessee Williams, Eugene O'Neill, and Thornton Wilder. The playhouse produced Wilder's *Our Town* and *The Skin of Our Teeth,* with Wilder himself in featured roles. Yet a production of *Pinafore* was a highlight of the 2001 season.

Leading lights in the theater appear regularly, from a young Katharine Hepburn in 1930 to Joanne Woodward in 1996.

The last two decades have been a period of growth and refocusing for BTF. In the spring of 1976, the building was entered on the National Register of Historic Places. Since then, gradual refurbishment has continued, with a new paint job and, most noticeably, all new seats. The Berkshire Theatre Festival has expanded its educational and rehearsal facilities, principally upon the gift of the Lavan Center, a few miles north of the playhouse. Interns and apprentices live at the center and rehearse there while pursuing a program of classes in acting, voice, movement, and design.

BTF also features performances at its 100-seat Unicorn Theatre, a showcase for younger artists. These are becoming increasingly substantial, recently being highlighted by the painterly *Mississippi Nude,* by John Reaves, one artist's life in living color. The educational aspect, called "The BTF Plays," reaches out to local schools.

### SHAKESPEARE & COMPANY

413-637-1194; fax 413-637-4274.
www.shakespeare.org.
70 Kemble St., Lenox, MA 01240.
Season: Summer, fall.
Tickets: Vary.

Shakespeare is revitalized on stage in Lenox, having moved uptown to Springlawn, where world-class performances are offered in Founders' Theatre and Spring Lawn Theatre, along with other special programs outdoors on the grounds. Under the powerful artistic guidance of English actor-director Tina Packer and her artistic associate, Dennis Krausnick, Shakespeare & Company, 29 years old in 2006, has brought new light, feeling, and clarity to Shakespeare, making the works more accessible to many people. Shakespeare & Company works in area schools in winter, spreading the wonder of the Bard even farther.

Part of the dramatic impact derives from the actors' ability to treat the audience as their alter ego, always privy to secrets of the drama. The plays are staged all around the seating area; intimacy with the action is inevitable, with stage and lighting design creating magical effects. Wrote the *New York Times* critic Ben Brantley of the company's performance of *A Midsummer Night's Dream:* "The overall result is vulgar, over scaled and loud. And it works. . . . There are few productions of Shakespearean comedy in which the meaning of every joke (whether intended by Shakespeare or not) reads so clearly, and the audience was responsive to each one."

While Shakespeare & Company attends to its namesake, it has also produced Edith Wharton–oriented plays and contemporary plays. Under the aegis of its Arden Institute, the company has toured, offering free workshops and demonstrations. It also runs programs for young actors. Under construction in Lenox is a replica of the Rose Playhouse, where Shakespeare's *Henry VI* and *Titus Andronicus* were first performed.

Shakespeare & Company is a "must see" for locals and visitors alike.

### WILLIAMSTOWN THEATRE FESTIVAL & '62 CENTER FOR THEATRE AND DANCE

413-597-3400; administration 413-458-3210; fax 413-458-3147.
www.wtfestival.org.
1000 Main St., P.O. Box 517, Williamstown, MA 01267.
Season: Summer; '62 Center year-round.
Tickets: Vary.

For former Producer Michael Ritchie the challenge was not to be "the best summer theater but the best theater in America." Williamstown Theatre Festival took a giant step in that direction in the summer of 1999, exciting the theater world with Academy Award winner Gwyneth Paltrow in *As You Like It*, followed by an extraordinary production of Arthur Miller's *The Price*. Stellar WTF plays regularly move on to Boston or Broadway. In 2002 WTF received a regional Tony Award for 48 years of sustained excellence, the first summer theater in the nation to be so recognized. Roger Rees's first season, 2005, had a mixture of standards and innovation, with the fresh and invigorating production of *Picnic* the most critically successful.

*Elizabeth Banks, originally from Pittsfield, starred in the Williamstown Theatre Festival's 2005 production of* Bus Stop. Richard Feldman

*The '62 Center for Theatre and Dance is home to the undergraduate performances, professional performances in the school year, and the Williamstown Theatre Festival in summer.* Robert Benson

Each summer, in addition to full-scale productions with first-rate sets and costumes on the Main Stage at the sparkling '62 Center for Theatre and Dance, WTF offers other more intimate theater experiences. There are the four productions mounted at the smaller Downstage. Late-night musical cabarets provide surprise cameo appearances by Main Stage celebrities like inveterate songster and raconteur Dick Cavett. Catch Staged Readings; Free Theater, usually outdoors at the Buxton School in Williamstown; Act I Performance Projects by the WTF young actor training ensemble, at work in Goodrich Hall on the Williams Campus; and the Greylock Theatre Project, which connects economically disadvantaged young people from North Adams with professional theater artists.

It's no mistake, then, that *Newsweek* ranked WTF as "the best of all American summer theaters" with "the cream of America's acting crop." And in its new facility, the fly's the limit!

The '62 Center, meanwhile, carries on a full program of student and professional theater and dance during the fall, winter, and spring.

## Other Theater

There are more than a dozen other theater companies in and about Berkshire.

### South County

The biggest little theater in South County is **Mixed Company** (413-528-2320; at the Granary, 37 Rosseter St., Gt. Barrington, MA 01230), where fall-off-the-seat comedy alternates with moving drama. Under the direction of playwright Joan Ackermann, Mixed

Company has built a solid following, often leading to competition for the theater's few dozen seats. Ackermann's award-winning *Zara Spook and Other Lures* premiered here, as did her droll *Bed and Breakfast,* in which she played an addled Mrs. Digby. The **DeSisto Estate Cabaret** (413-298-4032; DeSisto School, Rte. 183, Stockbridge, MA 01230) hosts dinner theater Tuesday through Thursday evenings in the summer, cabaret performances Friday and Saturday following dinner, and additional cabaret after some Friday and all Saturday Tanglewood concerts. The venerable **Mahaiwe Theater** (413-664-9040) in Gt. Barrington has reopened as a performing arts center, with a full schedule of local and touring talent.

### Central County

The theater scene in Central County has never been livelier. The Berkshire Community College Players regularly appear at the **Robert Boland Theater** at BCC (413-499-0660 when performances are staged; 1350 West St., Pittsfield, MA 01201). The Town Players (413-443-9279; www.berkshire.net/townplayers; mail: P.O. Box 765, Pittsfield, MA 01201), more than 85 year old, present a fall, winter, and spring production, with occasional special shows. **The News in Revue** (888-401-6397; www.newsinrevue.com; mail: P.O. Box 2336, Westport, CT 06880) performs political satire summers at several locations. Ambitious plans for the **Colonial Theatre** (413-448-8048; 111 South St., Pittsfield, MA 01201) call for a busy performance space, once the renovations are completed.

### North County

North County is especially theatrical. Besides the Williamstown Theatre Festival, in Williamstown, the **Starlight Stage Youth Theatre** (413-458-4246; http://myvanwy.tripod.com/ssyt.html; 57 Linden St., Williamstown, MA 01267), a hands-on theater experience for youth from 8 years to 18, performs summers at the First Congregational Church. In fall and winter, slack is picked up by **Williamstheatre**, the Williams College theater group (413-597-2342; www.williams.edu/theater; '62 Center for Theatre and Dance, 1000 Main St., Williamstown, MA 01267), producing impressive revivals and new plays. The drama department at **Massachusetts College of Liberal Arts** (413-662-5000) presents additional performances. **Trova Theater Arts** (413-663-3240) presents intimate, live theater at Main Street Stage, 57 Main St., N. Adams. **Topia** (413-743-9600; 27 Park St., Adams, MA 01220) exists at this writing as a café whose owners have a bold plan for theater in the old Adams movie theater and artists' lodging.

### Outside the County

In neighboring Chatham, New York, the **Mac-Haydn Theatre** (518-392-9292; mail: P.O. Box 204, Chatham, NY 12037; on Rte. 203,) has been offering 15-week-long summer seasons of robust Broadway musicals since 1969. Productions are staged in the round. Their high-energy casts are guaranteed to deliver a supercharge of musical theater—less than truly sophisticated, perhaps, but usually a whole lot of fun. In New Lebanon, New York, at the **Theater Barn** (518-794-8989; www.theaterbarn.com; mail: P.O. Box 39, New Lebanon, NY 12125; on Rte. 20), producers Joan and Abe Phelps zero in on musical comedy, with an occasional murderous dose of Agatha Christie thrown in. **Proctor's Theatre** in Schenectady (518-382-1083; www.proctors.org; 432 State St., Schenectady, NY 12035), and the **Egg** in Albany (518-473-1061; www.theegg.org; mail: P.O. Box 2065, Albany, NY 12220; at the Empire State Plaza), both provide stages for national acts, shows, and dramas. Up in Bennington, Vermont, the **Oldcastle Theater Company** (802-447-0564; www.oldcastle.org; mail: P.O. Box 1555, Bennington, VT 05201; at the Bennington Center for the Arts) can always be counted on for enjoyment, controversy, or both. Back in Massachusetts, the **Miniature Theatre of Chester** (413-354-6565; www.miniaturetheatre.org; mail: P.O. Box 722, Chester, MA 01011; at Chester Town Hall), hosts large-as-life drama.

## SEASONAL EVENTS

A number of special Berkshire events are tuned to the calendar. The Berkshire year wouldn't unfold properly without them. Literally leading the parade are Pittsfield's **Home Town Parade** on July 4 and North Adams's **Fall Foliage Parade** on the Sunday before Columbus Day.

Additional information about these and other seasonal events is available from listings under "Tourist Information" in chapter 9. See also "Festival Frenzy," above. County newspapers carry the specifics of just when this year the event will take place.

*A spring street festival in Gt. Barrington and an impromptu parade of the Berkshire Bateria Scuola de Samba. The Bateria offers free drumming workshops for the public and plays outdoors in Gt. Barrington throughout the summer.* Judith Monachina

### Spring

**Sheep to Shawl**, Williamstown Rural Lands Foundation's sheepsheering and weaving demonstration shows how alive old arts remain. Held at WRLF's Lewis Center on Cold Spring Rd., Williamstown.

**Jazztown**, Williamstown's salute to the authentic, takes place all around town in April, with Williams College and the town's chamber of commerce collaborating on a musical blowout. Performing are college big bands from the East, distinguished pros, and alumni groups.

**Riverfest** is North County's favorite outdoor event every May, celebrating the revitalized Hoosic River, which threads through Adams, North Adams, and Williamstown. Environmental art along the riverbanks, raft rides, food, and music at Cole Field, Williamstown.

### Summer

**Adams Agricultural Fair** is the old-fashioned kind, with a midway of rides, noisy big trucks, and judging of produce and animals. For a weekend in August it takes over the fairgrounds off the Curran Highway just south of the Adams–North Adams line. Other notable fairs in the area include those of **Cummington**, **Schaghticoke**, **Altamont**, and the **Eastern States Exposition** (the Big E), Springfield.

**Berkshire Crafts Fair** is a mid-August event, held at Monument Mountain Regional High School (413-528-3346; Rte. 7, between Stockbridge and Gt. Barrington). Top craftspeople offer their extraordinary creations, from handmade paper to handblown glass, from handwoven clothing to exotic woodenware.

**The Berkshires Summer Arts Festival,** held at Butternut Ski Area in early July. American Crafts Marketing, affiliated with American Craftsmen galleries (New York City and Stockbridge) presents a 3-day juried crafts show, with music, food, and children's events.

**Fireworks over Stockbridge Bowl** are spectacular because of echoes from the hills. The biggest bangs and most colorful starbursts come from Tanglewood, on the Fourth of July, and following *The 1812 Overture* at the end of Tanglewood on Parade, a highlight of the BSO Berkshire season.

**The Monument Mountain Author Climb** is a literary event commemorating the August day in 1851 when Melville, Hawthorne, Holmes, and friends scaled the Great Barrington peak. They imbibed a good deal of champagne, weathered a thunderstorm, read William Cullen Bryant's poem about the Indian maiden who threw herself in sorrow from the top, and began a lasting friendship. Also a fixture is the annual reenactment of **Henry David Thoreau's climb up Mount Greylock,** on or about July 20. Watch the *Berkshire Eagle* for announcements.

**Susan B. Anthony Celebration & Adams Street Fair** is held every July on Park Street, which is closed off for the event. Features are the "Pedal & Plod" bike- and footrace, food, and much more. For information, call the Adams Chamber of Commerce (413-743-1881).

## Fall

**Great Josh Billings RunAground** is Berkshire's great 1-day party, an athletic extravaganza that involves thousands of participants and many more admiring, supportive spectators. This late-September biking-canoeing-running triathlon takes its name from Lanesborough's Henry Wheeler Shaw, an inveterate 19th-century prankster-humorist writing under the pen name of Josh Billings. "If a fellow gets to going down hill, it seems as if everything were greased for the occasion," wrote Billings (more or less); and every fall at the RunAground the bike racers, shooting down that last hill on Route 183 to Stockbridge Bowl, prove how right old Josh was. After the race, there's a huge party at Tanglewood with food, drink, dancing, and Berkshire camaraderie.

**Greylock Ramble.** On Columbus Day the Adams chamber celebrates the height of fall foliage. It provides 3,000 or more people of every dimension an opportunity to hike the big hill and certificates for those who do. Other hikes and climbs to and around the lofty top of Mount Greylock in North County are sponsored by the Department of Conservation and Recreation, beginning at Greylock Glen in Adams, the Visitors Center in Lanesborough, the Sperry Road Campground, or Bascom Lodge, often narrated by well-informed guides.

**Harvest Festival** at the Berkshire Botanical Garden, Stockbridge, is an early-October event packed with cider and doughnuts, apples and pumpkins, hay wagon and fire engine rides, plants and seeds, and mayhem of all sorts appealing to children and grown-ups. A highlight of the Berkshire calendar, this 2-day event includes a live-performance tent featuring the likes of the Bluestars. Besides a great plant sale and flea market, a book sale and secondhand-clothes mart, the festival has also attracted a greater number of craftspeople selling an increasingly refined collection of handcrafts.

**Hopkins Forest Fall Festival** is the destination on an October Sunday at Hopkins Memorial Forest, at the top of Bulkley Street, Williamstown, where old-time crafts are practiced, timeless music is performed, and tempting cider and applesauce are produced.

**Lenox Apple Squeeze** takes place in the week after the Tub Parade (below). Many shops have major sales; there are crafts and food booths, as well as demonstrations, live music, and more.

**Octoberzest** is a fall foliage festival of music and ballet, presented at Simon's Rock by the Barrington Performing Arts. Mixing and matching poets with musicians, dancers with actors, into various ensemble pieces really does add a zesty élan to the southern Berkshire fall.

**Tub Parade** is one of Berkshire's oldest annual events, dating back to the Gilded Age. This late-September parade has been revived with a hitch—that is, with the hitches that attach show ponies to the ornate, flower-decked carts they pull. Under the auspices of the Lenox Village Association and the Colonial Carriage and Driving Society, the Tub Parade gives a glimpse back into turn-of-the-previous-century Berkshire, when dogs with ruffled collars rode next to their masters. Brief but brilliant.

## Winter

**Chesterwood** holds its Christmas open house from the first weekend in November through Veterans Day. Tours of the house and studio, shops open, refreshments, demonstrations.

**Holiday Walk** in Williamstown opens Spring and Water streets to horses and wagons, which carry spectators to shops where musical and dramatic groups perform, town and gown. Nonprofit organizations present festive exhibits in the Williams College gymnasium, and crafters exhibit in the Towne Field House.

**Holly-Days** is Lenox's 4-day celebration of the holiday season, with the arrival of Santa, a gingerbread house contest, holiday entertainment (such as the Albany Berkshire Ballet), a pancake breakfast, and an ecumenical candlelight service on Sunday.

**Naumkeag at Christmas** is extra special because that's when the Choates' Christmas decorations are taken out, and the house is made to look ever so festive. Looking in on a quiet turn-of-the-last-century Christmas can make the viewers merrier. The historic "cottage" in Stockbridge (described under "Historic Homes" in this chapter) offers this opportunity to the public on an irregular basis.

**Stockbridge Main Street at Christmas,** the first weekend in December, salutes Christmas and Norman Rockwell. Arts and crafts, readings by actors from the Berkshire Theatre Festival, house tours, luminaria, carolers, a gala concert, and a reenactment of Rockwell's painting Stockbridge Main Street at Christmas (1956) with vintage cars. Information at the Stockbridge Chamber of Commerce (413-298-5200; www.stockbridgechamber.org; 6 Elm St., P.O. Box 224, Stockbridge, MA 01262).

**The Tea Ceremony** at Great Barrington Pottery is a moving meditation, a highly stylized form of social communion for both the Tea Mistress and those she serves. Enter the Chashitsu (Japanese Ceremonial Teahouse and Formal Garden) at Richard Bennett's Great Barrington Pottery (described in chapter 8, "Shopping") to return to 14th-century Japan.

## Video Rentals

The following video rental outlets stock the standard Hollywood movies and a smattering of foreign art titles. There may be other outlets. Public libraries in the county lend videos.

### South County

**AVC Video Showcase** (413-229-2910; 231 Main St., Sheffield, MA 01257; Rte. 7 next to Sheffield Pub).

**Elm Street Market** (413-298-3040; 4 Elm St., Stockbridge, MA 01262).

**Housatonic Corner Market** (413-274-3500; 266 Pleasant St., N. Housatonic, MA 01236).

**Impoco's** (413-528-9162; 54 State Rd., Gt. Barrington, MA 01230; Rte. 7).

**Lee Video** (413-243-3636; 23 Park Plaza, Lee, MA 01238).

**North Star Video of Great Barrington** (413-528-1067; 224 State Rd., Gt. Barrington, MA 01230; Rte. 23).

**West Stockbridge Video** (413-232-7851; 20 Main St., W. Stockbridge, MA 01266).

### Central County

**Blockbuster Video** (413-442-2818; 1 Dan Fox Dr., Pittsfield, MA 01201).

**East Street Video** (413-443-2000; 10 Lyman, Pittsfield, MA 01201).

**Hollywood Video** (413-4690; 690 Merrill Rd., Pittsfield, MA 01201).

**Hollywood Video** (413-442-4805; 455 Dalton Ave., Pittsfield, MA 01201).

**Variety Video** (413-637-2046; 26 Housatonic St., Lenox, MA 01240).

**Video Studio 12** (413-447-7595; 180A Elm St., Pittsfield, MA 01201).

### North County

**Movie Gallery** (413-664-7880; North Adams Plaza, N. Adams MA 01247).

**Movie Gallery** (413-663-7282; 854 State Rd., N. Adams, MA 01247).

**Video Studio** (413-743-7007; 1 Myrtle St., Adams, MA 01220).

*A quiet spot for relaxing at Canyon Ranch* Judith Monachina

# 6

# Body & Spirit

## Spas & the Spiritual Life

**The Berkshire landscape** has long attracted the traveler in search of beauty. The rolling hills, mountains and farms, open landscapes, and intimate scenes are the backdrop for relaxation and rejuvenation, creativity and renewal. Sculptor Daniel Chester French called the Berkshires "heaven," and the land is well known for attracting artists and those who like to be where the artists are. Here there is a long-standing connection of the land to the creative.

But less well known is the even longer attraction of this place to other kinds of seekers—those whose lifelong vocation was spiritual search and, more recently, those looking for the new ways, through the disciplines that begin with the body, to rejuvenate the mind and spirit. The Berkshires, then, is also a place where the physical—the land and the health of the body and mind—is connected to the spiritual. The area has become a mecca, not only for music, dance, and art lovers but also for yoga enthusiasts and macrobiotic and healing-arts practitioners of all kinds. In many cases the homes of these organizations started out as "cottages" for wealthy summer residents, later becoming centers for the Jesuits, Franciscans, and other Western religious groups. Now they are home to Sufis, virtually all kinds of yoga practitioners, and those who practice the Chinese disciplines of Chi Kung and Tai Chi.

A Franciscan monastery has become the Kushi Institute, a well-known macrobiotic center in Becket. The Kripalu Center for Yoga and Health was first a massive 100-room home, then a Jesuit seminary; now people from all over the world come to learn about yoga. Their international network of Kripalu-trained yoga teachers includes many countries, and the natural effect of this yoga center on the Berkshires means an abundance of classes in all approaches to yoga. The most luxurious of these health centers, Canyon Ranch of the Berkshires, was first an elegant house (modeled after Le Petit Trianon in France), then a seminary; now people come from all over the world to learn to nurture their bodies and spirits.

### Spas & Wellness Centers

**CANYON RANCH IN THE BERKSHIRES**
413-637-4400.
www.canyonranch.com.
92 Kemble St., Lenox, MA 01240.

Live, transform, choose: These three words quietly flash on the Web site screen for Canyon Ranch in the Berkshires, and they sum up the experience of a stay at this luxury spa.

Several years ago health entrepreneurs Mel and Enid Zuckerman took their highly successful Tuscon, Arizona, Canyon Ranch formula and transferred it to the sculptured hills of Lenox. Here they transformed and built upon Giraud Foster's splendid "cottage," Bellefontaine, a replica of Le Petit Trianon in France, to create a world-class spa. It is a spectacular facility, smoothly run by a group of skilled and friendly professionals. Whether used for a short cool out, a vacation, a chance to drop a few pounds, an invigorating change of pace, or a whole new start, Canyon Ranch lives up to its billing as "the spa that never leaves you," or their slogan: "The power of possibility." With over 50 fitness classes to choose from daily, swimming, racquet sports of all kinds, and a state-of-the-art gymnasium, the spa complex offers a customized physical workout.

In addition, hiking, mountain biking, and cross-country skiing provide indoor/outdoor fitness possibilities unimaginable at the average spa. Besides steam rooms and saunas and an indoor pool, Canyon Ranch provides a wide range of medical and personal services. Personal services include massages, herbal wraps, and various exotic treatments to revitalize inside and out.

Prices vary seasonally but are always substantial. Access to the facility is limited to guests.

### CRANWELL, RESORT SPA & GOLF

413-637-1364.
www.cranwell.com.
55 Lee Rd., Lenox, MA 01240; Rte. 20.

This massive spa features 16 treatment rooms with well over 50 treatments, including seaweed, remineralizing and thermal clay therapies, stone therapy, Swedish and deep-tissue massage, reflexology, sport-specific massage, prenatal, duet (for two), and in-room massage. Among classes offered are yoga, Pilates, Nordic walking, and spinning. Day and overnight packages are available.

### KRIPALU CENTER FOR YOGA AND HEALTH

413-448-3400, 800-741-7353.
www.kripalu.org.
Mail: P.O. Box 793,Lenox, MA 01240.
West St., Rte. 183, in Stockbridge, S. of Tanglewood.

One of the grandest of the Berkshire summer "cottages" was Shadowbrook, a 100-room Tudor mansion built by Anson Phelps Stokes. Later a Jesuit seminary, the original building burned to the ground, and the Jesuit brothers built an equally large but much more modest building to replace it. Though modern and functional, the estate—with its breathtaking views of Stockbridge Bowl and the mountains beyond—continues to move its many guests. It's hard to imagine a more complete line of yoga workshops and classes than can be found at Kripalu. The catalogue includes listings for such classes as Hatha Yoga, Kundalini Yoga, Bikram Yoga, Restorative, Kripalu and Kitchen Chair Yoga, Kripalu Yoga Teacher Training, Chakra Yoga, Meditation, Raw Juice Fasting—and that is a small fraction of the offerings at this center, which caters to beginners as well as those well as advanced yoga training. The offerings don't stop with yoga, however, and well-known wellness experts are among those who have offered weekend workshops in their specialties. Facilities include Danskinetics and yoga studios, saunas and whirlpools, 300 acres of forest, meadows, meditation gardens, miles of woodland trails and a private beach on Stockbridge Bowl, a bookstore and gift shop, special health services, and a natural-foods kitchen serving tasty well-balanced meals. Health services include bodywork therapies. Kripalu's environment is nurturing. Clients sign on for short-term or longer-term visits. Prices are moderate, and a special 20 percent discount applies to guests who bring a friend.

*Yoga at Kripalu* | Judith Monachina

### MEPAL SPA

413-229-3490.
100 Stone Manor Dr.; New Marlborough, MA 01244; at Gedney Farm.

The luxurious spa offers yoga, Pilates, facials, haircuts and color treatments, aromatic body touch, indoor and outdoor hot tub and relaxation deck. Spa packages available.

## Macrobiotics & Health

### THE KUSHI INSTITUTE

800-975-8744.
www.kushiinstitute.org.
P.O. Box 7, Becket, MA 01223.

The quietist of the healthful learning places in the Berkshires lies just outside the village of Becket, about 5 miles from Jacob's Pillow dance Festival. Once a Franciscan monastery, the Kushi Institute now attracts people from all over the world who want to learn about this approach to health.

Michio and Aveline Kushi founded this institute in 1978 in Brookline, Massachusetts, and gradually moved all programs out to Becket by 1990. The internationally known macrobiotic center attracts people who wish to learn more about the macrobiotic way of life. The basic philosophy includes a whole-foods diet and an appreciation of other natural elements for a healthy lifestyle. These include exercise, body care, household products, and livelihood. Macrobiotics has been popularized through books and various media that have detailed its effects on health recovery from debilitating disease. Many people choose the macrobiotic way of life and a natural approach to recovery and optimal health maintenance. The macrobiotic approach can be embraced by people of any philosophy or religion.

The basic institute program, offered year-round, is the weeklong "Way of Health." Kushi offers a macrobiotic career training program and annual summer conferences. Guests can enjoy the walking trails on this mostly wooded 600-acre property.

## MONASTERIES & RETREAT CENTERS

### THE ABODE OF THE MESSAGE

518-794-8095.
www.theabode.net.
Abode Rd., New Lebanon, NY 12125.

Just a stone's throw from the Massachusetts border, this former New Lebanon Shaker settlement on 400 acres is now home to a Sufi community. This group invites the public to attend its weekly universal worship services and participate in various programs throughout the year. While theirs is a community of members who have embraced the ideas of Sufism, all religions are respected and many of those who participate in programs here come from other paths. The community puts on events—musical, spiritual, and artistic—throughout the year and from various traditions, including Sufi, Buddhist, and others. It hosts yoga, dance, and music workshops as well.

Accommodations for those who stay at the Abode include cabins and rooms. Meals are healthy and hearty; rates are reasonable. Groups may rent facilities as well.

### SISTERS OF THE VISITATION MONASTERY

413-243-3995.
14 Beach Rd., Tyringham, MA 01264.

In the beautiful Tyringham Valley, this monastery is home to a small group of women who relocated here from Delaware some time ago. They built their monastery at the end of Beach Road on a hill overlooking meadows and fields, and cleared walking trails in the meadows. These sisters live in a cloister, and individual women retreatants are invited into the cloister for private retreats of meditation and prayer. They are asked, therefore, to observe the silence of the monastery and the schedule, which includes a great silence after the 8 PM service. There is room for two retreatants at any given time. Retreatants are invited to attend the services, at which the sisters sing the Hours of the Office five times per day. Visitors are not obligated to attend the services or the morning mass but are invited to do so and are given assistance in using the various books for following the prayers and singing. The prayerful voices of the sisters during services can be appreciated by guests at the nearby chapel, which is not part of the cloister, and which is open to the public on most days from the morning Mass on. The meadows and trails are open to retreatants once inside the cloister.

## OTHER YOGA, DAY SPAS & RELATED PLACES

**Balance Wellness Center** (413-637-1877; 67 Church St., Lenox, MA 01240) Various kinds of massage, including shiatsu, reflexology, and aromatherapy as well as energy therapy, body treatments, holistic health counseling, and yoga classes.

**Berkshire Mountain Yoga** (413-528-5333; 30 Elm Ct., Gt. Barrington, MA 01230) Year-round yoga classes of various kinds, including Astanga, Hatha, Flowing Hatha, Yoga Basics, Power Vinyasa Yoga, and classes such as Heart Dance.

**Body & Soul** (413-528-6465; 184 Maple St., Gt. Barrington, MA 01230) Massage, Dr. Hauschka facials, body treatments, cosmetics, skincare, bath and body products.

**Essencials Day Spa** (413-443-6260; www.BerkshireSpas.com; 439 Pittsfield Rd., Lenox, MA 01240). Offers hair and body treatments, sauna rooms, a fireplace for sipping teas, treatment rooms, makeup, waxing, and massage.

**Kali Ray Tri-Yoga Center** (413-229-3399; www.triyoga.com/centers; Rte. 7, Sheffield, MA, 01257) This style of flowing Hatha yoga focuses on breath and posture and was founded over 20 years ago by Kali Ray.

**Michele's Day Spa** (413-528-9999; www.michelessalon.com; 54 Stockbridge Rd., Gt. Barrington, MA 01230) Full-day escapes or just one service, including salt glow massage, dermatological facials, manicure, and pedicure. These services and others by appointment.

**Phoenix Rising Yoga Therapy** (800-288-9642; www.pryt.com; 5 Albany Rd., W. Stockbridge, MA 01236) Michele Lee, founder of the modality of Phoenix Rising, describes it as a body, mind, and health program based on yoga. Thus it is spiritual as well as physical. It offers professional certification programs as well as healing touch therapeutic massage and yoga for the general public. They emphasize professional training, and they offer retreats.

**Spanda Holistic Center** (413-442-0123; www.spanda.com; 823 North St., Pittsfield, MA 01201) The philosophy of Spanda is that health comes from the balanced flow of chi—life force in the body mind and spirit. They offer acupuncture and other healing modalities, as well as workshops, including Chi Quong, Healing the Spirit, Chinese Herbs, and Energy Psychology, among others.

## Ymcas & Fitness Centers

**Berkshire Nautilus** (413-499-1217; 42–56 Summer St., Pittsfield, MA 01201) Nautilus equipment and instruction; stationary bikes, rowing and treadmill, StairMaster, whirlpool sauna and steam, certified instruction, a rock climbing wall, and free weights.

**Berkshire West** (413-499-4600; Dan Fox Dr., Pittsfield, MA 01201) Nautilus and free weights, bikes, also tennis and racquetball, aerobics, classes, saunas and steam rooms, pools and certified instruction. Nursery available. Massage therapy and yoga have also been added to their list of client services.

**In Touch Day Spa** (413-458-3235; 84 Water St., Williamstown, MA 01267) Offers massage, skin care, outside hot tub rentals, full-service hair salon in downtown Williamstown. Tagged "a spa like no other," In Touch is located in a bright and warm nine-sided wood frame building that was once a gristmill. The back decks, where massages are offered in-season, run along the Green River.

**Lenox Fitness Center** (413-637-9893; www.lenoxfitnesscenter.com; 90 Pittsfield Rd., Lenox, MA 01240) Life fitness training, stationary bikes and rowing machines,

StairMasters, aerobics, steam rooms, tanning booths, free weights, yoga, and certified instruction. Spa services include: manicure, pedicure, massage, facial waxing, reflexology, manual dermabrasion, and Pilates.

**Pittsfield YMCA** (413-499-7650; 292 North St., Pittsfield, MA 01201) At the North Street YMCA, the range of fitness and sports includes aerobics, swimming, racquetball, and squash. Nautilus equipment and programs, special classes for kids, saunas and a steam room. Call for information about summer camps, programs, and activities. Other Y memberships are honored with a small surcharge. Short-term guest passes can be arranged.

**North Berkshire YMCA** (413-663-6529; 22 Brickyard Ct., N. Adams, MA 01247) North County's Y is another center of vitality. There is a six-lane pool, full gymnasium, weight room, gymnastics room for children, and two racquetball/handball courts, all with programs to match. As with the Pittsfield Y, other Y memberships are honored with a small surcharge, and short-term guest passes can be arranged.

**Kilpatrick Health Center** (413-528-7777; www.simons-rock.edu: click on "Kilpatrick" link; 84 Alford Rd., Gt. Barrington, MA 01260). Open to the public. Full fitness, Nautilus, free weights, cardiovascular, Olympic pool, indoor track, basketball and tennis, racquetball and squash, rock climbing wall; an aerobics studio, water fitness, yoga and Pilates classes. The center has 3-, 6-, and 12-month family memberships. Guests may purchase daily and weekly passes.

**Berkshire South Regional Community Center,** (413-528-2810; www.berkshiresouth.org; Crissey Rd., Gt. Barrington, MA 01260) Local residents and visitors alike may utilize the facility by buying a membership or paying admission, although the center is open to all regardless of ability to pay. Pool, exercise pool, and kids' splash playground; a fitness center, gymnasium, game room and pre-school; auditorium with dance floor that includes nightclub lights and sound; a lounge, kitchen, and babysitting center. Classes are offered throughout the year. Rental and conference facilities are available for groups, parties, and special events.

**Please note:** New day spas and healing-arts practices open with regularity, making it impossible to give a full listing of the literally hundreds of private practices around the county. Also, many massage therapists, Reiki and other technique practitioners, acupuncturists, and others operate solo businesses and can be found by looking at various brochures and newspapers, and the Yellow Pages, *The Women's Times*, *The Artful Mind*, and the *Shoppers Guide* are sources of information about these professionals.

# 7

# Outdoor Recreation

## *For the Fun of It*

**Berkshire beckons** bikers, boaters, hikers, horseback riders, runners, skaters, skiers, swimmers, and nearly every other variety of sportsperson to come outside. Although nature left the area shy of large bodies of water, 19th-century industrialists dammed well, to some degree making up the deficiency. Mountains and trails, lakes and rivers, and Berkshire valley air—which can be breathed without chewing—invigorate. The ski areas assure groomed winter sport with extensive snowmaking and, in warmer weather, Berkshire's golf courses and tennis courts draw sports lovers from all quarters.

For the spectators among us, school sports teams are competitive and fun in fall, spring, and winter, including downhill and Nordic skiing. The hills are alive with bouncing balls, from youth programs to secondary school teams to college leagues. Three of the four Berkshire colleges—**Berkshire Community** in Pittsfield, **Massachusetts College of Liberal Arts** in North Adams, and **Williams** in Williamstown—field men's and women's teams in soccer, basketball, baseball, and softball. Williams perennially ranks among the best in the nation in NCAA Division III soccer, field hockey, football, cross country, basketball, ice hockey, track, tennis, squash, volleyball, swimming, lacrosse, and crew. In 1996, 1997, and 1999–2005, Williams copped the Sears Cup for having the best small-college athletic record in the nation. The athletic departments of the colleges provide schedules.

### Sporting Goods Stores

The following stores provide sporting goods for a range of activities. Additional listings are provided under individual sports, e.g., bicycling, skiing.

#### South County

**Gerry Cosby & Co.** (413-229-6600; fax 413-229-3492; www.cosbysports.com; Undermountain Rd., Sheffield, MA 01257; Rte. 41)

**Housatonic River Outfitters, Inc.** (413-528-8811; fax 413-528-5054; www.dryflies.com; 684 S. Main St., Gt. Barrington, MA 01230)

#### Central County

**Arcadian Shop** (413-637-3010; fax 413-637-4112; www.arcadian.com; 91 Pittsfield–Lenox Rd., P.O. Box 1637, Lenox, MA 01240; Rte. 7)

*Williams men's soccer players warm up.*

**Champ Sports** (413-448-2123; www.champsports.com; mail: Old State Rd., Lanesborough, MA 01237; Berkshire Mall, Rte. 8)

**Dave's Sporting Goods** (413-442-2960; 1164 North St., Pittsfield, MA 01201)

**Dick Moon Sporting Goods** (413-442-8281; fax 413-448-2718; 114 Fenn St., Pittsfield, MA 01201)

**Plaine's Bike Snowboard Ski Shop** (413-499-0294; 55 W. Housatonic St., Pittsfield, MA 01201; Rte. 20)

**Porter's Sporting Goods** (413-442-9967; 370 Pecks Rd., Pittsfield, MA 01201)

NORTH COUNTY

**Berkshire Outfitters** (413-743-5900; fax 413-743-3359; www.berkshireoutfitters.com; Grove St., Adams, MA 01220; Rte. 8)

**Goff's Sports** (413-458-3605, 800-424-3747; www.williams-shop.com; 15 Spring St., Williamstown, MA 01267)

**The Mountain Goat** (413-458-8445; www.themountaingoat.com; 130 Water St., Williamstown, MA 01267)

**The Sports Corner** (413-664-8654; www.northadams.com; 61 Main St., N. Adams, MA 01247)

## Baseball & Softball

The first collegiate baseball game ever was played in Pittsfield, July 1, 1859—Amherst defeated Williams 73–32 in a 26-inning marathon (the rules have since changed). Williams won a companion chess match.

Professional baseball in the Berkshires began later in the 19th century, but it wasn't till the Roaring Twenties that the hardball action was continuous. The Pittsfield Hillies played some admirable ball in the A-level Eastern League, winning a couple of pennants. When the Depression came, baseball went. Through some of the 1940s, the Pittsfield Electrics played to large home crowds, finally being short-circuited by the advent of televised baseball. Then in 1965 a Red Sox farm club came to play at Pittsfield's Wahconah Park. The Pittsfield-Berkshire Red Sox played in the AA Class of the Eastern League. Starring George "Boomer" Scott and Reggie Smith (both of whom went on to shine with the Sox), the club drew nearly 80,000 fans for the season. The Red Sox farm club moved from the Berkshires in 1976.

Now the Berkshires host two pro teams in the New England Collegiate Baseball League (www.necbl.com ). The **SteepleCats** play at Joe Wolfe Field in North Adams. The **Dukes** perform in Pittsfield at Wahconah Park (105 Wahconah St., Pittsfield, MA 01201). Unlike minor leaguers, neither team's players belong to major-league teams. Players are hotshots in or just graduated from college, playing with wooden bats. They'd like to move up. Intercounty competition is spirited. The fast balls are wicked, homers are truly belted, and the playing fields are real dirt and grass.

Women's softball is a feature of Berkshire colleges and secondary schools in the spring. Nowhere is the action thicker than at the **Berkshire County Softball Complex** (413-499-1491; 1789 East St., Pittsfield, MA 01201). This three-field park sees at least six games a night during the summer. The complex is also home to the Berkshire County Slow Pitch Softball League, a 30-team men's league sponsored by local businesses. To facilitate matters, the complex has a two-story clubhouse with bar and restaurant.

## Bicycling

How sweet the cycling! And how the number of cyclists has increased in the Lance Armstrong years. For the views, the rolling terrain, and the variety of roadways, Berkshire is made for de rider and derailleur. A major push is underway to create a north–south bikeway through the county, the first completed segment of which is the Ashuwillticook Rail Trail. An 11-mile off-road section is open, from Pittsfield to Adams—and later on from there, maybe, to North Adams and Williamstown. The Ashuwillticook is good for family biking, walking, and all other manner of person-powered activity. For racers, there's the **Josh Billings Run-Aground** in September, and an annual July race around Brodie Mountain. The Williams College cycling team holds a **Criterion** in the spring. The

Greylock Cycling Club sponsors an annual **Greylock Hill Climb,** a 9.2-mile, decidedly uphill race. There is also a race around Mt. Greylock. The Hoosic River Watershed Association offers a three-state tour in late August.

For those who are touring, the back roads are tranquil, and some main roads have wide shoulders. The varied terrain intrigues cyclists; stunning views are followed by exhilarating descents that call for *well*-tuned equipment—especially brakes.

Mountain bikers thrive in these hills, 21-speeders rolling through the picturesque landscape, leaving the blacktop behind. Not too steep, not too tortuous, the Berkshire Hills beckon those who have enough brawn, coupled with the right machine. Mountain bikers frequently gather at the **Mountain Goat** in Williamstown, taking to the hills for some "undulating all-terraining." Mountain bikers should remember that some hiking trails are not open to bikers.

Similarly, cyclists out on the roadways should remember that, until the revolution, motorists in their quaint way still claim the right-of-way. It seems wise to oblige. So: right-hand riding, single file. After dark: a headlight, a red rear reflector, and side and pedal reflectors. In traffic, turns require hand signals with the left hand: extended straight out for left turn, raised 90 degrees for right turn, held down diagonally for stopping. Helmets help, in a crisis, to keep us from losing our heads. Bicycles should be registered at local police departments, so they can help locate a lost one.

The Massachusetts Department of Conservation and Recreation and MassHighway published *Berkshire Bike Touring,* a guide to county routes (available at MassHighway's Lenox office or the DCR South Mountain, Pittsfield, office). Pittsfield resident Lewis Cuyler, avid bike rider and writer, sums it all up in *Bike Rides in the Berkshire Hills,* available at bookstores and sports stores.

## Bicycle Dealers

It is fair to say the county boasts some of the best bike shops anywhere.

### South County

**Berkshire Bike and Blade** (413-528-5555; fax 413-528-1776; www.bikeandblade.com; 326 Stockbridge Rd., Great Barrington, MA 01230; Rte. 7) Also bike repairs.

**Harland B. Foster** (413-528-0546; fax 413-528-5474; 15 Bridge St., Gt. Barrington, MA 01230)

### Central County

**Arcadian Shop** (413-637-3010, 800-239-3391; www.arcadian.com; 91 Pittsfield Lenox Rd., P.O. Box 1637, Lenox, MA 01240)

**Mean Wheels** (413-637-0644; 57A Housatonic St., Lenox, MA 01240)

**Mike's Bike Shop** (413-443-1166; www.mikesbikesshop.com: 555 North St., Pittsfield, MA 01201)

**Ordinary Cycles** (413-442-7225; www.ordinarycycles.com; 247 North St., Pittsfield, MA 01201)

**Plaine's Bike Snowboard Ski Shop** (413-499-0294; 55 W. Housatonic St., Rte. 20, Pittsfield, MA 01201)

*Athletic Center, Simon's Rock College, Gt. Barrington* Judith Monachina

North County

**Berkshire Outfitters** (413-743-5900; fax 413-743-3359; www.berkshireoutfitters.com; Grove St., Rte. 8, Adams, MA 01220)

**The Mountain Goat** (413-458-8445; www.themountaingoat.com; 130 Water St., Williamstown, MA 01267)

**The Spoke Bicycles** (413-458-3456; www.thespoke.com; 279 Main St., Williamstown, MA 01267)

**The Sports Corner** (413-664-8654; 61 Main St., N. Adams, MA 01247)

## Boating

When Henry Ward Beecher called Berkshire the American Lake District, he was comparing the number of writers settled here to England's home of the Romantic poets. Nevertheless, while we have no water body the size of Lake Windermere, we have nearly 100 ponds, lakes, and one "bowl." Big boats may wish to plow larger seas, but the Otis Reservoir, at 1,056 acres, is the largest recreational freshwater body in the state. Mainly we have water bodies for small craft, from outboards down to inner tubes. Or shells: Spring and fall we can watch the Williams College crews on Lake Onota and on almost any still day we can see individuals sculling. Berkshire scullers win more than their share of races.

**Berkshire Outfitters** (see under "Sporting Goods Stores") rents canoes and kayaks. Or one can row. Lew Cuyler founded **Berkshire Sculling Inc.** (413-496-9160), which provides rentals and lessons; or purchase at Stockbridge Bowl, by appointment. Lew says: "It takes but an hour to learn the fundamentals. The rest is practice."

South County

**Benedict Pond, Beartown State Forest** (413-528-0904; Blue Hill Rd., Monterey) Sylvan pond suitable for canoe or rowboat only.

**Goose Pond** (Tyringham Rd., Lee) Boat rentals.

**Lake Buel** (Rte. 57, Monterey)

**Lake Garfield** (Kinne's Grove, Rte. 23, Monterey) Boat rentals.

**Laurel Lake** (Rte. 20, Lee) Boat rentals.

**Otis Reservoir, Tolland State Forest** (413-528-0904; Reservoir Rd., off Rte. 8, Otis) The largest of Berkshire's lakes. Small fishing boats, canoes, Sunfish, and sailboats for rent and a small family restaurant at **J&D Marina** (413-269-4839; 1367 Reservoir Rd., E. Otis, MA 01029). **Miller Marine** (413-269-6358; Reservoir Rd., E. Otis, MA 01029) provides moorings, sales, and service but no rentals. Summer weekends the water is crowded.

*The prospect from Mt. Prospect, part of the Greylock massif* Lauren R. Stevens

**Prospect Lake** (413-528-4158; fax 413-528-3666; e-mail: prospectlk@aol.com; Prospect Lake Rd., N. Egremont, MA 01252) Canoe, paddleboat, rowboat, and sailboard rental and instruction at a private-access family campground and lake.

**Stockbridge Bowl** (Rte. 183, Stockbridge) Public launching site on one of the county's prettiest lakes, just below Tanglewood.

**York Pond, West Lake,** and **Abbey Lake, Sandisfield State Forest** (413-258-4774; New Marlborough and Sandisfield).

Central County

**Buckley-Dunton Pond, October Mountain State Forest** (Yokum Rd., Becket) An intriguingly remote spot.

**Greenwater Pond** (Pleasant Point, Becket) Boat rentals.

**Lake Onota** (Onota Blvd., Pittsfield) Free launching area for motorboats. Good windsurfing. **Onota Boat Livery** (413-442-1724; 455 Pecks Rd., Pittsfield, MA 01201) rents small powerboats.

**Pontoosuc Lake** (Rte. 7, Pittsfield) The YMCA's **Ponterril** (office: 413-499-0640; East Acres Rd., Pittsfield, MA 01201) offers sailboat and canoe rentals. **U-Drive Boat Rentals** (413-442-7020; 990 Valentine Rd., Pittsfield, MA 01201) on Route 7 features ski boats and Jet Skis.

**Richmond Pond** (Swamp Rd., Richmond) Boat rentals.

North County

**Cheshire Reservoir** (Hoosac Lake)
(Rte. 8, Cheshire) Launching site at
Rte. 8.

**Mauserts Pond,** Clarksburg State Forest (413-664-8345; Middle Rd., Clarksburg)
A bit weedy.

**North Pond,** Savoy Mountain State Forest (413-663-8469, summer only; for camping reservations, call 877-I-CAMP-MA; off Rte. 2 in Florida, in Savoy) North Pond and **South Pond** are two jewels in the hills; remote, rarely busy.

**Windsor Lake** (413-662-3047; access via Bradley St. or Kemp Ave., in N. Adams) Launch site.

## Camping

See "Walking, Hiking, Camping, and X-C Skiing."

## Canoeing & Kayaking

Besides all of Berkshire's lovely lakes to canoe and kayak, paddlers have four rivers to choose from, with stretches varying from lazy flat water to rushing rapids. The Housatonic River rises in Washington and the lakes near Pittsfield, flowing southward between the

*Lew Cuyler sculls on Onota Lake* Lauren R. Stevens

Taconic Range and the Berkshire Plateau, heading for Long Island Sound near Stratford, Connecticut. Four Berkshire trips down the Housatonic are recommended by the Appalachian Mountain Club: Dalton to Lenox (19 miles); Lenox to Stockbridge (12 miles); Stockbridge to Great Barrington (13 miles); and Great Barrington to Falls Village, Connecticut (25 miles). Send for *The AMC River Guide to Massachusetts, Connecticut and Rhode Island* ($9.95, from AMC, 5 Joy St., Boston, MA 02108), or ask local booksellers.

*A Canoe Guide to the Housatonic River: Berkshire County*, a nifty little booklet published jointly by Housatonic supporters and the Berkshire Regional Planning Commission, contains line drawings, a history of the river and its flora and fauna, and dozens of access points. Highly recommended for Housy paddling; at local booksellers. Hilary Bashara's **Berkshire Canoe Tours** (413-442-2789) provides canoes and offers day and evening guided tours of the Housatonic.

In **South County**, the stretch on the Housatonic from Great Barrington to Bartholomew's Cobble in Ashley Falls is classic lazy river paddling. Canoes can be purchased and rented in Sheffield at **Gaffer's Outdoors** (413-229-0063; 216 Main St., Sheffield, MA 01257; on Rte. 7).

For lovely lake paddling, canoes can be rented on **Prospect Lake** (413-528-4158; Prospect Lake Park, 50 Prospect Lake Rd., N. Egremont, MA 01252) and **Lake Garfield** (413-528-5417; www.kinnesgrove.com; Kinne's Grove, Rte. 23, Monterey, MA 01245).

In the fall, when the dam on Otis Reservoir is opened, the West Branch of the Farmington River swells. The stretch south of Route 23, along Route 8 in Otis and Sandisfield, is the site of an annual Olympic kayak-racing event. In early spring, this stretch is a Class III rapids, making for exciting whitewater paddling and great viewing. The Westfield offers whitewater racing in the spring.

Up in **North County**, the Hoosic River flows northward, and in those parts, **Berkshire Outfitters** (see "Sporting Goods Stores"), canoe and kayak specialists, rents craft and offers sound advice on the best in area boating. The Hoosic River Watershed Association has put out a recreational map of the river to the Hudson, available at sports stores.

## Croquet

In the Berkshires, croquet has had a small but tenacious group of followers, willing to risk the indignity of their ball being sent to the periphery of the lawns at the Lenox Club. This is not the back yard variety of croquet, but serious stuff with national rankings. The Lenox Club annually hosts the Berkshire Invitational. The Lenox Club offers classes and Blantyre, also in Lenox, offers resident guests the use of imported equipment and lessons by a certified professional, during a season running from July to September. (See chapter 3, "Lodging," for more information on Blantyre.)

## Cross-Country Skiing

See "Walking, Hiking, Camping, and X-C Skiing."

## Downhill Skiing

Berkshire downhill ski areas date back to the 1930s. Evidence suggests that three significant advances in modern skiing had their origins here: The surface ski lift, snowmaking, and the ski bar—referring, of course, to the part of the lift chair that locks in the rider rather than the après-ski appliance. Berkshire ski areas continue to be innovative, always questing for better and more consistent conditions over a longer season.

But it's not the technology that makes Berkshire skiing so appealing, so popular. The Berkshire Hills are challenging yet picturesque, without being imposing. From the summits of the area's ski mountains, the vistas are splendid—mountains on the horizon (like the Catskills, seen from atop Butternut) and skinny bands of civilization below. With six major ski areas in the region to choose from, skiers in the Berkshires can pick their mountain for a week or tour the hills and ski a different area each day. Each ski mountain has its own character; each caters to a slightly different skier yet welcomes all. Jiminy Peak and Berkshire East have the highest proportion of trails suited to advanced skiers; but Butternut, Catamount, and even Bousquet have dicey runs, demanding enough for many experts. And for the best deal for the dollar, the Mount Greylock Ski Club shines. Every Berkshire ski area offers instruction; Bousquet with its ski school and Otis Ridge with its ski camp emphasize youth instruction.

Snowboarding is familiar and accepted on Berkshire slopes. Popular especially with younger enthusiasts, snowboards offer both thrilling sport and a challenge to one's skills and coordination. Most Berkshire ski areas can rent or sell a board and follow up with instruction. Some areas segregate snowboarders from skiers; all require courtesy and safety from everyone descending the slopes. Tubing is also growing in popularity; some areas have tubing parks, and Brodie is all tubing.

## Berkshire Ski Information

From outside Massachusetts: 800-237-5747.

**Berkshire Ski Conditions**: 413-499-7669. New England Ski Council reports are broadcast twice daily from radio station **WBEC-AM (1420)** and **FM (105.5)** on the dial, Pittsfield.

## Where to Buy and Rent Equipment

Besides the ski areas themselves, all of which have fully stocked ski shops renting and selling equipment, the following specialty shops sell skis and related paraphernalia. Price-cautious skiers should keep their eyes open in the fall for ski and skate sales of used equipment such as the one at Jiminy Peak that benefits the Hancock Fire Department and the one at Pine Cobble School in Williamstown.

Some of these same stores rent snowshoes, for those who prefer that sport (see "Walking," later in this chapter).

### SOUTH COUNTY

**Expeditions** (413-528-7737; 276 Main St., Gt. Barrington, MA 01230)

**Kenver Ltd**. (413-528-2330; Rte. 23, S. Egremont, MA 01258)

**Mechangers Ski & Snowboard Service** (413-528-9668; 309 Main St., Gt. Barrington, MA 01230)

### CENTRAL COUNTY

**Arcadian Shop** (413-637-3010; www.arcadian.com; 91 Pittsfield Rd., P.O. Box 1637, Lenox, MA 01240)

**Plaine's Bike Snowboard Ski Shop** (413-499-0294; 55 W. Housatonic St., Pittsfield, MA 01201)

**Ski Fanatics** (413-443-3023; 241 North St., Pittsfield, MA 01201; also at Brodie)

*Cross-country skiing at Canyon Ranch* Judith Monachina

North County

**Berkshire Outfitters** (413-743-5900; fax 413-743-3359; www.berkshireoutfitters.com; Grove St., Adams, MA 01220; Rte. 8)

**Goff's Sports** (413-458-3605, 800-4243747; www.williams-shop.com; 15 Spring St., Williamstown, MA 01267)

**The Mountain Goat** (413-458-8445; www.themountaingoat.com; 130 Water St., Williamstown, MA 01267)

**The Sports Corner** (413-664-8654; www.northadams.com; 61 Main St., N. Adams, MA 01247) Bearing in mind that Berkshire areas are less expensive than those in northern Vermont, New Hampshire, and Maine, we call our top price category—$35 to $50 for an adult weekend and holiday pass—"Moderate." Below $35 we call "Inexpensive." Skiers should contact ski areas for a more elaborate breakdown, which often includes lower rates for weekdays, for night skiing, for junior and seniors. Bousquet's offers free skiing to those 65 and older.

South County

### BUTTERNUT BASIN

413-528-2000.
Ski conditions: 800-438-SNOW.
www.skibutternut.com.
Rte. 23, Gt. Barrington, MA 01230.
2 mi. E. of town, toward Monterey.
Trails: 22 downhill (20 percent novice, 40 percent intermediate, 30 percent expert); also 8 km of X-C trails.
Lifts: 6 chairlifts (quad, triple, 4 doubles), puma, rope tow.
Vertical Drop: 1,000 ft.
Snowmaking: 100 percent of area.
Tickets: Moderate.
Open: Mon.–Fri. 9–4; Sat., Sun. 8:15–4.
Ski School Pro: Einar Aas.

Ski-resort developer Channing Murdoch was lucky. Few entrepreneurs can realize their business dreams in their own backyards as he did. His son, Jeff, now carries on the business. Murdoch designed and built Butternut Basin Ski Area on a site that has become one of the Berkshires' premier winter recreation meccas. At Butternut, challenging downhill runs, a separate beginner's slope, and extensive cross-country ski trails offer ideal options for every kind of skier—from first-timer to serious racer.

But Butternut is more than terrific trails and the welcoming charm of its two lovely lodges. From the top of Warner Mountain extend extraordinary views of the distant Catskills in the west and of Mount Greylock at the northern end of Berkshire County. The mountain's timed slalom course is open to everyone, making a potential Olympic-class racer—at least in fantasy—out of even a beginner. Butternut's personable ski pro, Einar Aas, and his team of expert ski instructors, can aid advanced skiers or those on the slopes for their debuts. Two snowboard parks have been opened. Plus Butternut's ski shop is one of the most extensive and stylish at any Berkshire mountain.

Butternut's quadruple fixed-grip lift, food facilities at the base—including an area exclusively devoted to their Ski Wee kids' program—and outside "Cruiser" barbecue deck show that the resort remains at the skiing edge. From the mogul fields of the expert run, Downspout, to the meandering path of the novice Pied Piper's Trail, Butternut is a delight to the eye as well as a refreshing test of athletic skill.

### CATAMOUNT

413-528-1262, 518-325-3200.
www.catamountski.com.
Rte. 23, S. Egremont, MA 01258.
On NY border.
Trails: 28 downhill (novice to expert).
Lifts: 4 chairlifts, T-bar, J-bar.
Vertical Drop: 1,152 ft.
Snowmaking: 96 percent of area.
Tickets: Moderate.
Open: Weekends, holidays 8:30–4; midweek 9–4; night skiing Wed.–Sat. 3–10.
Ski School Director: Jen Brown.

"On the cutting edge of Berkshire ski country," as *Skiing* magazine put it, Catamount straddles two states and offers magnificent views of four: Massachusetts, New York, Connecticut, and Vermont. The slopes are primarily novice and intermediate, but seasoned skiers can find quite a bit of challenge through the glades near the summit and down on through the Flipper and Dipper trails. For snowboarders there's the Megaplex park.

Called by some a vest-pocket Killington, Catamount is convenient, especially to New Yorkers. Not the trendiest, competition-minded ski resort, although it does offer an extensive race season, it cultivates a pleasant quaintness, right down to the Swiss Hütte restaurant at the mountain's base. Snowmaking equipment at Catamount has been overhauled and expanded, firing state-of-the-art equipment at virtually all trails and slopes. Catamount has installed an additional 22 airless snowmakers mounted on towers. Night skiing and an area for kids are attractions.

The Upper and Lower Sidewinder is a new skiing trail a mile long. For borderline skiing in the Berkshires, there's no better.

### OTIS RIDGE

413-269-4444.
www.otisridge.com.
Rte. 23, Otis, MA 01253.
Trails: 11 (3 novice, 5 intermediate, 3 expert).
Lifts: Double chairlift, T-bar, pony-bar, 2 rope tows.
Vertical Drop: 400 ft.
Snowmaking: 90 percent.
Tickets: Inexpensive.
Open: Weekends, holidays 9–4; midweek 9:30–4; night skiing Tues.–Sun. 5–10.
Ski School Pros: Dave Day and Terri Dunn.

Otis Ridge is the molehill among the mountains, but few slopes do so much to cater to beginners and youngsters, with two ski-school heads. Famous for its winter ski camp, the area takes on a special character on frosty weekends and holiday periods when camp's in session, starting the day after Christmas.

Central County

### BOUSQUET

413-442-8316.
www.bousquets.com.
101 Dan Fox Dr., Pittsfield, MA 01201.
Access from South St. (Rte. 7) or Swamp Rd.
Trails: 21 downhill (novice to expert); all-terrain area.
Lifts: 2 chairlifts, 2 rope tows; snowboarding half-pipe; tubing park.
Vertical Drop: 750 ft.
Snowmaking: 98 percent of area.
Tickets: Inexpensive; free tickets for 65 and older.
Open: Weekdays 10 AM–10 PM, weekends 9 AM–10 PM, Sun. 9 AM–4 PM; night skiing Mon.–Sat. 4–10 PM
Ski and Snowboard School Pro: John Koch.

In 1932 a group of winter enthusiasts approached Clarence Bousquet about using the slopes of his Bousquet Farm for skiing. Three years later the fledgling Bousquet Ski Area put together one of the Berkshires' great travel promotions: Ski trains from New York to Pittsfield (with bus connector to Bousquet) for $2 round-trip.

Now, over 70 years later, the Berkshires' oldest ski area continues to provide friendly slopes, primarily for novice and intermediate skiers. There are, however, several very demanding runs. As a plus, from the summit of Bousquet, a skier has a fine view of Mount Greylock's whalelike profile (nearly the same view that so inspired Herman Melville; see "Arrowhead" in chapter 4, "Arts & Pleasures"). Bousquet is well known for its effective ski school, a corps of some 50 teachers. The state may purchase this facility.

### JIMINY PEAK

413-738-5500.
www.jiminypeak.com.
Corey Rd., Hancock, MA 01237.
Access from Rte. 7, Lanesborough, or Rte. 43, Hancock, via Brodie Mtn. Rd.
Trails: 43 downhill (novice to expert), 18 lighted.
Lifts: 8 chairlifts.
Vertical Drop: 1,140 ft.
Snowmaking: 95 percent of area.
Tickets: Moderate.
Open: Weekdays 9 AM–10:30 PM, weekends 8:30 AM–10:30 PM
Ski School Pro: Chuck Seymour.

Jiminy is committed to long seasons of well-groomed slopes. To that end, it goes to extraordinary lengths, frequently opening early in November and staying open well into March, utilizing advanced snowmaking equipment. It has completed a multimillion-dollar expansion program, opening up a new mountain, East Peak, and a cluster of five buildings called Bentley Brook.

This is one of the area's most demanding mountains, with 40 percent of its trails being suitable for advanced skiers only. Those with such talents will greatly enjoy the North Glade, Upper Lift Line, and Whirlaway. For Intermediates, there's the 360, the WestWay, and the Ace of Spades. These last two trails reveal a magnificent vista of the Jericho Valley, northward toward Vermont. Two expert glades, an expanded beginners' area with a triple chair, and always and improving snowmaking complete the picture.

In addition to a full calendar of races, clinics, and demonstrations, Jiminy runs a race team just for children, a more serious tri-state race team, a freestyle team, a night adult program, and a ski school. Those who ski at Jiminy spend most of their time skiing: Lift lines are carefully monitored so that skiers rarely have to wait more than 12 minutes. Jiminy closes the parking lots when the area nears its capacity.

Jiminy offers facilities and activities to compete with resorts in Vermont. It continues to add more beds (ski-in, ski-out), new lifts, and snowmaking improved to operate at higher temperatures.

## NORTH COUNTY

### BERKSHIRE EAST

413-339-6617.
www.berkshireeast.com.
Rte. 2 Charlemont, MA 01339.
Trails: 45 (12 novice, 14 intermediate, 14 expert).
Lifts: 3 double chairlifts, 1 triple, J-bar, rope tow; snowboarding half-pipe.
Vertical Drop: 1,180 ft.
Snowmaking: 100 percent.
Tickets: Moderate.
Open: Sun.–Tues. 9 AM–4:30 PM, Wed.–Sat. 9 AM–10 PM.

Berkshire East bills itself as "Southern New England's most challenging ski area," and its steep terrain lives up to that claim. With more than 40 percent of its trails suited to experts, this mountain is demanding—especially down the steep Flying Cloud and Lift Line trails, both of which are over 4,000 feet long. For beginners, three separate open slopes around the west lodge provide plenty of room to learn the basics. From the summit of Berkshire East, amid the evergreens, skiers can get a fine view of the steep-sided Deerfield River valley to the east.

The area offers day and night skiing, accompanied by a rustic lodge with a bar upstairs.

### SNOWY OWL RESORT

413-443-4752.
www.skibrodie.com.
Rte. 7, New Ashford, MA 01237.
Trails: Snow tubing park; snowshoeing.
Snowmaking: 98 percent of area.
Tickets: Inexpensive.
Open: Fri. 4:30 PM–9 PM, Sat. and holidays 10:30 AM–9 PM, Sun. 10:30 AM–7:30 PM. At the present time the former Brodie is closed for skiing but remains open for tubing and snowshoeing. Plans are in the works for resort development. One of the oldest ski areas in the Berkshires, Brodie Mountain started out under the direction of Gregory Makeroff, acquir-

ing a different flavor under the guidance of the Kelly clan. It became "Kelly's Irish Alps." In the fall of 1999, Jiminy Peak purchased Brodie, to be run as a "separate but cooperative corporation." Brodie will continue to be a fun area, and has always had tremendous appeal to singles and younger snow enthusiasts.

After tubing, Brodie keeps the fun going off the slopes with the Blarney Room and Kelly's Irish Pub.

### MOUNT GREYLOCK SKI CLUB

413-458-3060; 413-445-7887 (ski conditions).
Roaring Brook Rd., Williamstown, MA 01267
In south Williamstown, turn east on Roaring Brook Rd. beside Rte. 7 state DPW garage.
Continue up gravel road that, in-season, is one-way until 2:30 PM.
Trails: 16 (4 novice, 9 intermediate, 3 expert).
Lifts: 2 rope tows.
Vertical Drop: 500 ft.
Tickets: Very inexpensive membership.
Open: Weekends and holidays when snow permits (no snowmaking).
Features: Lodge, outhouses, ski lessons available.

Mount Greylock Ski Club is a cooperative, which means that in exchange for low rates (family membership is about $100 for a season, including children up to 21), everyone works. Jobs range from helping to take care of the wood-heated lodge to cutting brush on the trail to running the antique Ford and GMC engines that power the lifts. It is a fine place for a family because the adults look out for all the kids. The very young amuse themselves by the hour, sliding near the lodge while parents ski. Members ski patrol and teach.

The area, which has a base altitude of 1,200 feet, faces north and holds snow well, but if the snow doesn't fall . . . well, then, members get to enjoy the social events and work parties the club sponsors. If the one-way traffic is daunting, the alternative is a pleasant 0.5 mile walk.

## Football

High-school teams and pickup touch football games carry on throughout the county, but only in Williamstown can one see collegiate gridiron action, as presented by the Williams College Ephmen (named after their school founder, Ephraim Williams). This is football at its sweetest: No athletic scholarships; studies really do come first, and competition with the likes of Amherst is even and spirited.

**Williams College Football** (413-597-2344; www.williams.edu: click on "sports information"; Weston Field, Williamstown).

## Golf

In 1895 Joseph Choate Jr., son of the prominent Stockbridge lawyer, returned from a Canadian trip with three rudimentary golf clubs. Using tomato cans for holes, he made a course in his backyard at Naumkeag, establishing golf in the Berkshires. Three years later, having perfected his swing, Choate won the National Championships with a record low score. (A variation on the tomato can tale cites the Taconic as the first course in the county.)

Nowadays hardy sports folk tee up on 16 courses countywide from March through November. Every course and club runs tournaments. A call or visit will provide exact dates. Long-distance driving options have expanded, too. First there were wood woods, then metal woods, and now—developed from Pittsfield-GE engineered resins—Lexan woods. And for those who just have to hit some in the dark of night, **Baker's Driving Range & Miniature Golf** (413-443-6102; Rte. 7, Lanesborough, MA 01237) keeps its driving range open from 10 AM till 10:30 PM.

Possibilities in the miniature division: **Par 4 Family Fun Center** (413-499-0051; Rte. 7, Lanesborough, MA 01237), **Jiminy Peak** (413-738-5500; Corey Rd., Hancock, MA 01237), and in South County there's **Rainbow's End Miniature Golf** (413-528-1220; 109 Stockbridge Rd., Gt. Barrington, MA 01230; Rte. 7) inside—yes, inside!—Cove Bowling Lanes.

## Golf Clubs

**Price Code—Greens Fees (weekends; some include cart)**

| | |
|---|---|
| Inexpensive | Under $30 |
| Moderate | $30 to $45 |
| Expensive | Over $45 |

### SOUTH COUNTY

**Egremont Country Club** (413-528-4222; Rte. 23, S. Egremont, MA 01258) Price: moderate; 18 holes, par 71, 5,900 yards; pro: Marc Levesque.

**Greenock Country Club** (413-243-3323; 220 W. Park St., Lee, MA 01238 Price: inexpensive; 9 holes, par 35, 6,140 yards; pro: Michael Bechard.

**Stockbridge Golf Club** (413-298-3423; Main St., P.O. Box 223, Stockbridge, MA 01262) Price: expensive; 18 holes, par 71, 6,294 yards; pro: Jim Walker. Must be introduced by a member.

**Wyantenuck Country Club** (413-528-3229; Sheffield Rd., Gt. Barrington, MA 01230) Price: moderate; 18 holes, par 70, 6,223 yards; pro: Tom Sullivan. Private club.

### CENTRAL COUNTY

**Bas-Ridge Golf Course** (413-655-2605; Plunkett Ave., Hinsdale, MA 01235) Price: inexpensive; 18 holes, par 70, 5,164 yards.

**Berkshire Hills Country Club** (413-442-1451; Benedict Rd., Pittsfield, MA 01201) Price: moderate; 18 holes, par 72, 6,606 yards; pro: Bob Meheran. Must be introduced by a member.

**Country Club of Pittsfield** (413-447-8504; 639 South St., Pittsfield, MA 01201) Price: moderate; 18 holes, par 71, 6,100 yards; pro: Brad Benson. Must be introduced by a member.

**Cranwell Golf Course** (413-637-1364; www.cranwell.com; 55 Lee Rd., Rte. 20, Lenox, MA 01240) Price: expensive; 18 holes, par 70, 6,346 yards; pro: David Strawn.

**General Electric Athletic Association** (413-443-5746; 303 Crane Ave., Pittsfield, MA 01201) Price: inexpensive; 9 holes, par 36, 6,205 yards; pro: Jay Aba.

**Pontoosuc Lake Country Club** (413-445-4217; Ridge Ave., Pittsfield, MA 01201) Price: inexpensive; 18 holes, par 70, 6,305 yards.

**Skyline Country Club** (413-445-5584; 405 S. Main St., Lanesborough, MA 01237) Price: inexpensive; 18 holes, par 72, 6,643 yards; pro: Jim Mitus.

**Wahconah Country Club** (413-684-1333; Orchard Rd., Dalton, MA 01226) Price: expensive; 18 holes, par 71, 6,541 yards; pro: Paul Daniels. Public restricted on weekends.

North County

**Forest Park Country Club** (413-743-3311; Forest Park Ave., Adams, MA 01220) Price: inexpensive; 9 holes, par 34, 5,183 yards.

**North Adams Country Club** (413-663-7887; River Rd., P.O. Box 241, Clarksburg, MA 01247) Price: inexpensive; 9 holes, par 36, 5,681 yards; pro: Jack Tosone.

**Taconic Golf Club** (413-458-3997; Meacham St., P.O. Box 193, Williamstown, MA 01267) Price: expensive; 18 holes, par 71, 6,614 yards; pro: Rick Pohle. Open to public Tues.–Fri.

**Waubeeka Springs Golf Links** (413-458-8355; New Ashford Rd., Rte. 7, Williamstown, MA 01267) Price: moderate; 18 holes, par 72, 6,394 yards; pro: Eric Tiele.

Golfers live in anticipation of a new course, at **Donnybrook** in Lanesborough.

## Hiking

See "Walking, Hiking, Camping, and X-C Skiing."

## Horseback Riding

Over meadow and under mountain, there are a slew of riding academies and stables in and around Berkshire County. A quick look in the Yellow Pages under "Riding Academies" or "Stables" opens the barn door to information on horse breeders, dealers, trainers, farriers, and saddle shops. The following is a partial list of riding stables.

**Bonnie Lea Farm** (413-458-3149; 511 North St., Williamstown, MA 01267; Rte. 7) Private and group lessons; English and western; indoor and outdoor rings, guided trail rides; year-round.

**Horsesense at Golden Hill Farm** (413-637-1999; 87 Golden Hill Rd., Lenox, MA 01240) Private and group lessons; English; indoor and outdoor rings; year-round.

**Oakhollow** (413-458-9278; 651 Henderson Rd., Williamstown, MA 01267) English lessons; trails, indoor and outdoor rings; therapeutic riding program; year-round.

**Overmeade School of Horsemanship** (413-499-2850; 940 East St., Lenox, MA 01240) Private and group lessons; English; year-round.

**Riverbank Farm** (413-684-3200; 619 East St., Dalton, MA 01226) Summer riding program; English and western lessons; year-round.

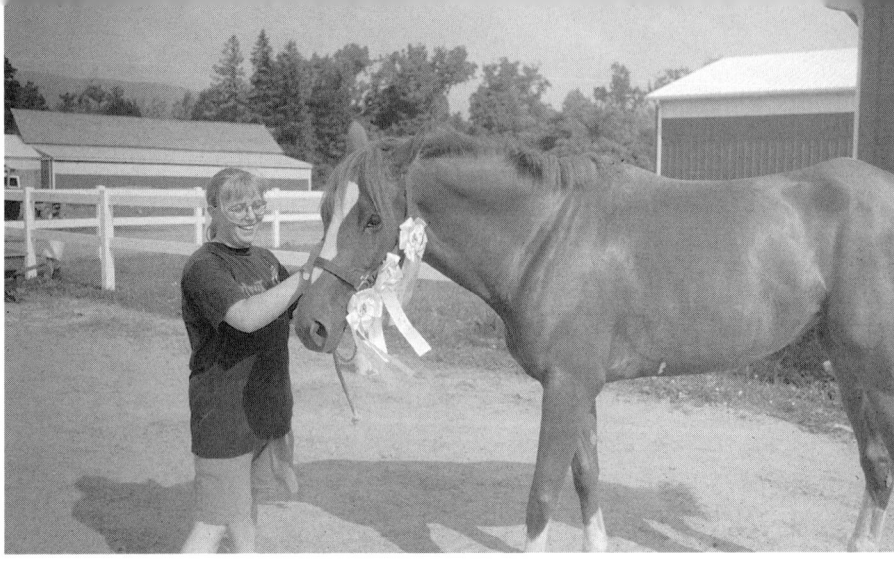

*Maybe not a blue ribbon, but pretty darn good!* Lauren R. Stevens

**Undermountain Farm** (413-637-3365; Undermountain Rd., Lenox, MA 01240; English lessons; English and western trail rides; spring through fall.

**Windy Knoll Farm** (413-243-0989; 40 Stringer Ave., Lee, MA 01238) Stable management and riding lessons (weather permitting) for beginners; horse-drawn wagon rides; open May 1–Dec. 1.

## Hunting & Fishing

The first settlers found Berkshire teeming with fish and game; wildlife is now more plentiful than it has been in 150 years. Deer visit town to devour ornamental shrubbery; wild turkey and beaver have been successfully reintroduced; and bear, pheasant, quail, rabbit, raccoon, fox, coyote, and gray squirrel are sufficient to satisfy nearly every hunter's aim. In Berkshire's waters, large- and small-mouth bass, northern pike, white and yellow perch, horned pout, and trout of all persuasions swim in abundance. Numerous brooks, rivers, ponds, and lakes are stocked with trout each year.

Essential equipment for any hunting or fishing is a pamphlet containing abstracts of the *Massachusetts Fish and Wildlife Laws*, available free at local sporting goods shops; from the **Division of Fisheries and Wildlife** (617-626-1590; www.state.ma.us/dfwele; 251 Causeway, Suite 400, Boston, MA 02114); or from the **Western Wildlife District Manager**, (413-447-9787; 400 Hubbard Ave., Pittsfield, MA 01201). This pamphlet carefully outlines the rules and regulations of Massachusetts fishing and hunting. Also essential is a license, which can be obtained through either city or town clerks, through the Division of Fisheries and Wildlife at the Boston address above, or through many local sporting goods stores (see the list at the beginning of this chapter).

A license permits hunting, fishing, or trapping on property that is not posted, although some towns also require owner permission. State lands are open with a few exceptions, such as a three-quarter-mile radius around the tower on Mount Greylock. No hunting is allowed anywhere on Greylock during the summer and early fall. As deer season varies by a few weeks between Massachusetts and neighboring states, hunters are responsible to know what state they are in.

## A List of Trout-Stocked Berkshire Waters

(In the spring; bodies of water that are stocked spring and fall are in italics.)

### South County

**Alford:** Green River, Seekonk Brook.

**Egremont:** Green River, Hubbard Brook, Karner Brook.

**Great Barrington:** Green River, Lake Mansfield, Williams River, West Brook.

**Lee:** Beartown Brook (W. branch), *Goose Pond,* Greenwater Brook, Hop Brook, Laurel Lake, Washington Mountain Brook.

**Monterey:** *Lake Buel,* Lake Garfield, Konkapot River.

**New Marlborough:** Konkapot River, Umpachene Brook, York Pond.

**Otis:** *Big Benton Pond,* Little Benton Pond, Farmington River, *Otis Reservoir.*

**Sandisfield:** Buck River, Clam River, Farmington River.

**Sheffield:** Hubbard Brook, Innworks Brook, Konkapot River.

**Stockbridge:** Konkapot Brook, Larrywaug Brook, *Stockbridge Bowl.*

**Tyringham:** *Goose Pond,* Goose Pond Brook, Hop Brook.

**West Stockbridge:** Cone Brook, Williams River.

### Central County

**Becket:** Greenwater Pond, Shaker Mill Brook, Walker Brook, Westfield River (W. branch), Yokum Brook.

**Dalton:** Housatonic River (E. branch), Sackett Brook, Wahconah Falls Brook.

**Hancock:** Berry Pond, Kinderhook Creek.

**Hinsdale:** Bennet Brook, Housatonic River (E. branch), Plunket Reservoir.

**Lanesborough:** Sachem Brook, Town Brook.

**Lenox:** *Laurel Lake,* Yokum Brook.

**Peru:** Trout Brook.

**Pittsfield:** Daniels Brook, Housatonic River (S.W. branch), Lulu Cascade Brook, *Lake Onota, Pontoosuc Lake,* Sackett Brook, Smith Brook.

**Richmond:** Cone Brook, Furnace Brook, *Richmond Pond.*

**Washington:** Depot Brook.

**Windsor:** Westfield Brook, Westfield River (E. branch), Windsor Brook, Windsor Jambs Brook, Windsor Pond.

### North County

**Adams:** Hoosic River (S. branch), Tophet Brook.

**Cheshire:** Dry Brook, Hoosic River (S. branch), Kitchen Brook, South Brook.

**Clarksburg:** Hoosic River (N. branch), Hudson Brook.

**Florida:** *Deerfield River, North Pond,* Cold River.

**North Adams:** Natural Bridge Pond, *Windsor Lake.*

**Savoy:** Chickley River, Cold River, Westfield River (E. branch).

**Williamstown:** Broad Brook, Green River, Green River (W. branch), Hemlock Brook, Roaring Brook.

## Fish, Exclusive of Trout, in Berkshire Waters

| TOWN | WATER | NP | LMB | SMB | CP | WP | YP | BB |
|---|---|---|---|---|---|---|---|---|
| SOUTH COUNTY | | | | | | | | |
| **Egremont** | Prospect Lake | | | | X | | X | X |
| **Lee** | Goose Pond | | X | X | X | | X | X |
| **Lee** | Laurel Lake | | X | | X | X | X | X |
| **Monterey** | Benedict Pond | | X | | | | X | X |
| **New Marlborough** | Thousand Acre Swamp | | | X | X | | X | X |
| **Otis** | Benton Pond | | | X | X | X | X | X |
| **Otis** | East Lake Reservoir | X | X | X | X | X | X | X |
| **Stockbridge** | Stockbridge Bowl | | X | X | X | | X | X |
| CENTRAL COUNTY | | | | | | | | |
| **Becket** | Center Pond | | X | X | X | X | X | X |
| **Becket** | Yokum Pond | | X | | | | X | X |
| **Hinsdale** | Ashmere Lake | | X | X | | | X | |
| **Pittsfield** | Onota Lake | X | X | | X | | X | X |
| **Pittsfield** | Pontoosic Lake | | X | | X | | X | X |
| **Pittsfield** | Richmond Pond | | X | X | X | | X | X |
| **Windsor** | Windsor Pond | | X | | X | | X | X |
| NORTH COUNTY | | | | | | | | |
| **Cheshire** | Cheshire Reservoir | X | X | | X | | X | X |
| **Clarksburg** | Mauserts Pond | | | | | X | | X |

**Abbreviations**

**NP:** Northern Pike
**LMB:** Largemouth Bass
**SMB:** Smallmouth Bass
**CP:** Chain Pickerel
**WP:** White Perch
**YP:** Yellow Perch
**BB:** Brown Bullheads

*The Stockbridge skateboard park is the most popular spot for kids in town.* Judith Monachina

## Kids Only

Although the county may be low on video arcades, bumper cars, skating centers, or amusement parks, as far as most kids are concerned, Berkshire is cool. Almost all the recreational and cultural activities in this book are suitable for children. In addition, some kids do the mall crawl, some hang out on shopping streets. The Ashuwillticook Rail Trail and baseball parks are area destinations. Hills and lakes beckon. Besides the dozens of children's camps here, most of the ski slopes operate ski schools for kids. In between the summer camping and winter skiing, the Berkshire cultural icons offer a wide range of kid programs, from after school, school to vacation, to summer day camps. Most local libraries have story hours, most of the community centers, museums, and playgrounds have kids' programs, and many of the local theaters have innovative children's productions. In addition, bulletin boards and signs at all kinds of locations—inns, local stores, libraries, post offices, and the like—keep viewers current. Web sites at local museums and other institutions provide the newest news. **Berkshire Resources for Child Care** (413-443-7830; 152 North St., Suite 230, Pittsfield, MA 01201) puts out a listing of camps and activities.

Most of what follows is aimed primarily at summer activities.

### South County

In Great Barrington, at the Cove Bowling Lanes on Route 7, is the **Rainbow's End Miniature Golf Course** (413-528-1220, 800-352-4398; fax 413-528-5295), an indoor extravaganza to test even the deftest little putter. Out in New Marlboro, **Four Colors**

*Late afternoon at Stockbridge Bowl* Judith Monachina

**Company** presents theater workshops for kids of all ages at the **Flying Cloud Summer Camp** (413-528-5614; S. Sandisfield Rd.).

**Berkshire South Regional Community Center** (413-528-2810 ext. 34; 15 Crissy Rd., Gt. Barrington, MA 01230) offers a day camp. The **Stockbridge Library** (413-298-5501; Main St., Stockbridge; Rte. 7) has a large and cozy children's section, with story hours as a regular event. During the summer, the **Berkshire Theatre Festival** (413-298-5536; 6 E. Main St., Stockbridge, MA 01262; Rte. 102, E. of jct. Rte. 7) gives Children's Theatre performances of plays written by local kids. It also offers an acting class for students 12 to 14. The **Norman Rockwell Museum** (413-298-4100; P.O. Box 309, Stockbridge, MA 01262; on Rte. 183, 0.6 mi. S. of jct. Rte. 102) offers a variety of activities geared to kids, one the best being its Family Day. Admission prices are lowered, and special guides are provided to inform both parents and kids. The **Berkshire Botanical Garden** (413-298-3926; www.berkshirebotanical.org; P.O. Box 386, Stockbridge, MA, jct. Rtes. 183 and 102,) holds a wonder-filled day camp for kids in summer, offering children in grades one through six the opportunity to explore the world of nature. Their early October Harvest Festival has lots of kids' activities, too. Art classes are a part of the **IS183** program (413-298-5252; www.is183.org; 13 Willard Hill Rd., Stockbridge, MA 01262), with special courses for children 8 to 17.

### CENTRAL COUNTY

In Pittsfield, **Buster's Entertainment Center** (413-499-7500; www.bustersforfun.com; 457 Dalton Ave., Pittsfield, MA 01201) is the place to be. There are more than 100 arcades, plus "Blue Skies & Rainbows" for 1- to 6-year-olds and "Adventure Crawl" for children up to 12 years.

The **Lenox Library** (413-637-0197; 18 Main St., Lenox, MA 01240) has a terrific children's room, which always seems to be brimming with kid energy. **Lenox Community Center** (413-637-5530; 65 Walker St., Lenox, MA 01240) offers a day camp, while

**Shakespeare & Co.** (413-637-1199 ext. 172; 70 Kemble St.) provides Riotous Youth at Lenox High School. **Pleasant Valley Wildlife Sanctuary** (413-637-0320; www.massaudubon.org; 472 W. Mountain Rd., Lenox, MA 01240) runs a History Day Camp, 1- and 2-week sessions, featuring exciting educational outdoor activities for boys and girls grades 1 through 12.

Central County's other Massachusetts Audubon Society property, **Canoe Meadows Wildlife Sanctuary** (413-637-0320; www.massaudubon.org; mail: 472 W. Mountain Rd., Lenox, MA 01240; on Holmes Rd., Pittsfield), in conjunction with the Berkshire Museum, runs a 1-week Native American camp for boys and girls, ages three, four, and five. During the summer, **Hancock Shaker Village** (413-443-0188, 800-817-1137; www.hancockshakervillage.org; mail: P.O. Box 927, Pittsfield, MA 01201; on Rte. 20, Hancock) offers a hands-on experience in its Discovery Room, where children can try on Shaker-style clothes and participate in such facets of 19th-century life as spinning wool, weaving, or writing with a quill pen at a Shaker desk. Outside, children can see the farm animals and demonstrations of sheepshearing or sheepherding trials. Hancock Shaker Village also conducts School Vacation Crafts Workshops in basket making, cooking, and textiles in February and April.

The **Robbins-Zust Family Marionettes** often perform a full range of "classic tales for children of all ages." Bringing out the heavyweight dramas such as *Three Little Pigs, Rumpelstiltskin* and *The Emperor's New Clothes,* the Robbins-Zust troupe often performs in Lenox and Pittsfield. These are well-crafted marionettes: All their clothes are made by the troupe. For more information, call the Marionettes themselves (413-698-2591; www.berkshireweb.com/zust; East Rd., Richmond, MA 01254). They are "the smallest, established, permanent, floating repertory company in America."

In downtown Pittsfield, the children's library at the **Berkshire Athenaeum** (413-499-9483; www.berkshire.net/PittsfieldLibrary; 1 Wendell Ave., Pittsfield, MA 01201; at East St.) has a wide range of programs, from story hours to films. The **Berkshire Museum** (413-443-7171; www.berkshiremuseum.org; 39 South St., Pittsfield, MA 01201; Rte. 7) also has an extensive series of educational children's events—theater, dance, and storytelling for the whole family. **Berkshire Music School** (413-442-1411; 30 Wendell Ave., Pittsfield, MA 01201) offers several programs for budding muscians. There's even a circus camp at **Berkshire Community College** (413-499-4660 ext. 375; 1350 West St., Pittsfield, MA 01201).

At **Dalton Community House** (413-684-0260; 400 Main St., Dalton, MA 01226) kids will find a positive plethora of fun activities, including several day camps. Then there's miniature golf in Lanesborough to keep little hands busy at **Baker's Golf Center** (413-442-6102; 658 S. Main St., Lanesborough, MA 01237) and the **Par-4 Family Fun Center** (413-499-0051; Rte. 7, Lanesborough, MA 01237). Up-county a ways, at **Jiminy Peak** (413-738-5500; Rte. 43, Hancock, MA 01237), the fun goes right into summer with the **Alpine Slide,** a scenic 15-minute ride up, and an exhilarating 5-minute slide down. Jiminy also has a miniature golf course, trout fishing, and a separate tennis program.

### North County

Over in North Adams, at the **Heritage Gateway State Park** (413-663-6312; 9 Furnace St. Bypass, N. Adams, MA 01247) a Junior Ranger's program is active. In Williamstown, there's an extensive summer playground program at the public schools, along with swimming lessons and a Nature Program at **Margaret Lindley Park.** Information can be had by calling the **Youth Center** (413-458-5925; Cole Ave., Williamstown, MA 01267). A summer playground program and a score of winter recreational programs are also offered through the Youth Center. **Williamstown Rural Lands Foundation** (413-458-9771; 671 Cold Springs Rd., Williamstown, MA 01267) usually offers a children's nature day camp. **Starlight Stage** (413-4584273; 57 Linden St., Williamstown, MA 01267) provides hands-on theater experience ending in a production at the First Congregational Church. The **Massachusetts Department of Environmental Management** (413-442-8928) and **Nature's Classroom** offer scores of children's programs at several sites on Mount Greylock, including The Glen, in Adams. And treasure hunts, along with children's workshops on various artists, are a few of the offerings for kids at the **Clark Art Institute** (413-458-8109; 225 South St., Williamstown, MA 01267). The **Williams College Museum of Art** has imaginative children's programs, while **Massachusetts College of Liberal Arts** (413-662-5543; 375 Church St, N. Adams, MA 01247) hosts kid technology programs. **Kidspace @ MASS MoCA** is a combined effort of the Clark, WCMA, and MASS MoCA to provide a program for children and families who have had little exposure to art. The college's science departments invite children in for imaginative exposure to natural phenomena. The **Williamstown Public Library** offers read-a-louds and a summer reading program. Children's tennis and soccer camps are available on the **Williams College** campus in the summer; call the Conference Office (413-458-2229). The **Williamstown Theatre Festival** (413-458-3200) runs a program for North Adams youth.

## Camps

There's a colorful list of overnight, resident summer camps in the Berkshires—some specializing in sports, some tuned to the arts, some with other enthusiasms. If youngsters are interested in dance or the theater, hiking or canoeing, tennis or gymnastics, dressmaking, or computers, Berkshire has a camp for them. Most camps take advantage of the beauty of their natural settings, and for many of them that includes lakes and mountains. Warm days and cool nights make for season-long aquatics and sound sleeping. Berkshire cultural life also enriches campers' time here, with Tanglewood and Jacob's Pillow being two of the more popular side trips.

The Indians were the first campers in the Berkshires, and many of its camps bear Indian names. Following is a list of addresses and telephone numbers. "Full program" indicates availability of both arts and sports activities.

### South County

**Camp Ashmere** (413-655-2650 summer, 413-663-3780 winter; Hinsdale, MA 01235) Religious; residential and day; special units.

**Camp Danbee** (413-655-8115; www.campdanbee.com; Rte. 143, Hinsdale, MA 01235) Girls residential; full program.

**Camp Half Moon** (413-528-0940; www.camphalfmoon.com; 400 Main St., P.O. Box 108, Gt. Barrington, MA 01230) Coed day and resident camp; full program.

**Camp Hi Rock YMCA** (413-528-1227; www.camphirock.com; RD 3 Box 49, Mt. Washington, MA 01258) Sessions for coed groups and adults; full program.

**Camp Kingsmont** (413-232-8518; www.campkingsmont.com; RFD 2, W. Stockbridge, MA 01266) Coed; nutrition and dietary education program; physical fitness.

**Camp Lenox** (413-243-2223 summer, 413-269-6036 winter; www.lenox.com; Rte. 8, Otis, MA 01238) Coed day; sports.

**Camp Nawaka** (413-269-4296; www.nawaka.org; Reservoir Rd., Otis, MA 01253) Camp Fire Boys and Girls.

**Camp WaWa Segowea** (413-229-8613; www.wawasegowea.com; Foley Hill Rd., Southfield, MA 01259) YMCA; coed residential; full program.

**Crane Lake Camp** (413-232-4257 summer, 201-804-9700 winter; www.eisnercamp.org/cranelake; State Line Rd., W. Stockbridge, MA 01266) Coed; run by URJ; full program and Jewish education.

**Eisner Camp** (413-528-1652 summer, 201-804-9700 winter; www.eisnercamp.org/eisner; Brookside Rd., P.O. Box 569, Gt. Barrington, MA 01230) Coed children's and adult retreats; run by URJ; full program and Jewish education.

**Madden Open Hearts Camp** (413-528-2229; www.openheartscamp.org; 250 Monument Valley Rd., Gt. Barrington, MA 01230) Coed for children who have had open-heart surgery or heart transplants; full program.

**New England Keswick** (413-528-9588; www.nekeswick.com; Chestnut Hill Rd., P.O. Box 156, Monterey, MA 01245) Evangelical Christian camp and retreat center.

### Central County

**Belvoir Terrace** (413-637-0555; www.belvoirterrace.com; 80 Cliffwood St., Lenox, MA 01240; winter: 212-580-3398; 101 W. 79 St., New York, NY 10024) Girls day; fine and performing arts.

**Camp Becket** (413-623-8972; www.bccymca.org/becket; Becket, MA 01223) Boys; full program; operated by Two-State YMCA. Becket and Chimney Corners also run a day camp.

**Camp Bonnie Brae** (413-269-4481; Algerie Rd., E. Otis, MA 01253) Girls; full program; run by Girl Scouts of the Pioneer Valley.

**Camp Chimney Corners** (413-623-8991; www.bccymca.org/chimney; Becket, MA 01223) Girls; full program; operated by Two-State YMCA, sister camp to Camp Becket. Becket and Chimney Corners also run a day camp.

**Camp Emerson** (413-655-8123 summer, 914-779-9406 winter; www.campemerson.com; 212 Longview Ave., P.O. Box 808, Hinsdale, MA 01235) Coed 7–15; full program.

**Camp Greylock** (413-623-8921 summer; www.campemerson.com; Rte. 8, Becket, MA 01233; winter: 212-582-1042; 200 W. 57th St., Suite 307, New York, NY 10019) Boys; full program.

**Camp Mah-Kee-Nac** (413-637-0781 summer, 201-429-8522 winter; www.campmkn.com; 6 Hawthorne Rd., Lenox, MA 01240) Boys; sports and outdoor-adventure programs.

**Camp Mohawk** (413-443-9843; www.campmohawk.org; 300 Old Cheshire Rd., Lanesborough, MA 01237) Coed day; run by YMCA.

**Camp Romaca** (413-655-2715 summer, 800-779-2070 winter; www.romaca.com; Long View Ave., Hinsdale, MA 01235) Girls; full program.

**Sports School Day Camp** (413-637-3463; Lenox, MA 01240).

**Camp Stevenson Witawentin** (413-445-5850; http://girlsinc-berkshires.org/camp; Churchill Rd., Pittsfield, MA 01201) Girls day; sports; through Girls Inc.

**Camp Taconic** (413-655-2717 summer, 914-762-2820 winter; www.camptaconic.com; Hinsdale, MA 01235) Coed sleepaway; full program.

**Camp Watitoh** (413-623-8951 summer, 914-428-1894 winter; www.campwatitoh.com; Center Lake, Becket, MA 01223) Coed; full program.

**Camp Winadu** (413-447-8900 summer, 407-994-5500 winter; www.campwinadu.com; Churchill St., Pittsfield, MA 01201) Boys; full program.

North County

**Manice Education Center** (413-663-8463; www.christodora.org: under "Programs"; 68 Savoy Rd., Florida, MA 01247) Coed; full programs; for inner-city youth.

## Racquet Sports

### Racquetball

There's a lively racquetball scene in Berkshire, with courts in Lenox, Pittsfield, New Ashford, and North Adams, and at Williams College. The **Northern Berkshire YMCA** (413-663-6529; www.northernberkshireymca.org; 22 Brickyard Ct., N. Adams, MA 02147) has two fine courts. **Pittsfield YMCA** (413-499-7650; www.pittsfieldymca.org; 292 North St., Pittsfield, MA 01201) has four; and **Berkshire West** (413-499-4600; www.berkshirewest.com; 100 Dan Fox Dr., P.O. Box 2188, Pittsfield, MA 01201) has four. Both Pittsfield facilities offer top-flight teaching programs. Williams's is located at the football field.

### Squash

For the sporting type—as opposed to the garden variety—many squash courts do exist; most are open only to people associated with the private schools maintaining them. Memberships are available at Williams College, which has increased the size of its courts. For travelers: the **Pittsfield YMCA** (see above). Luckily the Y's court is also new, well built, and lively.

### Tennis

In the Gilded Age of the Berkshires at the close of the 19th century, tennis was played on lawns, close cropped and lined with lime. Wheatleigh was an especially favored site. The lawn tennis parties there featured men in white-linen trousers and ladies in ankle-length tennis dresses. Most of the grass courts are front lawns now, and though a few Berkshire connoisseurs still play on turf, tennis—here as elsewhere—is now played principally on clay, composites, and hard courts.

Several tournaments are annual events and can be counted on to test the best skills or provide exciting viewing. A senior tournament in midsummer honors the fabled former Williams College coach Clarance Chaffee and his tennis partner, Billy Hart. Starting in late summer, tournaments are run by the YMCA's **Ponterril** (413-499-0687, 413-499-0640; Pontoosuc Lake, Pittsfield, MA 01201; Rte. 7).

Southern Berkshire has traditionally been lacking in public tennis courts, but **Monument Mountain High School** and the **Berkshire Hills Tennis Association** have created seven hard courts at the school, for both scholastic and community play. The courts are open to the public, with priority given to the school's tennis teams' needs.

## Tennis Facilities

### South County

**Monument Mountain Motel** (413-528-3272; Rte. 7, Gt. Barrington, MA 01230; opposite Friendly's) Lighted all-weather court; fee. Call for reservation.

**Monument Mountain Regional High School** (413-528-3346; Rte. 7, Gt. Barrington, MA 01230) 7 hard courts, used by school students on weekdays from 3 PM.

**Greenock Country Club** (413-243-3323; W. Park St., Lee, MA 01238) 2 clay courts. Fee.

**Prospect Lake Park** (413-528-4158; http://prospectlakepark.com; Prospect Lake Rd., P.O. Box 78, N. Egremont, MA 01252) 2 courts; fee.

**Simon's Rock College of Bard** (413-528-0771; 84 Alford Rd., Gt. Barrington, MA 01230) 4 hard courts plus backboard; summer memberships available.

**Stockbridge Golf Club** (413-298-3838; Main St., Stockbridge, MA 01262; behind Town Hall) 3 clay, 2 hard-surface courts; nonmembers may arrange for lessons only.

**Stockbridge Public Courts** for town residents and registered hotel guests; **Pine St.:** 2 hard courts; **The Plain School**, Main St. (Rte. 7) 2 hard courts.

### Central County

**Berkshire West** (413-449-4600; Dan Fox Dr., Pittsfield MA 01201) 6 outdoor courts and 5 indoor hard courts; memberships available.

**Cranwell Resort** (413-637-1364; 55 Lee Rd., Lenox, MA 01240; Rte. 20) 2 Har-Tru courts. Fee.

**Jiminy Peak** (413-738-5500; Hancock, MA 01237) 7 outdoor courts; instruction, tournaments. Fee.

**Herberg Middle School** (Pomeroy Ave.) 4 courts.

**Lakewood Park** (Newell St.) 2 courts.

**Pittsfield High School** (East St.) 4 courts.

**Pittsfield Public Courts** free to the public when school is not in session; asphalt courts.

**Taconic High School** (Valentine Rd.) 4 courts.

**Ponterril/YMCA** (413-499-0687; Pontoosuc Lake, Pittsfield, MA 01201; Rte. 7) 6 outdoor clay courts; members have priority, nonmembers may use them for a fee; summer memberships available.

### North County

**Greylock Recreation Field** (Protection Ave.; off Rte. 2) 2 courts.

**Noel Field** (State St. behind Child Care of the Berkshires; Rte. 8A) 2 courts.

**North Adams Public Courts** are free; asphalt.

**Williams College** (413-597-3131; Linde Lane, Williamstown; bet. Park St. and Cole Ave.) 24 clay and hard-surface courts; summer memberships available: Apply to Buildings and Grounds Department.

**Williamstown Public Court** (off E. Main St. near Colonial Village) first come, first serve (ah!).

## RUNNING

Runners have run into the right neck of the woods in the Berkshires. With terrain and roadways of all types, clean mountain air, and inspiring vistas, Berkshire draws out the relaxed runner, that meditative runner who can run almost forever. Most back roads and byways have little traffic. Running may be even more pleasant on trails. For the rugged cross-country runner, some of the trails outlined under "Walking" are suitable. Racers or wannabes should check in with the **Western Massachusetts Athletic Club** (413-743-5124; www.runwmac.com; P.O. Box 1517, N. Adams, MA 01247) for events and society.

## SKATING

For ice-skaters, the Berkshires offer many smooth and slippery possibilities, most of them framed by hills. Three rinks are open to the public: one at the **Pittsfield Boys Club** (413-448-8258; 16 Melville St., Pittsfield, MA 01201), open Sat. and Sun., 2–3:45; another at Williams College's **Lansing Chapman Rink** (413-597-2433; 76 Latham St.) in Williamstown; and the third in North Adams at the **Vietnam Veterans Memorial Skating Rink** (413-664-9474; S. Church St.), managed by Massachusetts College of Liberal Arts. All the rinks offer low-priced children's programs. Outdoor skating on flooded fields is a Berkshire tradition. During the colder months, public works crews groom ice at the Common in Pittsfield, by the Dalton Community House, and on the Stockbridge Town Field. Lake and pond skating is exquisite in Berkshire when the water freezes before the snow flies.

For those who prefer their skating on wheels, many of the county's smoother back roads make for ideal blacktop cruising. In-line skating has taken off big here, and 'bladers can now be seen skating the hills three seasons a year. In fact, many skiers now tune up during the warmer weather on roller skies. Some towns have developed skateboard parks, while others bother about how to keep skateboarders off the sidewalks. The Ashuwillticook Rail Trail, as smooth as smooth can be, is ideal for wheels of any configuration.

## SOARING

Attitude controls speed, which ideally is 51 mph. In this unearthly quiet half a mile up, the Berkshires seem like a Swiss landscape, all rolling patterns of farm and woodland.

The **Mohawk Soaring Club** operates out of Harriman West Airport, North Adams (413-458-8650). Those wishing to soar should hang out with the glider pilots at the far edge of the airstrip on weekends. Those who watch and ask a few questions could end up floating on air.

Should an aircraft seem an encumbrance to soaring, people with wings regularly jump off the top of Mount Greylock in Adams and just as often off the Western Summit of the Mohawk Trail, in Florida, relying on lightweight hang gliders to support their flight. We take no position on such Icarian activity.

## Swimming

Berkshire is blessed with countless magical swimming spots, some secluded and known only to the likes of otter and some quite public. There are sizable lakes and ponds, rushing green rivers, and deep, chilly quarries. In winter, and for those who prefer their water sports in a more controlled setting, there are numerous swimming pools both indoor and out. Most state and municipal ponds have day-use and inexpensive season passes available to residents and nonresidents.

### South County

**Benedict Pond, Beartown State Forest** (413-528-0904; Blue Hill Rd., Monterey; off Rte. 23 E. of Gt. Barrington or off Rte. 102, S. Lee) Beach; bathhouse with showers; picnicking, 12,000-acre state forest. Day fee.

**Green River** (off Rte. 23, 1 mi. W. of Gt. Barrington) Clearest of the clear, greenest of the green, purest of the pure—a summer treat not to be missed. Neighbors deserve consideration, especially in parking.

**Lake Garfield, Kinne's Grove** (Rte. 23, Monterey).

**Lake Mansfield** (413-528-6080; off Christian Hill Rd., Gt. Barrington).

**Oak n' Spruce Resort** (413-243-3500; 190 Meadow St., S. Lee; off Rte. 102) Heated outdoor and indoor pools, saunas, whirlpool bath, physical fitness room. By membership.

**Otis Reservoir, Tolland State Forest** (413-269-6002, 413-269-7268; Tolland Rd., Otis; off Rte. 23) Swimming, picnicking; 10,000-acre state forest.

**Prospect Lake** (413-528-4158; Prospect Lake Rd., N. Egremont; 0.75 mi. W. of Rte. 71) Camping, day picnics, adult lounge; open daily to 6 PM.

**Spectacle Pond** (Cold Spring Rd., Sandisfield).

**York Lake, Sandisfield State Forest** (413-258-4774, 413-229-8212; York Lake Rd., Sandisfield; off Rte. 57) Swimming, picnicking, 8,000-acre state forest.

*Wading at North Pond, Savoy* Lauren R. Stevens

### CENTRAL COUNTY

**Ashmere Lake** (Ashmere Beach, Rte. 143, Hinsdale).

**Berkshire West** (413-499-4600; Dan Fox Dr., Pittsfield) Indoor/outdoor pool, bathhouse, snack bar, showers; memberships available.

**Boys & Girls Club** (413-448-8258; 16 Melville St., Pittsfield) Under 18; indoor pool open to members only; memberships available. Free swimming early evenings, weekdays; Saturday 1–3 PM.

**Lake Onota** (Onota Blvd., Pittsfield) Free municipal beaches, supervised, 12–8 PM daily.

**Pittsfield Girls' Club** (413-442-5174; 165 East St., Pittsfield) Indoor pool open for recreational swimming evenings, Monday–Friday; Saturday 1–2:15.

**Pittsfield State Forest** (413-442-8992; Cascade St., Pittsfield) Swimming (lifeguards on duty 10 AM–6 PM), picnicking, 10,000-acre state forest.

**Pittsfield YMCA** (413-499-7650; 292 North St., Pittsfield).

**Plunkett Lake Lion's Club Beach** (Church St., Hinsdale).

**Ponterril** (413-499-0647; Pontoosuc Lake, Rte. 7, N. of Pittsfield) Operated by Pittsfield YMCA; pool open to members only. Season memberships available.

**Pontoosuc Lake** (Rte. 7, Pittsfield) Free municipal beach.

**Windsor State Forest** (413-684-0948; Windsor; follow signs from Rte. 9 in W. Cummington or Rte. 116 in Savoy) Swimming, picnicking.

### NORTH COUNTY

**Cheshire Reservoir** (The Causeway, Farnam's Road, Cheshire).

**Clarksburg State Park** (Mauserts Pond, Rte. 8, Clarksburg, near Vermont line) Swimming, picnicking, 3,400-acre state park.

**Hoosac Valley High School** (413-743-5200; Rte 116, Cheshire) Indoor pool open September through June.

**Jiminy Peak** (413-738-5500; Corey Rd., off Rte. 7, Hancock) Outdoor pool.

**Margaret Lindley Park** (Rte. 7 where Rte. 2 leaves Williamstown) Swimming pond open during school summer vacation.

**Northern Berkshire YMCA** (413-663-6529; Brickyard Ct., N. Adams) Indoor pool.

**North Pond, Savoy Mountain State Forest** (413-663-8459; Central Shaft Rd., Savoy; follow signs from Rte. 2 in Florida or Rte. 116 in Savoy) Swimming, picnicking, 11,000-acre state forest.

**Sand Springs Pool and Spa** (413-458-5205; off Rte. 7, Williamstown; near Vermont line) Mineral pool with year-round temperature of 74 degrees; 2 mineral whirlpools, mineral showers, sauna, shuffleboard, picnic area, beach. Pavilion for private party use.

**Windsor Lake** (413-662-3047; N. Adams; access via Bradley St. from Mass. College or via Kemp Ave. from E. Main St.) Municipal swimming area; supervised daily.

*Country road, take me home.* Lauren R. Stevens

## Walking, Hiking, Camping, X-C Skiing

*If you would be happy in Berkshire, you must carry mountains in your brain.*
—Oliver Wendell Holmes

It is possible to approximate the opportunities with numbers. Massachusetts may be the sixth smallest state in the union, but its forest and park system is the sixth largest. And of the state's quarter-million protected acres, nearly 150,000 are in Berkshire County. Of the 606,000 total county acres, those owned publicly include 97,000 managed by the Department of Conservation and Recreation, Division of Forests and Parks, and 12,500 by the Division of Fisheries and Wildlife. The county boasts 21 state parks, all of which have interesting tales and trails. Berkshire nature centers each have scenic paths. In addition, 86 miles of the Appalachian Trail run up through Berkshire County, entering near Bartholomew's Cobble in Ashley Falls and exiting from Clarksburg.

The real pleasures are qualitative, however. With trails along lake and riverside, up hills and steep mountains, the Berkshires offer all types of terrain that provide multiple opportunities, from an afternoon's jaunt to a full-fledged pack trip.

Now some enthusiasm: It would be difficult to find a spot with the variety of trails from light walks to heavy hikes, suiting any available amount of time, convenient from anywhere in the county, and open to the public. These trails are marked and maintained by volunteers, who give of their time because they love this remarkable place and want visitors to like it, too.

Although a compass and maps are advisable for any deep-woods hiking, it's comforting to know that in Berkshire County, no matter how wild the surroundings, hikers are never more than 5 miles from a paved road. Nevertheless, for walks of any length, and especially for those taken alone, hikers should notify a friend of plans, including estimated hour of return. Carry water.

Those who want to use snowshoes in winter can rent them at many of the same stores that supply ski equipment. See the list of stores in this chapter under "Downhill Skiing."

## Properties with Maintained Trails

State properties with campgrounds are marked with an asterisk (*). For camping reservations call 877-I-CAMP-MA (422-6762) or visit www.reserveamerica.com. Type-1 campgrounds have running water, Type-2 do not. For more properties, see under Trustees of Reservations, below.

### SOUTH COUNTY

#### State Owned

***Beartown State Forest** (413-528-0904; Blue Hill Rd., Monterey) 12,000 acres; Benedict Pond; 12 Type-1 campsites; mountain biking, nonmotorized boating, boat ramp, fishing, hiking, hunting, horseback riding trails, picnicking, x-c skiing, snowmobiling, swimming; beach and restrooms handicapped accessible.

**Campbell Falls State Park** (Campbell Falls Rd. leaves Norfolk Rd. at the Connecticut line in New Marlborough) A lovely little falls in a two-state park.

**Mount Everett State Reservation** (413-528-0330; East St., Mt. Washington) 1,356 acres; Guilder Pond, nonmotorized boating, boat ramp, fishing, horseback riding trails, picnicking, hiking, three-state views, Appalachian Trail, and a road that approaches summit but may not be open (2,600 feet).

***Mount Washington State Forest** (413-528-0330; East St., Mt. Washington) 4,169 acres; 15 Type-2 wilderness campsites; mountain biking, canoeing, fishing, hiking, horseback riding trails, picnicking, hunting, nonmotorized boating, boat ramp, snowmobiling, x-c skiing. **Bash Bish Falls**, on Bash Bish Falls Rd., 0.5 mile from the lower parking lot; celebrated by painters of the Hudson River school and poets, these falls say their name to those who listen carefully.

***October Mountain State Forest** (413-243-1778, 413-243-9735; Woodland Rd., Lee) 16,127 acres; 50 Type-1 campsites, mountain biking, fishing, hiking, nonmotorized boating, Appalachian Trail, horseback riding trails, hunting, x-c skiing. Restrooms and some campsites and trails handicapped accessible.

**Sandisfield and Cookson State Forest** (413-258-4774; York Lake Rd., Sandisfield/New Marlboro) 7,785 acres; York Lake, boat ramp, nonmotorized boating, fishing, hiking, hunting, x-c skiing, snowmobiling, swimming, picnicking.

***Tolland State Forest** (413-269-6002, 413-269-7268; Rte. 8, Otis) 10,305 acres; 93 Type-1 campsites, some overlooking Otis Reservoir; mountain biking, boating, fishing, hiking, hunting, horseback riding trails, picnicking, x-c skiing, snowmobiling, swimming. Handicapped-accessible restrooms.

*Bash Bish Falls* Lauren R. Stevens

### Other Natural Places with Trails

**Bartholomew's Cobble** (413-229-8600; www.thetrustees.org; Weatogue Rd., Ashley Falls; off Rte. 7, 1.1 mi. S. of Sheffield center) Bartholomew's Cobble, a National Natural Landmark, is a 294-acre sanctuary with limestone outcroppings about 500 million years old. The terrain supports wildflowers, trees, and ferns in great variety and number. Bird flyway. It's a fine place to view the Housatonic River and its surrounding valley. On the site is the **Bailey Museum of Natural History**, open daily 9–5 year-round except holidays. Grounds open sunrise to sunset year-round. Group tours on request; picnic privileges available. Adults $4, children 6–12 $1, free to members of The Trustees of Reservations.

**Berkshire Botanical Garden** (413-298-3926; www.berkshirebotanical.org; jct. Rtes. 102 and 183, Stockbridge) The foremost botanical complex in the county for more than 50 years spreads over 15 acres of gently rolling land. The plantings include exotic flowers, primroses, conifers, daylilies, perennials, and shrubs. A terraced herb garden, a rose garden, and raised-bed vegetable gardens all delight the eye and other senses. The greenhouses (one of them passive solar) grow seedlings, cuttings, and plants of all sorts. A visitors center, garden gift shop, and herb products shop offer information, practical garden items, and invigorating odors. Berkshire Botanical Garden runs a full schedule of activities year-round, ranging from flower shows and herb symposiums to lectures on flower arranging and English country gardens. The Botanical Garden calendar culminates with its annual Harvest Festival in early October, offering fun and food for both children and adults. Its fine reference library offers books, magazines, and the latest seed catalogs.

**Ice Glen** (Ice Glen Rd., Stockbridge) Cross the footbridge over the Housatonic River and follow the trail southward to walk a primeval path of glacial boulders. Not recommended for the weak of knee.

**Race Brook Falls** (Rte. 41, Sheffield) The pullover at the side of the road is marked and usually full of cars. A couple miles of hiking leads to cascades or, farther on, the Appalachian Trail.

## Central County

### State Owned

***Mount Greylock State Reservation** (413-499-4263, 413-499-4262; visitors center: Rockwell Rd., Lanesborough; also accessible from Notch Rd., N. Adams) 12,500 acres. *La crème de la crème* of Berkshire hiking, with state's highest peak (3,491 feet), Appalachian Trail, 100-mile-view from War Memorial Tower. (For **Bascom Lodge**, see lodging chapter.) 35 Type-2 campsites, 45 miles of trails, x-c skiing, hunting, mountain biking, snowmobiling, interpretive programs (wheelchair accessible), picnicking.

***Pittsfield State Forest** (413-442-8992; Cascade St., Pittsfield) 10,000 acres. Streams, waterfalls, views. 31 Type-1 and Type-2 campsites. Boating (electric motors only), canoeing, x-c skiing, ski lodge, bicycling, mountain biking, fishing, picnicking, hiking, horseback riding trails, hunting, interpretive programs, snowmobiling, swimming; wheelchair-accessible picnic area and trails, restrooms. Includes **Balance Rock** (Balance Rock Rd.): Of the county's glacial erratics—apparently about to tip off their small bases—this is the most dramatic.

*Henry David Thoreau Hike participants assembled on Mt. Greylock* Lauren R. Stevens

**Wahconah Falls** (Rte. 9, Dalton) One of the county's largest cascades.

***Windsor State Forest** (413-698-0948; winter 413-442-8928; River Rd., Windsor) 1,743 acres. 24 Type-2 campsites; mountain biking, fishing, hiking, horseback riding trails, hunting, picnicking, swimming, x-c skiing, snowmobiling. Includes **Windsor Jambs**, a spectacular gorge.

### Other Natural Places with Trails

**Canoe Meadows Wildlife Sanctuary** (413-637-0320; www.massaudubon.org; Holmes Rd., Pittsfield) 262-acre preserve of forest, ponds, streams, the Housatonic River banks and floodplain; owned and managed by the Massachusetts Audubon Society. Fee.

**Dorothy Frances Rice Sanctuary** (South Rd., Peru; off Rte. 143) 300-acre preserve of woodland trails. Owned and managed by the New England Forestry Foundation.

**Notchview Reservation** (413-684-0148; Rte. 9, Windsor) 3,000 acres of forest, crossed by miles of trails; holds snow for x-c skiing. Owned and managed by The Trustees of Reservations. Fee.

**Pleasant Valley Wildlife Sanctuary** (413-637-0320; www.massaudubon.org; 472 W. Mountain Rd., Lenox; off Rte. 7, opposite the Quality Inn) 1,400 acres of forest, field, ponds (beaver dams with real beaver), and streams with 7 miles of trails; educational programs. Owned and managed by the Massachusetts Audubon Society. Fee.

**Yokum Ridge** (off Lenox Rd., Lenox) An assemblage of properties and trails, including Pleasant Valley, mapped by the Berkshire Natural Resources Council (413-499-0596).

## NORTH COUNTY

### State Owned

***Clarksburg State Park** (413-664-8345 summer, 413-442-8928 winter; Middle Rd., Clarksburg) 3,421 acres. Mauserts Pond for swimming. 47 Type-2 campsites; boating (electric motors only), canoeing, x-c skiing, fishing, hiking, hunting, snowmobiling, picnicking. Wheelchair-accessible campsites and restrooms.

**Natural Bridge State Park** (413-663-6392; Natural Bridge Rd., N. Adams; N. of downtown on Rte. 8) Waters tumble over a marble dam and then course beneath a natural marble bridge; x-c skiing, too. Newly completed visitors center.

***Savoy Mountain State Forest** (413-663-8469; Central Shaft Rd., Savoy; off Rte 2, Florida, and Rte. 116) 11,118 acres; 45 Type-1 campsites and three cabins with fireplaces on South Pond. North Pond for swimming, boating, and fishing. Tannery Falls. Picnicking, mountain biking, canoeing, hiking, x-c skiing, interpretive programs, snowmobiling. Wheelchair-accessible restrooms, campsites, swimming, and trails.

**Taconic Trail State Forest** (413-499-4263; adjacent to Taconic Trail, Rte. 2, Williamstown) Hiking, hunting, x-c skiing.

### Other Natural Places with Trails

**Bear Swamp Hydroelectric Project** (413-424-5213; River Rd., Florida) A stop at the visitors center reveals how pumped storage works; a call ahead can result in a tour of the works deep in the mountain.

**Duvall Nature Trail** (Hoosac Valley High School, Rte. 116, Adams) 2 miles of nature trails overlooking the Greylock Range.

**Hopkins Memorial Forest** (413-597-2346; www.williams.edu/ces; P.O. Box 637, Williamstown, MA 01267; Bulkley St., off Rte. 7) 2,500 woodland acres on the slopes of the Taconic Range with miles of hiking trails. Hunting by permit, dogs on leashes. No camping, fires, wheeled vehicles (including bikes). Rare plants, historic relics: barn, sugar shack, carriage house with exhibits on past use of land; Victorian garden. Guided walks by appointment (413-597-4353.)

**Mountain Meadow** (Access either from Mason St, off Rte. 7 across from the Chef's Hat or up White Oaks Rd. to Benedict Rd.) Innumerable routes through an area once heavily logged and mined but now returning to a natural state; be alert to Lyme ticks.

For more detailed information on the county's state parks, contact: **Massachusetts Department of Conservation and Recreation,** Division of Forests and Parks (617-727-9800; www.mass.gov/dcr; 100 Cambridge St., Boston, MA 02202) or its Region V office (413-442-8928; Box 1433, Pittsfield, MA 01202).

There are several hiking clubs in the Berkshires. Of these, the **Appalachian Mountain Club** (413-528-6333), **Taconic Hiking Club** (45 Kately St., Albany, NY 12208) and the **Williams (College) Outing Club** (413-597-2317) are the most active. Each organizes hikes through the county.

**Greylock Discovery Tours** (413-637-4442; 800-877-9656; www.greylocktours.com; P.O. Box 2231, Lenox, MA 01240) will guide groups of eight or more along the Appalachian and

**History of The Trustees of Reservations**

In 1890, before the present national interest in the environment, a young landscape architect returned from study in Europe with a deepening concern for the need to preserve the natural beauty and historic sites of his community.

Charles Eliot (1859–1897), just 31 years old and son of Charles W. Eliot, then president of Harvard University, proposed the establishment of an organization "empowered to hold small and well distributed parcels of land . . . just as the Public Library holds books and the Art Museum pictures for the use and enjoyment of the public."

**The Trustees of Reservations** was incorporated by the Massachusetts General Court a year later, 1891, the first independent organization in the United States established for the purpose of preserving land.

Many of the properties are listed under "Historic Homes" in chapter 5, "Arts & Pleasures." Excellent hiking and x-c skiing opportunities await at the following properties of The Trustees of Reservations in the county or nearby:

**Bartholomew's Cobble:** Weatogue Rd. (Rte. 7A), Ashley Falls (Sheffield).

**Chapelbrook:** Williamsburg Rd., Ashfield.

**Chesterfield Gorge:** River Rd., Chesterfield.

**Field Farm:** Sloan Rd., off Rte. 7 at the Five Corners in Williamstown.

**Glendale Falls:** Clark Wright Rd., Middlefield.

**McLenan Reservoir:** Sun Rd., Tyringham and Otis.

**Monument Mountain:** Stockbridge Rd. (Rte. 7), Gt. Barrington.

**Mountain Meadow Preserve:** Mason St. off Rte. 7, or Benedict Rd., Pownal, Vermont, or off White Oaks Rd., Williamstown.

**Notchview Reservation:** Rte. 9, Windsor.

**Questing:** New Marlborough Hill Rd., New Marlborough.

*Climbing Tyringham Cobble* Lauren R. Stevens

**Tyringham Cobble:** 413-298-3239; Jerusalem Rd., Tyringham.

For more information about any of these or any other holdings, write: The Trustees of Reservations, 1 Sargeant St., Stockbridge, MA 01262; call 413-298-3239; or visit their excellent Web site: www.thetrustees.org.

Taconic Range trails in half- or whole-day hikes, arranging food, lodging, and cultural events as well.

Cogent books on Berkshire hiking are available: *Hikes & Walks in the Berkshire Hills* by Lauren R. Stevens; focusing on the Williamstown environs, *The Williams College Outing Club Northern Berkshire Outdoor Guide*, first published in 1927 and completely new in 1999. Stevens's book covers not only a wide variety of challenging hikes for the energetic and ambitious but also a large number of easy strolls for those with less time or gumption. A section outlines walks for the blind and physically handicapped.

In addition to its vast forests, Berkshire is blessed with many interesting outdoor sites, each of which shows off natural features, such as waterfalls, unusual geology, or plant life. For a description of natural places in the county, see the book of that name by René Laubach, and *Nature Walks in the Berkshire Hills* by Charles W. G. Smith.

## Camping

### State Parks

Campsites in **state parks** can be reserved by calling 877-I-CAMP-MA (877-422-6762) or visiting www.reserveamerica.com. As well, some of the sites at each property are available first come, first serve. For further information but *not* reservations, contact the **Massachusetts Department of Conservation and Recreation**, Region Five Headquarters (413-442-8928) Box 1433, Pittsfield, MA 01201.

Fees at state parks with swimming: *Day use:* $5 per car per day; $6 out of state; annual pass $35/$45; *Camping:* wilderness free; unimproved $5/$6; flush toilets with showers $10/$12; cabins $25 or $35, depending on size. These are likely to rise. **Public campgrounds (see list beginning on page 226)** are designated with an asterisk (*); private campgrounds follow.

### Private Campgrounds

#### SOUTH COUNTY

**Camp Overflow** (413-269-4036; Box 645, Otis, MA 01253; on Otis Reservoir, 5 mi. from Rte. 8) 100 sites, electric hookups, dumping station, camp store, fishing, swimming, boating, seasonal rates.

**Klondike Campground** (413-269-6010; Rte. 8, Otis, MA 01029).

**Laurel Ridge Camping Area** (413-269-4804; Old Blandford Rd., E. Otis, MA 01029) Electric and water sites.

**Maple Glade Campground** (413-243-1548; 165 Woodland Rd., Lee, MA 01238; across from October Mountain State Forest) 70 sites; hookups available; small store, swimming pool.

**Prospect Lake Park** (413-528-4158; Prospect Lake Rd., N. Egremont, MA 01252) 140 sites; tennis, swimming, boat rentals, basketball court, volleyball; snack bar, playground.

#### CENTRAL COUNTY

**Bissellville Estate & Campground** (413-655-8396; Washington Rd., Hinsdale, MA 01235; Rte. 8) 13 campsites with sewer hookups, 18 with water and electricity, 13 with all three. Closed Labor Day–May 15.

**Bonnie Brae Cabins and Campsites** (413-442-3754; 108 Broadway St., Pittsfield, MA 01201; 3 mi. N. of downtown Pittsfield, off Rte. 7 at Pontoosuc Lake) Full hookups, free showers, trailer rentals, pool; cabin rentals May 1–Oct. 31. Closed Nov.–Apr. 30.

**Bonnie Rigg Campground** (413-623-5366; P.O. Box 14, Chester, MA 01011-0014; corner of Rtes. 8 & 20 in Becket) 200 campsites, by owner/membership only (call for information); adult lounge, playground, swimming pool, sauna, Jacuzzi.

**Bucksteep Manor** (413-623-5535; Washington Mountain Rd., Becket, MA 01223; 10 mi. E. of Pittsfield, across from October Mountain State Forest) 15 sites, 9 cabins; showers, swimming pool, tennis, hiking, x-c skiing, weekend restaurant.

**Fernwood Forest Campground** (413-655-2292; 41 Plunkett Reservoir Rd., Hinsdale 01235; 1 mi. from Appalachian Trail) 30 campsites with water, toilets, showers, electricity; recreation field. Closed mid-Oct.–May 1.

**Ponterril** (413-499-0640; North St., Pittsfield, MA 01201; Rte. 7, off E. Acres Rd. at Pontoosuc Lake N. of Pittsfield) 12 campsites, swimming pool, tennis, sailing and sailing instructions. Operated by Pittsfield YMCA.

**Summit Hill Campground** (413-623-5761; Summit Hill Rd., Washington, MA 01235) 110 campsites for tents and trailers, 83 sites with electricity and water; adult lounge, swimming pool, and recreation hall. Closed in winter.

**Fun in the Hills**

In the 1860s and 1870s Williams College professor Albert Hopkins organized summer-long Camp Fern at what's now the Sperry Road Campground on Mount Greylock. Borrowing tents from a Methodist meeting and hiring a local Irish girl to cook, families stayed for weeks, with members returning to town as necessary. The boys descended to the Bacon farm in the Hopper early in the morning for milk, eggs, and other perishables. Most of the time Fern campers explored the mountain, but other adventures included organized games, skits, poetry, painting, journal writing, berrying, fishing, singing around the campfire and, oh yes, courting in the hills. Did people know how to have more fun in the 19th century?

North County

**Historic Valley Park Campground** (413-662-3198; Box 751, N. Adams, MA 01247; on Windsor Lake) 100 campsites with electric and water hookups; laundry, camp store, recreation hall, hiking trails; public and private beaches with lifeguards.

**Privacy Campground** (413-458-3125; Hancock Rd., Hancock, MA 01267; on Rte. 43, 5 mi. S. of Rte. 7) 475 acres, 35 sites, 4 small cabins; waterfall, pond, 10 miles of hiking trails, paddleboats, volleyball, badminton, horseshoes, tether ball, basketball, campfires, waterwheel, windmill, trolley car, playground, sauna.

## Cross-Country Skiing

Several of the resorts listed under "Downhill Skiing" also offer cross-country skiing. Berkshire is made for cross-country (also known as Nordic) skiers—from flat runs along the Housatonic to steep trails up Mount Greylock; from tours in town, such as Kennedy Park in Lenox and Historic Valley Campground in North Adams, to wilderness paths like the one around North Pond in Savoy Mountain State Forest.

With no lines, no chairlifts, and (generally) no fees, Berkshire X-C depends only on the whims of the weather. However, since Nordic skiing has gained in popularity, private touring centers have multiplied in the Berkshires. For a small fee, enjoy groomed trails and warm waxing huts at half a dozen such places. Cranwell even offers snowmaking.

It's best to ski accompanied, especially in a wilderness area. Those skiing in a state forest should check in at forest headquarters first. Maps and helpful hints are available; besides, it's a good precaution for staff to know that a skier's out there. Along with snacks and water, skiers would be well advised to carry a compass and extra clothes on the trail. The well-prepared also carry a first-aid kit, knife, whistle, flashlight, and space blanket. Hypothermia is the greatest danger; if 20 minutes of exercise doesn't warm the blood, it's time to head home.

Although many x-c skiers profess to dislike snowmobiles because of their growl and their tendency to prowl in packs, the going is easier if those creatures have packed the trail. And sometimes a cross-country skier in trouble might appreciate a snowmobiler's assistance. We recommend friendly relations with snowmobilers and, on their part, courtesy to skiers.

**Berkshire County Land Trust**

The Berkshire County Land Trust and Conservation Fund is an offshoot of Berkshire Natural Resources Council (BNRC), a private, not-for-profit environmental advocacy group established in 1967. Led by president Tad Ames, this group believes that the wealth of Berkshire lies in its quality of life, natural environment, and cultural heritage. The council works with state and local agencies to ensure that those lands are protected from abuse.

There are about 200 land trusts in America, many of them in New England. By all counts, the BNRC and its offspring in several Berkshire towns are some of the more successful. In Pittsfield the trust was responsible for increasing Pittsfield State Forest by 1,800 acres. Along the Housatonic, south of Pittsfield, the Resources Council is coordinating the creation of a 12-mile-long river park, reaching to Woods Pond in Lenox. The BNRC facilitated the preservation of Gould Meadows, that gorgeous 95-acre pasture reaching from Tanglewood to Stockbridge Bowl. The Stockbridge–Yokun Ridge Reserve is another land corridor the trust is assembling to remain forever wild, an 8-mile-long, 6,300-acre spread of Berkshire park.

For more information, contact Berkshire County Land Trust and Berkshire Natural Resources Council, 20 Bank Row, Pittsfield, MA 01201; 413-499-0596; www.bnrc.net.

Most of the properties listed above are available to skiers. A selection of trails is described below, with sufficient directions for a short tour. Skiers should know that if snow is not good in Berkshire, just over the line in Vermont a natural snowbelt provides some of the best cover in the East. **Prospect Mountain** (802-442-2575; Rte. 9, 8 mi. E. of Bennington) benefits from nature's largess. Trails are groomed; snowshoeing is available. Rentals and retail. The food offered at the base lodge ranges from vegetarian to burgers. Fee.

Many trails in **Mount Washington State Forest** offer quintessential Berkshire ski touring. No snowmobiles are allowed, so the whistle of the wind will be the loudest noise. From the forest headquarters on East Street, the Ashley Hill Brook Trail runs south along the brook toward New York State, a 4-mile, slightly uphill trip suitable for intermediate skiers. Nearby, from the parking lot just outside the Mount Everett Reservation, skiers can ski up 2,600-foot-high Dome of the Taconics. The climb up the mountain is gentle, passing

Guilder Pond; the run down, long and exhilarating with plenty of room to maneuver.

**Bartholomew's Cobble** in Ashley Falls (Sheffield) has an interesting system of trails, with the runs on the far side of Weatogue Road being the best. Some spots are wet in marginal weather. A map is posted in the parking lot. Donation box: $3 per person.

**Beartown State Forest** in Monterey has some lovely trails, starting at Benedict Pond and circling through the 12,000-acre forest preserve. Maps are available at the **State Forest Headquarters** (413-528-0904; Blue Hill Rd., off Rte. 23). Triangular red blazes or wooden markers designate the ski-touring trail in Beartown, with a blue-blazed trail circling Benedict Pond, the white-blazed Appalachian Trail passing through, and the orange-blazed trails for snowmobilers.

The West Lake area of **Sandisfield State Forest** is a fine site for Nordic skiing. No snowmobiles are allowed on the Abbey Hill Foot Trail (marked with blue blazes). From the state forest headquarters and parking area, just off West Street, a beautiful tour of about 2 hours circles Abbey Lake, up Abbey Hill (1,810 feet), and then down past West Lake.

Skiers can follow the Knox Trail in **Otis State Forest.** Take Route 23 to Nash Road in Otis. Where Nash joins Webb Road is a good place to wax up. Skiers should watch for red *K*s and red blazes marking the trail.

In Great Barrington, **Butternut Basin** (413-528-2000; Rte. 23) has 8 kilometers of groomed novice and intermediate trails, lovely lodges, and a pondside warming hut. **Otis Ridge** (413-269-4444; Rte. 23, Otis) has over 8 kilometers of packed, but not tracked, trails.

Lenox is graced with beautiful ski-touring areas, the most popular of which is **Kennedy Park.** Its 500 acres were once the site of the grand old Aspinwall Hotel (which burned to the ground in 1931). Now its long rising driveway and bridle paths are used for ski touring. The Main Trail (white blazes) is the widest and simplest, with Lookout Trail (red blazes) being more of a challenge. Stately oaks dot this pretty highland, with access either at the Church on the Hill (Main St., Rte. 7A), near the state DPW garage, or behind the Lenox House Restaurant (north of town on Rte. 7). Equipment available from the Arcadian Shop up the road on Route 7.

**Woods Pond** area in Lee and Lenox has a pretty, mostly flat trail running along the southern shore of Woods Pond, then north along the eastern bank of the Housatonic River for just over 2 miles. A footbridge spans the Housatonic River. Enter via Woodland Street in Lee. The trail is best skied on weekdays due to weekend snowmobile traffic. **Canoe Meadows,** a Massachusetts Audubon area, also has some lovely trails, open except Monday. A small fee includes a map.

For more advanced Nordic skiers, the **Honwee Mountain–Turner Trail** circuit in Pittsfield State Forest is a challenge. Parking just off Cascade Road in Pittsfield State Forest, skiers should check in at forest headquarters, get oriented, and then start up the Mountain Trail, initially marked in orange, then white. This trail has some great views, tough climbs, and steep descents. Closer to the center of the city, **Sackett Brook Park** (Williams Street), has 4 miles of marked trails.

On Route 9 lies **Notchview Reservation,** in the town of Windsor. Generally the best snow in Berkshire can be found here. Twenty miles of trails are well marked and maintained, with a modest charge for touring. Maps are available for 50 cents. The Budd Visitor Center is open daily as a warming and waxing shelter. Notchview is owned by The Trustees of Reservations. Further information is available at www.thetrustees.org.

South of Lenox on Route 20, **Cranwell** (413-637-1364; 55 Lee Rd., Lenox) has a network of trails, crisscrossing the golf course. It ventured into snowmaking in the winter of

1996–97. Open to the public; fee charged.

In the hill town of Washington, **Bucksteep Manor** (413-623-5535; Washington Mt. Rd.) operates a long ski-touring season. Set on over 250 acres at 1,900 feet, Bucksteep has 25 kilometers of looped, interconnecting trails. There's a waxing room, a ski shop that sells and rents, and on-site lodging and dining. Nearby in Becket, **Canterbury Farm** (413-623-8765; Fred Snow Rd.) grooms 11 miles of trails for its inn guests and daily cross-country ski guests. There is a ski shop for rentals, and lessons are available. Fee.

Up at 2,000 feet, where the snows come early and stay late, **Savoy State Forest** has miles of cross-country trails, best navigated with a map obtainable at **State Forest Headquarters** (413-663-8469; Florida Rd.). Enter the forest from Route 2 (Florida) or Route 116 (Savoy), and park at North Pond. A 3.1-mile-long trail, North Pond Loop makes a challenging circuit up and over a ridge. In North Adams, **Historic Valley Park** offers ski touring quite close to downtown. The trail starts at the parking area next to Windsor Lake and is well marked by blue blazes and signs that even describe the degree of difficulty of the next stretch of trail.

On **Mount Greylock**, many opportunities for fine ski touring exist. Here again, though, it's best to ski during the week because weekends tend to draw heavy snowmobile traffic. (The snowmobiles are supposed to stick to the roads.) Check in at the visitors center on Rockwell Road off Route 7, Lanesborough. Depending on skills and fitness, there's an 8-mile round-trip up Rockwell Road to Jones Nose and back, 15-mile round-trip to Stony Ledge, or 17-mile round-trip to the summit. The views are breathtaking, the skiing sometimes testing, and the weather more dramatic than experienced below. Take extra warm clothing and some snacks. A ski shelter is open off the summit parking lot, with firewood, for the skiers who brings matches.

The area in and around **Williamstown** is striped with trails, ranging from novice or intermediate to demanding, like the **RRR Brooks Trail.** For Brooks, and the **Taconic Crest Trail** attached to it, begin either at Bee Hill Road, west of Route 2, or Petersburgh Pass, at the top of Route 2 west of town. The **Taconic Golf Club** course, which Williams College grooms, and the 4-mile **Stone Hill Loop** in Williamstown are the area's most popular: relatively easy while offering all the splendor of the best ski touring. The golf course trail begins at the clubhouse on Meacham Street. Stone Hill starts and finishes in the Clark Art Museum parking lot (South Street), circling the 1,100-foot Stone Hill, with its wonderful views. At **Hopkins Forest**, Williams College maintains a network of trails just off Northwest Hill Road. The trails are groomed, and maps are available at the forest Carriage House. Many other trails exist, the best of which are described in the *Williams Outing Club's Northern Berkshire Outdoor Guide.* See also the **Mount Greylock Ski Club** under downhill skiing.

*Browsing the window at Farshaws in Great Barrington* Judith Monachina

# 8

# Shopping

## *Fancy Goods*

**Antiques,** books, clothing, handcrafts, home furnishings—those shopping for the necessities and the accessories of life will find ample scope in the Berkshires, on still-vital downtown streets and at a variety of retail destinations. They'll find an ever-changing mix of the currently "hot" collectibles along with the genuinely old, and the timeless—sometimes all in one shop. They'll also find imaginative wares designed and made in the Berkshires as well as goods from the farthest corners of the world. There are some chain stores, outlets, and discount centers, too. Note: Many Berkshire shops have been in place for generations; others sprang up last week and will have moved on by next Monday. It's helpful to call ahead before making a special trip and important to keep an eye open for the newest additions to the shopping scene!

### Antiques

From formal 18th-century furniture to bold art deco tableware, with country primitive carvings and High Victorian accessories in between, antiques in the Berkshires are varied and abundant. Whether you hanker after museum-quality pieces of a specific style and period or whether you simply enjoy exploring unique home furnishings, you'll find plenty to choose from. The antiques scene here includes furniture large and small; vintage clothing, textiles, and jewelry; prints, paper, and other ephemera; trunks and lamps, clocks and rugs, and baskets and wicker; and "kitchenalia" and militaria. European and Asian antiques specialists have also found their way to the Berkshires. A number of antiques shops also include new furnishings and accent pieces that complement their antiques; many offer custom decorating services.

South County in particular is an antiques center, with Route 7 the main artery for an array of multidealer shops, specialists, and generalists. They know their merchandise, and their prices reflect their knowledge. In Central County and North County, prices are more flexible, but finding a bargain takes some looking.

Those who extend antiques hunting to auctions or—the sign of the true diehard—to yard sales and flea markets, should check listings in the helpful free weekly shoppers' guides (such as the *Berkshire Penny Saver*), which are stacked up at supermarket entrances and newsstands around the county. The *Berkshire Eagle*, the largest daily paper in the county, also carries classified listings for antiques, tag sales, and auctions. A list of auctioneers is also given below. The annual brochure of the *Berkshire County Antique Dealer's Association* lists dealers and locations, with business hours, telephone numbers, and a brief description of what they offer. Members of this association "take pride in their merchandise and guarantee its authenticity." Their brochure is available in member shops or by mail (send a SASE to: BCADA Directory, P.O. Box 95, Sheffield MA 01257).

Several rare book specialists also make their home here; they're listed in the next section, "Books."

## South County

GREAT BARRINGTON

**Asian Antiques** (413-528-5091, phone/fax; 199 Stockbridge Rd., Gt. Barrington, MA 01230; Rte 7) High-quality Asian, Korean, Japanese, and Indonesian antiques, furniture for home or garden, handcrafts, art, and gifts. For those who have always wanted an opium bed or a temple gong, this is the place to find it.

**Berkshire Home & Antiques** (413-644-9262; 107 Stockbridge Rd., Gt. Barrington, MA 01230) Lots of space housing an eclectic collection of furnishings, of which 85 percent is imported. Architectural salvage, plumbing fixtures, and an in-house refinishing, painting, and upholstery service make this a perfect one-stop-shopping experience.

**Bygone Days** (413-528-1870; 969 S. Main St., Gt. Barrington, MA 01230; Rte. 7) Country and formal furniture, large and small, especially for bedrooms and dining rooms; farm tables and chairs, armoires, nightstands, hutches, and china closets and more. Open 11–4 daily, "sometimes earlier; sometimes later."

**Carriage House Antiques** (413-528-6045; 389 Stockbridge Rd., Gt. Barrington, MA 01230) Tables, chairs, other furniture—even sets of doors can be found here. Antique furniture restoration, repair, stripping, refinishing, and custom cabinetry by Eric Schutz are specialties in the newly enlarged quarters.

**Coffmans' Country Antiques Market** (413-528-9282; Stockbridge Rd., Gt. Barrington, MA 01230; at Jenifer House Commons) Two buildings (yellow and red) of high-quality wares, pre-1949, from 200 New England and regional dealers. The large assortment is appealingly arranged in cases and room settings, and includes ephemera and prints, kitchenware, primitives, wood, pottery, furniture, tools, quilts, rugs, baskets, folk art, stoneware, glassware, and tin, brass, and copper.

**Corashire Antiques** (413-528-0014; Rte. 7/23, Gt. Barrington, MA 01230; at Belcher Square) In the red barn: American country furniture and accessories.

**Country Dining Room and Tea Garden Antiques** (413-528-5050; 178 Main St., Gt. Barrington, MA 01230; Rte. 7) Complete accoutrements for dining in style, formal or country. In lavishly coordinated rooms, dining tables boast elaborate place settings of china, silver, glass, crystal, porcelain—down to the matching damask napkins with silk rose napkin rings. Chairs, rugs, paintings, and other furnishings and accessories complete the look. For a less formal but still elegant approach, Tea Garden Antiques, upstairs, offers more place settings, linens, and other accents. Country Dining Room's own Sheila Chafetz wrote two stunning books that show how to put it all together: *Antiques for the Table* and *Modern Antiques for the Table.*

*It's easy to find just about any kind of antique in Sheffield but also in Egremont, Lenox, Gt. Barrington, and other towns.* Judith Monachina

**Elise Abrams Antiques** (413-528-3201; 11 Stockbridge Rd., Gt. Barrington, MA 01230; Rte. 7) Large selection of 18th-, 19th-, and 20th-century china, porcelain, and stemware, plus decorative accessories and fine linens, silver, art, and dining-room furniture. They even maintain a bridal registry.

**Emporium Antique Center** (413-528-1660; 319 Main St., Gt. Barrington, MA 01230) A variety of dealers offer estate and costume jewelry, crystal, silver, accessories, furniture, and furnishings. **The Kahns' Antique and Estate Jewelry** is now located here, as well. June–Oct., open daily; Nov.–May. Closed Tues. and Wed.

**Great Barrington Antiques Center** (413-644-8848; www.greatbarringtonantiquescenter.com; 964 S. Main St., Gt. Barrington, MA 01230; Rte. 7) A group shop of 50 dealers, featuring realistically priced quality country furniture, Oriental rugs, and everything in-between displayed in a large (5,000 square feet) open space conducive to browsing. Open 7 days a week, 10–5.

**Le Perigord** (413-528-6777; 964 S. Main St., Gt. Barrington, MA 01230; Rte. 7) A great source for French furniture, and pottery, garden, and architectural accents from the 18th century through the 1960s. Open weekends.

**Metropolitain** (413-644-8868; 631 S. Main St., Gt. Barrington, MA 01230) A charming shop exhibiting a certain Gallic insouciance, specializing in antique furnishings, lighting, garden accessories, and decorative objects from France. They also offer interior design services.

**Donald McGrory Oriental Rugs** (413-528-9594; 24 Railroad St., Gt. Barrington, MA 01230) Antique and decorative Oriental rugs. Open Tues.–Fri. 11–4, Sat. 11–5

**Mullin-Jones Antiquities** (413-528-4871; 525 S. Main St., Gt. Barrington, MA 01230; Rte. 7) The fragrance of lavender pervades this importer of 18th- and 19th-century country farmhouse to formal French furniture and accessories. Closed Tues.; call ahead in winter.

**Olde—An Antiques Market** (413-528-1840; Stockbridge Rd., Gt. Barrington, MA 01230; at Jenifer House Commons) Two floors in the greenhouse are jam-packed with potential treasures. Fifty dealers offer a variety of collectibles. Open 7 days a week, 10–5.

**Paul and Susan Kleinwald, Inc.** (413-528-4252; 578 S. Main St., Gt. Barrington, MA 01230) The concentration here is on 18th- and 19th-century American and English antique furniture, fine art, accessories; appraisals. Closed Tues.

**PW Vintage Lighting** (www.pwvintagelighting.com; 413-644-9150; 2 State Rd., Gt. Barrington, MA 01230; Rte. 7) Interesting collection of 19th- and 20th-century light fixtures and lamps, from funky to fabulous, in a large shop just before the bridge.

**Snyder's Store** (413-528-1441; 945 Main St., Gt. Barrington, MA 01230) What's inside: funky furniture and accessories, with rustic pieces, tramp art, jewelry, linens, garden accents, and architectural elements. Open most weekends 12–5; weekdays by whim.

### Lee

**The Greylock Cottage** (413-243-1115; 52 Main St., Lee, MA 01238) Lovely, immaculate shop where, while shopping, one can garner lots of wonderful ideas for using and displaying antiques. The emphasis is on cottage and country collectibles. The prices are fair, and the owners are charming. A visit here is a trip down memory lane with something for everyone to enjoy.

**Henry B. Holt** (413-243-3184; 125 Golden Hill, P.O. Box 699, Lee, MA 01238) Specialist in 19th- and early-20th-century American paintings. Call for an appointment regarding appraisal, purchase, sale, or restoration.

### Sheffield

**Centuryhurst Antiques** (413-229-8131; 173 Main St., P.O. Box 486, Sheffield, MA 01257; Rte. 7) Specializing in antique clocks and Wedgwood; with 18th- and 19th-century furniture, glass, china, paintings, prints, and accessories.

**Corner House Antiques** (413-229-6627; P.O. Box 411, Sheffield, MA 01257; Rte. 7 and Old Mill Pond Rd.) Specialists in antique wicker furniture—including whole sets; a variety of styles and finishes. A well-chosen selection of American country furnishings and accessories, as well. Open most days.

**Cupboards & Roses Antiques** (413-229-3070; fax 412-229-0257; P.O. Box 426, Sheffield, MA 01257; Rte. 7) Beautifully displayed antique and reproduction paint-decorative 18th- and 19th-century furniture, featuring capacious armoires and chests from Europe and Scandinavia. Decorative accessories, old and new, including wedding baskets, paint decorated bride boxes, textiles, and ceramics. Closed Tues.

**Darr Antiques and Interiors** (413-229-7773; S. Main St., Sheffield, MA 01257; Rte. 7) Two buildings of elegant room settings displaying formal 18th- and 19th-century American,

English, Continental, and Oriental furniture and accessories, with a focus on dining-room furnishings. Open 10–5 Sat. and 12–5 Sun.; or by appointment.

**Dovetail Antiques** (413-229-2628; 440 Sheffield Plain, Sheffield, MA 01257; Rte. 7) A select collection of American clocks, country furniture, including pieces with original paint or finish, and spongeware, stoneware, and redware. No glass or china. Open daily 11–5; Tues. by chance.

**Falconwood Antiques** (413-229-7745; 176 S. Undermountain Rd., Sheffield, MA 01257; Rte. 41) Country furniture and accessories, with a good selection of brass, copper, pewter, woodworking tools, and treen (small wooden pieces).

**Frederick Hatfield Antiques** (413-229-7986; 99 S. Main St., Sheffield, MA 01257; Rte. 7) Antiques and collectibles from the 18th through 20th centuries, with country and formal furniture, paintings, silver, paper items, jewelry, architectural elements, and other treasures from New England homes.

**Good & Hutchinson Associates, Inc.** (413-229-8832, 413-258-4555; Main St., Sheffield, MA 01257; Rte. 7 on the Green) Specialists in fine antiques and decorative arts from the 18th and 19th century, with American, English, and Continental furniture, Chinese export porcelain, paintings, brass, lamps; for the discriminating buyer. Open June–Oct., Wed.–Sat. 10:30–4, Sun. 11–4. Closed Tues. Open Nov.–May by chance.

**Kuttner Antiques** (413-229-2955; fax 413-229-6000; N. Main St., P.O. Box 741, Sheffield, MA 01257; Rte. 7) Formal and high country American and English furniture and decorative accessories from the 18th and 19th centuries. Open 10:30–5; closed Tues.

**Le Trianon** (413-528-0775; trianon@vgernet.net; 1854 N. Main St., Sheffield, MA 01257; Rte. 7) 17th-, 18th- and 19th-century French and Continental furniture, carpets, tapestries, and accessories. Open daily 10:30–5:30.

**Ole T. J.'s Antique Barn** (413-229-8382; 640 S. Main St., Sheffield, MA 01257; Rte. 7) Antiques and collectibles on two floors from all over, some of it gathered by the owners on their travels in the Far East and Africa, also Early American and European furniture, jewelry, paintings, rugs, lamps, and other accessories. Thurs.–Mon., by chance, or by appointment.

**Painted Porch** (413-229-2700; www.paintedporch.com; 102 S. Main St., Sheffield, MA 01257; Rte. 7) Wonderful collection of country antiques displayed in both the Victorian house and outbuilding. The antique furnishings are interspersed with sofas and chairs from Urban Country so one can see how old and new complement one another. Open Thurs.–Mon. 10–5, Tues. and Wed. by appointment.

**Saturday Sweets Antiques and Design** (413-229-0026; satsweet@bcn.net; 755A N. Main St., P.O. Box 814, Sheffield, MA 01257; Rte. 7) 20th-century decorative arts with an emphasis on art deco, including furniture, accessories, and vintage costume jewelry. Open Fri.–Sun. or by chance or appointment. Call ahead in winter.

**Susan Silver Antiques** (413-229-8169; N. Main St., P.O. Box 621, Sheffield, MA 01257; Rte. 7) English furnishings from the 18th and 19th centuries. One specialty is library furniture. Closed Tues.

**Vintage Linens** (413-229-3549; Main St., Sheffield, MA 01257) Right in the heart of Sheffield, this charming little shop features linens, as one might expect, but also a changing collection of accessories: including buttons, dishes, and glassware.

### SOUTH EGREMONT

**Geffner/Schatzky Antiques** (413-528-0057; Rte. 23, S. Egremont, MA 01258; at the sign of the Juggler) 19th-century to 1950s furniture and accessories, jewelry, architectural elements. Open May–Aug., daily 10:30–5; Sept.–Apr., Fri.–Sun. 10:30–5, during the week by chance or appointment.

**Howard's Antiques** (413-528-1232; Rte. 23, P.O. Box 472, S. Egremont, MA 01258; 2 _ west of the center of the village) Specialists in American lighting. Antique lighting fixtures from the late 1890s to the 1930s have been wired for present uses. Nineteenth-century dining-room tables and chairs are also offered, as are other country-style antique furniture. Open daily 10–5 except Tues. and Thurs.

**Red Barn Antiques** (413-528-3230; 72 Main St., Rte. 23, P.O. Box 25, S. Egremont, MA 01258) Restored antique lighting from the early 19th century and onward, including kerosene, gas, and early electric fixtures. Repair and restoration of antique lamps on-site; metal polishing.

**The Splendid Peasant** (413-528-5755; Rte. 23, S. Egremont, MA 01258; at Old Sheffield Rd.) 18th- and 19th-century painted country furniture and folk art, all stunningly displayed in a fascinating series of galleries and niches. Original paint a specialty. Open 9:30–5:30 daily.

### SOUTHFIELD

**The Buggy Whip Factory Antique Market Place** (413-229-3576; Main St., Southfield, MA 01259) An antiques market of 95 dealers featuring country to formal furniture, architectural pieces, kitchenware, tools, china, sterling, glassware, jewelry, and books. Closed Tues. and Wed.

**Kettering Antiques** (413-229-2859; 135 Main St., P.O. Box 17, Southfield, MA 01259) Formal English and American 18th- and 19th-century furniture and decorative porcelain and brass. Cabinet restoration and polishing available. Winter hours vary; please call before you stop; appointments available.

### STOCKBRIDGE

**Hillary Beadell** (413-298-8102; 6 Elm St., Stockbridge, MA 01262) Tiny shop with great window displays. Lots of interesting pieces here to add a bit of Continental flair to one's décor. Pricing is realistic, and the owner is both knowledgeable and friendly.

### WEST STOCKBRIDGE

**Ebenezer II Antiques and Gifts** (413-232-7017; 2 Main St., W. Stockbridge, MA 01266) Eclectic assortment of antiques and collectibles, also Turkish rugs and copper.

**Sawyer Antiques** (413-232-7062; 1 Depot St., W. Stockbridge, MA 01266) In a Shaker-built gristmill, Early American furniture and accessories in a variety of styles: formal, Shaker, country. In-season open Fri.–Sun. 10–5; other days, call ahead.

## Central County

### LENOX

**Charles L. Flint Antiques Inc.** (413-637-1634; www.cflint.org; chazma@vgernet.net; 52 Housatonic St., P.O. Box 971, Lenox, MA 01240) This shop features furniture, oil paintings, accessories, folk art, Shaker items. The owner is a noted local historian who has a genuine knowledge of and enthusiasm for his wares. Mon.–Sat. 9–5 or by appointment.

**Past and Future** (413-637-2225; 63 Church St., Lenox, MA 01240) 19th- and 20th-century silver and small antiques and collectibles; including scales, inkwells, perfumes, sewing items, and sporting antiques. Open. Apr.–Jan., daily; Jan.–Mar., weekends and by appointment.

**Stone's Throw Antiques** (413-637-2733; 57 Church St., Lenox, MA 01240) American, French, English, and Asian 19th- and early-20th-century furniture, accessories, and collector's items, including china, glass, silver, prints. Open Apr.–Dec., daily 10–5; Jan.–Mar., weekends.

### PITTSFIELD

**Berkshire Hills Coins and Estate Jewelry** (413-499-1400; 222 Elm St., Pittsfield, MA 01201) Specializing in collectible coins, estate gold, and sterling and costume jewelry. Open Mon.–Fri. 10–5:45, Sat. 10–4.

**Berkshire Pedlar** (413-236-5600; 288 Tyler St., Pittsfield, MA 01201) A huge warehouse full of goodies. The proprietress is delightful, and one can often find unexpected treasures.

**Nora's Estate Goods** (413-499-0927; 446 Tyler St., Pittsfield, MA 01201) Housed in the former Memory Lane shop and run by the daughter of the owner, this shop sells used furniture, antiques, and vintage linens. It is the newest outpost of the Bargain Box, Martin's former shop in Pittsfield. Closed Tues. and Sun.

## North County

### NORTH ADAMS

**Mary Ann-tiques & Gifts** (413-663-7803: 615 Ashland St., N. Adams, MA 01247) Small but charming shop filled to the rafters with gifts and antiques. Teacups and tea accessories predominate, but there are lots of unexpected treasures, such as vintage hats, lady's slipper chairs, and jewelry.

**Skiddoo Vintage & Modern** (413-664-8007; 38 Eagle St., N. Adams, MA 01247) Open Thurs.–Sat. 12–6, Sun. and Mon. 12–4.

**Stormy Crandall Antiques** (413-663-5050; 437 W. Main St., N. Adams, MA 01247) A funky shop in a building that was once a neighborhood market. Stormy Crandall has collected an eclectic group of antiques and fun stuff. A fun browse and a potential source for just the right accent piece for any home.

### CHESHIRE

**Winterbrook Farm Antiques** (413-743-2177; www.winterbrookfarm.com; 450 N. State Rd., Cheshire, MA 01225; Rte.8) Late 19th- and 20th-century restored and refinished furniture and accessories. Howard's refinishing products and replacement hardware in stock. Open Mon.–Fri. 10:30–5; weekends by chance or appointment.

WILLIAMSTOWN

**Collector's Warehouse** (413-458-9686; 723 Rte. 7, Williamstown, MA 01267) Antiques; collectibles, including glassware, jewelry, frames, dolls, linen, and furniture. Deborah Elder's Collector's Warehouse is now located on Rte. 7. Open Mon., Wed.–Sat. 10–5, Sun. 12–5. Closed Tues.

**LiAsia Gallery** (413-458-1600; 31 Spring St., Williamstown, MA 01267) A fine collection of antique Chinese furniture, primarily 18th and 19th century; also offers an extraordinary selection of Chinese architectural elements. Open Mon.–Sat., 10–6, Sun. 12–5.

**Auctioneers**

**William Bradford Auction Galleries** (413-229-6667; Rte. 7, Sheffield, MA 01257)

**Roy C. Burdick** (413-664-6055; 24 S. County Rd., Florida, MA 01247)

**John and Dina Fontaine** (413-448-8922, 1485 W. Housatonic St., Pittsfield, MA 01201)

**Ralph Fontaine & Heritage Auctions** (413-442-2537; 94 Dawes Ave., Pittsfield, MA 01201)

**T.A. Gage** (413-528-0076, 413-528-4771; Rte. 23, S. Egremont, MA 01258)

**LuJohns Auctioneers** (800-243-4420; www.lujohns.com; 2130 Cape St., Lee, MA 01238)

**The Library Antiques** (413-458-3436; www.libraryantiques.com; 70 Spring St., Williamstown, MA 01267) Old and new items, artfully displayed in a series of rooms, including jewelry, furniture, writing supplies, housewares, pillows, prints, books, international décor pieces, silver, dishes, pottery, fabrics, and textiles. They welcome browsers. A great place for gifts for others or just for ourselves.

**Saddleback Antiques** (413-458-5852; 1395 Cold Spring Rd., Williamstown, MA 01267; Rte. 7) Furniture, glass, pottery, prints, posters. A group shop in an old schoolhouse with a bell tower. Inventory changes weekly and includes a fine selection of pieces at realistic prices. Open Mon.–Sat. 10–5 or 6; Sun. 12–5.

## BOOKS

The Berkshires' literary traditions are upheld by a number of excellent bookstores, selling new and used books, each with its own distinct character. Specialists, rare book, and antique book dealers are also listed.

### South County

GREAT BARRINGTON

**The Bookloft** (413-528-1521; Barrington Plaza, Stockbridge Rd., Gt. Barrington, MA 01230; Rte. 7) A thoughtfully chosen selection of books and tapes, both music and books. It's also a good source for Berkshire-related titles. With its wooden bookcases and pleasant atmosphere, this is one of the nicest places in South County for browsing and consulting with fellow book lovers, particularly owner Eric Wilska.

**Yellow House Books** (413-528-8227; 252 Main St., Gt. Barrington, MA 01230) Bob and Bonnie Benson offer a fine selection of used and rare books in three rooms of a house that is more than 100 years old. Specialties include photography, Native American topics, literature, art, music, children's illustrated books, cooking, and metaphysical topics.

LEE

**Media Merchant** (413-243-3359; 50 Water St., Lee, MA 01238; at Prime Outlets) This is a discount book and media outlet. Can be a good source for bargain books. They also have a shop in Prime Outlets dedicated to children's books.

SHEFFIELD

**Berkshire Book Co.** (413-229-0122, 800-828-5565; 510 S. Main St., Sheffield, MA 01257; Rte. 7) The ideal used-book store for the reader, with an extensive and well-organized collection. Co-proprietor Esther Kininmonth truly knows and loves her stock and its authors, and it's a pleasure to consult with her about various writers and editions. Categories include literature, travel, biography, children's books, art, and antiques.

SOUTH EGREMONT

**B&S Gventer Books** (413-528-2327; P.O. Box 298, S. Egremont, MA 01258; Tyrrell Rd. and Rte. 23) "Tons of books" from the 15th century to the 19th. Medieval manuscript and Renaissance pages on vellum and various pages from books published from 1300 to 1600; 19th-century hand-colored engravings. Knowledgeable owner Bruce Gventer can tell their stories. June–Oct., Wed.–Sun.; occasional weekends in winter.

**Farshaw's Fine Old Books** (413-528-1890; 43 A Main St., S. Egremont, MA 01258) Formerly on Railroad Street in Great Barrington, Farshaw's still offers select antique used or out-of-print titles for the reader, collectors, and bibliophile in a well-organized, browser-friendly shop. The owners, Helen and Michael Seltzer, established Bibliofind—a large inventory of used and rare books—on the Internet.

STOCKBRIDGE

**Stockbridge Booksellers** (413-298-3329; www.stockbridgebooksellers.com; 10 Elm St., Stockbridge, MA 01262) An excellent new bookstore featuring new and used books, including political, historical, local interest, poetry, literary fiction, and much more; sizeable children's collection. Offers engaging author discussions and other events. Open Mon., Tues., Thurs. 11–7; Fri., Sat., and Sun 10–7; hours may change seasonally.

## Central County

LANESBOROUGH

**Waldenbooks** (413-499-0115; Berkshire Mall, Lanesborough, MA 01237; off Rte. 8) Berkshire County's entry for this well-known chain, stocking current hardcover and softcover best sellers as well as representative collections in various categories, including children's books and books of local interest. Books, tapes, magazine section.

LENOX

**The Bookstore** (413-637-3390; 9 Housatonic St., Lenox, MA 01240) A literate and imaginative selection of new fiction, old fiction, and nonfiction. There are collections of small-

*The Bookstore in Lenox* Judith Monachina

press titles and books by local and regional authors, plus well-chosen children's and young-adult titles. The Bookstore is a community center, too, presided over by owner Matt Tannenbaum with grace and humor. Matt and his assistants know their books and are happy to converse with you about them; they organize book-signing parties and special events, too. "The world's oldest, permanent literary establishment, serving the community since last Tuesday."

PITTSFIELD

**Barnes & Noble** (413-496-9051; 555 Hubbard Ave., Pittsfield, MA 01201; at Berkshire Crossing Mall) This chain "superstore" has a large selection of the most popular titles, along with book CDs and tapes, plus some musical scores. The in-store café features Starbucks coffee and other goodies.

## North County

NORTH ADAMS

**Papyri Books** (413-662-2099; 49 Main St., N. Adams, MA 01247) This shop carries mostly used books, some new; excellent programs of music and readings.

WILLIAMSTOWN

**Water Street Books** (413-458-8071; 26 Water St., Williamstown, MA 01267) A large selection in just about every category, displayed on classy architectural shelving. The help is hip and friendly. There are sale books and children's books, and the Williams College bookstore is in the back. A book lover's paradise.

**Book Dealers**

These specialist book dealers do business by catalog or appointment:

**Found at the Bookloft** (413-232-0251; 14 Main St., W. Stockbridge, MA 01266) An outpost of The Bookloft; rare and used books. Also, all-new books, maps, and guides of the Berkshires.

**Howard S. Mott** (413-229-2019; Rte. 7, Sheffield, MA 01257) First editions, books from the 16th to the 20th centuries, autographs.

**Iron Kettle Books** (413-738-5362; Rte. 43, Hancock, MA 01237) By catalog; occasional open houses.

**John R. Sanderson Antiquarian Bookseller** (413-298-5322; P.O. Box 844, Stockbridge, MA 01262) Rare and fine books.

**North Star Rare Books and Manuscripts** (413-644-9595; 684 S. Main St., Gt. Barrington, MA 01230; Rte. 7) Specializing in 18th-, 19th-, and 20th-century historical literary manuscripts and rare volumes. Open 7 days a week in a shop located next to Grape Finds wine emporium!

Farther afield but a destination for a good browse: **Librarium** (518-392-5209; 126 Blackbridge Rd., E. Chatham, NY 12060; off Rte. 295, 1 mi. E. of E. Chatham) More than 25,000 secondhand, out-of-print books "for all interests and ages." Sept.–June, open most days 10–5 by chance or appointment only. July and Aug., Fri.–Mon 10–6 and by appointment or chance.

## CLOTHINGS & ACCESSORIES

We can outfit ourselves in just about any style of our choice in the Berkshires: classic, traditional, designer, funky, all-natural, English country squire, buckaroo—it's all here. Some boutiques also feature designs and concepts that have been created in the Berkshires, too. For clothing factory outlets, and there are a number of them, check the listings below plus the "Shopping Streets, Mews & Malls" section.

### South County

GREAT BARRINGTON

**Barrington Outfitters** (413-528-0021; 289 Main St., Gt. Barrington, MA 01230) A good selection of shoes for men, women, and kids along with casual clothes for men and women.

**Byzantium** (413-528-9496; 32 Railroad St., Gt. Barrington, MA 01230) The sweaters in chenille, wool, and cotton will catch the eye first, but it doesn't stop there. Stylish and easy women's dresses, blouses, skirts, and ensembles, casual to dressy. Lots of lovely lingerie and sleepwear, too, plus jewelry, throws, and other accessories.

**Church Street Trading Company** (413-528-6120; 4 Railroad St., Gt. Barrington, MA 01230) Featuring mainly trendy and natural-fiber clothes, this eclectic shop also offers jewelry, men's and women's accessories, and home furnishings, attractively arranged.

**Gatsby's** (413-528-9455; 25 Railroad St., Gt. Barrington, MA 01230) Useful and funky stuff, including cotton nightgowns, Doc Martins, Teva sandals, Birkenstocks, denim, socks and turtlenecks, and housewares. Gatsby's covers the territory with shops in Williamstown (413-458-5407; 31 Spring St.) and Lee (413-243-3412; 62 Main St.).

**Especially for Children**

**Gifted Child** (413-637-1191; 80 Church St., Lenox, MA 01240) Children's clothing, newborns to preteens, with a contemporary flair; high-quality toys and gifts. Camp care packages—what a great idea. And don't miss the sale barn. Also in Great Barrington at 23 Railroad St. (413-528-1395), featuring clothes from newborn to size 6X.

**M. Lacey** (413-528-5991; 12 Railroad St., Gt. Barrington, MA 01230) A beautiful selection of clothing for infants and children, much of it imported. The whimsical designs are sure to delight both wearer and buyer.

**Matruska** (413-528-6911; 252 Main St., Gt. Barrington, MA 01230) Toys and books that have been chosen to enhance a child's imagination and sense of beauty. Wonderful dolls from Holland that only absorb a child's love.

*A funny fellow before Tom's Toys, Gt. Barrington*
Judith Monachina

**Persnickety** (413-662-2990; 13 Eagle St., N. Adams, MA 01247) This is a tiny treasure trove of unique gifts for baby and child, including delightful outfits, hand-knit cap and sweater sets, along with wonderful finger puppets and toys.

**Tom's Toys** (413-528-3331; 307 Main St., Gt. Barrington, MA 01230) A happening place for kids that carries all the most popular toys and a great selection of inexpensive trinkets to amuse even the most bored young traveler.

Other spots for clothes, toys, and gifts for children include **Mary Stuart** (413-637-0340; 69 Church St., Lenox, MA 01240), for exquisite clothes designed for grandmothers to give. And several area museums and galleries, particularly the **Berkshire Museum** in Pittsfield, have gift shops with sections devoted to educational items disguised as toys.

**Hildi B** (413-528-0331; 320 Main St., Gt. Barrington, MA 01230) Natural-fiber clothes, including batik sweaters, skirts, blouses, and dresses. Plus handcrafted jewelry and other crafts, leather items, oils, and soaps.

**Jack's Country Squire** (413-528-1390; 316 Main St., Gt. Barrington, MA 01230) Family clothing and shoes, including Nike, Woolrich, Reebok, Levi.

**Main Street** (413-528-0702; 322 Main St., Gt. Barrington, MA 01230) An excellent selection of designer women's clothing for work and weekend.

LEE

**Ben's** (413-243-0242; 68 Main St., Lee, MA 01238) A friendly store packed with clothing and footwear for the entire family.

**Zabian's Ltd.** (413-243-0136; 19 Main St., Lee, MA 01238) Clothing for men with an emphasis on personal service.

**Prime Outlets at Lee** (413-243-8186; 50 Water St., Lee, MA 01238; Exit 2 off the MassPike at Rte. 20) Over 60 discount and factory-outlet stores, featuring women's clothing **(Jones New York, Liz Claiborne)**, leather goods **(Coach)**, sporting goods, menswear, and shoes **(Johnson & Murphy, Haggar)**, **Polo**, and **Brooks Brothers.**

STOCKBRIDGE

**Greystone Gardens** (413-298-0113; www.greystonegardens.com; Main St., Stockbridge, MA 01262; in the Mews) Antique clothing for men and women. See the description under "Pittsfield."

**Sweaters Etc.** (413-298-4287; 5 South St., Stockbridge, MA 01262; Rte 7) The third house behind the Red Lion Inn contains a veritable feast of sweaters in wool and cotton. Some are high fashion, while others are more casual. Many are hand knit, and all sweaters are discounted.

**Vlada Boutique** (413-298-3656; Elm St., Stockbridge, MA 01262) Retail therapy for sure! Selling sophisticated women's clothing with an emphasis on comfort, witty gifts and accessories, lovely and outrageous cards, and clever contemporary jewelry.

WEST STOCKBRIDGE

**Out of Vietnam at Truc Orient Express Restaurant** (413-232-4204; 3 Harris St., W. Stockbridge, MA 01266) The owners of this wonderful Vietnamese restaurant have a shop adjacent that specializes in lacquerware and silk accessories for the home, along with some Asian-inspired clothing and accessories. Open during restaurant hours, 5–9 PM daily except Tues., or by appointment.

## Central County

LANESBOROUGH

**Berkshire Pendleton Store** (413-443-6822; 100 Williamstown Rd., Lanesborough, MA 01237; Rte. 7 between Pittsfield and Williamstown) Classic wool clothes and accessories for the complete look. Men's sport shirts and sweaters, too, and a large selection of American Indian trade blankets and robes. They also have an outlet basement.

**The Berkshire Mall** (413-445-4400; Old State Rd., Lanesborough, MA 01237; off Rte 8) Comprises many and varied clothes-shopping options for men, women, teens, and children: **The Gap, Old Navy, American Eagle Outfitters, EMS, Eddie Bauer**, and **Filene's.**

LENOX

**Casablanca** (413-637-2680; 21 Housatonic St., Lenox, MA 01240) Men's and women's clothes, stylishly displayed in a gallery setting.

**Evviva!** (413-637-9875; 22 Walker St., Lenox, MA 01240) Sophisticated dresses, separates, and accessories by designers "well known and undiscovered." They also have shoes to complete the outfit!

**Glad Rags** (413-637-0088; 66 Church St., Lenox, MA 01240) Clothes with an emphasis on easy fit and easy care in a variety of fabulous fabrics. Wonderful hats, scarves, and other accessories and jewelry.

**Purple Plume** (413-637-3442; 35 Church St., Lenox, MA 01240) A large selection of fun and unusual clothing, some batiked or hand-painted, featuring the latest looks and natural fibers. The amazing array of accessories includes jewelry, headbands, and scarves. Gifts and cards, too.

**Shooz** (413-637-1118; 44 Housatonic St., Lenox, MA 01240) Another shop run by the owners of Casablanca featuring—what else?—shoes to complement today's contemporary look in clothing. They also have great handbags and wonderful jewelry.

**Talbot's** (413-637-3576; 46 Walker St., Lenox, MA 01240) Classic women's clothing and accessories, and a special petites section.

**Tanglewool, Inc.** (413-637-0900; 28 Walker St., Lenox, MA 01240) Sophisticated clothing, shoes, gorgeous sweaters (from Issey Miyake, Yoji Yamamoto, Patricia Roberts, and other well-known designers) for the fashion conscious.

**Weaver's Fancy** (413-637-2013; 65 Church St., Lenox, MA 01240) One-of-a kind clothing and hats in hand-created fabrics, along with beautiful hand-painted silks and luscious rayon chenille. The whimsical hats provide both warmth and wit.

*Tanglewool, an exclusive clothing shop in Lenox* Judith Monachina

PITTSFIELD

**The Cottage** (413-447-9643; 31 South St., Pittsfield, MA 01201) A popular shop where women's clothing shares space with home and gift items.

**Deidre's** (413-499-9959; 75 North St., Pittsfield, MA 01201) Women's clothing for any day, especially those special days. Wedding gowns, mother-of-the-bride dresses, bridesmaids dresses, cocktail outfits—even tuxedo rentals for the man in one's life.

**Greystone Gardens** (413-442-9291; www.greystonegardens.com; 436 North St., Pittsfield, MA 01201) An emporium of timeless treasures. Victorian and vintage clothing, accessories, jewelry, and linens for men and women. The long, high-ceilinged shop has floral carpeting, velvet-curtained dressing rooms with antique mirrors, stacks of old-fashioned hatboxes, swanky fashion prints, and vintage songs being crooned in the background—the perfect setting for '40s evening gowns, sporty rayon dresses, lacy camisoles and wedding gowns, vintage tuxedos, top hats, tweed jackets and coats, bowling shirts, fringed scarves, and more, all eminently wearable. Owner Carla Lund, creator of this outpost of nostalgia, is a genius at putting it all together. Cards, soaps, and other niceties, too. Not to be missed—it or the sister shop in The Mews in Stockbridge.

**Fabrics and Weavers**

For your home or self, two sources of special textiles and fabrics:

**Sam Kasten's SKH Gallery** (413-528-3300; 46 Castle St., Gt. Barrington, MA 01230; in the Train Station) The old Great Barrington Train Station houses the looms of Sam Kasten's nationally renowned architectural fabrics firm. Wall coverings, upholstery fabrics, and carpeting almost too fine to tread upon are the mainstay of his business, but shawls and wraps in exotic and unusual yarns are available, too. Call for hours.

**Undermountain Weavers** (413-274-6565; 311 Gt. Barrington Rd., W. Stockbridge, MA 01266; Rte. 41) In a restored barn, on century-old hand looms, traditional Shetland Island patterns take shape. Purchase by the yard, or tailoring can be arranged.

**Steven Valenti** (413-443-2569; 157 North St., Pittsfield, MA 01201) Menswear for these times in a well-appointed store, with up-to-date styles by Perry Ellis, Jhane Barnes, and other contemporary designers. Shirts, sweaters, suits, jackets, and coats here feature fine fabrics and colors ranging from traditional to fashion-forward styles. An outstanding collection of silk ties.

**U.S. Bluesware** (413-442-5533; 141 North St.; Pittsfield, MA 01201). U.S. Bluesware has been recognized by eBay for their quality of gently used designer clothing—Armani, BCBG, Chanel, Dior . . . all the way to Yves Saint Laurent—and stellar customer service. The garments are conveniently organized by size.

## North County

NORTH ADAMS

**Galadriel's** (413-664-0026; 105 Main St., N. Adams, MA 01247) Imported women's clothing, accessories, and jewelry.

WILLIAMSTOWN

**The Cottage** (413-458-4305; 24 Water St., Williamstown, MA 01267) Specialty fabrics and apparel from designers like April Cornell, Vera Bradley, Putamayo, and Crabtree & Evelyn (nightwear).

**Williams Shop** (413-458-3605; 15 Spring St., Williamstown, MA 01267) A large selection of items bearing the Williams College logo, as well as athletic and sporting goods.

**Zanna** (413-458-9858; 41 Spring St., Williamstown, MA 01267) Contemporary women's clothes and accessories, featuring natural fibers and up-to-the-minute looks. There is also a selection of sophisticated but comfortable shoes.

## GIFT & SPECIALTY SHOPS

### South County

GREAT BARRINGTON

**Bella Collections** (413-528-3936; 152 Main St., Gt. Barrington, MA 01230) A fine collection in an intimate space offering distinctive gifts, primarily fine jewelry and art. Open Wed.–Mon. 11–5, Tues. by appointment.

**Crystal Essence** (413-528-2595; 39 Railroad St., Gt. Barrington, MA 01230) Geodes, jewelry, gemstones, ceramics, clothes, books, and other items for enhancing a New Age lifestyle.

**Farmhouse** (413-528-6452; 635 S. Main St., Gt. Barrington, MA 01230) "Fresh country style" for the home. A mix of antiques, furniture, dinnerware, bedding and bath products ,and more. Open Mon.–Sat. 10–5; Sun. 12–5. Closed Tues.

**The Gingham Rabbit** (413-528-0048; 389 Stockbridge Rd., Gt. Barrington, MA 01230; Rte. 7) A pastel palate predominates in this two-story shop that sells wonderful cards, pillows, gift items, infant clothing, lingerie, and bath products. They specialize in Berkshire-related gift items.

**La Pace** (413-528-1888; 313 Main St., Gt. Barrington, MA 01230) A beautifully conceived and decorated store full of luxurious bath items imported from all over Europe, with an emphasis on Italy. Linen hand towels, chic shower curtains, bath pillows, even rubber duckies for the tub.

**Mistral's** (413-528-1618; 7 Railroad St., Gt. Barrington, MA 01230) "Provence in the Berkshires" is the way the owners describe their shop. French wire baskets, lamps, and vases as well as jacquard-patterned napkins, Provençal olive oil, faience plates, cutlery, and serving pieces, all guaranteed to win a Francophile's heart. Upstairs are bath and bedroom products.

**Nahual** (413-528-2423; 9 Railroad St., Gt. Barrington, MA 01230) Handcrafted items from Mexico and Africa. Only open Thurs.–Sun. afternoons.

**The Red Door** (413-528-1899; 3 Railroad St., Gt. Barrington, MA 01230) Behind the red door is a tiny shop carrying a variety of gift items both old and new.

**Sappa** (413-528-9592; 308 Main St., Gt. Barrington, MA 01230) An elegant store with style and wit. The very charming young owner has a great sense of design and an eye for the unusual. Gifts and accessories from Europe join American antiques and interesting artworks in an ever-changing display of beautiful objects.

**Seeds & Co., Inc.** (413-528-8122; 34 Railroad St., Gt. Barrington, MA 01230) Simplicity and sophistication of design are the hallmarks of this store. Home and bath accessories with wit and charm share space with those having a 21st-century edge.

**T. P. Saddle Blanket and Trading Co.** (413-528-6500; 304 Main St., Gt. Barrington, MA 01230) An outpost for the Southwest look, from cowboy-motif pajamas to saddle blankets for your living room, with a colorful abundance of shirts, vests, boots, belts, pillows, books, candles, bedding, dishware, and furniture accents.

**Wonderful Things** (413-528-2473; 232 Stockbridge Rd., Gt. Barrington, MA 01230; Rte. 7) Deb and Harry Sano offer the largest selection of yarn, needlework, handcrafted gifts, and crafts supplies in the Berkshires, in a friendly and casual atmosphere. You'll find novice knitters practicing under the watchful tutelage of Deb, who generously shares her expert advice when time permits.

### LEE

**Hats and Jewels** (413-243-2506; 83 Center St., Lee, MA 01238) Don't wait to attend Ascott to find a reason to purchase an attractive hat—this shop offers tastefully embellished hats for both special and everyday wear. The millinery is paired with jewelry, both locally made and vintage in a range of price points.

**Pamela Loring Gifts & Interiors** (413-243-2689; 151 Main St., Lee MA 01238) Tastefully decorated shop in a renovated Victorian house. Each room is filled with carefully chosen merchandise. There's an emphasis on seasonal gifts and decorations. Besides household decorative items there are candles, bath oils, soaps, potpourris, and charming gifts for children.

### SHEFFIELD

**Bits and Pieces** (413-229-9996; 116 Main St., Sheffield, MA 01257) Rustic country treasures from artisans all across the country.

**Campo de Fiori** (413-528-9180; 1815 N. Main St., Sheffield, MA 01257; Rte. 7) A wonderful source for garden ornaments, pots, botanical prints, interesting soaps, plants, and containers. A very sophisticated touch of European country in the Berkshires.

### STOCKBRIDGE

**Red Lion Inn Gift Shop** (413-298-3134; 30 Main St., Stockbridge, MA 01262; at the Red Lion Inn) A lovely shop with gifts, cards, and accessories, featuring Berkshire items.

**Seven Arts** (413-298-5101; Main St., Stockbridge, MA 01262) A concentration of items with Rockwell motifs, also T-shirts, jewelry, and gifts.

**Williams & Son Country Store** (413-298-3016; Main St., Stockbridge, MA 01262) A Stockbridge institution, with jams and jellies, soaps, candy, gourmet foods, glassware, gifts, cards, and various nostalgia items. Enjoyable old tins are displayed behind the counter.

**Yankee Candle** (413-298-3004; Main St., Stockbridge, MA 01262) A huge selection of candles in a variety of shapes, colors, and scents.

West Stockbridge

**Charles H. Baldwin & Sons** (413-232-7785; 1 Center St., W. Stockbridge, MA 01266) Not only is this an outlet for Baldwin's flavoring extracts along with table and maple syrup, it is also a general store with seasonal gifts, cards, candy, and inexpensive toys for children. *Martha Stewart Living* featured this store.

**Hotchkiss Mobiles Gallery** (413-232-0200; 8 Center St., W. Stockbridge, MA 01266) Open Sat.–Sun., or call for an appointment. Contemporary mobiles for your home or office.

## Central County

Lenox

**B. Mango & Bird** (413-637-2611; 48 Main St., Lenox, MA 01240) An eclectic mix of home furnishings and accessories in a dramatic, high-ceilinged store, with an outdoor patio where garden gifts and furniture are displayed.

**Colorful Stitches** (413-637-8207; 48 Main St., Lenox, MA 01240) A rainbow of fine yarns in wools, silks, cottons, and blends. Wonderful patterns, buttons, and all the necessary needles and other supplies. There are regular weekend instruction sessions.

**Mary Stuart** (413-637-0340; 69 Church St., Lenox, MA 01240) A chic shop carrying accessories for gracious country living, including china, glassware, linen, needlepoint, and toiletries; lingerie and sleepwear; books and cards. A small but beautiful selection of clothing for infants and toddlers is displayed at the rear of the shop. A small but sophicated collection of Kit's clothing.

**Pine Cone Hill** (413-496-9700; Rte. 7, Lenox, MA 01240) Housed in the Lenox Shops compound, this is an outlet store for the Pine Cone Hill brand of bedding and table linens for which local Annie Selke is responsible. These items are sold elsewhere for much higher prices. Styles complement both country and contemporary interiors.

**Villager Gifts** (413-637-9866; 68 Main St, Lenox, MA 01240) An engaging variety of gifts and collectibles, featuring jewelry, pottery, stationery, candles, and cards. This is the largest area dealer for the Cats' Meow Village houses and custom pieces. A Christmas Shop is downstairs.

**Yankee Candle** (413-499-3626; 639 Pittsfield–Lenox Rd., Lenox, MA 01240; Rte. 7) Candles, gifts, bath accessories. Also on Main St. in Stockbridge.

Pittsfield

**The Cottage** (413-447-9643; 31 South St., Pittsfield, MA 01201) Attractive tableware, including glasses, vases, dinnerware, table linens, baskets, frames, and soaps, along with clothes and jewelry.

**Museum Facsimiles Outlet Store** (413-499-0020; 117 Fourth St., Pittsfield, MA 01201) Here one can find hand-printed greeting cards and stationery sold in the finest museums, along with frames and mirrors to give as gifts or to grace the home. Open Mon., Wed., and Fri. 12–5, Sat. 10–5.

**Pasko Frame & Gift Center** (413-442-2680; 243 North St., Pittsfield, MA 01201) The new owner carries on the tradition set by Ann Pasko of offering Berkshire landscapes by Walter Pasko, the Berkshire map, superb custom framing, prints, and posters. They still have a lovely selection of gifts and handcrafts from around the world. Largest area dealer of P. Buckley Moss prints. Open until 8 on Thurs.

## North County

### ADAMS

**The Crafter's Cottage** (413-743-2640; 9 Grove St., Adams, MA 01220) Unique handcrafted gifts and seasonal offerings in a range of prices. This is an outlet for crafters whose work is often only seen at crafts fairs or holiday boutiques.

### NORTH ADAMS

**Berkshires' Best . . . Locally Produced Products** (413-663-6040, 888-663-6040; fax (413- 664-8162; 85 Union Street, P.O. Box 788, N. Adams, MA 01247) A recent addition to the North Adams streetscape, specializing in locally produced products, handmade toys, paintings and photographs, food products, and period lighting fixtures.

**Moulton's Country Store** (413-664-7770; 77 Main St., N. Adams, MA 01247) Large, bright space filled with locally made gifts, baked goods, toys, cards, seasonal items, even an ice-cream bar, overseen by a friendly staff, just like in an old-fashioned country store.

**Tala's Quilt Shop** (413-664-8200; Heritage State Park, Bldg. #2, N. Adams, MA 01247) From the reports of accomplished quilters, this is a wonderful source for supplies and ideas. Classes available.

**Wigwam & Western Summit Gift Shop** (413-663-3205; fax 413-663-3205; wigwamsummit@aol.com; Rte. 2, 2350 Mohawk Trail, P.O. Box 7, N. Adams, MA 01247) Fine gifts, Fenton Art Glass, jewelry, moccasins, T-shirts in a shop with a panoramic view of North Adams, Williamstown, and Mount Greylock from gift shop and cottages.

### WILLIAMSTOWN

**The Cottage** (413-458-4305; 24 Water St., Williamstown, MA 01267) A variety of gift items including tableware and table linens, cards, children's gifts, photo frames, toiletries from Crabtree & Evelyn, and women's clothes from designers like Putumayo. This is an independently owned Cottage store!

**Where'd You Get That!?** (413-458-2206; www.wygt.com; 100 Spring St., Williamstown, MA 01267) This fun store aims to provide gifts and toys to tickle the brain, the fancy, and the funnybone—and it succeeds. Open daily.

## HANDCRAFTS

See chapter 5 "Arts & Pleasures," for additional listings of galleries with handcrafted art.

## South County

GREAT BARRINGTON

**Evergreen** (413-528-0511; 291 Main St., Gt. Barrington, MA 01230) Contemporary American crafts include vases, tableware, pottery, clocks, and handcrafted jewelry.

**Kaolin Pottery** (413-528-1531; 80 Rte. 71, Gt. Barrington, MA 01230; near Gt. Barrington airport) Contemporary ceramics, from whimsical to elegant, at the artists' studio and showroom.

**October Mountain Stained Glass** (413-528-6681; 343 Main St., Gt. Barrington, MA 01230) A vivid array of lampshades, window panels, and glass accessories. Custom design work is a specialty, including commissions for homeowners, builders, and architects. Beveling, sandblasting, repairs, and supplies are also offered. Closed Mon.

**Wonderful Things** (413-528-2473; 232 Stockbridge Rd., Gt. Barrington, MA 01230) Handcrafted gifts, or make our own with yarn, needlework accessories, beads, feathers, stencils, paint, other crafts supplies.

HOUSATONIC

**The Great Barrington Pottery** (413-274-6259; www.gtbarringtonpottery.com; Rte. 41, Housatonic, MA 01236) Potter Richard Bennett uses a Japanese wood-burning kiln for firing pottery designs that combine East and West in a beautiful garden setting. Visit the pottery showroom or participate in an ancient tea ceremony. (See "Seasonal Events" in chapter 5, "Arts & Pleasures.")

MONTEREY

**Joyous Spring Pottery** (413-528-4115; 20 Art School Rd., Monterey, MA 01245) Potter Michael Marcus fires his climbing kiln once a year for a 10-day period for his Japanese-inspired unglazed ceramics.

SHEFFIELD

**Sheffield Pottery** (413-229-7700; www.sheffield-pottery.com; P.O. Box 399, Sheffield, MA 01257; Rte. 7) New England potters' ware, including mugs, teapots, platters, tureens; terra-cotta items. Supplies and equipment, too.

STOCKBRIDGE

**An American Craftsman** (413-298-0175; 36 Main St., Stockbridge, MA 01262) Browse among the unique glass, wood, and jewelry boxes made by some of America's best craftspeople.

WEST STOCKBRIDGE

**Hoffman Pottery** (232-4646; 103 Rte. 41, Gt. Barrington Rd., W. Stockbridge, MA 01255) Hand-thrown, hand-painted functional works that dance with energy.

## Central County

LENOX

**Concepts of Art** (413-637-4845; 67 Church St., Lenox, MA 01240) Fine crafts and local artisans, with lamps and other glass, wood sculpture, jewelry, throws. There is an emphasis on Judaica.

**Recordings, Classical and Jazz**

Compact discs, cassette tapes, and even those dinosaurs, records, are available throughout the county, in various chain stores and other retail outlets. Most places here with CDs and tapes have a small classical music selection, but for those looking for more than the Three Tenors or the *Four Seasons*, visit the **Tanglewood Music Store,** at Tanglewood in Lenox, open for Tanglewood audiences, and featuring the music and performing artists of that week, plus much more. The **Berkshire Record Outlet** (413-243-4080; www.berkshirerecordoutlet.com; Rte. 102, Lee, MA 01238) has classical remainders listed in a catalog—send for one for $2—containing thousands of classical CDs, tapes, and LPs, at closeout prices. On Saturdays from 10 to 5:30, customers can also browse through an eclectic selection of recordings in the small retail room, being sure to turn up something they've always wanted.

A well-chosen selection of classical, jazz, and blues is available at **Tune St.** (413-528-4999; 294 Main St., Gt. Barrington, MA 01230) along with pop, folk, New Age, and world music recordings. They also sell electronic gear (stereo equipment, etc.) and do custom home installations. A low-key, but vital business since 1979, **White Knight Records** (413-528-9466; 288 Main St., Gt. Barrington, MA 01230) carries a broad range of CDs and tapes. They have been complimented by out-of-towners for their collection of classical music and will do special orders.

Jazz enthusiasts in particular will enjoy **Toonerville Trolley Records** (413-458-5229; 131 Water St., Williamstown, MA 01267) and its array of CDs, tapes, and LPs, out-of-print and current. In addition to jazz, there's rock, folk, and reggae.

For musically related gift items, including instruments, try **The Music Store** (413-528-2460; Rte. 7, Gt. Barrington, MA 01230; at Jenifer House Commons).

**Cose D'Argilla** (413-637-8886; 93 Church St., Lenox, MA 01240) The owner is Italian with a real flair for picking out the best in contemporary Italian crafts pieces, including pottery and glass.

**Inspired Planet** (413-637-2836; www.inspiredplanet.com; 36 Pittsfield–Lenox Rd., Lenox, MA 01240; Rte. 7 at Brushwood Farm Shops) This abundant collection of distinctive "cross-cultural art" includes high-quality paintings, jewelry, primitives, rugs, icons, textiles, masks, pottery, carved wooden animals, and other sculpture. These handcrafted items with symbolic meaning are "gifts that connect." Call ahead for hours.

**Lydia Mongiardo Collection** (413-637-0809; 51 Church St., Lenox, MA 01240) Furniture by Nicholas Mongiardo, a specialist in 20th-century French designs, plus stunning jewelry and accessories for the home, are beautifully displayed.

## HOUSE & HOME

### South County

#### GREAT BARRINGTON

**Bridlewood Home Furnishing** (413-528-5825; 434 Stockbridge Rd., Gt. Barrington, MA 01230) Simple country furniture displayed in a wonderful converted barn. Closed Tues. and Wed.

**The Chef's Shop** (413-528-0135; 31 Railroad St., Gt. Barrington, MA 01230) A hardware store for serious cooks, featuring innovative kitchen equipment, including top-of-the-line cookware and knives. From garlic peelers to pasta pots, the Chef's Shop has it all. Also pottery serving pieces and cookbooks.

**Gatsby's** (413-528-9455; 25 Railroad St., Gt. Barrington, MA 01230) In addition to wearables, there are futons, wicker and other furniture, bedclothes, and housewares.

**Hammertown Barn** (413-528-7766; 325 Stockbridge Rd., Gt. Barrington, MA 01230) Once only in Pine Plains, New York, Hammertown Barn's owners expanded to Great Barrington. Country chic is the theme; comfort is the name of the game. They carry Mitchell Gold furniture, lots of great pillows, rugs, and bedding. One-stop shopping for everything for the home, from kitchen to bath.

**Out Of Hand** (413-528-3791; 81 Main St., Gt. Barrington, MA 01230) Every size, shape, and color of basket you ever needed or imagined—one upstairs room is full of them—plus rugs, throws, pillows, glassware in a rainbow of colors, toys, candlesticks, clothing. A great place for accessorizing the home!

**The Lamplighter** (413-528-3448; 162 Main St., Gt. Barrington, MA 01230) An exceptional lighting store with a wide selection and knowledgeable staff. Chandeliers, floor and table lamps, and outdoor lighting in all shapes, sizes, and styles, from Colonial to art deco to contemporary. Lampshades and other accessories.

**Phoebe** (413-528-1166; 325 Stockbridge Rd., Gt. Barrington, MA 01230) Visit this shop for "luxe" linens, including custom-order bedding, tablecloths, placemats, napkins, and rugs. There are also some great gift items.

**Wingate Ltd.** (413-644-9960; 420 Stockbridge Rd., Gt. Barrington, MA 01230) Importers of antique and reproduction furniture displayed in room-like settings, with design services offered on the premises.

### Stockbridge

**Country Curtains** (413-298-5565; 30 Main St., Stockbridge, MA 01262; at the Red Lion Inn) Manufacturer's shop offering curtains and matching bedding from the manufacturer, displayed in charming room vignettes. Select from a variety of styles and fabrics.

### West Stockbridge

**Anderson & Sons' Shaker Tree** (413-232-7072; Main St., W. Stockbridge, MA 01266) Exquisite Shaker reproduction furniture, with quilts, herbs, and other wares. The craftsmanship is so highly regarded that the Andersons were entrusted with permission to measure the Shaker pieces in the noted Andrews' collection at the Metropolitan Museum of Art. The showroom is not always open; call ahead.

## Central County

### Hancock

**Hancock Union Store** (413-738-5072; Main St., P.O. Box 1009, Hancock, MA 01237) Fine reproductions of American period furniture—tables, chairs, sofas, and beds. Michael Boulay, cabinetmaker. Call for appointment.

LENOX

**Different Drummer's Kitchen** (413-637-0606; 568 Pittsfield–Lenox Rd., Lenox, MA 01240; Rte. 7) All manner of equipment and accessories for kitchen and table, from coffeepots to measuring spoons.

**Michael Charles Cabinetmakers** (413-637-3483; 53 Church St., Lenox, MA 01240) Fine handcrafted furniture in a variety of finishes, all beautiful in their stylish simplicity.

**Tassels** (413-637-2400; fax 413-637-1836; 36 Pittsfield–Lenox Rd., Lenox, MA 01240; at Brushwood Farm Shops, Rte. 7) Fine furniture and accessories in room settings in a variety of styles. A division of Designers Furniture Showcase, Ltd.

PITTSFIELD

**Haddad's Rug Company** (413-443-4747; 32 Bank Row, Pittsfield, MA 01201; in Park Square) Specialists in Oriental and Oriental-style rugs, new and antique, plus carpeting and other types of rugs.

**Homegoods** (413-236-6996; 676 Merrill Rd., Pittsfield, MA 01201) This is a huge discount emporium (a division of TJX), with everything for the home, including furniture on occasion.

**Paul Rich & Sons Home Furnishings** (413-443-6467, 800-723-7424; 242 North St., Pittsfield, MA 01201) A large and well-chosen selection of traditional, contemporary, and country furniture and accent pieces.

**Pittsfield Furniture Company** (413-499-1106; www.pittsfieldfurniture.com; 2 Brown St., Pittsfield, MA 01201) A move to the space formerly occupied by New England Furniture has given Pittsfield Furniture room to expand. Lots of affordable furniture for all style homes. Open late Thurs.

## North County

ADAMS

**Interior Alternative** (413-743-1986; 5 Hoosac St., Adams, MA 01220) A home furnishings center with seconds and discontinued famous-brand upholstery and curtain fabric, wallpaper, Oriental carpets, hooked rugs, area rugs, bedspreads, comforters, pillows. Custom sewing available on the second floor of this huge old mill.

NORTH ADAMS

**Berkshire Fabric & Wallpaper Outlet** (413-664-9514; www.berkshirefabricwallpaper.com; N. Adams Plaza, Rte. 8, 1679 Curran Highway, N. Adams, MA 01247) Featuring the largest selection of first-quality designer fabrics and wallpaper in the Berkshires, all at deeply discounted prices.

**International Outlet** (413-664-4580; 115 State St., N. Adams, MA 01247; at Western Gateway Heritage Park) A good source for imported crystal, glassware, dinnerware, kitchen utensils, wicker furniture, rugs, brass, table and kitchen linen, candles, pottery, cookware, and terra-cotta pots. They advertise "upscale goods at deeply discounted prices."

## Jewelry

For additional jewelry options, check the listings in "Antiques," "Gifts & Specialty Shops," and "Handcrafts."

**925 Silver** (413-644-6412; in the Barrington House next to Helsinki Café, Gt. Barrington) The owners advertise that this is the finest collection of silver jewelry in the world. They may be right!

**Berkshire Classic Leather and Silver** (413-637-0727; www.berkshireclassic.com; 74 Main St., Gt. Barrington, MA 01230) The emphasis is on leather goods and silver jewelry. They also carry some Judaica and gift items for both men and women.

**Heirlooms Classic Jewelry** (413-298-4436; www.heirloomsendure.com; P.O. Box 515, Stockbridge, MA 01262; in the Mews, off Main St.) A glittering treasure box of a shop, offering an international selection of elegant—and affordable—jewelry. Open daily 10 – 6.

**McTeigue and McClelland** (413-528-6263; 597 S. Main St., Gt. Barrington, MA 01230) This little gem in a tiny, renovated Victorian house emphasizes estate and consignment jewelry but also offers jewelry from prominent contemporary artists.

**R. W. Wise Goldsmiths** (413-637-1589; 81 Church St., Lenox, MA 01240) Richard Wise finds gemstones from all over the world—traveling recently in Brazil, Africa, and Tahiti—and offers them superbly crafted in contemporary fine art jewelry. Imaginative and unique combinations of gems and precious metals. Custom design service. Closed Mon. in winter.

**Sienna Gallery** (413-637-8386; 80 Main St., Lenox, MA 01240) A very contemporary décor provides the appropriate atmosphere for stunning and expensive jewelry from the most talented new designers. The owner's father is a well-known glass artist, and the artistic eye is very much in evidence here.

## Shopping Streets, Mews & Malls

Many of the shops described in this chapter are, happily, on Berkshire downtown Main Streets. There, real people actually walk along the sidewalks, go to the hardware store and post offices, get books at libraries, pick up groceries, run into friends, and stop for lunch or coffee or ice cream against a backdrop of mostly 19th-century civic architecture, highlighted by a few notable historic buildings. For beyond-the-downtown shopping experiences, short and usually scenic drives lead to clusters of destination shops, some in genuinely venerable buildings, others where the quaintness is of more recent vintage. And, yes, there are even some malls. Following is a roundup of where to find favorite shops and shopping settings. More detailed listings of many of the establishments in these centers may be found in relevant sections of chapters 4, 5, and 7—"Dining," "Arts & Pleasures," and "Outdoor Recreation."

### South County

**Southfield's Buggy Whip Factory** (Main St., Southfield; Rte. 272) Driving there from anywhere is a ride through classic New England scenery. The huge two-centuries-old building houses a large antiques center.

**Downtown Great Barrington** is a happening place, with a true Main Street atmosphere created by a lively combination of shops and boutiques, antiques stores, bookstores, an outstanding selection of eateries, a first-rate coffee place, and theaters (for movies, opera, and other performances). The action centers around Railroad Street and Main Street and takes in other side streets, too. Great Barrington hosts downtown food and music events

**Cultural Shopping**

Many Berkshire museums, and other institutions devoted to the arts and culture or to historical preservation, fund and publicize their operations with their own gift and book shops. They are excellent sources for unique Berkshire gifts, books about a wide range of historical subjects and the visual and performing arts, and fun and educational items for children. Institution members often get discounts at the shop.

**Berkshire Museum Shop** (413-443-7469; 39 South St., Pittsfield, MA 01201) An excellent array of items reflecting the scope of the museum's collections: books, cards, plates (including the reproduction Spode blue and white "Pittsfield" plate), and other home accessories, international crafts, and jewelry. There is a treasure trove of small and creative items for children, from the artistic to the scientific, reflecting the museum's natural-history collection. Shop staff, mostly volunteers, are helpful and personable.

**The Museum Store at the Clark Art Institute** (413-458-9545; www.clarkart.edu; 225 South St., Williamstown, MA 01267) features items based on the Clark's collection and those of museums and art galleries around the world: cards, posters, and prints, matted and framed; fine art books; jewelry; and great toys, from basic to upscale. The selection of books has been greatly enlarged in the past few years to include an extensive collection of art books and regional titles.

**Ex Libris: The Lenox Library Shop** (413-637-0197; 18 Main St., Lenox, MA 01240) This pocket-sized shop offers cards, postcards, toys, T-shirts, bookplates, bookmarks, games, tote bags, sealing wax, and various Berkshire-related items.

**Hancock Shaker Village Shop** (413-443-0188; www.hancockshakervillage.org; Rte. 20, Pittsfield, MA 01201) The spacious gift shop in the new visitors center offers books, clocks, Shaker reproduction furniture, and other items, in kits or assembled—even the Shaker cloak. Prints of drawings of the Hancock Shaker community and of Shaker "spirit drawings," and wonderful children's toys and kits, too.

**The Norman Rockwell Museum** (413-298-4100; www.nrm.org; Rte. 183, Stockbridge, MA 01262) A well-designed center for books, prints, and cards; the children's section has books and toys and art-related things to do. There are limited-edition artist's proofs signed by Rockwell and other items related to current exhibits and programs.

Additional cultural shopping options include the shop at the **Massachusetts Audubon Sanctuary,** Pleasant Valley; **Chesterwood,** particularly for their selection of National Trust publications; **Tanglewood**'s gift shop, with lots of Tanglewood-logo wearables and other items; the **Arrowhead Museum** shop, with books about Melville and county history, and cards and gifts; the **Garden Gift Shop** at the **Berkshire Botanical Garden**; the **Mount** (former home of Edith Wharton and current home of **Shakespeare & Co.**); **Williams College Museum of Art**; **MASS MoCA;** the **Berkshire Theater Festival;** and even the **Berkshire Scenic Railway Museum** (books, toys, T-shirts).

throughout the year. There is a fabulous Farmer's Market each Saturday from May to the end of the growing season.

**Great Barrington**'s **Jenifer House Commons** (Rte. 7, Stockbridge Rd.) is just north of the town center. This cluster of multilevel barns and buildings—some old and some new—houses an extensive group of antiques dealers' wares and a restaurant/brewery. Do lunch there or nearby. Open daily.

**Main Street, Stockbridge** still looks like—and is—Norman Rockwell territory, even though the Rockwell Museum has moved (but not far; see chapter 5, "Arts & Pleasures"). The welcoming expanse of the Red Lion Inn shares the scene with the gracious library, an excellent market, and several stores. Connected to Main Street is the **Mews,** a cozy cul-de-sac of shops offering clothes, jewelry, and gifts. Many Stockbridge shops offer Rockwelliana in one form or another, from T-shirts to signed prints. Also around the corner from Main Street is Elm Street, with more shops, eateries, and the post office. Note: Main Street and the Mews can seem overrun during high-season weekends; if possible, weekday visits may be better.

A side trip to the small downtown of **West Stockbridge** will reward with several galleries, good restaurants and cafés, and antiques—not to mention a hardware store and a shop devoted to flavoring extracts. The gallery scene offers outdoor sculptures on display, handcrafted jewelry, mobiles, stained glass, and reproduction Shaker furniture, and many other options for contemporary art and craftswork. A vintage depot houses a café and studios; a Shaker mill building is home to antiques. A small concentration of excellent restaurants, including a sophisticated Italian take-out food store, is sure to please.

A relatively new offering on the Berkshire shopping scene is **Lee**'s **Prime Outlets.** These shops are all stocked with discounted (and, some say, last year's) merchandise. Shoes, clothing, leather goods, cards, gourmet food, and watches are all available from top-of-the-line manufacturers to those more trendy and inexpensive. Conveniently located near Exit 2 of MassPike, the shopping village's visibility attracts out-of-town shoppers as well as locals. Local controversy over the design notwithstanding, it is an attractive, well-landscaped area. Shops include **Coach, Liz Claiborne, Jones New York, Tommy Hilfiger, Ralph Lauren, Harry & David, Mikasa, Gap,** and **Carter's** among others.

## Central County

**Downtown Lenox** still maintains a "real" downtown flavor, though the boutique and gallery contingent seems to be in the ascendancy. The appealing variety of architecture—neoclassic and Victorian-cottage predominate—is home to inns and taverns, restaurants, an exceptional library and bookstore, and the aforementioned boutiques and galleries. A number of clothing shops, mostly for women, cover the style territory from fine to funky, from classic to casual; art and handcrafts galleries offer Berkshire scenes and world-renowned jewelry and other creations.

**Downtown Pittsfield** was once the commercial and civic hub of the Berkshires, and though the glory of its main thoroughfare, North Street, has somewhat faded, it still hosts a number of services and shops. The downtown area includes several large churches and buildings that will interest the architecture buff, plus the **Berkshire Museum** and the **Berkshire Athenaeum** (the public library). Besides, occasionally in the summer a free concert downtown is offered.

**Berkshire Crossing Mall** is the newest addition to the mall scene in the Berkshires. Located off Route 9 between **Pittsfield** and **Dalton**, it has a **Barnes & Noble** store, a **Staples**, a **Pier One**, and the ubiquitous **Home Depot** and **Wal-Mart** along with crafts, supermarket, and clothing stores.

**Berkshire Mall** in **Lanesborough** can supply basic mall needs, with a multiscreen cinema complex, clothing, and shoe stores—among them **Filene's** and **Old Navy**—a food court and sit-down restaurants, a bookstore, and so forth.

## North County

**Spring Street** and **Water Street** in **Williamstown** roughly parallel to each other and are across from the main Williams College campus. Both easily walkable, they offer handcrafts, clothing, books, tapes and CDs, places to eat, antiques and accessories, sports gear, and all the Williams memorabilia the most purple Williams College shopper could ever need.

## Outside the County

A recommended destination just outside the county is **Chatham, New York.** Main Street shops include the **Dakota** for high-end clothes; the **Chatham Bookstore**; **American Pie**, a contemporary general store; the **Handcrafters** for fine handcrafted gift items as well as art supplies; and the **Warm Ewe** for knitting supplies.

# 9

# Information

## *Practical Matters*

**We** offer here a small encyclopedia of useful information to help facilitate everyday life for residents and visitors in the Berkshires.

### Ambulance, Fire, Police

The general emergency number for all Berkshire communities is **911.** The county-wide set of emergency numbers is:

| | |
|---|---|
| **Ambulance, Fire, Police** | 911 |
| **Poison Control** | 800-222-1222 |
| **Rape Crisis Hotline** (Central County) | 413-443-0089/413-663-7459 |

### Area Codes & Town Halls

#### Area Codes

The area code for all of Berkshire County is **413.** Area codes for adjacent counties are as follows:

**Massachusetts**
Franklin (most towns), Hampshire, and Hampden counties: **413.**

**Connecticut**
Litchfield County: **860.**

**New York**
Columbia and Rensselaer counties: **518.**

**Vermont**
All Vermont: **802.**

#### Town Halls

All Berkshire communities have town or city halls as the seats of local government. Most townships are governed by boards of selectmen; several also have town managers. For general information, call the town offices at the following numbers or write to the Town Clerk, c/o Town Hall.

*The P.O. in full bloom, Williamstown* Lauren R. Stevens

| TOWN | ZIP CODE | TOWN HALL OFFICE |
|---|---|---|
| Adams | 01220 | 413-743-8320 |
| Alford | 01230 | 413-528-4536 |
| Ashley Falls | 01222 | 413-229-8752 (Sheffield) |
| Becket | 01223 | 413-623-8934 |
| Cheshire | 01225 | 413-743-1690 |
| Clarksburg | 01247 | 413-663-5282 |
| Dalton | 01226 | 413-684-6111 |
| Egremont | 01258 | 413-528-0182 |
| Florida | 01247 | 413-662-2448 |
| Glendale | 01229 | 413-298-4714 (Stockbridge) |
| Gt. Barrington | 01230 | 413-528-3140 |
| Hancock | 01237 | 413-738-5225 |
| Hinsdale | 01235 | 413-655-2301 |
| Housatonic | 01236 | 413-528-3140 (Gt. Barrington) |
| Lanesborough | 01237 | 413-442-1167 |
| Lee | 01238 | 413-243-5505 |
| Lenox | 01240 | 413-637-5506 |
| Lenoxdale | 01242 | 413-637-5506 (Lenox) |
| Middlefield | 01243 | 413-623-8934 (Becket) |

| | | |
|---|---|---|
| Mill River | 01244 | 413-229-8116 (New Marlborough) |
| Monterey | 01245 | 413-528-1443 |
| Mt. Washington | 01258 | 413-528-2839 |
| New Ashford | 01267 | 413-458-5461 |
| New Marlborough | 01244 | 413-229-8116 |
| N. Adams | 01247 | 413-662-3011 |
| N. Egremont | 01252 | 413-528-0182 (Egremont) |
| Otis | 01253 | 413-269-0101 |
| Peru | 01235 | 413-655-8027 |
| Pittsfield | 01201; 01202 (P.O. Boxes) | 413-499-9361 |
| Richmond | 01254 | 413-698-3882 |
| Sandisfield | 01255 | 413-258-4771 |
| Savoy | 01256 | 413-743-4290 |
| Sheffield | 01257 | 413-229-8752 |
| S. Egremont | 01258 | 413-528-0182 (Egremont) |
| S. Lee | 01260 | 413-243-5505 (Lee) |
| Southfield | 01259 | 413-229-8116 (New Marlborough) |
| Stockbridge | 01262 | 413-298-4714 |
| Tyringham | 01264 | 413-243-1749 |
| Washington | 01223 | 413-623-8878 |
| W. Stockbridge | 01266 | 413-232-0300 |
| Williamstown | 01267 | 413-458-9341 |
| Windsor | 01270 | 413-684-3811 |

*Waiting for a bus near the Lee information booth* Judith Monachina

## BANKS

Several Berkshire County banks are linked electronically to banking systems elsewhere in the United States. Visitors may find these options helpful—especially if they need extra cash or traveler's checks.

**Adams Co-operative Bank** 93 Park St., Adams, 413-743-0001; 545 S. Main St., Lanesborough, 413-443-4070; 31 Eagle St., N. Adams, 413-664-4571.

**Banknorth Massachusetts** 800-322-3264 (connecting all branches). **Offices:** 10 Center St., Adams, 413-743-3000; 431 Main St., Dalton, 413-684-2466; 271 Main St., Gt. Barrington, 413-528-2323; 90 Main St., N. Adams, 413-663-6561; 99 West St,. Pittsfield, 413-499-3000; 200 Elm St., Pittsfield, 413-499-7850; 600 Merrill St., Pittsfield, 413-449-7687; 1 Dan Fox Dr., Pittsfield, 413-499-0551; 57 Spring St., Williamstown, 413-458-8321.

**Berkshire Bank** 413-443-5601, 800-773-5601 (connecting all branches). **Pittsfield offices:** 66 Allen St., 413-236-3160; 43 East St., 413-499-0150; Allendale Shopping Center, 413-499-1068; 165 Elm St., 413-447-1880; 66 West St., 413-445-8365. **Great Barrington branches:** 244 Main St., 413-644-3520; 255 Stockbridge Rd., 413-528-1664. **Other offices:** 1 Park St., Lee, 413-243-1800; 37 Main St., N. Adams, 413-664-4061; 103 N. Main St., Sheffield, 413-229-8516; 32 Main St., Stockbridge, 413-298-5526; 2 Depot St., W. Stockbridge, 413-232-8542.

**Citizens Bank,** Pittsfield: 600 Merrill Rd., 413-442-0136; 1 Dan Fox Dr., 413-442-0848; 555 Hubbard Ave., 413-443-2351.

**Greylock Credit Union,** 150 West St., Pittsfield, 413-236-4000. **Other Pittsfield offices:** 75 Kellogg, 413-443-5114; 660 Merrill Rd., 413-445-5555. **Offices outside Pittsfield:** 2 Park St., Adams, 413-743-7333; 312 Main St., Gt. Barrington, 413-528-4567; 250 Stockbridge Rd., Gt. Barrington, 413-664-9234; 47 Main St., Lee, 413-243-2121; 66 Main St., N. Adams, 413-664-4477.

**Hoosac Bank** 93 Main St, N. Adams, 413-663-5353; 269 Main St., Williamstown, 413-458-9503.

**Lee Bank** 75 Park St., Lee, 413-243-2196; Elm St., Stockbridge, 413-298-3611; 279 Main St., Gt. Barrington, 413-528-5531.

**Legacy Banks** 800-292-6634, 413-443-4421 (connecting all branches). **Pittsfield offices:** 99 North St.; 480 W. Housatonic St.; 734 Williams St.; 609 Merrill Rd. **Lenox offices:** 25 Main St.; 2 Holmes Rd. **Other offices:** 700 Main St., Gt. Barrington; 76 Park St., Lee; 102 Main St., N. Adams; 30 E. Otis Rd., Otis.

**Pittsfield Co-operative Bank** 888-447-7314. **Pittsfield offices:** 70 South St., 413-447-7314; 110 Dalton Ave., 413-395-9626. **Other offices:** 448 Main St., Dalton, 413-684-1551; 325 Main St., Gt. Barrington, 413-528-2840.

**Salisbury Bank & Trust** 51 Main St., Egremont, 413-528-5100.

**South Adams Savings Bank** 2 Center St., Adams, 413-743-0040; State Rd., Cheshire, 413-743-0270; 273 Main St., Williamstown, 413-458-2141.

**Williamstown Savings Bank** 795 Main St., Williamstown, 413-458-8191.

## BIBLIOGRAPHY

Here are two lists of books about the Berkshires, many of which we used in researching this book.

"Available Titles" shows books obtainable either through Berkshire bookshops, bookstores elsewhere, or from the publishers. For information on Berkshire booksellers, see "Books" in chapter 8, "Shopping."

"Harder to Find" suggests a wealth of other reading in publications no longer in print. Some of the more rarefied material on this list does not circulate outside of libraries, and usage may be restricted to those with professional credentials. Several popular items here will especially interest history buffs. The best sources for book borrowing are described under "Libraries" in chapter 5, "Arts & Pleasures."

### Available Titles

#### COOKBOOKS

Chase, Suzi Forbes. *The New Red Lion Inn Cookbook.* Woodstock, VT: The Countryman Press, 2000. 272 pp., photos, $23.95.

Cook, Janey, ed. *Berkshire Victuals.* Stockbridge, MA: Berkshire County Historical Society, 1993. 208 pages, illus., $19.95. Historical and contemporary recipes.

Hopley, Claire. *New England Cooking: Seasons & Celebrations.* Woodstock, VT: The Countryman Press, 2002. 272 pp., photos, $24.95.

Levitt, Atma Jo Ann. *The Kripalu Cookbook.* Woodstock, VT: The Countryman Press. 448 pp., $16.95. Recipes featured at the Kripalu Center in Lenox, tailored for home use.

Vanderstigchel, Armand, and Robert E. Birkel Jr. *Adirondack Cuisine.* Woodstock, VT: The Countryman Press, 2002. 292 pp., photos, $24.95. Recipes from the region adjacent to—and easily accessible from—the Berkshires.

Williamstown Theatre Festival. *As You Like It.* Williamstown, MA: Williamstown Theatre Festival Guild, 1993. 222 pp., illus, $15.00. Recipes from the festival's stars, directors, writers, and associates.

#### LITERARY WORKS

*The Berkshire Review.* Pittsfield, MA: The Berkshire Writers Room. Literary annual devoted to poetry, fiction, plays, and essays by Berkshire authors.

Howard, Walter. *Sisyphus in the Hayfield: Views of a Berkshire Farmer.* Tyringham, MA: Cobble Press, 1988. 128 pp., photos, $14.00.

Melville, Herman. *Great Short Works of Herman Melville.* New York, NY: Harper & Row, 1969. 507 pp., bibliog., $18.50.

Metcalf, Paul, ed. *October Mountain: An Anthology of Berkshire Writers.* Williamstown, MA: Mountain Press, 1992. 163 pp., $11.95.

Nunley, Richard, ed. *The Berkshire Reader.* Woodstock, VT: The Countryman Press. 544 pp., illus., $29.95.

Wharton, Edith. *A Backward Glance.* New York, NY: Charles Scribner's Sons, 1985 reprint. 379 pp., index, $13.95.

—. *Ethan Frome.* New York, NY: Scribner's, 1988 reprint. $5.95.

—. *Summer.* New York, NY: Scribner's, 1988 reprint. $10.00.

*A winter scene in Richmond* Judith Monachina

## LOCAL HISTORIES

Babcock, Richard, and Lauren R. Stevens. *Old Barns in the New World.* Woodstock, VT: The Countryman Press, 1996. 192 pp., photos, $21.95.

Burns, Deborah E. *Shaker Cities of Peace, Love, and Union: A History of the Hancock Bishopric.* Hanover, NH: University Press of New England, 1993. 246 pp., $45; $19.95 pap.

Cahill, Timothy, Mae G. Banner, Richard Nunley, and Fred Sokol. *Muses in Arcadia: Cultural Life in the Berkshires.* Woodstock, VT: The Countryman Press, 2000. 272 pp., illus. $19.95.

Chapman, Gerard. *Eminent Berkshire Women*. Gt. Barrington, MA: Attic Revivals Press, 1988. 32 pp., $5.00.

—. *Great Barrington.* Gt. Barrington, MA: Gt. Barrington Historic Society, 1999. illus. $49.95.

Drew, Bernard A. *Berkshire Further Off the Trail*. Gt. Barrington, MA: Attic Revivals Press, 1992. 56 pp., illus., $7.50.

—. *A History of Notchview Reservation: The Arthur D. Budd Estate in Windsor, Massachusetts*. Gt. Barrington, MA: Attic Revivals Press, 1986. 48 pp., illus., maps, $5.00.

—. *History of The Mahaiwe Theatre in Great Barrington, Massachusetts*. Gt. Barrington, MA: Attic Revivals Press, 1989. 48 pp., illus., $5.00.

—. *Spanning Berkshire Waterways*. Gt. Barrington, MA: Attic Revivals Press, 1990. 32 pp., photos, maps, $5.00.

—. *William Cullen Bryant's "A Border Tradition."* Gt. Barrington, MA: Attic Revivals Press, 1988. 32 pp., bibliog., $6.50.

Drew, Bernard A., and Donna M. Drew. *Mapping the Berkshires*. Gt. Barrington, MA: Attic Revivals Press, 1985. 48 pp., illus. maps, $5.00.

Lee, Laura. *Arlo, Alice & Anglicans: The Lives of a New England Church*. Woodstock, VT: The Countryman Press, 2000. 240 pp., illus., $16.95.

Miller, Amy Bess. *Hancock Shaker Village/The City of Peace: An Effort to Restore a Vision 1960–1985*. Hancock, MA: Hancock Shaker Village, 1984. 170 pp., illus., photos, appendices, bibliog., index, $19.95.

Murray, Stuart, and James McCabe. *Norman Rockwell's Four Freedoms*. Woodstock, VT: The Countryman Press, 1993. 176 pp., illus., $14.95.

Owens, Carole. *The Berkshire Cottages: A Vanishing Era*. Stockbridge, MA: Cottage Press, 1984. 240 pp., photos, illus., index, $29.95.

Pincus, Andrew L. *Scenes from Tanglewood*. Boston, MA: Northeastern University Press, 1989. 287 pp., photos, $14.95.

*A History of the Red Lion Inn in Stockbridge, Massachusetts*. Stockbridge, MA: Red Lion Inn, 1987. 54 pp., illus., $12.00.

*The Stockbridge Story: 1739–1989*. Stockbridge, MA: Town of Stockbridge, 1989. 209 pp., illus., photos, index, $25.00.

## PHOTOGRAPHIC STUDIES

Bazan, John. *Rails Across the Berkshire Hills. Railroad Photography, 1890–1984*. Pittsfield, MA: The Author, 1984. Photos, $9.95.

Chefetz, Sheila. *Antiques for the Table*. New York, NY: Viking-Penguin, 1993. 232 pp., 275 color photos, bibliog., Berkshire resource directory, index. Many photographs of Berkshire summer cottages.

Gilder, Cornelia Brooke. *Views of the Valley: Tyringham 1739–1989*. Tyringham, MA: The Hopbrook Community Club, 1989. 142 pp., photos, $15.

Resch, Tyler, ed. *Images of America: Bill Tague's Berkshires*. Dover, NH: Arcadia Publishing, 1996. 128 pp., map, photos, $16.99. A Berkshire photographer's work from the 1950s to the 1980s.

—. *Images of America: Bill Tague's Berkshires*, Vol. II. Dover, NH: Arcadia Publishing, 1998. 128 pp., photos, $16.95.

Scott, Walter. *The Norman Rockwell Bicycle Tours of Stockbridge*. Stockbridge, MA: SnO Publications, 1980. 32 postcards, $10.95.

## RECREATION & NATURE

*A Canoe Guide to the Housatonic River, Berkshire County*. Pittsfield, MA: Berkshire County Regional Planning Commission. Illus., maps. Updated in 1994.

*Appalachian Trail Guide to Massachusetts-Connecticut*. Harpers Ferry, WV: Appalachian Trail Conference, 1990. 189 pp., maps, $18.95.

Cuyler, Lewis C. *Bike Rides in the Berkshire Hills*. Revised and updated edition. Woodstock, VT: The Countryman Press, 1995. 200 pp., illus., maps, $9.95.

Laubach, Rene. *A Guide to Natural Places in the Berkshire Hills*. Second edition. Woodstock, VT: The Countryman Press, 1997. 288 pp., illus., maps, $17.95.

Lyon, Steve. *Bicyclist's Guide to the Southern Berkshires*. Lenox, MA: Freewheel Publications, 1993. 256 pp., pap., $16.95.

Stevens, Lauren R. *Hikes & Walks in the Berkshire Hills*. Third edition. Woodstock, VT: The Countryman Press, 2004. 236 pp., maps, $14.95.

Strauch, Joseph G., Jr. *Wildflowers of the Berkshire & Taconic Hills.* Woodstock, VT: The Countryman Press, 1995. 160 pp., maps, illus., $12.95.

**TRAVEL**

*The Berkshire Hills: A WPA Guide*, with a new foreword by Roger Linscott. Boston, MA: Northeastern University Press, 1987. 390 pp., illus., photos, maps, lore, history, $14.95.

Bryan, Clark, W. *The Book of Berkshire*. N. Egremont, MA: Past Perfect Books, 1993 reprint. 304 pp., engravings, index, large color map of county, $24.95. A splendid reprint of the first guide to the Berkshires.

Davenport, John. *Berkshire-Bennington Locator*. Madison, WI: First Impressions, 1988. 112 pp., maps, $10.95.

*The River Walk in Gt. Barrington is evidence of a growing awareness of the natural beauty of the Housatonic River. A River Walk garden is devoted to W. E. B. DuBois, Gt. Barrington native son.*

Judith Monachina

Whitman, Herbert S. *Exploring the Berkshires*. New York, NY: Hippocrene, 1991. 240 pp., illus., $9.95.

## Harder to Find

Annin, Katherine Huntington. *Richmond, Massachusetts: The Story of a Berkshire Town and Its People, 1765–1965*. Richmond, MA: Richmond Civic Association, 1964. 214 pp., photos, illus., index. Only complete, readable history of town.

Birdsall, Richard. *Berkshire County, A Cultural History*. New York, NY: Greenwood Press, 1978 reprint. 401 pp., notes, bibliog., index. Only cultural study of region; emphasis on first half of the 19th century. Chapters cover development of law, newspapers, education, religion. Special attention to the literary heritage.

Bittman, Sam, and Steven A. Satullo, eds. *Berkshire: Seasons of Celebration*. Pittsfield, MA: Either/Or Press, 1982. 112 pp., photos.

Boltwood, Edward. *The History of Pittsfield, Massachusetts from the Year 1876 to the Year 1916*. Pittsfield, MA: The City, 1916. Covers history of most important county communities to early 20th century.

Brooks, Robert R. R., ed. *Williamstown: The First Two Hundred Years*. Williamstown, MA: The Town, 1953. 458 pp., 69 illus. A model of its kind.

Bulkley, Morgan. *Mountain Farm: Poems From the Berkshire Hills*. Chester, MA: Hollow Springs Press, 1984. 95 pp., illus.

*Collections of the Berkshire Historical and Scientific Society*. Pittsfield, MA: Sun Printing Co., 1892–1899. Papers on historical topics read at society meetings. Often composed by local authorities, subjects range from Berkshire geology to glass manufacture in Berkshire. Often unique and usually reliable.

Burns, Deborah, E., and Lauren R. Stevens. *Most Excellent Majesty: A History of Mount Greylock*. Lee, MA: Berkshire County Land Trust and Conservation Fund, 1988. 128 pp., photos.

Consolati, Florence. *See All the People: Or, Life in Lee*. Lee, MA: The Author, 1978. 442 pp., photos, bibliog., index. Colorful, quaint history of the town and its citizens.

Coxey, Willard D. *Ghosts of Old Berkshire*. Gt. Barrington, MA: The Berkshire Courier, 1934. Legends and folktales of Berkshire people and places.

Drew, Bernard A. *Berkshire Between Covers: A Literary History*. Gt. Barrington, MA: Attic Revivals Press, 1985. 32 pp., illus., bibliog. Brief biographical sketches of deceased fiction writers with significant connections to the Berkshires.

—. *Berkshire Off the Trail*. Gt. Barrington, MA: Attic Revival Press, 1982. 96 pp., illus., index. Informal history of less traditional subjects.

Emblidge, David, ed. *The Third Berkshire Anthology: A Collection of Literature and Art*. Lenox, MA: Berkshire Writers, Inc., 1982. 185 pp., illus.

Field, Stephen, ed. *A History of the County of Berkshire, Massachusetts*. Pittsfield, MA: Samuel W. Bush, 1829. Perhaps the first history of the Berkshires, sponsored by the Berkshire Association of Congregational Ministers. A general history of the county, followed by accounts of individual towns, each written by its minister.

Jones, Electa F. *Stockbridge, Past and Present: Or, Records of an Old Mission Station*. Springfield, MA: Samuel Bowles & Co., 1854. History of Indian mission and Stockbridge Indians.

Kupferberg, Herbert. *Tanglewood*. New York, NY: McGraw-Hill, 1976. 280 pp., photos, bibliog., index. Thorough history of the Berkshire Music Festival.

Lewis, Joseph W. *Berkshire Men of Worth*. 4 vols. Scrapbook of newspaper articles. From 1933 until well after Lewis's death in 1938, over 300 columns on Berkshire notables were published in the *Berkshire Evening Eagle*. Series featured penetrating biographical sketches of men whom Lewis regarded as important historical figures. Perhaps the most comprehensive biographical treatment of historical Berkshire figures.

Oakes, Donald, ed. *A Pride of Palaces: Lenox Summer Cottages, 1883–1933*. Lenox, MA: Lenox Library, 1981. 83 pp., illus., photos.

Perry, Arthur L. *Origins in Williamstown*. New York, NY: Charles Scribner's Sons, 1896. Detailed, well-researched history of early Williamstown and other segments of northern Berkshire.

Preiss, Lillian E. *Sheffield, Frontier Town*. Sheffield, MA: Sheffield Bicentennial Comm., 1976. 188 pp., photos, illus., bibliog., index. Good, traditional town history.

Resch, Tyler, ed. *Berkshire, The First Three Hundred Years 1676–1976*. Pittsfield, MA: Eagle Pub. Co., 1976. 163 pp., photos, illus., maps, bibliog., index. Photographs and illustrations of significant and interesting historical events and people, with concise captions.

Sedgwick, Sarah Cabot, and Christina Sedgwick Marquand. *Stockbridge, 1739–1939: A Chronicle*. Stockbridge, MA: The Authors, 1939. 306 pp., photos, illus., bibliog. Popular, readable history.

Smith, J. E. A., ed. *History of Berkshire County, Massachusetts, With Biographical Sketches of Its Prominent Men*. 2 vols. New York, NY: J. B. Beers & Co., 1885. Wide-ranging history covering every aspect of Berkshire life. Nine chapters on individual towns. Most comprehensive, reliable history of the first 200 years of Berkshire development.

—. *The History of Pittsfield (Berkshire County), Massachusetts, From the Year 1734 to the Year 1800*. Boston, MA: Lee, Shepard, 1869. *The History of Pittsfield (Berkshire County), Massachusetts, From the Year 1800 to the Year 1876*. Springfield, MA: C.W. Bryan & Co., 1876. The most detailed, thorough town histories for the county. Smith had access to much material since lost; covers surrounding communities as well.

Taylor, Charles J. *History of Great Barrington (Berkshire), Massachusetts 1676–1882. Part II, Extension 1882–1922* by George Edwin MacLean. Gt. Barrington, MA, 1928. Detailed, accurate history of town, particularly the Taylor segment.

Wood, David H. *Lenox, Massachusetts Shire Town*. Lenox, MA, 1968. Similar to Sedgwick history of Stockbridge but more detailed.

## Climate & Weather Reports

### Climate

How the Berkshire climate strikes us depends on what we're used to. People visiting from outside the region may be helped by the following information.

In general, while summers are blessedly mild due to the elevation of the Berkshire Hills, winters can be cold and snowy with tricky driving conditions. Of course, what someone who doesn't ski finds annoying in a New England winter greases the skis for another. Summer visitors should remember that nights can be cool; bring sweaters. And those in search of great snow should note that spring comes to South County well before it does up north and up higher.

### Temperature & Precipitation

#### AVERAGE TEMPERATURE

| | |
|---|---|
| October | 48.4° F |
| January | 20.4° |
| April | 43.4° |
| July | 68.3° |

#### AVERAGE ANNUAL TOTAL PRECIPITATION

| | |
|---|---|
| Rainfall plus water content of snow | 44.15" |
| Snow | 75.7" |

For people who are really into statistics or are interested for business or investment purposes, the source for this information and a great deal more, *The Berkshire County Data Book*, is available (for $100) from the Berkshire County Regional Planning Commission (413-442-1521; Dunham Mall, Pittsfield, MA 01201).

### Weather Reports

| | |
|---|---|
| Great Barrington | 413-528-1118 |
| Pittsfield | 413-499-2627 |
| North Adams | 413-663-6264 |

## Guided Tours

For those wanting to be bused directly to Berkshire's high spots by an informed guide, there are hosts of possibilities, some based here in the hills, some coming from New York and Boston. From the big cities, there are fall-foliage tours, Tanglewood tours, and ski tours, all of which provide transport, tickets, meals, and lodging plus background on the sites. For an individual, these tours offer a taste of the area's delights in a perfectly packaged form. For groups, the tours turn a possible logistical nightmare into a fun-filled holiday.

In New York City or Boston, a travel agent may be helpful in choosing the right tour. The best of the commercial tour companies belong to the National Tour Association. The best of the charter bus companies belong to the American Bus Association. Here are a few of the most experienced Berkshire guided-tour companies operating from New York City and Boston.

### New York City

**Parker Tours:** 516-349-0575, 800-833-9600; 255 Executive Dr., Plainview, NY 11803.

**Tauck Tours:** 203-226-6911, 800-468-2825; 276 Post Rd. W., Westport, CT 06880.

### Boston

**Collette Tours:** 401-728-3805, 800-752-2655 (in New England, exc. Maine), 800-832-4656; 162 Middle St., Pawtucket, RI 02860.

### Within the Berkshires

Within Berkshire, there are also a number of guided-tour options. For something relatively brief and informal, a local cab driver can usually be persuaded to drive around, adding colorful histories that only a cabbie might know. For more organized, detailed tours, consider the following:

**Berkshire Canoe Tours** (413-442-2789) Hilary Bashara provides canoes and offers day and evening guided tours of the Housatonic River.

**Berkshire Tour Company** (413-443-5778; 86 Sampson Pkwy., Pittsfield, MA 01201) Berkshire native Nancy C. Hickey provides a wide range of tour services, including group tours of Berkshire County sites (a favorite is the Berkshire Cottages tour), plus walking tours of the Main Streets of Stockbridge, Lenox, and Williamstown. She also provides customized tours, including lunch or dinner at local restaurants, excursions to Tanglewood and other music and theater festivals, and combinations of tours for individuals or any size group. Phone for prices and schedules.

**Greylock Discovery Tours** (413-637-4442; www.greylockdiscoverytours.com; P.O. Box 2231, Lenox, MA 01240) See "Walking, Hiking, Camping, X-C Skiing" in chapter 7, "Outdoor Recreation."

## Services for the Disabled

Although Berkshire is a region with lots of rough terrain, the disabled will find access quite easy to most cultural sites and events, to many lodgings and restaurants, and to most shops. In chapter 3, "Lodging," we specify those places where we know handicapped access is feasible. Elsewhere, to confirm the situation, use the phone numbers we provide to get information.

**The Berkshire Visitors Bureau** (800-237-5747; www.berkshires.org; 3 Hoosac St., Adams, MA 01220) publishes an annual guide listing many Berkshire services and attractions, in many cases specifying access to the disabled. The *AAA Tour Guide,* available through **AAA Berkshire County** (413-445-5635; 703 W. Housatonic St., Pittsfield, MA 01201) also designates restaurants, lodging, etc. with universal access.

As for transportation, the **Berkshire Regional Transit Authority** (413-499-2782, or in county 800-292-2782) runs the public bus system throughout the major towns in the county and has buses equipped with wheelchair lifts. See "Getting Around the Berkshires" in chapter 2, "Transportation," for more information.

## HOSPITALS

GREAT BARRINGTON

**Fairview Hospital:** 413-528-0790; 29 Lewis Ave.

PITTSFIELD

**Berkshire Medical Center:** 413-447-2000; 725 North St.

**BMC Hillcrest Campus:** 413-443-4761; 165 Tor Ct.

NORTH ADAMS

**North Adams Regional Hospital:** 413-664-5000; Hospital Ave.

## LATE-NIGHT FOOD & FUEL

**Cumberland Farms** (food and fuel) Open all night: 70 Ashland St., N. Adams, 413-662-2721; 885 Dalton Ave., Pittsfield, 413-496-9774; 154 First St., Pittsfield, 413-443-4478; 707 Main St., Dalton, 413-684-1465.

**Dakota Restaurant** (food) Open till 11 PM, Fri.–Sat.: Pittsfield–Lenox Rd., Pittsfield, 413-499-7900.

**Dunkin' Donuts** (food) Open all night: 5 Union St., N. Adams, 413-662-2274; 18 First St., Pittsfield, 413-499-0371; 200 Housatonic St., Lee, 413-243-1676; open till midnight Mon.–Fri., 1 AM Sat.–Sun.: 480 W. Housatonic St., Pittsfield.

**Jimmy's** (food) Open till midnight Fri.–Sat.: 114 W. Housatonic St., Pittsfield, 413-499-1288.

**Lee Sunoco** (fuel) Pumps open all night: 15 Park St., Lee, 413-243-4356.

**Luau Hale** (food) Open till midnight Fri.–Sat.: Pittsfield–Lenox Rd., Lenox, 413-443-4745.

**O'Connell Convenience Plus** (food and fuel) Open all night: 84 Tyler St., Pittsfield, 413-499-1741; 241 Main St., Lee, 413-243-2399; open till midnight Mon.–Fri., 1 AM Sat.–Sun.: 480 W. Housatonic St., Pittsfield; 413-499-3675; open till 11 PM: South St., Stockbridge, 413-298-4036.

**P. J.'s Convenience Store** (food) Open till 11:30 PM Mon.–Sat.: 139 S. Main, Sheffield, 413-229-6610

**Papa Joe's Ristorante & Pizzeria** (food) Open till 11 PM Fri.–Sat.: 107 Newell St., Pittsfield, 413-499-2151.

**Price Chopper Supermarkets** (food) Open all night Mon.–Fri., Sat. till midnight: 121 Pittsfield Rd., Rte. 7, Lenox, 413-443-5449; open till midnight Mon.–Sat., till 7 PM, Sun:

300 Stockbridge Rd., Rte. 7, Gt. Barrington, 413-528-9262, and 88 W. Park St., Lee, 413-243-2238.

**Stop & Shop Supermarket** (food) Open all night Mon.–Fri.; Sat. till midnight: 600 Merrill Rd., Pittsfield, 413-499-0745.

## MEDIA

### Newspapers

*The Advocate* (413-664-6900; American Legion Dr., N. Adams, MA 01247; Thursday) Readable freebie, well-researched articles, mostly on community-related topics, for Berkshire and southwestern Vermont.

*The Berkshire Eagle* (413-447-7311; 75 S. Church St., Pittsfield, MA 01201; daily) The county's newspaper of record, 7 days, a Pulitzer Prize–winning publication with world, national, state, and local news, plus features and comics (*Doonsbury*). Thursdays for half the year the *Eagle* also publishes *Berkshires Week*, a supplementary magazine-in-newsprint containing a calendar of events and lots of ads from local dining and entertainment places.

*Berkshire Living* (413-528-3600; 47 Railroad St., Gt. Barrington, MA 01230; nine issues per year) Glossy, full-color regional lifestyle and culture magazine featuring people, places, and things to do in the Berkshires, available on newsstands or by subscription.

*Berkshire Penny Saver* (413-243-2341; 14 Park Pl., Box 300, Lee, MA 01238; Tuesday) Central County's free shopping guide, including classifieds, TV listings, nightlife, comprehensive business service listings.

*The Berkshire Record* (413-528-5380; 21 Elm St., Gt. Barrington, MA 01230; weekly) Southern Berkshire weekly features current affairs and articles of historic note.

*Berkshire Trade & Commerce* (413-447-7700; 137 North St., Pittsfield, MA 01201; monthly) This freebie is Berkshire's answer to the *Wall Street Journal*. Lively up-to-date news of Berkshire business doings.

*Country Journal* (413-667-3211; 25 Main St., Huntington, Hampshire County; Thursday) Covers 16 of the central hill towns.

*The Paper* (518-392-2674; P.O. Box 336, Chatham, NY 112037; monthly). A features freebie published the first Thursday of the month.

*The Pittsfield Gazette* (413-443-2010; 141 North St., Pittsfield; Thursday) Lively, even acerbic local Pittsfield news.

*Shopper's Guide* (413-528-0095; Bridge St., Box 89, Gt. Barrington, MA 01230; weekly) Southern Berkshire's shopping guide, including enticing sections on real estate and automobiles.

*The Transcript* (413-663-3741; American Legion Dr., N. Adams, MA 01247; weekday noons, Saturday morning) Local, some state and national news; covers northern Berkshire County and southern Vermont.

*The Women's Times* (413-528-5303; 323 Main St., Box 390, Gt. Barrington, MA 01230; monthly) A classy, well-written magazine-style paper, with articles by, for, and about Berkshire women. Free.

*Yankee Shopper* (413-684-1373; 839 Main St., Box 96, Dalton, MA 01226; weekly) Central and northern Berkshire's shopping guide, including scads of used cars, rototillers, computers, vacuum cleaners, and baby bunnies, as well as a business/professional services directory.

## Radio Stations

### NATIONAL PUBLIC RADIO

At least five stations receivable in the Berkshires:
**WBTN-FM** 94.3; 800-639-2192; Vermont Public Radio, Bennington, Vt.
**WAMC-FM** 90.3; 800-323-9262; Northeast Public Radio, Albany, NY.
**WAMQ-FM** 105.1; 800-323-9262; Northeast Public Radio, Albany, NY
**WFCR-FM** 88.5; 413-545-0100; Amherst, MA.
**WMHT-FM** 89.1; 518-356-1700; Schenectady, NY.

### OTHER LOCAL RADIO STATIONS

**WBEC-AM** 1420; 413-499-3333; Pittsfield. General.
**WBEC-FM** 105.5; 413-499-3333; Pittsfield. Rock music.
**WBRK-AM** 101; 413-442-1553; Pittsfield. General.
**WCFM-FM** 91.9; 413-597-2373; Williams College.
**WJJW-FM**, 91; 413-662-5405; Massachusetts College of Liberal Arts.
**WMNB-FM**, 100.1; 413-663-6567; N. Adams. General.
**WNAW-AM**, 1230; 413-663-6567; N. Adams. General
**WNAW-FM**, 100.0; 413-663-6567; N. Adams. General.
**WSBS-AM**, 860; 413-528-0860; Gt. Barrington. General.
**WUHN-AM**, 1110; 413-499-1100; Pittsfield. General.
**WUPE-FM**, 96; 413-499-1100; Pittsfield. Rock and other music.

## Television

Local public-access television, run mostly by community volunteers, brings important meetings, events, and opinion to listeners who subscribe to cable television.

In addition to live broadcast of town meetings, city council meetings, and other events of civil and local interest, the locally run stations in each region generate other programs such as live viewer call-ins, self-help, and religious programs, along with musical and dramatic entertainment by local performers.

### COMMUNITY-BASED TELEVISION CHANNELS

**Community Television for the Southern Berkshires (CTSB):** Channel 11 (413-243-0676).

**Pittsfield Community Television:** Warner Cable Channel 5 (413-443-4755).

**North Berkshire Community Television:** Adelphia Channels 15, 16, and 17 (413-664-4408).

**WilliNet (Williamstown):** Adelphia Channels 15, 16, and 17 (413-458-0900).

Consult the *Berkshire Eagle* for schedules.

## Real Estate

What's our dream house? An isolated cabin deep in the woods? A late-20th-century split-level suburban tract house? A lakeside condo for time-sharing? Or a 40-room Gilded Age mansion that just needs a couple of hundred grand in handyman repairs? Berkshire County has them all.

Those shopping for Berkshire real estate can obtain information as follows:

Lists of agents: Consult the Yellow Pages of the telephone book or contact any of the three chambers of commerce: **Southern Berkshire Chamber of Commerce** (413-528-1510; 362 Main St., Gt. Barrington, MA 01230); **Central Berkshire Chamber of Commerce** (413-499-4000; 66 West St., Pittsfield, MA 01201); **Northern Berkshire Chamber of Commerce** (413-663-3735; 69½ Main St., N. Adams, MA 01247). All three organizations will send a list of their realtor members. The seasonal tourist information brochures from the **Berkshire Hills Conference** (413-443-9186; 50 South St., Pittsfield, MA 01201) also list numerous realtors.

Potential buyers of land or a house should check with the local town government about zoning laws, building permits, and the like. Such regulations vary widely from town to town. See "Town Halls" in this chapter for telephone numbers.

Buyers can also follow the real estate market in the newspapers; see "Media" in this chapter. *The Berkshire Home Buyers Guide* is a free monthly publication, distributed in local shops or available from 413-243-2500; 80 Run Way, Lee, MA 01238.

## Religious Services & Organizations

Berkshire County has an active and unusually diverse religious community. The best source for information about church and synagogue services is the Saturday edition of the *Berkshire Eagle*. Berkshire County telephone books have a comprehensive list of all mainstream religious organizations, under the headings "Churches" and "Synagogues." Nontraditional groups should keep an eye on community bulletin boards at the area's colleges and in towns such as Great Barrington, Stockbridge, Lenox, Pittsfield, and Williamstown.

## Road Service

Emergency road service from **AAA**, anywhere in the county, can be obtained by calling 413-443-1635, Pittsfield. For non-AAA drivers, the following is a listing of emergency towing services:

### South County

**Bachetti's Auto:** Sheffield; 413-528-5410

**Decker's Auto Body:** Gt. Barrington; 413-528-1432 or 800-Tow Truck

**John's Garage:** Housatonic; 413-274-3328

**Mac's Garage:** Gt. Barrington; 413-528-1234

**R W's Inc.:** Lee; 413-243-0946

**Stockbridge Motors:** Stockbridge; 413-298-4780

CENTRAL COUNTY

**County Auto Wrecking:** Pittsfield; 413-443-6665

**Sayers' Auto Wrecking:** Lanesborough; 413-443-5200

**Scratch-A-Ticket Towing:** Pittsfield; 413-443-1754

**Southgate Motors:** Pittsfield; 413-445-5971

**Village Truck Sales:** Lanesborough; 413-442-0407

NORTH COUNTY

**Al's Service Center:** Adams; 413-743-7797

**Carpinello's Service Center:** Williamstown; 413-458-2528

**Dean's Quality Auto & Truck Repair:** N. Adams; 413-664-6378

**Mohawk Auto Wrecking:** N. Adams; 413-663-6835

**Sayers Auto Wrecking:** N. Adams; 413-663-9030

**T&M Auto Sales:** N. Adams; 413-664-6697

## SCHOOLS

### Public School Districts

SOUTH COUNTY

**Berkshire Hills Regional School District**, Stockbridge; 413-298-3711

**Farmington River Regional**; 413-269-7105

**Lee Public Schools**; 413-243-0276

**Southern Berkshire Regional School District**, Sheffield; 413-229-8778

CENTRAL COUNTY

**Central Berkshire Regional School District**, Dalton; 413-684-1330

**Lenox Public Schools**; 413-637-5550

**Richmond Consolidated Schools**; 413-698-2207

**Pittsfield Public Schools**; 413-499-9512

NORTH COUNTY

**Adams-Cheshire Regional School District**; 413-743-2939

**Berkshire Arts & Technology Charter School**, Adams; 413-743-7311

**Clarksburg School Department**; 413-664-8735

**Florida School Department**; 413-664-6023

**Lanesborough Schools**; 413-442-2229

**Mount Greylock Regional School District**; 413-458-9582

**New Ashford School Department**; 413-458-5461

**North Adams Public Schools**; 413-662-3225

**Northern Berkshire Vocational**; 413-663-5383

**Savoy School Department**; 413-743-1992

**Williamstown Public Schools**; 413-458-5707

## Private & Religious Schools

### SOUTH COUNTY

**Berkshire School**, Sheffield; 413-229-8511

**De Sisto School**, Stockbridge; 413-298-3776

**Frontline Church School**, Lee; 413-243-2673

**Eagleton School**, Gt. Barrington; 413-528-9881

**Great Barrington Rudolf Steiner School**, Gt. Barrington; 413-528-4015

**Great Barrington Waldorf High School**, Gt. Barrington; 413-528-8833

**Heartwood School**, Washington; 413-623-6677

**John Dewey Academy**, Gt. Barrington; 413-528-9000

**The Kolburne School**, New Marlborough; 413-229-8787

**St. Mary's School**, Lee; 413-243-1079

### CENTRAL COUNTY

**Berkshire Country Day School**, Lenox; 413-637-0755

**Berkshire County Christian School**, Pittsfield; 413-442-4014

**Berkshire Institue for Christian Studies**, Lenox, 413-637-4673

**Berkshire Institute for Life Long Learning**, Pittsfield; 413-443-1797

**Hillcrest Educational Centers**, Lenox, Gt. Barrington, Pittsfield, and Hancock.

**Miss Hall's School**, Pittsfield; 413-443-6401

**Sacred Heart School**, Pittsfield; 413-443-6379

**St. Agnes School**, Dalton; 413-684-3143

**St. Joseph's High School**, Pittsfield; 413-447-9121

**Sinai Academy of the Berkshires**, Pittsfield; 413-499-4167

NORTH COUNTY

**Buxton School**, Williamstown; 413-458-3919

**Institute for International Cooperation and Development**, Williamstown; 413-458-9460

**Pine Cobble School**, Williamstown; 413-458-4680

**St. Stanislaus**, Adams; 413-743-1091

### Colleges

**Berkshire Community College**, Pittsfield; 413-499-4660. In Gt. Barrington: 413-528-4521.

**Massachusetts College of Liberal Arts**, N. Adams; 413-662-5000

**Simon's Rock College of Bard**, Gt. Barrington; 413-644-4400

**Williams College**, Williamstown; 413-597-3131

## TOURIST INFORMATION

Volunteers in several Berkshire towns staff tourist information booths in the summer and early fall. Often information is available at the site even when the volunteers aren't. Year-round tourist information can be obtained from **The Berkshires Visitors Bureau** (800-237-5747; www.berkshires.org; 3 Hoosac St., Adams, MA 01220). The bureau is open Mon.–Fri., 8:30–4:30. Lodging information can be obtained from the **Berkshire Lodgings Association** (413-298-4760, 800-298-4760). Chambers of commerce, listed below, serve the commercial and business needs of the community and can be the source of information on special events.

SOUTH COUNTY

**Chamber of Commerce of South Berkshire:** Business office at 248 Main St., Gt. Barrington, MA 01230; 413-528-4284. Information booth at 362 Main St., Gt. Barrington; 413-528-1510. Lodging information: 413-528-4006.

**Lee Information Booth:** Main St. at the park; 413-243-0852.

**Massachusetts Turnpike Information:** Eastbound mile marker 8, Lee; 413-243-4929.

**Stockbridge Chamber of Commerce:** Business office at 7 Elm St.; 413-298-5200; www.stockbridgechamber.org. Information booth on Main St.; 413-298-5200. Lodging information: 413-298-5327.

**West Stockbridge Information Booth:** Corner Main St. (Rte. 102) and Depot St., next to Berkshire Bank.

CENTRAL COUNTY

**Chamber of Commerce of the Berkshires:** 66 West St., Pittsfield, MA 01201; 413-499-4000.

**Lenox Chamber of Commerce:** Information office at Lenox Academy, 65 Main St., P.O. Box 646; 413-637-3646, 800-25-LENOX; www.lenox.org. Summer: 48 Main St.

**Pittsfield Information Booth:** Bank Row, Park Square.

NORTH COUNTY

**Adams Chamber of Commerce:** at NBCC, below; 413-743-1881.

**Northern Berkshire Chamber of Commerce (NBCC):** Business office at 6 W. Main St., N. Adams; 413-663-3735. Information booth (summer and fall) on Union St.

**Williamstown Chamber of Commerce:** Gatehouse, foot of Spring St.; 413-458-9077. Information booth at Rte. 7 and Main St.; 413-458-4922.

# 10

# If Time Is Short

**Berkshire** offers so much to the visitor that longer sojourns are most rewarding, but sometimes that isn't possible. Here are some recommendations from the author, the publisher, and the editor from their personal favorites among the multitude of attractions that best exemplify the spirit of Berkshire County and might perfectly suit the visitor with only a weekend or a few days available for a first visit.

## Lodging

**The Orchards** (413-458-9611; 222 Adams Rd., Williamstown; off Rte. 2) A superb small luxury hotel offering a formal clublike atmosphere. Huge rooms, many with bay windows and fireplaces, plus an award-winning restaurant. The service throughout is honed to a fine edge.

**The Red Lion Inn** (413-298-5545; www.redlioninn.com; 30 Main St., Stockbridge) Satisfying meals, an excellent range of lodging options, and endless collections of fine furniture and antiques in a rambling, century-old inn in the old style, pleasing visitors and locals since 1793.

## Dining Out

**Castle Street Café** (413-528-5244; 10 Castle St., Gt. Barrington) An American bistro in South County in a charming, brick-walled café.

**Elm Court Inn** (413-528-0325; www.elmcourtinn.com; Rte. 71, N. Egremont) Pleasant inn in South County serving Continental cuisine in a cozy traditional setting.

**The Mill on the Floss** (413-458-9123; Rte. 7, New Ashford) One of the greater gourmet experiences in North County, offering excellent French cuisine in an informal setting.

**Old Inn on the Green** (413-229-7924; Rte. 57, New Marlborough, MA 01230) A combination of a superb chef in Peter Platt and all the ambiance one could ask at the Old Inn, including candlelight.

## Dining In

**The Store At Five Corners** (413-458-3176; jct. of Rtes. 7 & 43, S. Williamstown) A wonderful assortment of gourmet foods, wines, oils, jellies for gift baskets, prepared food for picnics, delicious ice creams and yogurt in a renovated Victorian building. Creative cooks will delight in the myriad offerings, and novice cooks will be inspired to experiment. They can even buy the newest cookbooks to assure culinary success. Devoted noncooks should just stock up on the delicious ready-made salads, casseroles, and baked goods.

## Culture

### Museums

**Hancock Shaker Village** (413-443-0188; www.hancockshakervillage.org; Rte. 20, near Pittsfield–Hancock line) Beautifully restored Shaker village, with numerous exhibits, Shaker buildings, and events for the whole family.

**MASS MoCA** (413-664-4481; www.massmoca.org; 87 Marshall St., N. Adams) The miraculous result of 12 years' work to convert an old mill into a "supercollidor of the best of today's visual, performing, and new media arts" (in director Joe Thompson's words). The 13-acre, 27-building campus houses art from the gigantic to the minimal and is home to performances of every stripe.

**Norman Rockwell Museum** (413-298-4100; www.nrm.org; Rte. 183, Stockbridge) Even connoisseurs of fine art find themselves captivated by Rockwell's evocations of America as we always wanted it to be. A guaranteed hit with every member of the family.

**The Sterling & Francine Clark Art Institute** (413-458-9545; www.clark art.edu; 225 South St., Williamstown) Among the museums in the county, the one with the longest-standing national reputation; renowned for its collection of impressionist paintings, especially by Renoir. Major expansion plans.

**Williams College Museum of Art** (413-597-2429; www.williams.edu/ WCMA; Main St., Williamstown; Rte. 2) One of the finest college museums in the country and a leading research center. Emphasis on early art and 20th-century American art, to complement the 19th-century collection at the Clark.

### Summer Music

**Tanglewood** (413-637-1666, 413-637-5165; www.bso.org; West St., Lenox; Rte. 183) The obvious choice for the visitor with but one evening or day. Shed concerts Friday and Saturday evenings and Sunday afternoons from early July through late August; Wednesday- or Thursday-evening recitals in Seiji Ozawa Hall; operas in the newly refitted Concert Hall. In addition to concerts by the Boston Symphony Orchestra and visiting soloists, students of Tanglewood's summer program aspiring professionals give numerous concerts in all venues 7 days a week. Popular or jazz artists take the stage at the end of August. The grounds, justly famous for their cultivated beauty, are great for a stroll or a picnic.

**Tannery Pond Concerts** (518-794-7887, or for reservations/tickets call 888-846-5848; Rte. 20, New Lebanon, NY) Five chamber concerts, about one a month between late May and early October. Superb rising stars along with internationally renowned performers, in a former Shaker tannery now converted to a rustic and acoustically excellent hall situated in a beautiful meadow on the grounds of the Darrow School.

**South Mountain Concerts** (413-442-2106; Rte. 7 & 20, Pittsfield) Chamber music for the serious listener, primarily string quartets but other combinations, too. Concerts are in a historic building built expressly for small ensembles, in a wooded setting above Pittsfield. Five Sunday-afternoon concerts during September and early October.

### Summer Theater

**Berkshire Theatre Festival** (413-298-5576, 413-298-5536 off-season; www.berkshiretheatre.org; E. Main St., Stockbridge; Rte. 102,) and **Williamstown Theatre Festival** (413-597-3400; www.wtfestival.org; Main St., Williamstown) The two granddaddies of American summer stock theater vie with each other to present superior theater in charming settings. Both offer main stage and studio presentations, traditional and new works from mid-June through Labor Day. Call ahead for schedules and reservations.

**Shakespeare & Company** (413-637-3353 box office, 413-637-1199 off-season; www.shakespeare.org; 70 Kemble St., Lenox) Shakespeare's classics and modern plays presented with feeling and clarity by the celebrated company led by Tina Packer. The company now has its own glorious—and growing—campus in downtown Lenox.

## RECREATION

**Monument Mountain Reservation** (413-298-3239; Stockbridge Rd., Gt. Barrington.; Rte. 7) 503 acres. A short but rugged climb up Squaw Peak, the reservation's most prominent feature, offers excellent views of three states from a summit 1,642 feet above sea level.

**Mount Greylock State Reservation** (413-499-4262; Rockwell Rd., Lanesborough; off Rte. 7, also accessible from Notch Road, N. Adams) 12,000 acres, including the state's highest peak, along with 45 miles of trails.

## SHOPPING

### Antiques

**The Painted Porch** (413-229-2700; 102 S. Main St., Sheffield; Rte. 7) A lovely new shop carrying French and English country furniture arranged in vignettes to help one visualize the pieces in one's own home.

**Greylock Cottage** (413-243-1115; 52 Main St., Lee) A charming shop with lots of collectibles displayed beautifully and priced fairly.

## Clothing

**Evviva!** (413-637-9875; 22 Walker St., Lenox) The clever window displays capture the sophistication and variety of clothing and accessories offered. Dresses for special events, romantic hats, unique jewelry, casual country clothes, and hand-painted silks combine to create a feast for the eye. The window displays (which change monthly) are fascinating in and of themselves. A recent expansion has added shoes to the mix.

**Steven Valenti** (413-443-2569; 157 North St., Pittsfield) A men's store with an emphasis on customer satisfaction and stylish yet comfortable clothes for all occasions.

**Zanna** (413-458-9858; 41 Spring St.) Contemporary women's clothes and accessories, featuring natural fibers and up-to-the-minute looks. Also a selection of sophisticated yet comfortable shoes.

## Books

**Bookloft** (413-528-1521; Barrington Plaza, Stockbridge Rd., Gt. Barrington) A popular source for best sellers and books about the Berkshires, with a knowledgeable staff in a pleasant setting.

**The Bookstore** (413-637-3390; 11 Housatonic St., Lenox) A most knowledgeable owner and a slightly 1970s air makes this a great place to browse and chat about books.

## Gifts

**B. Mango & Bird** (413-236-6996; 676 Merrill Rd., Pittsfield) Deep red walls set off an eclectic collection of accessories for home and table. Witty tapes, clever cards, and toys for adults round out the offerings in this shop.

**Hammertown Barn** (413-528-7766; 325 Stockbridge Rd., Gt. Barrington) Gifts for decorators, cooks, brides-to-be, or anyone on the list who is an aficionado of what's hot and hip for today's country lifestyle.

**Mistral's** (413-528-1618; 7 Railroad St., Gt. Barrington) A most elegant, sophisticated collection of tableware, linens, and home furnishings from France. The upstairs houses a collection of items for the bed and bath. A beautiful shop to visit for an infusion of French chic.

**Pamela Loring Gifts & Interiors** (413-243-2689; 40 Main St., Lee) Very attractive shop on Main Street with excellent service, they will wrap packages and provide gift cards. Mostly giftware with an emphasis on floral, pretty gifts for women, and seasonal merchandise.

## For Fun . . .

**Homegoods** (413-236-6996; 676 Merrill Rd., Pittsfield) and Sappa (413-528-9592; 308 Main St., Gt. Barrington) are at different ends of the spectrum in relationship to style, but each is fun in its own way for shopping.

**Where'd You Get That!?** (413-458-2206; www.wygt.com; 100 Spring St., Williamstown) a delightful store with books, toys, and unique gifts to tickle the funny bones of kids 3 years to 100!

# Index


## A

AA Transport Car Services, 31
AAA Berkshire County, 276
Abbey Lake, 201
Abbott's Limousine & Livery, 31
Abode of the Message, The, 192
accommodations. *See* hotels and resorts; inns and bed & breakfasts; motels
Adams. *See* North County
Adams Agricultural Fair, 184
Adams Chamber of Commerce, 284
Adams-Cheshire Regional School District, 281
Adams Co-operative Bank, 269
*Advocate, The*, 278
Aegean Breeze, 84
Affordable, 31
air travel, 29
Airport Limousine Service, 31
Albany Berkshire Ballet, 140
All Fired Up Gallery—Berkshire Center for Contemporary Glass, 145
Alpine Slide, 217
Al's Service Center, 281
Alston's Livery & Limo, 31
ambulance, 266
American Air Charter, 29
American Cab Co., 31
American Craftsman, An, 258
Amtrak, 28–29
Anderson & Sons' Shaker Tree, 260
annual events, 184–86
antiques stores, 239–46
Appalachian Mountain Club, 230
Appalachian Trail, 32
Apple Tree Inn, The, 57
Applegate Inn, 45
Arbor Rose Bed & Breakfast, 52
Arcadian Shop, 32, 195, 198, 204
architecture, 133–38
area codes, 10, 266
Arrow Taxi, 31
Arrowhead, 148
Art Center Theater (ARC), 142
Artifacts, 145
arts and entertainment: architecture, 133–38; cinema, 138–40; classes, 138; dance, 140–42; galleries, 142–48; historic homes, 148–57; libraries, 157–62; museums, 162–69; music, 169–76; nightlife, 176–78; overview of, 131–33; personal favorites, 287–88; seasonal events, 184–86; theater, 179–84; video rentals, 187
Ashintully Gardens, 148–49
Ashmere Lake, 224
Asian Antiques, 240
Asian Arts, 143
Asters, 104
Aston Magna, 169–70
Aubergine, 113–14
auctioneers, 246
Aunti M's Bed & Breakfast, 45
Avalon Transportation, 30
AVC Video Showcase, 187

## B

B. Mango & Bird, 256, 289
Babalouie's Sour Dough Pizza Co., 125
Bachetti's Auto, 280
Bagel Smith, 118
Bagels Too, 118
Bailey Museum of Natural History, 228
bakeries, 117–18
Baker's Driving Range & Miniature Golf, 210
Baker's Golf Center, 217
Balance Rock, 228
Balance Wellness Center, 192
Baldwin Hill Farm B&B, 42
Baldwin's Table Syrup, 127
Banknorth Massachusetts, 269
banks, 269
Barnes & Noble, 248
Barrington Brewery & Restaurant, 84
Barrington Coffee Roasting Co., Inc., 118
Barrington Court Travelodge, 76
Barrington Outfitters, 249
Barrington Stage Company, 179

Bartholomew's Cobble, 228, 231, 235
Bartlett's Orchard, 119, 126
Bas-Ridge Golf Course, 210
Bascom Lodge, 66–67, 228
baseball and softball, 197
B&B at the Egmonts, 60
Bear Swamp Hydroelectric Project, 230
Beartown State Forest, 226, 235
Beaver Pond, 145
Becket. *See* Central County
Becket Arts Center, 145
bed & breakfasts. *See* inns and bed & breakfasts
Bella Collections, 254
Bella Flora, 120
Belvoir Terrace, 219
Ben & Jerry's Ice Cream, 125
Benedict Pond, 200, 223
Bennington Museum, 169
Ben's, 251
Berger's Bakery and Deli, 120
Berger's Specialty Foods, 121–22
Berkshire Art Gallery, 143
Berkshire Arts & Technology Charter School, 281
Berkshire Athenaeum, 157–58, 217
Berkshire Aviation, 29
Berkshire Bach Society, 174
Berkshire Bagels, 118
Berkshire Bank, 269
Berkshire Berries, 126
Berkshire Bike & Blade, 32, 198
Berkshire Bistro, 118
Berkshire Blues Café, 177
Berkshire Book Co., 247
Berkshire Botanical Garden, 216, 228
Berkshire Canoe Tours, 202, 276
Berkshire Catering, 122
Berkshire Choral Festival, 170–71
Berkshire Classic Leather and Silver, 262
Berkshire Co-op Market, 124
Berkshire Coffee Roasting Company, 118
Berkshire Community College, 174–75, 217, 283
Berkshire Concert Choir, 175
Berkshire Country Day School, 282
Berkshire County Christian School, 282
Berkshire County Extension Service, 119
Berkshire County Land Trust, 234
Berkshire County Softball Complex, 197
Berkshire Crafts Fair, 184
Berkshire Crossing Mall, 265
Berkshire Dance Theater, 142
*Berkshire Eagle, The*, 278
Berkshire East, 208
Berkshire Fabric & Wallpaper Outlet, 261
Berkshire Grown, 119
Berkshire Hills Coins and Estate Jewelry, 245
Berkshire Hills Conference, 280
Berkshire Hills Country Club, 210
Berkshire Hills Country Inn, 66
Berkshire Hills Motel, 78
Berkshire Hills Regional School District, 281
Berkshire Hills Tennis Association, 221
Berkshire Home & Antiques, 240
Berkshire Ice Cream, 125
Berkshire Inn, 77
Berkshire Institute for Christian Studies, 282
Berkshire Institute for Life Long Learning, 282
Berkshire Limousine, 31
Berkshire Livery Service, 31
*Berkshire Living*, 278
Berkshire Lodgings Association, 283
Berkshire Lyric Theatre, 175
Berkshire Mall, The, 251, 265
Berkshire Medical Center, 277
Berkshire Mountain Bakery, 117, 126
Berkshire Mountain Spring Water, 126
Berkshire Mountain Yoga, 193
Berkshire Museum, The, 162, 177, 217, 250
Berkshire Museum Shop, 263
Berkshire Music School, 217
Berkshire Nautilus, 193
Berkshire Opera Company, 171
Berkshire Outfitters, 32, 196, 199, 203, 205
Berkshire Pedlar, 245
Berkshire Pendleton Store, 251
*Berkshire Penny Saver*, 278
*Berkshire Record, The*, 278
Berkshire Record Outlet, 259
Berkshire Regional Transit Authority, 30, 277
Berkshire Rent-A-Car, 31
Berkshire Resources for Child Care, 215
Berkshire Scenic Railway Museum, 162–63
Berkshire School, 282
Berkshire Sculling Inc., 199
Berkshire Ski Conditions, 204

Berkshire South Regional Community Center, 194, 216
Berkshire Symphony, 175
Berkshire Taxi, 31
Berkshire Theatre Festival, 135, 179–80, 216, 288
Berkshire Tour Company, 276
*Berkshire Trade & Commerce*, 278
Berkshire Visitors Bureau, 11, 276, 283
Berkshire West, 193, 220, 221, 224
Berkshires' Best . . . Locally Produced Products, 257
Berkshires Summer Arts Festival, The, 185
Best Value Inn, 76
Best Western Black Swan Inn, 45
bibliography (books about the area), 270–75
bicycling, 32, 197–99
Bidwell House, The, 149
Birch Hill Bed & Breakfast, 50
Birchwood Inn, 57–58
Birdhouse, 143
Bish Bash Falls, 226
Bissellville Estate & Campground, 232
Bistro Zinc, 98–99
Bits and Pieces, 255
Bizen, 84–85
B.J. Faulkner, 146
Blackinton Manor, 67
Blantyre, 40, 58, 98
Blockbuster Video, 187
Blue Willow, 52
Blueberries, 115
Blueberry Hill Farm, 121
BMC Hillcrest Campus, 277
boating, 199–201
Body & Soul, 193
Bogies Restaurant and Pub, 177
Bombay Bar & Grill, 90
Bonanza, 26, 28
Bonnie Brae Cabins and Campsites, 233
Bonnie Lea Farm, 211
Bonnie Rigg Campground, 233
Bookloft, The, 246, 289
Bookstore, The, 247–48, 289
bookstores, 246–49
Bousquet, 207
Boys & Girls Club, 224
Brewhaha!, 115
Briarcliff Inn, 76
Bridlewood Home Furnishing, 259
Broken Hill Manor, 50
Brook Farm Inn, 58–59
B&S Gventer Books, 247
Buckley-Dunton Pond, 201
Bucksteep Manor, 74, 233, 236
Buel, Lake, 200
Buggy Whip Factory Antique Market Place, The, 244
Burgner's Farm Products, 119
Burgner's Poultry Farm, 128
bus travel, 26, 28, 30
Buster's Entertainment Center, 216
Butler Sculpture Park, 144
Butternut Basin, 205–6, 235
Buxton Brook Farm, 68–69
Buxton Garden, 169
Buxton School, 283
Bygone Days, 240
Byzantium, 249

## C

Cafe Latino, 107–8
Café Lucia, 99
Caffe Pomo d'Oro, 116, 122
Cakewalk Bakery & Café, 118
Calvin Theatre, 178
Camp Ashmere, 218
Camp Becket, 219
Camp Bonnie Brae, 219
Camp Chimney Corners, 219
Camp Danbee, 218
Camp Emerson, 219
Camp Greylock, 219
Camp Half Moon, 218
Camp Hi Rock YMCA, 218
Camp Kingsmont, 218
Camp Lenox, 219
Camp Mah-Kee-Nac, 219
Camp Mohawk, 219
Camp Nawaka, 219
Camp Overflow, 232
Camp Romaca, 219
Camp Stevenson Witawentin, 220
Camp Taconic, 220
Camp Watitoh, 220

Camp WaWa Segowea, 219
Camp Winadu, 220
Campbell Falls State Park, 226
camping, cross-country skiing, walking and hiking, 225–36
Campo de Fiori, 255
camps, children's, 218–20
Canoe Meadows Wildlife Sanctuary, 217, 229, 235
canoeing and kayaking, 201–3
Canterbury Farm, 236
Canyon Ranch in the Berkshires, 189–90
car rentals, 30–31
Card Lake Country Inn, The, 55
Carey, 30
Carey Chauffeured Service, 30
Cariddi Catering, 122
Carol's, 116
Carol's Cookery, 120
Carpinello's Service Center, 281
Carriage House Antiques, 240
Carriage House Motel, 78
Casablanca, 251
Castle Street Café, 85, 124, 286
Catamount, 206
caterers and gourmet & deli markets, 121–24
Catherine's Chocolate Shop, 127
Celestial Bar, 177
Central Berkshire Chamber of Commerce, 280
Central Berkshire Regional School District, 281
Central County: antiques stores, 245; architecture, 135–37; art galleries, 145–47; bicycle dealers, 198; boating, 201; bookstores, 247–48; campgrounds, 232–33; children's camps, 219–20; children's recreation, 216–17; cinema, 139; clothing and accessories stores, 251–53; dance, 142; downhill skiing, 207–8; emergency road service, 281; fishing, 213–14; gift and specialty shops, 256–57; golf courses, 210–11; handcraft stores, 258–59; house and home stores, 260–61; inns and bed & breakfasts, 56–66; motels, 77–78; music, 174–75; nightlife, 177; private and religious schools, 282; public school districts, 281; restaurants, 97–106; shopping streets, mews, and malls, 264–65; ski shops, 204; sporting goods stores, 195–96; swimming, 224; tennis, 221; theater, 183; tourist information, 283–84; trails, 228–29; video rentals, 187
Centuryhurst Antiques, 242
Chamber of Commerce of South Berkshire, 283
Chamber of Commerce of the Berkshires, 283
chambers of commerce, 280, 283–84
Chambéry Inn, 45–46
Champ Sports, 196
Chapelbrook, 231
Chapin Library of Rare Books, 158
Charles H. Baldwin & Sons, 127, 256
Charles L. Flint Antiques Inc., 245
Charles Steinhacker Editions, 146
Cheesecake Charlie's, 122–23
Chef's Hat, 116
Chef's Shop, The, 260
Chen & Dancers, 142
Chenail's Farm Fresh Products, 119–20
Chenail's Farmstand, 119
Chesapeake Inn, 59
Cheshire. *See* North County
Cheshire Reservoir, 201, 224
Chester Air, 29
Chesterfield Gorge, 231
Chesterwood, 150–51, 186
Chez Nous, 90–91
Chez Vous Catering, 123
children's stores, 250
Chimney Mirror Motel, 78
Chocolate Springs Cafe, 127
Christine's B&B, 44–45
Chuck Davis African Dance Collective, 142
Church on the Hill, 137
Church Street Café, 99–100
Church Street Trading Company, 249
churches, 280
Churchill House Bed & Breakfast, 73
cinema, 138–40
Citizens Bank, 269
Citizens Hall, 135
city halls, 266–68
Clarksburg School Department, 281
Clarksburg State Park, 224, 230
Classic Coach Limo, 31
Clearwater Natural Foods, 124
Cliffwood Inn, 59
climate, 275

Close Encounters with Music, 174
clothing and accessories stores, 249–54
Club Helsinki, 176–77
Cobbleview B&B, 56
coffee specialists, 118–19
Coffmans' Country Antiques Market, 240
Collector's Warehouse, 246
colleges, 283
Collette Tours, 276
Colonel Ashley House, 149–50
Colonial Motor Lodge, 77
Colonial Theatre, 183
Colorful Stitches, 256
Comfort Inn, 77
Comfort Inn & Suites, 76
Common Grounds Coffee House, 177
Community Access, 142
Community Television for the Southern Berkshires (CTSB), 279
Concepts of Art, 146, 258
Congregational Church, 133, 135
Conroy's B&B, 52–53
Contemporary Artists Center, 147
convenience stores, 277–78
Corashire Antiques, 240
Cork N' Hearth, 90
Corn Crib, 120
Cornell Inn, 59–60
Corner House Antiques, 242
Cose D'Argilla, 259
Cottage, The, 253, 254, 256, 257
Country Club of Pittsfield, 210
Country Curtains, 260
Country Dining Room and Tea Garden Antiques, 240
*Country Journal*, 278
County Auto Wrecking, 281
County Catering, 123
Court Square Breakfast & Deli, 116
Cozy Corner Motel, 78
Crabtree Cottage, 46
Crafter's Cottage, The, 257
Crandell Theatre, 139
Crane Lake Camp, 219
Crane Paper Mills, 135
Cranwell Resort, Spa and Golf Club, 74, 137, 190, 210, 221, 235
Criterion, 197
Crooked Row Farm, 121
croquet, 203
cross-country skiing, walking, hiking and camping, 225–36
Crowne Plaza Hotel, 75
Crystal Essence, 254
culture. *See* arts and entertainment
Cumberland Farms, 277
Cup and Saucer Cafe, 119
Cupboards & Roses Antiques, 242
Curtis Hotel, 137
Curtisville Consortium, 174

## D

Daily Bread, 118
Dakota, 104, 277
Dalton. *See* Central County
Dalton Community House, 217
Dalton House, The, 56
dance, 140–42
Dark Ride, 147
Darr Antiques and Interiors, 242–43
Dave's Sporting Goods, 196
Days Inn, Gt. Barrington, 76
Days Inn of Lenox, 77
De Sisto School, 282
Dean's Quality Auto & Truck Repair, 281
Decker's Auto Body, 280
Deidre's, 253
Delftree Corporation, 127
deli & gourmet markets and caterers, 121–24
Depot, The, 177
DeSisto Estate Cabaret, 183
Devonfield B&B, 46
Dibble, Susan, 142
Dibble Dance, 142
Dick Moon Sporting Goods, 196
Different Drummer's Kitchen, 261
dining. *See* food purveyors; restaurants
disabilities, services for persons with, 276–77
Dolls & Dwellings, 120
Domaney's Discount Liquors, 128
Donald McGrory Oriental Rugs, 242
Dorothy Frances Rice Sanctuary, 229
Dovetail Antiques, 243
downhill skiing, 203–9

Dream Away Lodge, 177
Dukes, 197
Dunkin' Donuts, 277
Duvall Nature Trail, 230

## E

Eagleton School, 282
East, The, 85–86
East Side Café, The, 125
East Street Video, 187
Eastover Resort and Conference Center, 75
Ebenezer II Antiques and Gifts, 244
Echezeaux, A Country Bed & Breakfast, 66
Econo Lodge, 77
Econo Lodge Springs Motor Inn, 78
Egg, 183
Egremont. *See* South County
Egremont Country Club, 210
Egremont Inn, The, 40, 42–43, 82–83, 177
1896 House Country Inn & Motels, 69
Eisner Camp, 219
Elise Abrams Antiques, 241
Elizabeth's Borderland Café, 104–5, 125
Elm Court Inn, 40, 82, 286
Elm Street Market, 116, 187
emergency phone numbers, 266
emergency road service, 280–81
Emporium Antique Center, 241
Enterprise, 31
Esposito Flying Service, 29
Essencials Day Spa, 193
Evergreen, 258
Everything Art, 147
Evviva!, 252, 289
Ex Libris: The Lenox Library Shop, 263
Expeditions, 204

## F

Fairview Hospital, 277
Falcon Ridge Folk Festival, 178
Falconwood Antiques, 243
Fall Foliage Parade, 184
farm, orchard and produce markets, 119–21
Farmhouse, 254
Farmington River Regional, 281
Farshaw's Fine Old Books, 247
Federal House, The, 47–48
Fernwood Forest Campground, 233
Ferrin Gallery, 146
Field Farm, 231
fire, 266
Fireworks over Stockbridge Bowl, 185
First Congregational Church, 138
First Flight, 29
fish, poultry, and meat markets, 128
fishing, 212–14
fitness centers, 193–94
Florida School Department, 282
Flying Cloud Summer Camp, 216
food purveyors. *See also* restaurants: bakeries, 117–18; coffee specialists, 118–19; farm, orchard and produce markets, 119–21; gourmet & deli markets and caterers, 121–24; health/natural food stores, 124–25; ice cream shops, 125–27; local food and beverage specialties, 126–27; meat, fish, and poultry markets, 128; pizza, 125; wine and liquor stores, 128–29
football, 209
Forest Park Country Club, 211
Found at the Bookloft, 249
Four Acres Motel, 78
Four Colors Company, 215–16
Frederick Hatfield Antiques, 243
Frelinghuysen-Morris House & Studio, 164–65
Friendly's, 125
Frontline Church School, 282

## G

Gables Inn, The, 60
Gaffer's Outdoors, 202
Galadriel's, 253
galleries, 142–48
Garden Gables Inn, 60
Garfield, Lake, 200, 202, 223
Gateways Inn, 60–61, 100
Gatsby's, 249, 260
Gedney Farm and Maple Manor & Spa, 48–49
Geffner/Schatzky Antiques, 244
General Electric Athletic Association, 211
Gerry Cosby & Co., 195
Gideon's Fine Dining, 108
Gideon's Luncheon and Nightery, 178
gift and specialty shops, 254–57, 263

Gifted Child, 250
Gilly's Hot Vanilla, 126
Gingerbread House, 135
Gingham Rabbit, The, 254
Glad Rags, 252
Glendale Falls, 231
Glendale River Grille, 93–94
Goff's Sports, 196, 205
golf, 209–11
Good & Hutchinson Associates, Inc., 243
Goose Pond, 200
Gorham & Norton, 123, 128
Gould Farm's Roadside Store and Café, 122
gourmet & deli markets and caterers, 121–24
Gramercy Bistro, 108–9
Great Barrington. *See* South County
Great Barrington Antiques Center, 241
Great Barrington Downtown, 263
Great Barrington Pottery, The, 258
Great Barrington Rudolf Steiner School, 282
Great Barrington Waldorf High School, 282
Great Josh Billings RunAground, 185, 197
Green River, 223
Green River Produce & Stables, 120, 121
Green Valley Motel, 78
Greenock Country Club, 210, 221
Greenwater Pond, 201
Grey Fox Bluegrass Festival, 178
Greyhound, 26, 28
Greylock, Mount, 236
Greylock Cottage, The, 242, 288
Greylock Credit Union, 269
Greylock Discovery Tours, 230, 232, 276
Greylock Hill Climb, 198
Greylock Ramble, 185
Greylock Recreation Field, 221
Greystone Gardens, 251, 253
Griffin Hall, 138, 175
Gt. Barrington Bagel Co., 118
Guest House at Field Farm, 69
Guido's Fresh Marketplace, 120, 126
Guthrie Center, 177

## H

Habitat Galleries, 143
Haddad's Rug Company, 261
Hammertown Barn, 260, 289
Hampton Terrace, 61
Hancock. *See* Central County
Hancock Inn, 56–57
Hancock Shaker Village, 133, 165–66, 217, 287
Hancock Shaker Village Shop, 263
Hancock Union Store, 260
Hand of Man—A Craft Gallery, 146
handcrafts stores, 257–59
handicapped services, 276–77
Harbour House Inn, 67
Harland B. Foster, 198
Harrington's Restaurant & Inn, 107
Harrison Gallery, 147
Harrison House, 61, 151
Harry's Supermarket, 124, 128
Harvest Festival, 185
Hats and Jewels, 255
Hayloft Gallery and Studio, 144
health/natural food stores, 124–25
Heart of the Berkshires Motel, 77
Heartwood School, 282
Heirlooms Classic Jewelry, 262
Helen's Place, 123
Henry B. Holt, 242
Herberg Middle School, 221
Hickory Bill's Bar-B-Que, 123
High Lawn Farm, 127
hiking, camping, cross-country skiing and walking, 225–36
Hildi B, 250
Hillary Beadell, 244
Hillcrest Educational Centers, 282
Hillside, The, 92
Hinsdale. *See* Central County
Historic Deerfield, Inc., 169
historic homes, 148–57
Historic Merrell Inn, 48
Historic Valley Park, 236
Historic Valley Park Campground, 233
history: natural, 14–16; social, 16–23
Hoadley Gallery: Contemporary Crafts, 146
Hobson's Choice, 109–10
Hoffman Pottery, 258
Holiday Farm, 122
Holiday Inn Berkshires, 75
Holiday Inn Express Hotel & Suites, 76
Holiday Walk, 186

Holly-Days, 186
Hollywood Drive-In, 139–40
Hollywood Video, 187
Holsten Galleries, 145
Home Town Parade, 184
Homegoods, 261, 289
Homer's Variety, 118
homes, historic, 148–57
Honwee Mountain-Turner Trail, 235
Hoosac Bank, 269
Hoosac Tunnel, 137
Hoosac Valley High School, 224
Hopkins Forest Fall Festival, 186
Hopkins Forest Museum, 169
Hopkins Memorial Forest, 122, 169, 230, 236
Hopkins Observatory, 169
horseback riding, 211–12
Horsesense at Golden Hill Farm, 211
hospitals, 277
Hot Tomatoes, 125
Hotchkiss Mobiles Gallery and Studio, 145, 256
hotels and resorts, 74–76, 286. *See also* inns and bed & breakfasts; motels
Housatonic. *See* South County
Housatonic Corner Market, 187
Housatonic River Outfitters, Inc., 195
house and home stores, 259–61
House of Earth Studio Ge-raj Gallery, 144
House of India, 105
House on Main Street, The, 69–70
Howard Johnson Motel, 77
Howard S. Mott, 249
Howard's Antiques, 244
Hoyts Berkshire Cinema 10, 139
Hoyts North Adams Cinemas, 139
hunting, 212

## I

ice cream shops, 125–27
Ice Glen, 228
Image Gallery, 145
Images Cinema, 138
Impoco's, 187
In Touch Day Spa, 193
information booths, 11
Inn at Stockbridge, The, 53
Inn on Laurel Lake, 46
inns and bed & breakfasts. *See also* hotels and resorts; motels: Central County, 56–66; North County, 66–72; outside Berkshire County, 72–74; personal favorites, 286; South County, 42–56
Inspired Planet, 146, 259
Institute for International Cooperation and Development, 283
Interior Alternative, 261
International Outlet, 261
Ioka Valley Farm, 121
Iron Horse Music Hall, 178
Iron Kettle Books, 249
IS183—Art School of the Berkshires, 138, 145, 216

## J

Jack's Country Squire, 250
Jacks Grill, 89–90
Jack's Hot Dogs, 117
Jacob's Pillow Dance Festival, 140–41
Jae's Inn, 68, 109
Jaeschke's Brothers Farms, 120
Jazz Ensemble, 175
Jazztown, 184
J&D Marina, 200
Jenifer House Commons, 264
Jenkins Livery, 31
Jericho Valley Inn, 78
"Jerusalem," 135
jewelry stores, 262
Jilly's Ice Cream, 126
Jiminy Peak, The Mountain Resort, 75–76, 207–8, 210, 217, 221, 224
Jimmy's, 277
Joe's Diner, 91
John and Dina Fontaine, 246
John Andrew's, 83
John Dewey Academy, 282
John R. Sanderson Antiquarian Bookseller, 249
John Stritch, 146
John's Garage, 280
Jonathan Foote 1778 House, 47
Joyous Spring Pottery, 258
Juice n' Java, 116

## K

Kabot, 30
Kahns' Antiques and Estate Jewelry, The, 241
Kali Ray Tri-Yoga Center, 193
Kaolin & Co. Pottery, 143, 258
Kate Baldwin, 123
kayaking and canoeing, 201–3
Kemble Inn, The, 61–62
Kennedy Park, 235
Kenver Ltd., 204
Kettering Antiques, 244
Kidspace @ MASS MoCA, 218
Kilpatrick Health Center, 194
Kim's Dragon Restaurant, 106
Kitchen Store, The, 120
Klondike Campground, 232
Koi, 86
Kolburne School, The, 282
Koussevitzky Arts Center, 147
Kripalu Center for Yoga and Health, 190–91
Kushi Institute, The, 191–92
Kusika, 142, 175
Kuttner Antiques, 243

## L

La Bruschetta, 123, 125
La Pace, 254
Lakeview Orchard, 120
Lakewood Park, 221
Lamplighter, The, 260
Lampost Motel, 77
Lane, Dawn, 142
Lanesborough. *See* Central County
Lanesborough Mountain Motel, 77
Lanesborough Schools, 282
Lansing Chapman Rink, 222
Lantern House Motel, 76
LaPerla at Gregory House, 72
Laurel Hill Motel, 76
Laurel Lake, 200
Laurel Ridge Camping Area, 232
Le Jardin, 70, 110
Le Perigord, 241
Le Trianon, 243
Lee. *See* South County
Lee Bank, 269
Lee Information Booth, 283
Lee Public Schools, 281
Lee Sunoco, 277
Lee Video, 187
Lee's Prime Outlets, 264
Legacy Banks, 269
Lenox. *See* Central County
Lenox Academy, 137
Lenox Apple Squeeze, 186
Lenox Artisans Gallery, 146
Lenox Chamber of Commerce, 284
Lenox Community Center, 216
Lenox Downtown, 264
Lenox Fitness Center, 193–94
Lenox Gallery of Fine Art, 146
Lenox Inn, 77
Lenox Library, 137, 158–59, 216
Lenox Public Schools, 281
Lenox 218, 100–101
Lenox Wine Cellar and Cheese Shop, 128
LiAsia Gallery, 147, 246
libraries, 157–62
Library Antiques, The, 246
Lichtenstein Center for the Arts, 147
Lickety Split, 126
Liliana Gallery, 146
limousines, 30, 31
Linda's Cafe, 116
Linwood, 135
Lion's Den, 177
liquor and wine stores, 128–29
Liquor Mart, 128
Liquors Inc., 128
Little Cinema, 139
"Little Red House," 135
Locke, Stock and Barrel, 124, 128
lodging. *See* hotels and resorts; inns and bed & breakfasts; motels
Loring Gallery, 144
Luau Hale, 277
LuJohns Auctioneers, 246
Lydia Mongiardo Collection, 146, 259
Lyon Aviation, 29

## M

M. Lacey, 250
Mac-Haydn Theatre, 183
macrobiotic centers, 191–92

Mac's Garage, 281
Madden Open Hearts Camp, 219
Mahaiwe Theater, 183
Main Street, 250
Main Street Café, 116
malls, mews, and streets, 262–65
Manhattan Pizza Company, 125
Manice Education Center, 220
Mansfield, Lake, 223
Maple Glade Campground, 232
maple sugar and syrup, 122
Maple Terrace Motel, 79
Maplewood B&B, 57
maps: accessing Berkshire, 27; Berkshire County, 6; Berkshire towns, 11; Great Barrington, 34; Lenox, 36; North Adams, 39; Pittsfield, 37; Stockbridge, 35; Williamstown, 38
Margaret Lindley Park, 217–18, 224
Marian Fathers Seminary, 135
Marketplace, The, 123
Martin's, 116–17
Mary Ann-tiques & Gifts, 245
Mary Stuart, 250, 256
Massachusetts College of Liberal Arts, 142, 176, 183, 218, 283
Massachusetts Department of Conservation and Recreation, 230, 232
Massachusetts Department of Environmental Management, 218
Massachusetts Division of Fisheries and Wildlife, 212
Massachusetts Museum of Contemporary Art (MASS MoCA), 137, 142, 166–67, 177–78, 287
Massachusetts State Forest Headquarters, 235
Massachusetts Turnpike Information, 283
Masse's Seafood, 120, 128
Matruska, 250
Mauserts Pond, 201
Mayflower Motor Inn, 77
Mazzeo's Meat Center, 120, 128
McLenan Reservoir, 231
McLeod, Laurie, 142
McTeigue and McClelland, 262
Mean Wheels, 32, 198
meat, fish, and poultry markets, 128
Mechangers Ski & Snowboard Service, 204
media, news, 278–80
Media Merchant, 247
Mepal Spa, 191
Merrill Tavern, 135
Merwin House, The, 151–52
Metro North, 28
Metropolitan, 241
Mews, 264
Mezze, 110–11
Michael Charles Cabinetmakers, 147, 261
Michael's Restaurant, 111, 124
Michael's Restaurant & Pub, 94, 177
Michele's Day Spa, 193
Mike's Bike Shop, 32, 198
Milan at 55 Main, 109
Milham Planetarium, 169
Mill Brook Sugar House, 122
Mill House Inn, 74
Mill on the Floss, 107, 286
Mill River Studio, 143
Miller Marine, 200
Milne Public Library and House of Local History, 159
Miniature Theatre of Chester, 184
Miss Hall's School, 282
Mission House, The, 135, 152
Mistral's, 254, 289
Mixed Company, 182–83
Mohawk Auto Wrecking, 281
Mohawk Soaring Club, 222
Mohawk Trail Concerts, 176
monasteries and retreat centers, 192
Monterey. *See* South County
Monterey General Store, 124
Monument Mountain Author Climb, The, 185
Monument Mountain Motel, 76, 221
Monument Mountain Regional High School, 221
Monument Mountain Reservation, 231, 288
Moore Fine Food, 123, 124
Morgan House Inn, The, 47
motels. *See also* hotels and resorts; inns and bed & breakfasts: Central County, 77–78; North County, 78–79; South County, 76–77
Moulton's Country Store, 257
Mount, The, 152, 155
Mount Everett State Reservation, 226
Mount Greylock Regional School District, 282

Mount Greylock Ski Club, 209, 236
Mount Greylock State Reservation, 228, 288
Mount Washington State Forest, 226, 234–35
Mountain Goat, The, 32, 197, 198, 199, 205
Mountain Meadow Preserve, 230, 231
Mountain View Motel, 76
Movie Gallery, 187
Movie House, 140
movie theaters, 138–40
Mt. View Motel, 77
Mullin-Jones Antiquities, 242
Museum Facsimiles Outlet Store, 256–57
Museum Store at the Clark Art Institute, The, 263
museums, 162–69
music, 169–76
Music Mountain, 176
Music Store, The, 259
Myles Bradford Collection, 144

## N

Nahual, 254
Naoussa Gallery, 145
National, 31
Natural Bridge State Park, 230
natural/health food stores, 124–25
Nature's Classroom, 218
Naumkeag, 135, 155–56
Naumkeag at Christmas, 186
Nejaime's, 126
Nejaime's Stockbridge Wine Cellar, 128
Nejaime's Wine & Liquor, 128
New Ashford. *See* North County
New Ashford Motor Inn, 79
New Ashford School Department, 282
New Boston Inn, 40, 49–50, 93
New England Keswick, 219
New Marlborough. *See* South County
News in Revue, The, 183
news media, 278–80
newspapers, 278–79
nightlife, 176–78
925 Silver, 262
Noel Field, 222
Nora's Estate Goods, 245
Norfolk Chamber Music Festival, 176
Norman Rockwell Museum, 135, 167–68, 216, 263, 287
Norm's Limousine Service, 31
North Adams. *See* North County
North Adams Country Club, 211
North Adams Museum of History & Science, 168
North Adams Public Courts, 222
North Adams Public Library, 159–60
North Adams Public Schools, 282
North Adams Regional Hospital, 277
North Berkshire Community Television, 279
North Berkshire YMCA, 194
North County: antiques stores, 245–46; architecture, 137–38; art galleries, 147–48; bicycle dealers, 199; boating, 201; bookstores, 248–49; campgrounds, 233; children's camps, 220; children's recreation, 217–18; cinema, 139; clothing and accessories stores, 253–54; dance, 142; downhill skiing, 208–9; emergency road service, 281; fishing, 213–14; gift and specialty shops, 257; golf courses, 211; house and home stores, 261; inns and bed & breakfasts, 66–72; motels, 77–78; music, 175–76; nightlife, 177–78; private and religious schools, 283; public school districts, 281–82; restaurants, 107–13; shopping streets, mews, and malls, 265; ski shops, 205; sporting goods stores, 196–97; swimming, 224; tennis, 221–22; theater, 183; tourist information, 284; trails, 230, 232; video rentals, 187
North Egremont. *See* South County
North Pond, 201, 224
North Star Rare Books and Manuscripts, 249
North Star Video of Great Barrington, 187
Northern Berkshire Chamber of Commerce, 280, 284
Northern Berkshire Chorale, 176
Northern Berkshire Vocational, 282
Northern Berkshire YMCA, 220, 224
Northside Motel, 79
Notchview Reservation, 229, 231, 235

## O

Oak n' Spruce Resort, 223
Oakhollow, 211
O'Connell Convenience Plus, 277
October Mountain Stained Glass, 258
October Mountain State Forest, 226

Octoberzest, 186
Old Inn on the Green, 40, 92–93, 133, 286
Old Mill, 83–84
Oldcastle Theater Company, 183–84
Olde—An Antiques Market, 242
Ole T.J.'s Antique Barn, 243
Olga Dunn Dance Company, Inc., 141
Once Upon a Table, 94
1/2 Dozen or So, 147
Onota, Lake, 201, 224
Onota Boat Livery, 201
Orchard Shade, 50
Orchards, The, 178, 286
Orchards Hotel, The, 70
Ordinary Cycles, 32, 198
Origins Gallery, 145
Other Brother Darryl's, The, 128
Other Brother Darryl's Too, 128
Otis Poultry Farm, 128
Otis Reservoir, 200, 223
Otis Ridge, 206–7, 235
Otis State Forest, 235
Out Of Hand, 260
Out of Vietnam at Truc Orient Express Restaurant, 251
outdoor recreation. *See* recreation
Over the Rainbow, 125
Overmeade School of Horsemanship, 211

## P

Painted Porch, 243, 288
Pamela Loring Gifts & Interiors, 255, 289
Panda House, 101
Panorama, 29
Papa Joe's Ristorante & Pizzeria, 277
*Paper, The*, 278
Pappa Charlie's Deli Sandwich Shop, 112
Papyri Books, 248
Par 4 Family Fun Center, 210, 217
Park Taxi, 31
Parker Tours, 276
Parsonage on the Green, 47
Pasko Frame & Gift Center, 257
Past and Future, 245
Pasta Prima, 120, 124
Pasta's Wood-Fired Pizzas, 125
Paul and Susan Kleinwald, Inc., 242
Paul Rich & Sons Home Furnishings, 261
Pearl Street, 178
Pearl's, 86
Perfect Picnics, 123
Persnickety, 250
Peter Pan/Trailways, 28
Pete's Leasing, 31
Phoebe, 260
Phoenix Rising Yoga Therapy, 193
Pilgrim Inn, 76
Pillars Carriage House Restaurant, The, 114–15
Pine Cobble School, 283
Pine Cone Hill, 256
Pittsfield. *See* Central County
Pittsfield Boys Club, 222
Pittsfield Co-operative Bank, 269
Pittsfield Community Television, 279
Pittsfield Downtown, 264
Pittsfield Furniture Company, 261
*Pittsfield Gazette, The*, 278
Pittsfield Girls' Club, 224
Pittsfield High School, 221
Pittsfield Information Booth, 284
Pittsfield Public Courts, 221
Pittsfield Public Schools, 281
Pittsfield Rye Bakery, 126
Pittsfield State Forest, 224, 228
Pittsfield Travelodge, 77
Pittsfield YMCA, 194, 220, 224
pizza, 125
P.J.'s Convenience Store, 277
Plaine's Bike Snowboard Ski Shop, 32, 196, 198, 204
Pleasant Valley Motel, 76–77
Pleasant Valley Wildlife Sanctuary, 217, 229
Plum, 148
Plunkett Lake Lion's Club Beach, 224
police, 266
Ponterril, 201, 220, 224, 233
Ponterril/YMCA, 221
Pontoosuc Lake, 201, 224
Pontoosuc Lake Country Club, 211
Porches Inn, The, 68
Port Authority Bus Terminal, 26
Porter's Sporting Goods, 196
poultry, meat, and fish markets, 128
Powder Hounds Restaurant and Tavern, 97–98

President's House, 138
Price Chopper Supermarkets, 277–78
Prime Oulets at Lee, 251
Privacy Campground, 233
private and religious schools, 282–83
Proctor's Theatre, 183
produce, farm and orchard markets, 119–21
Prospect Lake, 201, 202, 223
Prospect Lake Park, 221, 232
Prospect Mountain, 234
public school districts, 281–82
Purple Plume, 252
PW Vintage Lighting, 242

## Q

Quaker Meeting House, 138
Quality Inn, 77–78
Queensborough Spirits, 128
Questing, 231

## R

R W's Inc., 281
Race Brook Falls, 228
Race Brook Lodge, 50–51
racquetball, 220
radio stations, 279
Railway Café, The, 178
Rainbow Taxi, 31
Rainbow's End Miniature Golf, 210, 215
Ralph Fontaine & Heritage Auctions, 246
Ramada Inn & Suites, 78
Ramblewood Inn, 51
Rawson Brook Farm, 126–27
real estate, 280
record stores, 259
recreation: baseball and softball, 197; bicycling, 197–99; boating, 199–201; camps for children, 218–20; canoeing and kayaking, 201–3; for children, 215–20; croquet, 203; downhill skiing, 203–9; fishing, 212–14; football, 209; golf, 209–11; horseback riding, 211–12; hunting, 212; personal favorites, 288; racquetball, 220; running, 222; skating, 222; soaring, 222–23; sporting goods stores, 195–97; squash, 220; swimming, 223–24; tennis, 220–22; walking, hiking, camping and cross-country skiing, 225–36
Red Barn Antiques, 244
Red Bird Inn, The, 49
Red Door, The, 254
Red Lion Inn, The, 40, 53–54, 94–95, 123, 286
Red Lion Inn Gift Shop, 255
religious and private schools, 282–83
religious services and organizations, 280
resorts and hotels, 74–76
restaurants. *See also* food purveyors: breakfast and lunch, 115–17; Central County, 97–106; late-night food, 277–78; North County, 107–13; outside Berkshire County, 113–15; personal favorites, 286–87; South County, 82–97
retreat centers and monasteries, 192
Richmond. *See* Central County
Richmond Consolidated Schools, 281
Richmond Performance Series, 174
Richmond Pond, 201
Richmor Aviation, 29
Rising Paper Mill, 133, 135
Rita Marie's Ice Cream, 126
River Bend Farm, 40, 70–71
Riverbank Farm, 211
Riverfest, 184
road service, emergency, 280–81
Robbins-Zust Family Marionettes, 217
Robert Boland Theater, 183
Rookwood Inn, 62–63
Rosenberg Center, 169
Rouge, 96
Roy C. Burdick, 246
RRR Brooks Trail, 236
running, 222
R.W. Wise Goldsmiths, 262

## S

Sackett Brook Park, 235
Sacred Heart School, 282
Saddleback Antiques, 246
Salisbury Bank & Trust, 269
Salmon Run Fish House, 91
Sam Kasten's SKH Gallery, 253
Samel's Deli and Catering, 123, 124
Sand Springs, 126
Sand Springs Pool and Spa, 224
Sandisfield. *See* South County

Sandisfield and Cookson State Forest, 226, 235
Sanford Smith Fine Art, 143
Santarella, 135
Sappa, 255
Saturday Sweets Antiques and Design, 243
Savoy Mountain State Forest, 230, 236
Savoy School Department, 282
Sawyer Antiques, 244
Sawyer Library, 160
Sayers Auto Wrecking, 281
schools, 281–83
Scratch-A-Ticket Towing, 281
Searles Castle, 156–57
seasonal events, 184–86
Seasons on Main B&B, 54
Sedgwick Inn, The, 72–73
Seeds & Co., Inc., 255
Seekonk Pines Inn B&B, 43
Seven Arts, 255
Seven Hills Inn, 63
Sevenars Music Festival, 176
1753 House, 138
Shaker Meadows Bed and Breakfast, 73–74
Shaker Mill Inn, 55
Shakespeare & Company, 180–81, 217, 288
Shamrock Village Inn, 78
Sheep to Shawl, 184
Sheffield. *See* South County
Sheffield Inn, 51
Sheffield Pottery, 258
Shiro Restaurant, 87
Shooz, 252
*Shopper's Guide, The*, 278
shopping: antiques, 239–46; books, 246–49; children's stores, 250; clothing and accessories, 249–54; gift and specialty shops, 254–57, 263; handcrafts, 257–59; house and home, 259–61; jewelry, 262; malls, mews, and streets, 262–65; personal favorites, 288–89; recordings, 259
Sienna Gallery, 262
Silver Screen, The, 124
Simon's Rock College of Bard, 135, 139, 143, 174, 221, 283
Simon's Rock Library, 160
Sinai Academy of the Berkshires, 282
Sisters of the Visitation Monastery, 192
'62 Center for Theatre and Dance, 142, 181–82
skating, 222
SKH Gallery, 143
Ski Fanatics, 204
Skiddoo Vintage & Modern, 245
skiing, 203–9, 225–36
Skyline Country Club, 211
Smith House Concert Series, 176
Snowy Owl Resort, 208–9
Snyder's Store, 242
soaring, 222–23
softball and baseball, 197
South Adams Savings Bank, 269
South County: antiques stores, 240–44; architecture, 133–35; art galleries, 143–45; bicycle dealers, 198; boating, 200–201; bookstores, 246–47; campgrounds, 232; children's camps, 218–19; children's recreation, 215–16; cinema, 139; clothing and accessories stores, 249–51; dance, 142; downhill skiing, 205–7; emergency road service, 280–81; fishing, 213–14; gift and specialty shops, 254–56; golf courses, 210; handcraft stores, 258; house and home stores, 259–60; inns and bed & breakfasts, 42–56; motels, 76–77; music, 174; nightlife, 176–77; private and religious schools, 282; public school districts, 281; restaurants, 82–97; shopping streets, mews, and malls, 262–64; ski shops, 204; sporting goods stores, 195; swimming, 223; tennis, 221; theater, 182–83; tourist information, 283; trails, 226, 228; video rentals, 187
South County (SoCo), 126–27
South Egremont. *See* South County
South Egremont Spirit Shoppe, 128
South Lee. *See* South County
South Mountain Concerts, 171–72, 288
South Pond, 201
Southern Berkshire Chamber of Commerce, 280
Southern Berkshire Regional School District, 281
Southfield. *See* South County
Southfield's Buggy Whip Factory, 262
Southgate Motors, 281
Spanda Holistic Center, 193
spas and wellness centers, 189–93
Spectacle Pond, 223

Spencer's Restaurant at the Thornewood Inn, 87–88
Spencertown Academy, 176
Spigalina, 101–2
Spirit Shop and Deli Station, 129
Splendid Peasant, The, 244
Spoke Bicycles, The, 32, 199
sporting goods stores, 195–97
sports. *See* recreation
Sports Corner, The, 32, 197, 199, 205
Sports School Day Camp, 220
Spring Street, 265
Sprout House, 125
squash, 220
St. Agnes School, 282
St. Joseph's High School, 282
St. Luke's Chapel, 137
St. Mary's School, 282
St. Paul's Church, 135
St. Paul's Episcopal Church, 135
St. Stanislaus, 283
Stagecoach Tavern, 93
Star City Taxi, 30
Starlight Stage Youth Theatre, 183, 218
Staveleigh House B&B, 51–52
Steep Acres Farm, 71
SteepleCats, 197
Sterling and Francine Clark Art Institute, 138, 163–64, 175, 178, 218, 287
Steven Valenti, 253, 289
Stockbridge. *See* South County
Stockbridge Booksellers, 247
Stockbridge Bowl, 201
Stockbridge Chamber Concerts, 174
Stockbridge Chamber of Commerce, 283
Stockbridge Golf Club, 210, 221
Stockbridge Library and Historical Room, 160–62, 216
Stockbridge Main Street, 264
Stockbridge Main Street at Christmas, 186
Stockbridge Motors, 281
Stockbridge Public Courts, 221
Stone Hill Loop, 236
Stone School Gallery, 146
Stone's Throw Antiques, 245
Stonover Farm, 63
Stop & Shop Supermarket, 278
Store at Five Corners, The, 123, 124, 126, 287
Stormy Crandall Antiques, 245
Strawberry Acres, 121
Sugar Llama, 127
Summit Hill Campground, 233
Sunflowers Natural Foods, 125
Sunset Farm Maple Products, 122
Sunset Motel, 77
Super 8 Motel, 77
Super Eight Motel, 78
Susan B. Anthony Birthplace, 137–38
Susan B. Anthony Celebration & Adams Street Fair, 185
Susan Silver Antiques, 243
Sweaters Etc., 251
Sweet Basil Grille, The, 91–92, 124
Sweet Pea and Petunia, 117
swimming, 223–24
Swiss Hütte Country Inn, 73, 114

## T

T.A. Gage, 246
Taconic Crest Trail, 236
Taconic Golf Club, 211, 236
Taconic High School, 221
Taconic Hiking Club, 230
Taconic Restaurant, 112–13
Taconic Trail State Forest, 230
Taft Farms, 120–21
Taggart House B&B, 54–55
Tala's Quilt Shop, 257
Talbot's, 252
Tanglewood, 172–74, 287–88
Tanglewood Music Store, 259
Tanglewool, Inc., 252
Tannery Pond Concerts, 176, 288
Tassels, 261
Taubman Piano Festival, 175
Tauck Tours, 276
Taxi Company, 31
taxis, 30, 31
Tea Ceremony, The, 186
television, 279–80
tennis, 220–22
Teo's Hot Dogs, 117
Thaddeus Clapp House, 65
Thai Garden, 113

theater, 179–84
Theater Barn, 183
Thornewood Inn, 43–44
T&M Auto Sales, 281
Tobi's Limousine Service, 31
Tokonoma Gallery & Framing Studio, 143
Tolland State Forest, 226
Tom's Toys, 250
Toonerville Trolley Records, 259
TOPIA Arts Center, 147, 183
tourist information booths, 11, 283–84
tours, guided, 275–76
town halls, 266–68
T.P. Saddle Blanket and Trading Co., 255
trails, 32
Trailways, 28
Train Station Gallery, 145
train travel, 28–29
*Transcript, The,* 278
Transport the People, 31
transportation: access map, 27; arriving by airplane, 29; arriving by bus, 26, 28; arriving by car, 25–26; arriving by limousine or taxi, 30; arriving by train, 28–29; bicycling, 32; car rentals, 30–31; emergency road service, 280–81; foot trails, 32; late-night fuel, 277–78; limousines, 30, 31; local bus service, 30; taxis, 30, 31
Trattoria Il Vesuvio, 102
Trattoria Rustica, 106
Triplex Cinema, 139
Trotta's Discount Liquors, 129
Trova Theater Arts, 183
Truc Orient Express, 96–97
Trustees of Reservations, 231
Tub Parade, 186
Tuckered Turkey, The, 57
Tune St., 259
Tunnel City Coffee, 119
Turner Farms Maple Syrup, 122
Turning Point Inn, 44
TV, 279–80
20 Railroad Street, 88
Tyringham. *See* South County
Tyringham Cobble, 231

## U

U-Drive Boat Rentals, 201
Undermountain Farm, 212
Undermountain Weavers, 253
Union Bar and Grill, 88, 177
U.S. Bluesware, 253
Utter Delight, 127

## V

Val's Pipe & Package Store, 129
Variety Video, 187
Ventfort Hall, 157
Verdura Cucina Rustica, 89
Vic's Seafood, 128
Victory Girl Productions, 142
video rentals, 187
Video Studio, 187
Video Studio 12, 187
Vietnam Veterans Memorial Skating Rink, 222
Village Inn, The, 40, 63–64, 102–3
Village Oven, The, 125
Village Truck Sales, 281
Villager Gifts, 256
Villager Motel, 79
Vintage Linens, 244
Viviani's, 89
Vlada Boutique, 251

## W

Wagon Wheel Motel, 78
Wahconah Country Club, 211
Wahconah Falls, 229
Wainwright Inn, 44
Waldenbooks, 247
Walker House Inn, 64
walking, hiking, camping and cross-country skiing, 225–36
Water Street, 265
Water Street Books, 248
Water Street Grill, 113
Waterside, 145
Waubeeka Springs Golf Links, 211
weather, 275
Weathervane Inn, The, 40, 43
Weathervane Motel, The, 78
Weaver's Fancy, 252
wellness centers and spas, 189–93

West College, 138
West Lake, 201
West Stockbridge. *See* South County
West Stockbridge Downtown, 264
West Stockbridge Information Booth, 283
West Stockbridge Video, 187
Western Gateway Heritage State Park, 137, 168, 217
Western Massachusetts Athletic Club, 222
Western Wildlife District Manager, 212
West's Package & Variety Stores, 129
West's Wines & Spirits, 129
Wheatleigh, 40, 64–65, 103–4
Where'd You Get That!?, 257, 289
Whistler's Inn, 65
White Hart Inn, The, 72
White Horse Inn, 65–66
White Knight Records, 259
Whitney's Beverage Shop, 129
Wigwam & Western Summit Cottages, 79
Wigwam & Western Summit Gift Shop, 257
Wild Oats Community Market, 125
William Bradford Auction Galleries, 246
William Cullen Bryant Homestead, The, 150
Williams & Son Country Store, 255
Williams Choral Society, 175
Williams College, 175, 218, 222, 283
Williams College Dance Department, 142
Williams College Football, 209
Williams College Museum of Art, 138, 168–69, 218, 287
Williams College Outing Club, 230
Williams Inn, 71, 178
Williams Shop, 254
Williamstheatre, 183
Williamstown. *See* North County
Williamstown Bed and Breakfast, The, 71–72
Williamstown Chamber Concerts, 175–76
Williamstown Chamber of Commerce, 284
Williamstown Film Festival, The, 139
Williamstown Public Court, 222
Williamstown Public Library, 138, 218
Williamstown Public Schools, 282
Williamstown Rural Lands Foundation, 218
Williamstown Savings Bank, 269
Williamstown Theatre Festival, 178, 181–82, 218, 288
Williamsville Inn, The, 40, 55–56, 97
WilliNet, 280
Willows Motel, The, 79
Wilson Wilde, 148
Windflower Inn, 44
Windsor Jambs, 229
Windsor Lake, 201, 224
Windsor State Forest, 224, 229
Windy Hill Farm, 121
Windy Knoll Farm, 212
wine and liquor stores, 128–29
Wingate Ltd., 260
Winterbrook Farm Antiques, 245–46
Wit Gallery, 147
*Women's Times, The*, 279
Wonderful Things, 255, 258
Woods Pond, 235
WTF Cabaret, 178
Wyantenuck Country Club, 210

## Y

Yankee Candle, 256
Yankee Inn, 78
*Yankee Shopper*, 279
Yasmin's at the Orchards, 111
Yellow House Books, 247
yoga, 192–93
Yokum Ridge, 229
York Lake, 223
York Pond, 201

## Z

Zabian's Ltd., 251
Zambezi Marimba Band, 142, 175
Zanna, 254, 289

# LODGING BY PRICE

**LODGING BY PRICE CODE**

| | |
|---|---|
| Inexpensive | up to $100 |
| Moderate | $100-$150 |
| Expensive | $150-$200 |
| Very Expensive | $200 or more |

**SOUTH COUNTY**

*Inexpensive-Moderate*

Briarcliff Inn, 76
Orchard Shade, 50
Super 8 Motel, 77
Turning Point Inn, 44

*Inexpensive-Expensive*

Aunti M's Bed & Breakfast, 45
Pleasant Valley Motel, 76–77
Sunset Motel, 77

*Inexpensive-Very Expensive*

Holiday Inn Express Hotel & Suites, 76

*Moderate*

Baldwin Hill Farm B&B, 42
Crabtree Cottage, 46
The Egremont Inn, 42–43
Lantern House Motel, 76
Staveleigh House B&B, 51–52

*Moderate-Expensive*

Arbor Rose Bed & Breakfast, 52
Best Value Inn, 76
The Card Lake Country Inn, 55
Days Inn, Gt. Barrington, 76
Historic Merrell Inn, 48
Laurel Hill Motel, 76
Monument Mountain Motel, 76
Mountain View Motel, 76
New Boston Inn, 49–50
Race Brook Lodge, 50–51
Seekonk Pines Inn B&B, 43
Sheffield Inn, 51

*Moderate-Very Expensive*

Chambéry Inn, 45–46

*Expensive*

Blue Willow, 52
Broken Hill Manor, 50
Christine's B&B, 44–45
The Federal House, 47–48
The Morgan House Inn, 47
Parsonage on the Green, 47
Pilgrim Inn, 76
Ramblewood Inn, 51
The Red Bird Inn, 49
Windflower Inn, 44

*Expensive-Very Expensive*

Applegate Inn, 45
Barrington Court Travelodge, 76
Birch Hill Bed & Breakfast, 50
Cobbleview B&B, 56
Comfort Inn & Suites, 76
Conroy's B&B, 52–53
Gedney Farm and Maple Manor & Spa, 48–49
The Inn at Stockbridge, 53
Inn on Laurel Lake, 46
Jonathan Foote 1778 House, 47
The Red Lion Inn, 53–54
Seasons on Main B&B, 54
Shaker Mill Inn, 55
Thornewood Inn, 43–44
Wainwright Inn, 44
The Weathervane Inn, 43
The Williamsville Inn, 55–56

*Very Expensive*

Best Western Black Swan Inn, 45
Devonfield B&B, 46
Taggart House B&B, 54–55

**CENTRAL COUNTY**

*Inexpensive*

Berkshire Hills Country Inn, 66

*Inexpensive-Moderate*

Colonial Motor Lodge, 77
Heart of the Berkshires Motel, 77
Lampost Motel, 77
Lanesborough Mountain Motel, 77

*Inexpensive-Expensive*
Days Inn of Lenox, 77
Mayflower Motor Inn, 77
Pittsfield Travelodge, 77
Wagon Wheel Motel, 78

*Inexpensive-Very Expensive*
Quality Inn, 77–78

*Moderate*
Bucksteep Manor, 74
Eastover Resort and Conference Center, 75
Echezeaux, A Country Bed & Breakfast, 66
Hancock Inn, 56–57
Maplewood B&B, 57
Shamrock Village Inn, 78
The Tuckered Turkey, 57
The Weathervane Motel, 78

*Moderate-Expensive*
Berkshire Inn, 77
The Dalton House, 56
Lenox Inn, 77
Mt. View Motel, 77
White Horse Inn, 65–66

*Moderate-Very Expensive*
Comfort Inn, 77
Howard Johnson Motel, 77
Ramada Inn & Suites, 78
Thaddeus Clapp House, 65
Walker House Inn, 64
Yankee Inn, 78

*Expensive*
B&B at the Egmonts, 60
Econo Lodge, 77
Super Eight Motel, 78

*Expensive-Very Expensive*
The Apple Tree Inn, 57
Birchwood Inn, 57–58
Brook Farm Inn, 58–59
Cliffwood Inn, 59
Cornell Inn, 59–60
Cranwell Resort, Spa and Golf Club, 74
Crowne Plaza Hotel, 75
The Gables Inn, 60
Garden Gables Inn, 60
Gateways Inn, 60–61
Hampton Terrace, 61
Harrison House, 61
The Kemble Inn, 61–62
Rookwood Inn, 62–63
Seven Hills Inn, 63
The Village Inn, 63–64
Whistler's Inn, 65

*Very Expensive*
Blantyre, 58
Chesapeake Inn, 59
Jiminy Peak, The Mountain Resort, 75–76
Stonover Farm, 63
Wheatleigh, 64–65

**NORTH COUNTY**
*Inexpensive*
Bascom Lodge, 66–67
Carriage House Motel, 78
Northside Motel, 79
Villager Motel, 79

*Inexpensive-Moderate*
New Ashford Motor Inn, 79
Wigwam & Western Summit Cottages, 79
The Willows Motel, 79

*Inexpensive-Expensive*
Steep Acres Farm, 71

*Moderate*
Chimney Mirror Motel, 78
Cozy Corner Motel, 78
Green Valley Motel, 78
Holiday Inn Berkshires, 75
The House on Main Street, 69–70
Jericho Valley Inn, 78
Maple Terrace Motel, 79
River Bend Farm, 70–71
The Williamstown Bed and Breakfast, 71–72

*Moderate-Expensive*
Berkshire Hills Motel, 78
Econo Lodge Springs Motor Inn, 78
Four Acres Motel, 78
Harbour House Inn, 67

*Moderate-Very Expensive*
1896 House Country Inn & Motels, 69

*Expensive*
Blackinton Manor, 67
Buxton Brook Farm, 68–69
Jae's Inn, 68

*Expensive-Very Expensive*
Guest House at Field Farm, 69
Le Jardin, 70
The Orchards Hotel, 70
The Porches Inn, 68
Williams Inn, 71

**CONNECTICUT**
*Expensive-Very Expensive*
The White Hart Inn, 72

**NEW YORK**
*Inexpensive-Expensive*
Shaker Meadows Bed and Breakfast, 73–74

*Moderate*
LaPerla at Gregory House, 72
Swiss Hütte Country Inn, 73

*Moderate-Expensive*
Mill House Inn, 74
The Sedgwick Inn, 72–73

*Expensive*
Churchill House Bed & Breakfast, 73

## DINING BY PRICE

**DINING BY PRICE CODE**

| | |
|---|---|
| Inexpensive | up to $15 |
| Moderate | $15-$30 |
| Expensive | $30-$50 |
| Very Expensive | $50 or more |

**SOUTH COUNTY**
*Inexpensive*
Joe's Diner, 91
20 Railroad Street, 88

*Inexpensive-Moderate*
Barrington Brewery & Restaurant, 84
Michael's Restaurant & Pub, 94
New Boston Inn, 93
Salmon Run Fish House, 91

*Moderate*
Bombay Bar & Grill, 90
Cork N' Hearth, 90
The East, 85–86
The Hillside, 92
Jacks Grill, 89–90
Koi, 86
Rouge, 96
Shiro Restaurant, 87
Stagecoach Tavern, 93
The Sweet Basil Grille, 91–92
Viviani's, 89

*Moderate-Expensive*
Aegean Breeze, 84
Bizen, 84–85
Castle Street Café, 85
The Egremont Inn, 82–83
Glendale River Grille, 93–94
John Andrew's, 83
Old Inn on the Green, 92–93
Old Mill, 83–84
Once Upon a Table, 94
Spencer's Restaurant at the Thornewood Inn, 87–88
Truc Orient Express, 96–97
Union Bar and Grill, 88

*Expensive*
Chez Nous, 90–91
Elm Court Inn, 82

*Continued on next page*

Pearl's, 86
The Red Lion Inn, 94–95
Verdura Cucina Rustica, 89
Williamsville Inn, 97

*Very Expensive*
Old Inn on the Green, 92–93

**CENTRAL COUNTY**
*Inexpensive*
Elizabeth's Borderland Café, 104–5
House of India, 105

*Inexpensive-Moderate*
Panda House, 101

*Moderate*
Asters, 104
Church Street Café, 99–100
Dakota, 104
Kim's Dragon Restaurant, 106
Lenox 218, 100–101
Powder Hounds Restaurant and Tavern, 97–98
Spigalina, 101–2
Trattoria Rustica, 106
The Village Inn, 102–3

*Moderate-Expensive*
Bistro Zinc, 98–99
Trattoria Il Vesuvio, 102

*Expensive*
Café Lucia, 99
Gateways Inn, 100

*Very Expensive*
Blantyre, 98
Wheatleigh, 103–4

**NORTH COUNTY**
*Inexpensive*
Michael's Restaurant, 111
Pappa Charlie's Deli Sandwich Shop, 112
Thai Garden, 113

*Inexpensive-Moderate*
Water Street Grill, 113

*Moderate*
Cafe Latino, 107–8
Gramercy Bistro, 108–9
Harrington's Restaurant & Inn, 107
Hobson's Choice, 109–10
Jae's Inn, 109
Milan at 55 Main, 109
Taconic Restaurant, 112–13

*Moderate-Expensive*
Mill on the Floss, 107
Yasmin's at the Orchards, 111

*Expensive*
Gideon's Fine Dining, 108
Le Jardin, 110
Mezze, 110–11

**NEW YORK**
*Moderate*
The Pillars Carriage House Restaurant, 114–15

*Moderate-Very Expensive*
Aubergine, 113–14

*Expensive*
Swiss Hütte, 114

# DINING BY CUISINE


**SOUTH COUNTY**

*American*
- Barrington Brewery & Restaurant, 84
- The Egremont Inn, 82–83
- Jacks Grill, 89–90
- Joe's Diner, 91
- John Andrew's, 83
- Michael's Restaurant & Pub, 94
- New Boston Inn, 93
- Old Mill, 83–84
- Once Upon a Table, 94
- Stagecoach Tavern, 93
- 20 Railroad Street, 88

*American, Innovative*
- Old Inn on the Green, 92–93

*American, New*
- Union Bar and Grill, 88

*American, Traditional*
- The Red Lion Inn, 94–95

*Chinese*
- The East, 85–86
- Koi, 86

*Continental*
- The Egremont Inn, 82–83
- Elm Court Inn, 82
- The Hillside, 92
- Old Mill, 83–84
- Pearl's, 86

*Continental, Country*
- Spencer's Restaurant at the Thornewood Inn, 87–88

*Continental-Contemporary*
- Castle Street Café, 85

*Eclectic*
- Glendale River Grille, 93–94

*French*
- Rouge, 96

*French Bistro*
- Chez Nous, 90–91

*German*
- Williamsville Inn, 97

*Greek*
- Aegean Breeze, 84

*Indian*
- Bombay Bar & Grill, 90

*Italian*
- The Sweet Basil Grille, 91–92
- Verdura Cucina Rustica, 89
- Viviani's, 89

*Japanese*
- Bizen, 84–85
- The East, 85–86
- Shiro Restaurant, 87

*New England Contemporary*
- Cork N' Hearth, 90

*Seafood*
- Salmon Run Fish House, 91

*Vietnamese*
- Truc Orient Express, 96–97

**CENTRAL COUNTY**

*American*
- Asters, 104
- Church Street Café, 99–100
- Dakota, 104
- Gateways Inn, 100
- Lenox 218, 100–101
- Powder Hounds Restaurant and Tavern, 97–98
- The Village Inn, 102–3

*Chinese*
Panda House, 101

*Country House*
Blantyre, 98

*French*
Blantyre, 98

*French, Contemporary*
Wheatleigh, 103–4

*French Bistro*
Bistro Zinc, 98–99

*Indian*
House of India, 105

*Italian*
Café Lucia, 99
Trattoria Il Vesuvio, 102
Trattoria Rustica, 106

*Italian, Northern*
Lenox 218, 100–101

*Mediterranean*
Spigalina, 101–2

*Pizza*
Elizabeth's Borderland Café, 104–5

*Regional Eclectic*
Church Street Café, 99–100

*Vietnamese*
Kim's Dragon Restaurant, 106

**NORTH COUNTY**
*American*
Michael's Restaurant, 111
Pappa Charlie's Deli Sandwich Shop, 112

*American, Contemporary*
Water Street Grill, 113

*American/French*
Harrington's Restaurant & Inn, 107
*Asian*
Jae's Inn, 109

*Eclectic*
Gideon's Fine Dining, 108
Yasmin's at the Orchards, 111

*French*
Le Jardin, 110
Mill on the Floss, 107

*Fusion*
Mezze, 110–11

*Greek*
Michael's Restaurant, 111

*International*
Gramercy Bistro, 108–9

*Italian*
Milan at 55 Main, 109

*New England*
Taconic Restaurant, 112–13

*Nuevo Latino*
Cafe Latino, 107–8

*Thai*
Thai Garden, 113

**NEW YORK**
*American/French*
Aubergine, 113–14

*Continental*
The Pillars Carriage House Restaurant, 114–15
Swiss Hütte, 114